American Government

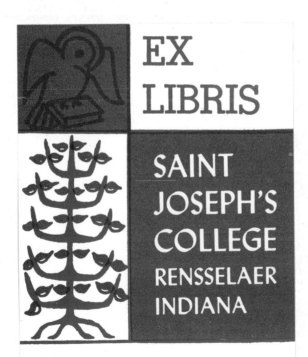

American Government
Brief Edition

GENERAL EDITOR
D. Grier Stephenson, Jr.
Franklin and Marshall College

Robert J. Bresler
Pennsylvania State University

Robert J. Friedrich
Franklin and Marshall College

Joseph J. Karlesky
Franklin and Marshall College

 HarperCollins*CollegePublishers*

Acquisitions Editor: Maria Hartwell
Developmental Editor: Richard Smith
Project Editor: Melonie Parnes
Design Supervisor: Mary Archondes
Text Design: Sheree L. Goodman
Cover Design: Mary Archondes
Cover Photo: Pete Saloutos, The Stock Market, New York City
Photo Researcher: Leslie Coopersmith
Production Manager/Assistant: Willie Lane/Sunaina Sehwani
Compositor: Ruttle, Shaw & Wetherill, Inc.
Printer and Binder: R. R. Donnelley & Sons Company
Cover Printer: The Lehigh Press, Inc.

American Government, Brief Edition

Library of Congress Cataloging-in-Publication Data

American government / general editor, D. Grier Stephenson ; Robert J.
  Bresler, Robert J. Friedrich, Joseph J. Karlesky.—Brief ed.
      p.   cm.
    Includes index.
    ISBN 0-06-500233-4
    1. United States   Politics and government.   I. Stephenson, D.
  Grier.   II. Bresler, Robert J., 1937-   .
  JK274.A5475   1993b
  320.973—dc20
                                                                    93-1308
93 94 95 96 9 8 7 6 5 4 3 2 1   CIP

Contents

Features

Preface

As the Brief Edition of *American Government* went into production, the administration of President Bill Clinton, the nation's forty-second chief executive, was well underway. Following 12 years of control of the White House by Republican presidents Ronald Reagan (1981–1989) and George Bush (1989–1993), Clinton is the first Democratic president since Jimmy Carter (1977–1981) and only the second since Lyndon Johnson (1963–1969). The transfer of power from one administration to another at noon on January 20, 1993, dramatically illustrated the ongoing importance of economics and ideology in American politics. Clinton had run in 1992 on a platform of economic change. A sign on the wall in his campaign headquarters read, "It's the economy, stupid." Moreover, on a host of issues his administration has signaled an ideological break with the Reagan-Bush years.

Economics, Ideology, and Politics

A distinguishing feature of this book is the explicit recognition that economics and ideology significantly influence American politics. No student or instructor in a course on American government is immune to the ideological and economic forces which help shape the perennial pursuit of power in a democracy. Nor is any class or instructor untouched by recurring problems ranging from budget deficits and health care to unemployment and the underclass. Economics and ideology, in one way or another, intersect nearly all of them.

This text highlights the importance of economics and ideology in the context of American government in several ways. Chapter 12, "Economic Policy, the National Budget, and the Deficit," explores the relationship between politics and *economics,* as does a series of "Politics and Economics" boxes (described below) throughout the rest of the book. Students see how economic decisions have political consequences and how political decisions affect the economy. This is essential information in a day when economic topics frequently dominate electoral campaigns, television news, and conversation at the dinner table. However, the text assumes *no* prior knowledge of economics, and references to economic policy are free of confusing jargon.

Understanding differences among political beliefs is likewise essential at a time when the labels "liberal" and "conservative," "left" and "right" are hurled about. Such terms can be baffling, particularly because their meaning has not been constant. Consequently, the text underscores the importance of *political ideology*—the ideas people have about what government should or should not do and what kind of government they should have. This emphasis is reflected in a series of "Politics and Ideas" boxes (described below), in Chapter 4, "Political Ideologies," and in Chapter 5, "Public Opinion, the Mass Media, and Political Participation." Chapter 4 is nearly unique among shorter volumes on American government because it draws a road map that guides students through intellectual debates, past and present, in American politics. Additionally, Chapter 3, "Civil Liberties and Civil Rights" probes ideological distinctions among Americans concerning fundamental freedoms. Such an encompassing survey of the spectrum of political ideas encourages students both to comprehend and to tolerate points of view other than their own, enabling them to gain further insight into political differences that exist nationwide.

Anatomy of this Brief Edition

The need persists for widespread mastery of the political system John Quincy Adams once described as "the most complicated on the face of the globe." To this end, we offer today's students a comprehensive, readable, and balanced study of the context, structure, and process of American politics.

Yet, writing a book on American government that is both lean and complete is a daunting challenge. The second edition of *American Government,* with which this book has a special kinship, contains 21 chapters with 700 pages of text. Clearly we believe all of it to be important. By contrast, this book contains 12 chapters with only slightly more than half the pages of the bigger book. A reader may fairly ask what we omitted. We answer this question by first noting what is present: full coverage, in discrete chapters, of the constitutional structure and the major institutions and processes of American government. These chapters include one each on the Constitution (Chapter 1), federalism (Chapter 2), political ideologies (Chapter 4), campaigns and elections (Chapter 7), Congress (Chapter 8), the presidency (Chapter 9), the bureaucracy and government regulation (Chapter 10), the judiciary (Chapter 11), and economic and budgetary policy (Chapter 12).

In addition, the book contains extensive, if somewhat reduced, coverage of several other subjects. Civil liberties and civil rights appear in a single chapter (Chapter 3), instead of in two; the political role of the mass media logically has been combined with public opinion and political participation (Chapter 5). Analysis of interest groups has been merged with political parties (Chapter 6). Omitted have been separate policy chapters on social welfare, science and technology, and foreign and defense policy. We supposed that instructors choosing a brief edition would probably not have time to cover such topics in depth. Readers familiar with the larger second edition of *American Government* will also note that we have reduced somewhat the number of special boxed features and photographs. We eliminated entirely some boxed features such as the personality profiles. Pedagogically useful, they are not essential to study of the subject at hand.

Pedagogical Features

This brief edition is not a "theme" or point-of-view book. Aside from emphasizing the importance of politics and political involvement, the book embraces no single ideological perspective; it does not attempt to make readers Democrats or Republicans, liberals or conservatives. To ensure a single voice in this presentation, one author has served as general editor.

The goals are knowledge of, and critical thinking about, American politics and government. Accordingly, we have designed the book to encourage students to *engage* the material. Passive reading is not enough. Understanding so important and complex a subject necessitates active intellectual involvement.

To aid in learning, the brief edition incorporates several serviceable pedagogical features.

- "Politics and Ideas" boxes appearing throughout the text explore ideological topics in depth. They demonstrate how ideological divisions generate different political consequences.
- "Politics and Economics" boxes appearing through the text highlight special economics topics, illustrating the relationship between economics and politics.
- "Contemporary Controversies" boxes are present in a few chapters to illustrate how the subject matter covered in the chapter carries over into disputes that divide the nation.
- Study questions conclude the special boxed features to encourage critical thinking and further inquiry.
- Tables, graphs, and maps appear throughout the text to display both quantitative and conceptual data. Some illustrations present new data, while others summarize information covered in the body of the chapter.
- A summary, key terms, and a description of suggested readings conclude each chapter. The summary contains in numbered form the main points presented in the chapter. Key terms, in boldface, are defined at the point at which they are introduced in the chapter. Suggested readings are widely available primary and secondary sources that students may consult in pursuing topics in the chapter.

Supplements

The following supplements are available from HarperCollins: Instructor's Manual, Test Bank, Computerized Testmaster, Transparencies, Study Guide, and Democracy in Action: American Government Simulations.

Acknowledgments

The authors express their gratitude for the many helpful criticisms and suggestions offered by colleagues who read various drafts of the manuscript. They include: Robert Albritton, Northern Illinois University; Peter Bergerson, Southeast Missouri State; Sam Hoff, Delaware State College; Willoughby Jarrell, Kennesaw State College; Gregory D. Lessig, Edinboro University of Pennsylvania; Alfreda McCullough, College of Charleston; Gerald Money, El Paso Community College; Richard K. Moore, Lewis-Clark State College; Daniel Sloan, University of Colorado, Boulder; Elliot Vittes, University of Central Florida; Mitchell Weiss, Mott Community College; and Norman Zucker, University of Rhode Island.

Deserving credit for their wisdom, guidance, and forbearance are the staff at HarperCollins. In particular, we thank Maria Hartwell, Political Science Editor; Art Pomponio, Director of Development; Richard Smith, Developmental Editor; and Melonie Parnes, Project Editor. Also, we are in debt to Chris Olson who first encouraged us to write a brief edition of the book that has occupied our minds for a decade.

Finally, special gratitude, as always, is owed to our families, whose love, encouragement, and understanding are essential ingredients in a project of this magnitude. Specifically, we thank Ellen, Todd, and Claire Stephenson; Jessica Bresler, Lin Carvell, and Jordan and Greg Rogoe; Rebecca, Philip, and Elizabeth Friedrich; and Audrey, Christopher, and Matthew Karlesky.

D. Grier Stephenson, Jr.
Robert J. Bresler
Robert J. Friedrich
Joseph J. Karlesky

Introduction

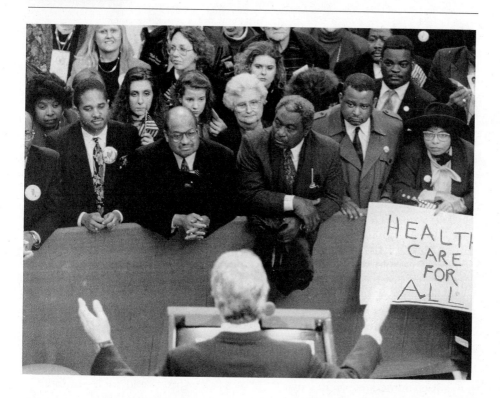

This book is an introduction to American politics and government. Its objective is not to convince readers that a particular political position is "best." It does not celebrate the virtues of capitalism or socialism or the free market or a planned economy. Nor does this book argue that taxes are too high or too low, abortion is right or wrong, social welfare policies are too generous or too stingy, or government is too big or too small. This book is not designed to create more liberals or conservatives or capitalists or socialists. Its task is to examine the American political system and to stimulate informed critical thinking about politics and government.

The fundamental purpose of this book is to explain why understanding politics and government is crucial to making one's way in our complex society and to clarify how the actions of politicians and the consequences of governmental decisions affect people's lives. The book highlights the importance of ideas and economic concerns in the resolution of political issues. Toward this end most chapters contain a special feature entitled either "Politics and Economics" or "Politics and Ideas."

What Is Politics?

What exactly is politics? For many people the word evokes negative feelings. "It's just politics," people say when they don't like a decision that's been made or when a friend loses out on a job promotion. The very mention of the word often conjures up the picture of a smooth-talking "wheeler-dealer" who uses cash to influence votes or a corrupt officeholder who exploits his or her position for financial gain. But politics is not all graft and kickbacks. Despite much of the current disillusionment with the political process, politics can be an honorable and noble profession. At its best it is a moral activity reconciling social and economic differences and constructing a way of governing society without chaos, tyranny, or undue violence.[1]

The ancient Greek philosopher Aristotle once called politics the "master science." He did not mean that politics explained all the mysteries of human life and nature. Rather, Aristotle meant that politics provided the means by which a community of people with differing views and interests could strive for collective survival and advancement. The drama of the American Civil War illustrated the importance of politics as being about ways to resolve differences without resorting to violence. All societies have differences. They are inevitable. The issue is how a society copes with, or settles, those differences. In this sense, politics is better described as the "necessary science."

With over 250 million people, the American nation is diverse. Some people are white and others black. Some are religious fundamentalists and others liberal humanists. Some are young, paying Social Security taxes, and some are old, receiving Social Security benefits. Some earn high incomes and others have little or no income at all. Some live in fashionable townhouses or suburbs and others live in blighted inner cities or on declining farms. Some make their living in high-tech industries and others in traditional smokestack industries.

The point need not be belabored. America is a complex, multicultural society in which consensus is often difficult to achieve. The process can strain the patience of the people; and different groups want different things and have different values. Such differences are at the root of the political process. In its best-known and most straightforward definition, **politics** is the study of "who gets what, when, and how."[2]

---

[1] Bernard Crick, *In Defense of Politics* (Chicago: University of Chicago Press, 1962), chap. 1.
[2] Harold Lasswell, *Politics: Who Gets What, When, How* (New York: McGraw-Hill, 1936).

Politics and Economics

Many of the conflicts that arise in a society—who has and who has not, who gives and who gets, who gains and who loses—are economic in their origins or their manifestations. Because money and material resources are limited and because human wants and demands are almost limitless, the need to make choices about spending money and using scarce resources becomes inevitable. Many of government's decisions are economic in nature because they affect the production, distribution, and consumption of wealth.

Even though our national government spends over $1.5 trillion annually, that amount is still not enough to satisfy all the demands and expectations on government. Every year the president and Congress wrestle over the budget. Should we increase the funding for the B-2 bomber or spend more on public transportation? Not all programs can be funded to the complete satisfaction of their supporters. Nor will everyone agree on who should provide the taxes to pay for them.

Politicians must make these choices under the pressure of people who clamor to advance their own interests. The elderly are likely to press for increases in Social Security, while the young are likely to be more interested in higher student aid grants for college expenses. Steel- and autoworkers favor quotas on foreign imports. Farmers who depend on the export market fear such quotas because foreign governments might retaliate against our agricultural products. Of course, not everyone takes predictable positions on every issue, nor is everyone motivated entirely by economic self-interest. Some of the wealthy are willing to pay higher taxes to help the poor, and some of the poor oppose higher social welfare spending. But, in general, when economic or occupational self-interest is at stake, most people press for programs that serve their self-interest. Politicians must resolve these conflicts.

In the face of scarcity, this task is difficult. Not all people will be satisfied, and few, if any, will be satisfied completely. Politics produces decisions that are almost guaranteed to be imperfect. Although the American system leaves most decisions about economics to the marketplace, it has never considered economic liberty an absolute right. Nor has America practiced any form of pure **capitalism,** an economic system based on private ownership of property and free economic competition among individuals and businesses. Minimum wage laws, child labor laws, and environmental regulations are a few examples of government restrictions on the functioning of the marketplace. From the beginning of the nation, government has provided certain infrastructural services (schools, roads, hospitals) in order for capitalism to flourish. And, since President Franklin D. Roosevelt's New Deal in the 1930s, the government has provided benefits for the elderly, the poor, and the unemployed. The American experience, particularly in the latter half of the twentieth century, has been witness to a strong central government that complements, coexists with, and regulates an economy largely in private hands. In the United States, economic and political power have historically been divided. But the line is always fluid and often hotly contested.

The genius of the American political experience comes from our ability, with the notable exception of the Civil War, to compromise claims and resolve differences without wrenching the system apart. But as the country grows more complex and diverse, the challenge becomes more formidable.

Politics and Ideas

Money and its uses have a magnetic attraction. But even if its supply were infinite (which it clearly is not), conflict would still be present. The political system is continually buffeted by debates over issues in which money and economic goods may be involved but in which they do not play a central role. These are debates over political ideas and the values that should be reflected in a nation's laws and political institutions. In other words, many political disputes are ideological in origin. **Ideology,** used interchangeably in this book with the term *political ideas,* refers to the kind of government people think they should have and what it should do. Ideology may include ideas about the economic system too. The prevailing political ideas have a lot to do with shaping the kind of life Americans enjoy, and ideological differences *among* Americans spark many political controversies.

For example, should abortion be allowed or banned? What a pro-choice group sees as the constitutional right of women to control their own bodies, a pro-life group sees as the murder of innocents. Other examples of disputes over values include the debates about the rights of homosexuals, the necessity of capital punishment, the censorship of pornography, and sex education and the teaching of evolution in the public schools.

Opposition to the sums spent on nuclear weapons, therefore, comes not just from the people who are concerned about the costs of defense but also from those who believe those awesome armaments to be immoral. Likewise, others call for increased government aid to the homeless because they believe that is the humane thing to do.

No amount of money can bring people together on these issues. They involve fundamentally different views about what is right and just. In these matters, as in economic questions, politicians must get people to settle for less than their ideal in this imperfect world. Politicians are the brokers of the claims we make and the values we insist on. Politics becomes an art when compromises are found where none seemed possible.

Why Government?

In casual conversation people frequently use the words *politics* and *government* interchangeably. Politics is a process. **Government** is the set of organizations within which much of that process takes place.

But why government? What is its purpose? No better answer to that question can be found than in the Preamble to the Constitution of the United States. In 1787, the framers summarized the answer in one paragraph, in fact, in one sentence:

We the People of the United States, in Order to form a more perfect Union, establish Justice, insure domestic Tranquility, provide for the common defence, promote the general Welfare, and secure the Blessings of Liberty to ourselves and our Posterity, do ordain and establish this CONSTITUTION for the United States of America.

"To Establish Justice, Insure Domestic Tranquility, . . . and Secure the Blessings of Liberty"

Government is essential to civilization. Only if people require restraint and decency among themselves is civilization possible. To government falls the task of trying to ensure such behavior. "Taxes," Justice Oliver Wendell Holmes (1902–1932)* wrote, "are what we pay for civilized society."[3] The English philosopher Thomas Hobbes wrote that in the absence of "the sovereign" or government, life among individuals would be "solitary, poor, nasty, brutish, and short."

Sovereign power is essential to protect people from one another, by force if necessary. If people attempt to kill one another or steal from one another or assault one another, government must intervene. If it does not, civilization is simply not possible. People could not enjoy the fundamental pleasures of life—a walk in the park, a baseball game, a concert—if their physical well-being were constantly threatened by others whose violent acts went unhindered or unpunished. Although anarchists would disagree, government is essential to human liberty.

Yet government cannot by itself guarantee civil behavior. Civilization is a precious and fragile state of human development that must be continually buttressed by the supporting values and beliefs of individuals in a society. Hobbes saw civilization as a thin veneer, beneath which surged a boiling caldron of human impulses.

Even in contemporary society the veneer is occasionally pierced. When social tensions reach a breaking point as they did in Los Angeles in 1992 after the first Rodney King verdict, antisocial forms of behavior frequently emerge—looting, robbing, assaulting, or killing. These threats to civil behavior must be resisted, and it is government that does the resisting.

"To Provide for the Common Defense"

Government must also protect its citizens against threats from other societies or governments. National defense is among the most important and visible functions of government. National security is essential to a society's preservation. The common defense has a long history, as any recounting of the wars in which the nation has engaged over the last two centuries will suggest. One of the principal concerns

---

* Throughout the book the dates in parentheses following the names of presidents and justices of the Supreme Court indicate their years in office.

[3] *Campanio de Tobacos* v. *Collector,* 275 U.S. 87, 100 (1904).

of the framers of the Constitution in 1787 was the creation of a stronger national government that could grapple more easily with the external threats and dangers of an uncertain world.

People may debate whether the government spends enough or too much on defense. But few will deny that the national government must be capable of defending the nation. Any organization or group calling itself a government that does not have that capability may be a symbol or a wish, but it is not a government.

"To Promote the General Welfare"

Government also exists to organize cooperative public efforts. Although some people believe in the adage "the government that governs least, governs best," few believe that government should do nothing. Throughout history government has subsidized railroads, constructed dams, protected the wilderness, provided for the needy, and built space shuttles. Such enterprises are **collective goods,** available for the benefit of all citizens, whether or not they paid taxes for them. These enterprises are generally too massive for private undertaking. They require a government that can tax and spend on a large scale.

The ideological debate over the size and scope of governmental enterprises has endured since the founding of our nation. Advocates of the **positive state** argue that government should play an active role in providing the goods, services, and conditions for a prosperous and equitable society. Adherents of the **minimalist state** argue that government is too inefficient and coercive and should be restricted to producing only goods that individuals themselves cannot provide.

What Is Democracy?

It is a basic axiom of American society that a government cannot be accountable merely to itself. The legitimacy of government in America rests on the consent of the governed. The Preamble to the Constitution states, "We the People of the United States . . . do ordain and establish this Constitution." This is a representative democracy, a system of government in which political authority is vested in the people. Its underlying ideology supposes that people are capable of controlling their own destiny, selecting their own leaders, and cooperating in creating a peaceful and wholesome society. Alexander Hamilton, a delegate from New York to the Constitutional Convention in 1787, thought the new American nation could answer "the important question whether societies . . . are really capable or not of establishing good government from reflection and choice, or whether they are forever destined to depend . . . on accident and force."[4]

---

[4] *Federalist,* No. 1.

Democratic Values and Goals

What makes a government democratic? **Democracy** requires a system of government based on four precepts:

1. *Majority rule* expressed in free, periodic elections
2. Full protection of *minority rights* against an irrational or tyrannical majority
3. Protection of *individual rights* to freedom of speech, press, religion, petition, and assembly
4. *Equality* before the law for all citizens, regardless of race, creed, color, gender, or national origin

The four objectives can be reached in different ways. Governments can vary in form and still be labeled *democratic*. In the United States, the head of state and the head of government are combined in one president, elected by the people. In other lands these roles may be vested in two people.

These four objectives are, to a degree, in conflict with one another. The achievement of one can entail limits on another. Minority rights limit the kinds of laws majorities in Congress or in the state legislatures may pass. Being in control of government in the United States does not give a majority unlimited power. If, for example, the Republicans lose an election to the Democrats, the latter have no authority to seize the property of the former or to say that Republicans no longer have the right to vote. Nor can members of a majority silence their critics (as much as they might like to) simply because they won an election.

Likewise, the command of equality before the law places limits on what a majority may do. Democratic governments may not design election laws so that some people have more votes than others. But the rule that everyone's vote counts equally does not guarantee everyone the same influence in public affairs. Citizens with money to contribute to the campaigns of certain candidates often have more influence than those who have less or who choose not to contribute. Equality before the law is often difficult to achieve in the face of economic inequality. For example, wealthier school districts often provide a better education than poor districts. Educational opportunities relate to one's income potential and full development as an informed citizen.

Yet, efforts to achieve equality may involve restraints on individual liberty. Laws banning certain forms of racial and gender discrimination, thus ensuring equal treatment for employees in the workplace, decrease the liberty of employers to hire and fire whomever they please. In turn, the protection of certain liberties may result in economic inequalities. For example, the liberty to keep one's property and earnings (subject, of course, to taxation) may result in vast disparities in wealth and income.

So, democracy American-style is not only, in Lincoln's immortal words, "government of the people, by the people, for the people." As we shall see in Chapter 1, American democracy also involves **constitutionalism**—the principle of limiting governmental power by a written charter. Our Constitution restricts the power of the state. It also establishes the basic idea that no official, no matter how high, is above the law. It is a point reaffirmed each time a president on Inauguration

Day promises to "preserve, protect, and defend the Constitution of the United States."

Making Democracy Work

For a democracy to function effectively, the people and their leaders must be willing to accept compromise and the notion that no one group will get all it desires. They must also accept democratic values and goals such as majority rule and minority rights. For democracy to work, the public must support the process by which agreement is reached. As one political scientist described it, "The American way is by compromise in little bits, by persuasion, by much talk and little bitterness."[5]

Generally through the avenues of open debate and free elections, those who lose a political battle get another opportunity. A minority faction in a democracy is more likely to accept defeat today if they know the way is open for them to become a majority tomorrow.

Why Do Politics and Government Matter?

Although Americans have had political institutions since colonial days, the nature of government in the United States has undergone radical change. Government at all levels—national, state, and local, but especially the national government—plays a much larger role in the life of the average citizen than it did 200 years ago during President Washington's administration, or even 130 years ago during President Lincoln's time.

Today, the national government pervades society, the economy, and the lives of its citizens. Its actions affect people all over the globe. Its trillion-and-a-half-dollar budget creates work for almost 5 million individuals (not including several million others indirectly supported by government grants and contracts). Governmental involvement is pervasive, regulating products from prescription drugs to toys. It insures banks, protects the air and drinking water, and warns against cigarette smoking.

With so broad a reach, the national government dwarfs every other organization in American society, including huge corporations like Exxon and IBM. Everyone who makes money must send some portion of it to the government in the form of taxes. In short, few people can get through a single day without being touched by the actions of the national government. These actions result from the process called politics. As the chapters that follow show, politics pervades American society, economy, and culture.

---

[5] Frank Tannenbaum, "On Certain Characteristics of American Democracy," *Political Science Quarterly* 60 (1945): 350.

Summary

1. Politics is about the resolution of conflict in society. Conflicts frequently arise over resource allocation and value preferences. Politicians, at their best, find compromises among these issues where none seemed available.
2. Government is essential to a civilized society. Its tasks are to ensure a peaceful society, to provide for the national defense, to secure basic freedoms, and to undertake cooperative enterprises for the general welfare.
3. American democracy means a government based on the consent of the governed, the protection of individual rights, and the equality of rights before the law. The Constitution, the basic charter of our government, preserves the principle of government under law.
4. In contemporary America, the tasks of government are extensive and varied. The national government spends over a trillion dollars a year and its activities pervade society. All Americans are directly affected by the policies and choices of government.

Key Terms

politics (p. 2)
capitalism (p. 3)
ideology (p. 4)
government (p. 4)
collective goods (p. 6)

positive state (p. 6)
minimalist state (p. 6)
democracy (p. 7)
constitutionalism (p. 7)

Readings for Further Study

Two classic discussions of politics are Harold Lasswell, *Politics: Who Gets What, When, How* (New York: McGraw-Hill, 1936), and Bernard Crick, *In Defense of Politics* (Chicago: University of ·Chicago Press, 1962). Richard Hofstadter, *The American Political Tradition* (New York: Vintage Books, 1954), remains a landmark study in American political history. A searching examination of politics in theory and practice can be found in Samuel P. Huntington, *American Politics: The Promise of Disharmony* (Cambridge, Mass.: Harvard University Press, 1981).

1 The Constitution of the United States

The politics of a nation is given a special cast by the kind of government it has as well as by the values of its citizens. This country is no exception. American politics has been shaped mightily by the Constitution and the institutions this document summoned into being. This chapter reviews the purposes of a constitution and traces the origins of ours from the Revolutionary War and the first experiment with a national government under the Articles of Confederation. Attention to the Philadelphia Convention of 1787 sheds light on what the framers wanted to avoid as well as what they wanted to achieve. Did they want to establish a democracy? What was the significance of dividing governmental authority among legislative, executive, and judicial branches? What is the unique relationship between the Supreme Court and the Constitution? How can a piece of parchment from the eighteenth century fit American needs on the eve of the twenty-first century? Exploring such questions is essential to understanding American government today, particularly when one considers that the Constitution of the United States is the oldest written national charter still in force.

What Is a Constitution?

"What is a constitution?" asked Supreme Court Justice William Paterson (1793–1806) nearly two centuries ago. "It is," he answered, "the form of government, delineated by the mighty hand of the people, in which certain first principles of fundamental laws are established." Like Paterson and his contemporaries, most Americans embrace **constitutionalism:** the belief in limiting governmental power by a written charter. This makes a constitution a very special document.

Constitutionalism

Constitutionalism has long been important in American politics. Each of the 50 states has a constitution. In January 1993, President Clinton (1993–   ), like all his predecessors back to George Washington (1789–1797), took an oath to "preserve, protect, and defend" the Constitution. Constitutionalism has also been contagious. Almost every country on Earth has a constitution, but constitutions take different forms in different lands. Most, like the U.S. Constitution, are single documents, usually with amendments. A few, like the British Constitution, are really made up of a series of documents and scattered major acts of Parliament (the British lawmaking body) that time and custom have endowed with paramount authority. The major difference between constitutionalism American-style and constitutionalism British-style is that the British Constitution can be changed by an act of Parliament. As described later in this chapter, the American Constitution can be formally altered, not by Congress alone but only by an elaborate amendment procedure that includes the states.

    American-style or British-style, a constitution is more than pieces of paper. It is a living thing that embodies much more than mere words can convey—it embodies intangibles that enable it to work and to survive. Moreover, it provides clues to the political ideas that are dominant in a nation. The U.S. Constitution, for example, includes a cluster of values in its Preamble: "to form a more perfect *Union,* establish *Justice,* insure domestic *Tranquility,* provide for the common *defence,* promote the general *Welfare,* and secure the Blessings of *Liberty*" [italics added].

Constitutional Functions

Constitutions matter because of what they do (or do not do) and what they are. First, a constitution *outlines the organization of government.* The outline may be long or short, detailed or sketchy, but a constitution answers key questions about the design of a government. Are executive duties performed by a monarch, prime minister, president, or ruling committee? Who makes the laws? Still, a constitution will probably not answer all the structural questions about a political system. The American Constitution, for instance, makes no mention of political parties. Yet a picture of American politics without them would be woefully incomplete. So, knowledge of a constitution may be a good starting place for a student of politics, but it is hardly the finishing point.

Second, a constitution *grants power.* Governments exist to do things, and under the idea of constitutionalism, governments need authority to act. For example, Article 1 of the Constitution (reprinted in the appendix) contains a long list of topics on which Congress may legislate, from punishing counterfeiters and regulating commerce "among the several States" to declaring war.

Grants of power imply limits on power. This is the principle of constitutional government in America: Rulers are bound by the ruled to the terms of a written charter. So, a constitution can also be a *mainstay of rights.* Constitutions commonly include a bill of rights or a declaration of personal freedoms that lists some of the things that governments may not do and proclaims that certain liberties are so valued that a society enshrines them in fundamental law.

Finally, a constitution may serve as a *symbol of the nation,* a repository of political values. When this happens, a constitution becomes more than the sum of its parts. More than a document that organizes, authorizes, and limits, it becomes an object of veneration. Americans have probably carried constitution veneration further than anyone else. This has had an impact on the political system that can hardly be exaggerated. Frequently, people debate policy questions not just in terms of whether something is good or bad, wise or foolish, but whether it is *constitutional.* Debate may rage over the meaning of the Constitution while contending forces accept the document as the fundamental law of the land. One group argues that the Constitution bans state-sponsored prayer in public schools, for example, while another argues just as vehemently that the Constitution permits it.

The Road to Nationhood

American government does not begin with the Constitution. Prior to 1787, there were many years of British rule, followed by the turbulence of revolution, and an experiment with national government under the Articles of Confederation.

The Declaration of Independence: The Idea of Consent

At least 13 years before the revolution, British leaders in London attempted to bring the American colonies under more direct control. Among other things, they wanted the colonials to pay a larger share of defense expenses. This policy, however, ran head on into colonial self-interest, revolutionary ideas, and a feeling of a new identity—an American identity as opposed to a purely British one. A series of events between 1763 and 1776 encouraged organized resistance to British authority and culminated in independence. Politics and reasoned debate within the British Empire soon gave way to armed revolt against it. Near the end of this period, colonial political leaders, meeting as the Second Continental Congress, considered a resolution moved by Richard Henry Lee of Virginia on June 7, 1776: "Resolved, that these United Colonies are, and of right ought to be, free and independent states." A declaration embodying the spirit of Lee's resolution and largely reflecting Thomas Jefferson's handiwork soon emerged from committee. Twelve states (New York abstaining) accepted it on July 2, with approval by all 13 coming on July 4.

At one level, the Declaration of Independence (reprinted in the appendix) itemized and publicized the colonists' grievances against British rule, now personified in King George III. The revolutionists felt obliged to justify what they had done. Reprinted in newspapers up and down the land, the document might, with luck, rally support at home and abroad to the cause of independence, especially for the military conflict under way. There was, after all, no unanimity within the colonies in 1776 on the wisdom of declaring independence. Loyalists were an active and hostile minority. Even among those who favored the break with England, some opposed fighting a war. Others were plainly indifferent.

In this effort to make the cause seem just and worth great sacrifice, the Declaration at another level said much about political thinking at the time. The

The American colonies' break with England in 1776 was precipitated by a series of events on both sides of the Atlantic. One of these was the Boston Tea Party, which protested the Tea Act that had given the East India Company a monopoly on all tea exported to the American colonies. On the night of December 6, 1773, the Sons of Liberty disguised themselves as Mohawk Indians, boarded several ships in Boston harbor, broke open 342 chests of tea, and heaved the contents into the water.

authors of the Declaration were steeped in the thinking of English and Scottish natural rights philosophers, such as John Locke, who were trying to find a new source of legitimacy for political authority. Formerly, justification of authority stemmed from the belief that governments were ordained by God. Consequently, rulers governed on the basis of a covenant with the Deity, which implied limits to a power, or on the basis of "divine right," which did not. If government was to have a secular basis, however, rulers could govern only by consent—not as an agent of God but as an agent of the people.

American leaders were also aware of precedents for rebellion in British history. Tensions between the Crown and Parliament had climaxed in the Glorious Revolution of 1688, which secured the supremacy of Parliament over the monarchy. They knew also of the series of political battles large and small over the centuries that had won particular rights for English subjects. They were familiar with the writings of the seventeenth-century English jurist Sir Edward Coke (whose name rhymes with *look*), who maintained that even actions of Parliament had to conform to "common right and reason" as embodied in the law of the land. Ironically, Coke's ideas eventually took root in America but not in England.

The Declaration of Independence drew heavily on these traditions. At least four themes emerge from its text. First, *humankind shares an equality.* All persons possess certain rights by virtue of their humanity. The Declaration called them "unalienable rights" and mentioned three specifically: "Life, Liberty, and the Pursuit of Happiness." These rights were bestowed by the Creator and were "self-evident."

Second, *government is the creation and servant of the people.* It is an institution deliberately brought into being to protect the rights that all naturally possess. It maintains its authority by consent of the governed. When government is destructive of the rights it exists to protect, citizens have a duty to revolt when less drastic attempts at reform fail. Citizens would then replace a bad government with a good one.

Third, *the rights that all intrinsically possess constitute a higher law binding government.* Constitutions, statutes, and policies must be in conformity with this higher law. That is, they must promote the ends that government was created to advance. Natural rights would become civil rights.

Fourth, *governments are bound by their own laws.* These laws must be in conformity with the higher law. No officer of government is above the law. To make this point, the authors of the Declaration detailed violations of English law by the king in a list that consumes more than half the text.

By eighteenth-century standards, the Declaration of Independence advanced objectives that were far removed from reality. Some newspapers of 1776 reprinted the Declaration alongside advertisements for slaves. Moreover, as a statement of American ideology, the Declaration's objectives remain unattained even today.

The Articles of Confederation: The Idea of Compact

If the Declaration of Independence proclaimed separation from England, it did little to knit the former colonies into a nation. Central political control disappeared in 1776. Something would now have to take its place for successful prosecution of the war and for development of the nation once liberty was won. Only eight days after adoption of the Declaration of Independence, a committee of Congress chaired by John Dickinson placed before the entire body a plan of union. The **Articles of Confederation** became the first American national constitution. Meeting in York, Pennsylvania, a safe distance from the British who had occupied Philadelphia, Congress approved Dickinson's Articles in amended form in November 1777 and referred them to the states for approval. All states, save one, gave assent by May 1779, with Maryland holding out until March 1781 because of a land dispute.

The main provisions of the Articles of Confederation are summarized in Table 1.1. Several features distinguished the document. First, *the Articles preserved state autonomy.* The document read more like a treaty between nations than a device to link component states. Describing the compact as "a firm league of friendship," the Articles stated clearly that "each state retains its sovereignty, freedom and independence, and every power, jurisdiction and right which is not by this Confederation expressly delegated to the United States in Congress assembled." The word *confederation* accurately described the arrangement: It was a loose union of separate states.

Second, *the Articles guaranteed equal representation for the states.* Congress represented the states, not the people. Whereas a state's delegation could range in size from two to seven, each state had one vote. The delegates were to be appointed "in such manner as the legislature of each state shall direct," and the states reserved the right to recall and replace their delegates at any time.

Third, *the Articles granted the central government only a few important powers.* Possessing control over foreign affairs and military policy, the central government was denied taxing power completely as well as the authority to regulate most trade. Revenues instead would be supplied by the states. If a state failed to make its proper payment, the Articles offered no remedy. Furthermore, most appropriations and laws of any significance required the affirmative vote of nine states.

Fourth, *the Articles provided for no separate executive and no national courts.* The rights of citizens lay in the hands of state courts. Congress was supposed to be the arbiter of last resort in disputes between states. The few executive duties permitted under the Articles were performed by officers appointed by Congress.

Fifth, *the Articles made amendment almost impossible.* Changes in the terms of the Articles needed approval not only of Congress but of the "legislatures of every state." For example, a single state could block any realignment of the balance the Articles struck between central direction and local autonomy. The states seemed destined to hold the dominant position for a long time to come.

The Making of the Constitution

Defects in the Articles of Confederation soon became apparent. Citizens who wanted change built their case on either of two deficiencies, and often on both. First was *an absence of sufficient power in the central government.* Absence of national taxation meant that Congress was hard-pressed to carry out even the

---

TABLE 1.1
An Overview of the Articles of Confederation

Article 1	Name of the confederacy: the United States of America
Article 2	Guarantee of the powers of the member states, except where the states expressly delegated powers to Congress
Article 3	Purposes of the confederation; defense and protection of the liberties and welfare of the states
Article 4	As they traveled from state to state, citizens of the several states were to enjoy the privileges each state accorded its own citizens; freedom of trade and travel between states
Article 5	Selection by state legislatures of delegates to Congress; voting by states in Congress
Article 6	States prohibited from engaging in separate foreign and military policies or using duties to interfere with treaties; recognition that each state would maintain a militia and a naval force
Article 7	Appointment by state legislatures of all militia officers of or under the rank of colonel
Article 8	National expenses to be paid by states to Congress, in proportion to the value of the land in each state; states retained sole power to tax citizens
Article 9	Sole power to make peace and war placed in Congress; restrictions on treaty-making power; Congress designated the "last resort" in all disputes between states; procedures spelled out for settling such disputes; power to establish a postal system and to regulate the value of money issued by state and central governments given to Congress; provision made for an executive committee of Congress called a "Committee of the States" to manage the government; stipulation that most major pieces of legislation would require the affirmative vote of nine states
Article 10	Committee of the States authorized to act for Congress when Congress was not in session
Article 11	Provision for Canada to join the United States
Article 12	Debts previously incurred by Congress deemed to be obligations of the government under the Articles of Confederation
Article 13	Obligation of each state to abide by the provisions of the Articles of Confederation and all acts of Congress; amendment by consent of the legislatures of every state

The Articles of Confederation provided for the dominance of the states in the political system and granted only a few powers to Congress.

---

limited responsibilities it had, such as national defense. Absence of control over interstate commerce meant trade wars between the states, with some states prohibitively taxing imports from others. Congress could do little to promote a healthy economic environment. Absence of power to compel obedience by the states meant that foreign countries had no assurance that American states would comply with treaties agreed to by the national government.

The second deficiency often mentioned was *the presence of too much power in the hands of the state governments.* Local majorities, unchecked by national power, could infringe an individual's property rights. Of particular concern were the "cheap money" parties that had been victorious in some of the states. The decade of the 1780s was generally one of economic depression. In the wake of the ravages of war and the loss of British markets, times were hard. In response, state legislatures suspended debts or provided for payment of debts in kind, not cash. Added to this was the circulation of different currencies issued by the states, even though the national government was supposed to have the monetary power. Printing additional money drove down its value, aiding debtors and hurting creditors. The economic picture was unsettled at best, chaotic at worst.

Prelude to Philadelphia

Heightening concern was **Shays's Rebellion** in Massachusetts in 1786–1787. Farmers in the Berkshire Hills failed to get the debt relief they had demanded from the legislature. Led by Daniel Shays, they closed local courts and forced the state supreme court at Springfield to adjourn before they were finally routed by a state military contingent of 4400 men. Although it was a military failure, the rebellion demonstrated that the central government under the Articles was powerless to protect the nation from domestic violence.

In September 1786, on the eve of Shays's Rebellion, delegates from five states attended the **Annapolis Convention** in Maryland to consider suggestions for improving commercial relations among the states. Alexander Hamilton was a delegate from New York. Along with Virginia's James Madison, Hamilton persuaded the gathering to adopt a resolution calling for a convention of all the states in Philadelphia the following May to "render the Constitution of the Federal Government adequate to the exigencies of the Union." In February 1787, Congress authorized the convention. All the states except Rhode Island selected delegates, but limited them to considering amendments to the Articles of Confederation.

Even though the Constitution soon replaced the Articles, the nation's first experiment with central government was not a complete failure. In one of its last actions, the Articles Congress enacted the **Northwest Ordinance** in June 1787. This statute provided for the government and future statehood of the lands west of Pennsylvania, laid the basis for a system of public education, and banned slavery in that territory.

The Philadelphia Convention

To appreciate fully what happened in Philadelphia in 1787, one must visualize America two centuries ago. That may not be easy. Today our nation is a global power—economically, militarily, and politically—with a population exceeding 250 million people in 50 states stretching from the Atlantic into the Pacific.

By contrast, the America of 1787 was a sparsely settled, weakly defended, and internationally isolated nation of 13 coastal states with a combined population of under 4 million. Philadelphia boasted a population of 30,000, making it the largest city in the land. Virginia and Massachusetts were the most populous states, with 747,000 and 473,000 inhabitants, respectively. Rhode Island and Delaware were the smallest, counting only 68,000 and 59,000 respectively. Three others had fewer than 200,000. The slave population, found mostly in the states from Maryland southward, numbered 670,000, or about 17 percent of the total.

It was in this context that the Philadelphia Convention assembled. By modern standards, the convention was not a large body: the legislatures of 12 states had selected 74 delegates, and 55 eventually took their seats. Of these, fewer than a dozen did most of the work. Quality amply compensated for numbers. Probably no other American political gathering has matched the convention in talent and intellect.

Who were the framers? Twenty-nine were college graduates, and the remaining 26 included notables such as George Washington and Benjamin Franklin. The youngest delegate, Jonathan Dayton of New Jersey, was 26. Franklin, of Pennsylvania, was the oldest, at 81. Thirty-four were lawyers; others were farmers and merchants. Some names were prominent by their absence. Thomas Jefferson was abroad. John Jay of New York was not chosen, even though he had been foreign affairs secretary for the Articles Congress. Patrick Henry of Virginia was chosen but declined because he "smelt a Rat." Richard Henry Lee, also of Virginia, and Samuel Adams of Massachusetts were likewise suspicious of what might happen and stayed away. Ten delegates were also members of the Articles Congress. Eight delegates had signed the Declaration of Independence, and the signatures of six appeared on the Articles of Confederation. But on balance, this was not a reassembling of the generation that had set the revolution in motion. Rather, the delegates came from a pool of men who were fast gaining a wealth of practical experience in the political life of the young nation. Most were also committed to making changes in the Articles of Confederation. Otherwise they would not have sacrificed the time and effort to attend.

May 14, 1787, was the appointed day for meeting, but the 10 delegates who convened that day at the Pennsylvania statehouse (now called Independence Hall) could do nothing until more arrived. Not only did the convention need its quorum of states, but each state delegation also needed a quorum because voting would be by state. Finally, on May 25 the Philadelphia Convention began its work. From then until September 17 the delegates conferred almost without stop, formally at the statehouse and informally at the City and Indian Queen taverns a short walk away.

In one of their first actions the delegates adopted a rule of secrecy. The delegates even closed the windows during the steamy Philadelphia summer to discourage eavesdroppers. Without secrecy, it is doubtful whether the group could have succeeded. With secrecy came the freedom to maneuver, explore, and compromise. Because no verbatim stenographic account was made at the time, knowledge of the proceedings has had to be built piece by piece over the years.[1] The

---

[1] See Max Farrand, *The Records of the Federal Convention of 1787,* 4 vols. (New Haven, Conn.: Yale University Press, 1966).

The Philadelphia Convention of 1787 contained many talented people, but it is doubtful that anyone had greater influence on the Constitution than James Madison (1751–1836) of Virginia. He earned the title "Father of the Constitution." Many of his political ideas are found in *The Federalist* which he cowrote with Alexander Hamilton and John Jay. Madison also deserves part credit for the Bill of Rights which, as a member of the House of Representatives, he persuaded Congress to propose in 1789. Unlike most American chief executives, Madison made his most noteworthy contributions to the nation *before* becoming president in 1809.

official journal of the convention was not made public until 1818. James Madison's notes on the proceedings, which are the most extensive account of what occurred, were not published until 1840.

On May 29 the Virginia delegation, led by Governor Edmund Randolph, seized the high ground for the discussion to follow. His 15 resolutions, largely Madison's handiwork, made it increasingly evident that replacement, not tinkering, awaited the Articles of Confederation. Called the **Virginia Plan** and depicted in Figure 1.1, the resolutions proposed a substantially stronger national government and a Congress based on numerical representation. This plan generated a counterproposal put forward by William Paterson of New Jersey. Known as the **New Jersey**

FIGURE 1.1
The Virginia Plan, the New Jersey Plan, and the Constitution

VIRGINIA PLAN

A two-house legislature, with numerical representation. Popularly elected lower house elects upper house.

Broad but undefined legislative power, with absolute veto over laws passed by state legislatures and taxing power.

Single executive elected by legislature for fixed term.

National judiciary elected by the legislature.

Council of Revision, composed of executive and judiciary, to review laws passed by national legislature.

NEW JERSEY PLAN

A one-house legislature, with equal state representation.

Same legislative power as under Articles, plus power to levy some taxes and to regulate commerce.

Plural executive, removable by legislature, on petition from majority of state governors.

Judiciary, appointed by executive to hear appeals on violations of national laws in state courts.

A "supremacy clause" similar to that found in Article 6 of present Constitution.

CONSTITUTION OF 1787

A two-house legislature, with numerical representation in popularly elected House and equal state representation in state-elected Senate.

Broad legislative power, including power to tax and to regulate commerce.

Single executive, chosen by electoral college.

National judiciary, appointed by president, confirmed by Senate.

Supremacy clause; no Council of Revision.

In the form signed by the framers on September 17, 1787, the Constitution reflected some features of the Virginia and New Jersey plans. Other features of the two plans were discarded during the summer's debates. The Great Compromise settled the issue of representation, drawing from both plans.

Plan (see Figure 1.1), it called for only modest change in the Articles of Confederation, keeping the state governments dominant.

What divided the delegates the most was the issue of representation, because in a legislature, representation translates into power. Would some states and interests have more votes than others in Congress? In late June and early July, the convention was deadlocked between delegates who favored representation in proportion to a state's population and those who wanted to keep equality between the states. Without settling this matter, the convention could not proceed.

This division is sometimes seen as the less populous states versus the more populous ones (small against large). True, a state such as Delaware would lose voting strength in the national legislature if population became the basis for representation. But the divisions were not always so simple. A majority of the New York delegation opposed numerical representation in either house because other states lay claim to extensive western lands with the potential for significant population growth. Besides, the Virginia Plan meant a greatly reduced role for *states as states* in the Union. Local leaders viewed centralizing tendencies as a threat to their own influence, regardless of their state's population.

Credit for a breakthrough went to Dr. William Samuel Johnson and Oliver Ellsworth, both delegates from Connecticut. Known as the **Great Compromise** or the Connecticut Compromise, their plan called for numerical representation in the lower house and equal state representation in the upper house. This compromise broke the deadlock, permitting the delegates to move along to other matters, and forms the basis of congressional representation today: by population in the House of Representatives, by states in the Senate.

There were other compromises too. The most notorious was the **three-fifths compromise,** which permitted slave states to count each slave as three-fifths of a person, thus enhancing these states' representation in the House while denying slaves, who were legally classified as property, the right to vote. Moreover, the Constitution let each state decide who could vote in national as well as state elections. As a result, a majority of Americans (women and all slaves) were denied basic rights of political participation for years to come. Property qualifications that existed in some states for a time barred the poorest white males as well from the polling places.

Ratification

Formal signing of the Constitution took place on September 17, 1787—109 days after the convention first met. Thirty-nine names appear on the document. Three delegates (Elbridge Gerry of Massachusetts and George Mason and Edmund Randolph of Virginia) refused to sign. Others, such as New York's Robert Yates, had gone home early because the Constitution included too many changes.

Approval by the country was surely on the framers' minds. Just as the delegates had taken liberty with their instructions to revise the Articles of Confederation, they proposed to bypass the rule of legislative unanimity for amendment. Article 7 of the Constitution stipulated in revolutionary fashion that the new government would go into effect when *conventions* in *nine* states gave their assent. On September 28, 1787, the Articles Congress resolved unanimously, though noncommittally, that the Constitution should be transmitted to the state legislatures "to be submitted to a convention of Delegates chosen in each state by the people thereof." Ironically, approval by popularly elected conventions meant that ratification of the Constitution would be more democratic than adoption of either the Declaration of Independence or the Articles of Confederation.

Supporters of the proposed Constitution called themselves **Federalists** and dubbed the other side the **Antifederalists,** thus scoring a tactical advantage by making it seem that opponents of ratification were against union altogether. Because ratification meant persuasion, both sides engaged in a great national debate in the months after the Philadelphia Convention adjourned. Not since the eve of the revolution had there been such an outpouring of pamphlets and essays. Most prominent among the tracts was ***The Federalist,*** a collection of 85 essays written, under the pen name Publius, by Alexander Hamilton, John Jay, and James Madison that originally appeared between October 27, 1787, and August 15, 1788, in newspapers in New York State. One of the most important expositions of American political theory, *The Federalist* achieved early recognition as an authoritative commentary on the Constitution.

Who were the Antifederalists? Most were not opposed to all change in the government. Some fought ratification because the Constitution was to become the supreme law of the land in an illegal manner, replacing the Articles of Confederation in violation of the Articles' own amendment procedure. For many, the Constitution was unacceptable because it would severely weaken state governments, leading eventually to a loss of local authority. Other opponents believed that individual liberty could be preserved only in "small republics," or states. If states were subordinated in the new government, it was only a matter of time before liberty would be lost, especially since the Constitution contained no bill of rights. As the governments closest to the people, states offered the best chance for self-government and so would promote, they thought, a virtuous citizenry. Conversely, a distant government endangered not just popular rule but citizenship itself. Moreover, the Constitution seemed designed to promote a commercial empire. This prospect threatened the agrarian values many of the Antifederalists shared.

For a time, ratification by the requisite number of states was in doubt, causing John Quincy Adams to observe a half-century afterward that the Constitution "had been extorted from the grinding necessity of a reluctant nation."[2] Not until June 21, 1788, did the ninth state (New Hampshire) ratify. Practically, however, the new government could not have succeeded had the important states of Virginia and New York not signed on. These states ratified on June 25 and 26, respectively—the latter by the close vote of 30 to 27. Some states ratified only on the promise that a bill of rights would soon be added to the Constitution, and it was, as Chapter 3 explains.

Meeting on September 13, 1788, the Articles Congress acknowledged ratification, set a date in February for electors to choose a president, and designated

---

[2] John Quincy Adams, *The Jubilee of the Constitution* (New York: Samuel Colman, 1839), p. 55.

"the first Wednesday in March next . . . for commencing proceedings under the said Constitution." The new House and Senate transacted their first business on April 2 and April 5, 1789, respectively, with George Washington's inauguration as president following on April 30. Legislation creating the Supreme Court and setting February 1, 1790, as the day of its first session was signed by Washington on September 24. Confirmation by the Senate of the first justices followed on September 26.

The Constitution is reprinted in the appendix. The main provisions of the Constitution, without amendments, are summarized in Table 1.2. Amendments, including the Bill of Rights, are summarized in Table 1.3.

Features of the Constitution

Several features, implicit or explicit in the document of 1787, plus its Bill of Rights, suggest why the Constitution was important for the framers. More important, they help to explain how the Constitution shapes American government today.

Republicanism, Divided Powers, and Federalism

The framers deliberately chose **republican,** or representative, **government** with divided powers. They feared the excesses of democracy, or pure majority rule, that they had seen in the politics of their own states. At the same time, recalling

---

TABLE 1.2
An Overview of the Constitution of 1787

Article 1	Establishment of legislative department; description of organization; list of powers and restraints; election of legislators
Article 2	Establishment of executive department; powers, duties, restraints; election of the president and vice-president
Article 3	Establishment of judicial department; jurisdiction of Supreme Court and other courts established by Congress; definition of treason; appointment of judges
Article 4	Relation of the states to the national government and to one another; guarantees of the states; provision for territories and statehood
Article 5	Amendment of the Constitution; assurance of equal representation of the states in the Senate
Article 6	Guarantee of national debts; supremacy of the national constitution, laws, and treaties; obligation of national and state officials under the Constitution; no religious test for national office
Article 7	Ratification of the Constitution

In the form in which it left the hands of the framers in 1787, the Constitution stressed the powers of the national government and did not include a bill of rights.

TABLE 1.3
Amendments to the Constitution by Subject

Individual Rights	1 (1791)	Free expression
	2 (1791)	Bearing arms
	3 (1791)	No quartering of troops
	4 (1791)	Searches, seizures, and warrants
	5 (1791)	Criminal procedure and fair trial
	6 (1791)	Criminal procedure and fair trial
	7 (1791)	Jury trials in civil suits
	8 (1791)	No cruel and unusual punishment
	9 (1791)	Recognition of rights not enumerated
	13 (1865)	Abolition of slavery
	14 (1868)	Restrictions on state interference with individual rights; equality under the law; also altered nation-state relations
Political Process	12 (1804)	Separate voting by electors for president and vice-president
	15 (1870)	Removal of race as criterion for voting
	17 (1913)	Popular election of U.S. senators
	19 (1920)	Removal of gender as criterion for voting
	23 (1961)	Enfranchisement of District of Columbia in voting for president and vice-president
	24 (1964)	Abolition of poll tax in federal elections
	26 (1971)	National voting age of 18 in all elections
Nation-State Relations	10 (1791)	Powers of the states
	11 (1798)	Restriction of jurisdiction of federal courts
Operation and Powers of National Government	16 (1913)	Income tax
	20 (1933)	Shift of start of presidential term from March to January; presidential succession
	22 (1951)	Two-term presidency
	25 (1967)	Presidential disability and replacement of vice-president
	27 (1992)	Limitation on timing of change in congressional salaries
Miscellaneous	18 (1919)	Prohibition of alcoholic beverages
	21 (1933)	Repeal of Eighteenth Amendment

Since the Bill of Rights (Amendments 1–10) was added in 1791, only 17 formal changes have been made in the Constitution. Most have occurred in periods of reform and have affected the manner in which officials are elected and the operation and powers of the national government.

the Declaration's insistence on "the consent of the governed," they knew that government had to be generally responsive to the people if ratification was to occur and revolution to be avoided. So, the Constitution blended democratic and antidemocratic elements: popular election—voters, as qualified by their states, directly elected only the members of the House of Representatives; indirect popular election—state legislatures chose members of the Senate, while specially designated electors selected the president; and appointment—the president picked the national judiciary (with the approval of the Senate).

In addition, the Constitution placed limits on what government can do. Implicit in the idea of a written constitution is that a government does not have unlimited power. As described later in this chapter, courts in the United States have assumed the role of deciding what those limits are and when they have been crossed. The Bill of Rights contains some of those restrictions. Sections 9 and 10 of Article 1 contain others.

The Constitution also diffused and dispersed power. Clearly concerned with the necessity of strengthening government, the framers divided power even as they added it. They were aware of an old dilemma: How does one construct a government with sufficient strength without endangering individuals' freedom? Madison put it this way in *Federalist* No. 51: "In framing a government, . . . the greatest difficulty lies in this: you must first enable the government to control the governed; and in the next place oblige it to control itself." The solution, thought the framers, lay in design: dividing power both horizontally among the different parts of the national government and vertically between the national government and the states.

To be avoided at all costs was tyranny, which Madison defined as "the accumulation of all powers, legislative, executive, and judiciary, in the same hands, whether of one, a few, or many, and whether hereditary, self-appointed, or elective." This threat could take at least two forms: domination of the majority by a minority or domination of a minority by the majority, with the latter running roughshod over the former in disregard of their rights. Ordinarily, the ballot box would give ample protection. The vote, after all, was the primary check on the rulers. But Madison saw the "necessity of auxiliary precautions."

Division of responsibilities at the national level among the three branches of government (Congress, president, and Supreme Court) would help but would not be enough. What was to keep one branch from grabbing all the power from the other two? Words on paper ("parchment barriers," Madison called them) would be inadequate, especially because experience had taught that the legislature might be too responsive to the popular will. The solution lay in juxtaposing power— "Contriving the interior structure of the government, as that its several constituent parts may, by their mutual relations, be the means of keeping each other in their proper places." Rather than counting on noble motives to ward off tyranny, the Constitution assumed the existence of less noble motives. "Ambition," wrote Madison, "must be made to counteract ambition."

This is the constitutional arrangement commonly called **checks and balances.** Power is checked and balanced because the separate institutions of the national government—legislative, executive, judicial—share some powers. As depicted in Figure 1.2, no one branch has exclusive dominion over its sphere of activity.

For example, a proposed law may pass both houses of Congress only to run headlong into a presidential veto, itself surmountable only by a two-thirds vote of each house. After scaling that obstacle, the law in question might well encounter a negative from the Supreme Court using its power of judicial review. Judicial review is not mentioned in the Constitution, but it soon joined the roster of

FIGURE 1.2
The Constitutional System of Checks and Balances

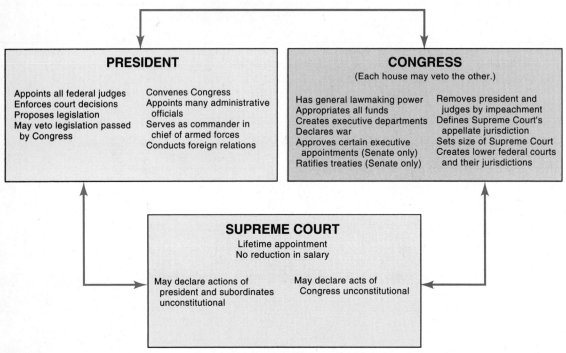

The framers designed the Constitution not just to divide governmental functions among three branches but to create a tension among the branches by allowing each some influence over the other two. American constitutional government means not just a separation of powers but separate institutions sharing some powers. The objective was to safeguard liberty by preventing a concentration of power.

Madison's "auxiliary precautions." Even the president's appointment and treaty-making powers require Senate cooperation. And although the president is designated commander-in-chief of the armed forces, Congress must declare war and appropriate money to finance the president's policies.

Securing liberty was also to be helped by **federalism,** the vertical division between national and state governments (explained in Chapter 2). The Constitution left the states with ample regulatory or police power—that is, control over the health, safety, and welfare of their citizens. As the second Justice Harlan (1955–1971) argued many years later, "We are accustomed to speak of the Bill of Rights and the Fourteenth Amendment as the principal guarantees of personal liberty. Yet it would surely be shallow not to recognize that the *structure* of our political system accounts no less for the free society we have."[3] Harlan echoed Alexander

[3] John Marshall Harlan, "Thoughts at a Dedication: Keeping the Judicial Function in Balance," *American Bar Association Journal* 49 (1963): 943 (emphasis added).

Hamilton's observation in *Federalist* No. 84 that the Constitution, even without amendments, "is itself, in every rational sense, and to every useful purpose, a Bill of Rights."

Coupled with divided power at the top, federalism was useful in guarding against majority tyranny. Some of the framers worried about "factions"—today we would call them tightly knit political parties or interest groups. The most productive source of factions, Madison acknowledged in *Federalist* No. 10, was economic inequality—rich versus poor, creditors versus debtors, and so forth. The Constitution was designed in part to limit the influence of factions. Minority factions could be outvoted. Majority factions would, with luck, exhaust themselves trying to fuse together what the Constitution had diffused. The Constitution would ultimately not prevent the majority from attaining its objectives, but the effort would have to be both long and hard. Short of this, the Constitution would work to insulate national policy from political fads that might capture majority sentiment in one or two states. The framers were especially concerned about movements like Shays's Rebellion that threatened the rights of political minorities.

Power divided horizontally and vertically was meant to cope with human ambition run amok. Measured by this standard, the Constitution has been largely successful, yet the scheme is by no means foolproof. The vaccination against tyranny has had some unpleasant side effects. First, the arrangements that held off the threats to the nation that Madison feared have sometimes made it more difficult to deal with threats to individual liberty in the states. As Chapter 3 describes, once the central government took a stand against continued racial and gender discrimination, fragmented powers and federalism hindered steps to alleviate existing wrongs. All checks, primary and auxiliary, failed to work for a long time. Second, the constitutional legacy of the framers makes difficult the task of governing a nation more than 200 years later. Separate national institutions and federalism have contributed to weak political parties. They all combine to tax the skills of any leader, including the president, who calls for concerted action. Power has to be amassed, it seems sometimes, in spite of the Constitution. The advantage always seems to lie with those who would delay, deflect, or derail. The framers institutionalized tension within the government. Yet on balance, the benefits of fragmented power have been worth the costs. American constitutional government is now in its third century.

A Single and Independent Executive

It was beyond doubt that the Philadelphia Convention would make provision for a legislature. Controversy converged instead on issues like representation and manner of selection. What is perhaps astonishing about the Constitution is that it provided for a single *and* independently elected executive. Neither the Virginia Plan nor the New Jersey Plan offered both, as Figure 1.1 illustrates. Understandably after 1776, executive authority was suspect, and the kind of executive the new government would have was a topic of debate throughout the summer. State constitutions of the day typically enhanced legislative power and kept governors on a short leash. Some delegates to the Philadelphia Convention favored a plural executive or a single executive responsible to a council or to Congress.

By unanimous vote of the electoral college, George Washington became the first president under the Constitution. His inauguration occurred on April 30, 1789, on the balcony
of Federal Hall, overlooking Wall Street in New York City. Because the first appointments
to the Supreme Court would not be authorized until the fall, Washington was sworn in by
Chancellor Robert Livingston of the New York state judiciary. Vice-President John Adams
had taken the oath of office earlier in the month.

The framers in Philadelphia put off a decision on selecting a president until
the end. Their choice represented a compromise. Creation of the electoral college,
discussed in Chapter 7, meant that the delegates could avoid direct election by
the people (a plan that allowed for too much democracy), election by Congress
(a plan that would make the executive subservient to the legislature), and election
by state legislatures (a plan that might make the executive a puppet of state
governments). By allowing for selection of a single individual by specially chosen
electors, the Constitution provided independence, strength, and, eventually, a
popular base of power for the president.

Adaptability

The significance of the Constitution today is ample reminder that the document is
a living charter, not just a relic from a bygone era. Yet the Constitution was written
by eighteenth-century men, with eighteenth-century educations, for an obscure
and fragile eighteenth-century nation. Formal amendment of the document, a
process to be discussed shortly, has taken place only 17 times since ratification of

the Bill of Rights in 1791. How, then, does the Constitution fit the needs of a world power approaching the twenty-first century? The answer is that the Constitution is adaptable. It is adaptable both because of particular characteristics built into it and because of the way the document has been regarded by successive generations.

The first factor is *brevity*. Including all 27 amendments, the Constitution of the United States contains fewer than 6000 words. This means a shortage of detail and an absence of reference to many things the framers could conceivably have included. (By contrast, the constitutions of the 50 states today tend to be long and detailed; many are also short-lived.) Tactically, brevity was wise in the face of the ratification debate, for, to a point, the less said, the less there was to arouse opposition. Later generations would have to flesh out the full potential of the document through interpretation and practice. For example, the "executive power" that Article 2 vests in the president is largely undefined.

Second, there is *elasticity* in the language of the Constitution. Some words and phrases do not have a precise meaning. Among Congress's list of powers in Section 8 of Article 1 is the regulation of commerce. But what does "commerce" include? In the 1960s Congress prohibited racial discrimination in hotels, restaurants, and other places of public accommodation. Its authority? The power to regulate commerce.[4]

Following the list of Congress's powers is the **elastic clause,** which authorizes Congress to pass "all Laws which shall be necessary and proper for carrying into Execution the foregoing Powers." So, to the itemization of things Congress can do is added an indefinite reservoir of implied powers. In different periods of American history this clause has enabled government to meet new challenges and the needs of a changing nation. For instance, as explained in Chapter 2, the Supreme Court long ago relied on the elastic clause to uphold Congress's authority to charter a national bank. According to Chief Justice John Marshall (1801–1835), the Constitution was "intended to endure for ages to come, and consequently to be adapted to the various crises of human affairs."[5]

Third, the Constitution exalts *procedure* over substance, containing far more about how policies are to be made than what policies are to be chosen. The Constitution stresses means over ends. The result has been to avoid tying the Constitution, for long periods of time at least, to a certain way of life—whether agrarian, industrial, or technological—or to a certain economic doctrine.

---

[4] *Heart of Atlanta Motel* v. *United States,* 379 U.S. 241 (1964). This is a citation to a Supreme Court decision. "U.S." stands for the *United States Reports,* the official publication containing decisions by the Supreme Court. The number 379 preceding "U.S." and the number 274 following "U.S." indicate the volume and page, respectively, of the *Reports* where the case can be found. For more information on Supreme Court decisions, see Chapter 11.

[5] *McCulloch* v. *Maryland,* 17 U.S. (4 Wheaton) 316, 415 (1819) (emphasis deleted). "Wheaton" was the name of the Supreme Court's reporter of decisions at this time. Until 1875, when the use of "U.S." became the rule, citations to Supreme Court decisions contained the reporter's name. Hence, this case was in volume 4 of the reports published by Henry Wheaton.

Amendment of the Constitution

The framers knew that the Constitution must allow for change in its terms if it was to be an enduring force. The near impossibility of amending the Articles, after all, drove the framers to scrap the rule of unanimity that the Articles required. Formal amendment is thus another means of ensuring adaptability.

Yet, of the more than 5000 amendments that have been introduced in Congress, only 27 amendments have been added to the document since 1789 (see Table 1.3). Article 5 of the Constitution says that three-fourths of the states can band together and bind the rest. Compared with the Articles of Confederation, amending the Constitution is easier, but it is still not easy. The national constitution is amended much less frequently than state constitutions.

As shown in Figure 1.3, the Constitution specifies two different tracks for its own amendment: initiation by Congress and initiation by state legislatures. Only the first has been employed successfully. Since 1789 Congress has submitted 33 amendments to the states for ratification. Until 1992, all but seven had been approved. Of those to fail, the most recent two were the District of Columbia Amendment, which would have given the district voting representation in Congress, and the Equal Rights Amendment, which would have banned discrimination by government on the basis of gender.

In 1992 an amendment, long known as the "lost amendment," became part of the Constitution upon ratification on May 7 by Michigan, the thirty-eighth state, and official, if grudging, acknowledgment by Congress. (Two additional states ratified later in May.) The Twenty-seventh Amendment declares: "No law, varying the compensation for the services of the Senators and Representatives, shall take effect, until an election of Representatives shall have intervened."

FIGURE 1.3
Formal Amendment of the Constitution

AMENDMENTS ARE PROPOSED

| By a two–thirds vote in both houses of congress | Usual route → By the legislatures of three–fourths of the states |

AMENDMENTS ARE RATIFIED

OR

Used once

OR

| By a national convention convened by Congress upon petition by two–thirds of the states | Never used | By conventions in three–fourths of the states |

Never used

The formal amendment procedure is prescribed by Article 5 of the Constitution. The General Services Administration certifies the ratification and keeps tally of the states.

Ironically, the newest amendment is, in one sense, among the oldest, as it was among the 12 amendments Congress submitted to the states in 1789. (Ten of this group of amendments became the Bill of Rights. Another, dealing with apportionment of the House of Representatives, was never ratified and is obsolete.) By December 1791, when the Bill of Rights amendments were ratified, only six states had approved the pay amendment. Only one additional state ratified it during all of the nineteenth century, but a drive to "revive" the amendment began in the late 1970s as many people became increasingly frustrated with Congress.

In modern times, Congress has set a time limit for ratification, usually seven years. An amendment that fails to obtain the required three-fourths approval by the specified date then "dies." But no such limit applied to the early amendments. Critics say that accepting the lost amendment as officially part of the Constitution is a dangerous precedent because allowing the ratification process to be spread over so long a period of time does not guarantee a contemporary national consensus. Others reply that the amendment would not have been revived had there not been such a consensus for setting this limit on congressional powers.[6]

The second track is the closest the Constitution comes to popular initiation of amendments. As depicted in Figure 1.3, the legislatures of two-thirds of the states first make application to Congress for an amendment. Congress then calls a convention, which in turn submits the amendment for ratification by the legislatures (or conventions) of three-fourths of the states. From time to time, people have attempted to amend the Constitution by campaigning for a second convention when Congress declined to propose the desired amendment in the usual way. Most recently, efforts to obtain an amendment along this second and untraveled track have been aimed at mandating a balanced budget for Congress. As of 1993, 32 states—two short of the proportion the Constitution requires—had petitioned Congress for a convention to propose the latter. This thrust from the states partly accounts for congressional interest in proposing a balanced-budget amendment. Using track one heads off the drive along track two.

Grave doubts persist over the wisdom of summoning a second convention. Many questions understandably remain unanswered. *Must* Congress call a convention when two-thirds of the states request one? Would such a convention be limited to proposing the amendment sought by the petitioning states, or could a convention propose other changes in the Constitution? Would the delegates vote as individuals, or would they cast the vote of a state, as was done in 1787? The Constitution does not say.

Aside from formal amendment and judicial interpretation (to be discussed next), the political system has also changed by custom. Even with the same words in the Constitution, the public's expectations of governmental institutions continue to evolve. Democratic values, socioeconomic conditions, industrialization, urbanization, and technology have all influenced attitudes and practices. For example, political parties, which developed early in our political history, are not mentioned in the Constitution. An even more obvious example of change by custom is the

---

[6] Marcia Coyle, "No Set Procedure for Amendments," *National Law Journal,* June 1, 1992, p. 10.

pledge of presidential electors to support their party's ticket, a practice the Constitution does not require. For a very long time members of the electoral college have not been expected to exercise an independent choice for president and vice-president (voters would feel both anger and betrayal if they frequently did) but merely to register the choice of the voters on election day.

Judicial Review Comes to the Supreme Court

Most changes to the Constitution since the beginning have resulted not from adding or deleting words but from applying new meaning to old words—a task that has largely fallen to the Supreme Court. Through interpretation, the Supreme Court sits as a kind of continuing constitutional convention. This is why Americans, more often than not, must look to court cases to know what the document means. Yet it is not entirely clear that the framers intended the Court to occupy a place of such prominence in the political system, a prominence that rests on the power of judicial review.[7]

Marbury v. *Madison:* The Case of the Undelivered Commissions

Following the presidential election in November 1800, the nation witnessed the modern world's first peaceful electoral transfer of political power from one party to another.[8] The "out group" of Democratic-Republicans led by Thomas Jefferson (1801–1809) captured the presidency and Congress, displacing the "in group" of Federalists led by President John Adams (1797–1801). Partisan tensions ran very high.

In the wake of the Adams defeat, Oliver Ellsworth (1796–1800) resigned as the third chief justice of the United States. If Adams moved swiftly, he, and not Jefferson, would be able to make the appointment. Adams offered the job to John Jay (1789–1795), who had been the first chief justice, but Jay declined because he doubted that the Court would ever amount to much. Adams turned next to his secretary of state, John Marshall, who accepted.

Several weeks before the switch in administrations, the Federalist-dominated Congress passed the District of Columbia Act, which authorized the appointment of 42 new justices of the peace. President Adams made the appointments, much to the displeasure of the Jeffersonians waiting in the wings. This series of events was possible because Congress convened annually in December in those days. This meant that members defeated in the November election (the "lame ducks") were still on hand to make laws. The newly elected Congress would not convene

---

[7] The Supreme Court as an institution is the subject of Chapter 11.
[8] Richard Hofstadter, *The Idea of a Party System* (Berkeley: University of California Press, 1969), p. 128.

until after the presidential inauguration in March of the following year, a practice that was not changed until ratification of the Twentieth Amendment in 1933.

In the waning hours of the Adams administration, John Marshall, who was still serving as secretary of state, failed to deliver all of the commissions of office to the would-be justices of the peace. Upon assuming office on March 4, 1801, Jefferson held back delivery to some of the Adams appointees and substituted a few of his own. Later that year, William Marbury and three others whom Adams had named justice of the peace filed suit against Secretary of State James Madison in the Supreme Court. They wanted the Supreme Court to issue a **writ of mandamus** to Madison, directing him to hand over the undelivered commissions. (A writ of mandamus is an order issued by a court to a public official directing performance of a ministerial, or nondiscretionary, act.) Thus, a case was in the works testing the power of the Supreme Court over another branch of government.

When the Court heard arguments in the case of ***Marbury* v. *Madison*** in February 1803, the Jefferson administration displayed its hostility to Marshall and the other Federalist justices by boycotting the proceeding.[9] It was by then apparent that Marshall and the five associate justices were in a predicament. If the Court issued the writ, Jefferson and Madison would probably disregard it. There would be no one to enforce the order, and the Court would seem powerless and without authority. For the Court to decide that Marbury and the others were not entitled to their judgeships would be an open acknowledgment of weakness and error.

Marshall's decision skillfully avoided both dangers and claimed added power for the Supreme Court, even though Marbury walked out the door empty-handed. First, in a lecture on etiquette to his cousin the president, Marshall made it clear that Marbury was entitled to the job. Second, he ruled that courts could examine the legality of the actions of the head of an executive department. Third, and dispositive, Marshall announced that Marbury was out of luck because the writ of mandamus he requested was not the proper remedy.

Why? Marshall acknowledged that Section 13 of the 1789 Judiciary Act gave the Supreme Court authority to issue a writ as part of the Court's original, as opposed to appellate, jurisdiction. (A court has **original jurisdiction** when a case properly starts in that court, **appellate jurisdiction** when the case begins elsewhere and comes to a higher court for review.) But, Marshall pointed out, the Supreme Court's original jurisdiction was specified in Article 3 of the Constitution and included no mention of writs of mandamus. By *adding* to the Court's original jurisdiction, Section 13 appeared unwarranted by the Constitution. Was the Court to apply an unconstitutional statute? No. To do so would make the statute (and Congress) superior to the Constitution. Section 13, therefore, was void, and the Court was obliged to say so.

The Significance of *Marbury*

Marbury v. *Madison* remains important because of what Chief Justice Marshall said about the Constitution and the Supreme Court. First, officers of the government were under the law and could be called to account in court. Second, statutes

---

[9] 5 U.S. (1 Cranch) 137 (1803).

contrary to the Constitution were not valid laws. Third, the Court claimed for itself the authority to decide what the Constitution means and to measure the actions of other parts of the government against that meaning. This is the power of **judicial review:** An electorally responsible agency of government is blocked by judges holding lifetime appointments. Alternatively, the lawmaking body (Congress) would be the judge of its own authority. Yet, to acknowledge the legitimacy of judicial review suggests that the judiciary, not the Constitution, is supreme. Fourth, Marshall was answering the rumblings of dissent heard in the **Kentucky and Virginia Resolutions** of 1798. Written, respectively, by Jefferson and Madison (the latter had by now become a foe of strong central government) as an attack on Federalist party policies, these resolutions claimed for the states final authority to interpret the Constitution. In their words lay the seeds for dismemberment of the Union. Marshall's reply was that the Court would have the final say on the meaning of the Constitution.

Judicial Review and the Framers

The novelty of the *Marbury* case is that it marked the first time the Supreme Court declared an act of Congress to be in violation of the Constitution. Did the framers intend the Court to have such power? The question cannot be answered with certainty. Some members of the Philadelphia Convention seemed to assume that the Court could set aside laws that ran counter to the Constitution. In *Federalist No. 78*, Alexander Hamilton made an argument in support of judicial review that Marshall followed closely in his *Marbury* opinion. References to judicial review abound in the records of the state ratifying conventions, and some state courts made use of the power well before Marshall did. Moreover, several Supreme Court decisions prior to *Marbury* assumed the existence of judicial review but neither explained nor applied it. Still, if the Court was to possess such a potentially important power, it is strange that the Constitution would be silent. Neither does the Constitution say anything about *how* its words are to be interpreted, a question that still divides political leaders and legal scholars. (See "Politics and Ideas: Whose Constitution Is It?")

It is probably safe to say that Marshall's opinion in *Marbury* would not have come as a great surprise to the authors of the Constitution. But it is also probably true that they did not envision the Court's becoming a major policymaker, a role that the doctrine of judicial review makes possible and that the Court enjoys today, as Chapters 3 and 11 show. In fairness to Marshall, he viewed judicial review as a modest power. Whereas Marshall was not hesitant to strike down state laws that he felt conflicted with the Constitution, it was not until the infamous Dred Scott case in 1857, 22 years after Marshall's death, that the Supreme Court again set aside an act of Congress as violating the Constitution.[10] (Inflaming abolitionist sentiment on the eve of the Civil War, this decision denied congressional authority to prohibit slavery in the territories and asserted that blacks were not intended to be citizens under the Constitution.)

---

[10] *Scott* v. *Sanford,* 60 U.S. (19 Howard) 393 (1857).

Politics and Ideas

Whose Constitution Is It?

What standard should guide justices of the Supreme Court in deciding what the Constitution means? One approach criticizes the justices for too often substituting their own values in place of those the Constitution explicitly contains. Because the Constitution says nothing about abortion, for instance, and because there is no evidence that those who wrote either the document of 1787 or later amendments intended to include abortion as a protected liberty, they believe the Court was plainly wrong when it ruled in *Roe* v. *Wade* (1973) that the Constitution protects a right to abortion (see Chapter 3). In place of excessive judicial creativity they rely on "original intent."[a] According to this view, the Supreme Court's task is to give the Constitution the meaning *intended* by those who wrote it. Whether abortions should be legal thus becomes a question for voters and legislators, not judges.

Others disagree and advance a different approach. Often the original intent is neither knowable nor clear, they argue. Even if it is, whose intent is supposed to matter most: those who wrote the words in the Constitution, those who voted on them at the Philadelphia Convention or (with respect to amendments) in Congress, or those in state ratifying conventions and legislatures? These questions aside, must the nation always be locked into an old way of thinking until the Constitution is formally amended? The Fourteenth Amendment, for example, commands that no state deny to any person the "equal protection of the laws." In its historic decision in *Brown* v. *Board of Education* (1954), discussed in Chapter 3, the Supreme Court concluded that these words prohibited racial segregation in public schools. Yet the same Congress that wrote and proposed the Fourteenth Amendment almost a century earlier also mandated racially segregated schools for the District of Columbia. It is hard to argue that the framers of the Fourteenth Amendment intended to ban a practice they were themselves requiring. Does this mean that the 1954 decision was wrong? No. And the reason is that the Constitution must be adaptive. According to opponents of "originalism," the Court's task should be one of applying principles, not specific intents. This approach sees in the Constitution the general principle of human dignity. One generation's understanding of human dignity will probably not be the same as another's. The question becomes not what the words meant in 1787 or 1868 but what the words mean in our own time.[b]

Even many proponents of original intent do not disagree with the result of *Brown.* Rather, they say that the Court can be faithful to the intent of the Fourteenth Amendment and still invalidate laws that require racial segregation because the framers of the Fourteenth Amendment, in laying down a command of "equal protection," did not foresee the harmful consequences of forced segregation.

If justices of the Supreme Court interpret the Constitution according to their understanding of the meaning of basic principles that the Constitution contains, how do they discover those principles? Why is their view of the values that the Constitution protects somehow superior to the views of state legislators or members of Congress? Should the fundamental law of the land be developed by elected representatives or by appointed judges?

[a] Robert H. Bork, *The Tempting of America* (New York: Free Press, 1990), pp. 143–160.

[b] William J. Brennan, Jr., "The Constitution of the United States: Contemporary Ratification," in Alpheus T. Mason and D. Grier Stephenson, Jr., *American Constitutional Law*, 8th ed. (Englewood Cliffs, N.J.: Prentice Hall, 1987), pp. 607–615.

Because of judicial review, the changes wrought by custom and formal amendment, and the needs of an expanding nation, what Americans mean by "the Constitution" today is vastly different from the document that emerged from the Convention in Philadelphia in 1787. Yet the Constitution, coupled with a commitment to constitutionalism, continues to play a vital part in the life of the third century of American government.

Summary

1. The Constitution of the United States is a living document, the charter of the nation, and thus has a presence that gives it a special place in American government.
2. The Declaration of Independence attempted to justify revolution against Great Britain by explaining the purposes of government. The Articles of Confederation represented the first effort at establishing a central government for the newly independent states, but the plan proved to be defective.
3. The Philadelphia Convention in 1787 produced a plan for a new national government that had to be approved by conventions in nine states before going into effect.
4. The Constitution was designed to achieve both effective and limited government: effective by granting powers sufficient for a strong union and limited by restraining and arranging those powers to protect liberty.
5. The possibility of amendment helps to explain how the Constitution remains current in its third century. The Constitution has also been remade through interpretation by the courts and through custom and usage.
6. *Marbury* v. *Madison* brought judicial review to the Constitution in 1803. As a result, the Supreme Court sits as the final authority on the meaning of the Constitution.

Key Terms

constitutionalism (p. 11)
Articles of Confederation (p. 15)
Shays's Rebellion (p. 17)
Annapolis Convention (p. 17)
Northwest Ordinance (p. 17)
Virginia Plan (p. 20)
New Jersey Plan (p. 20)
Great Compromise (p. 21)
three-fifths compromise (p. 21)
Federalists (p. 22)
Antifederalists (p. 22)

The Federalist (p. 22)
republican government (p. 23)
checks and balances (p. 25)
federalism (p. 26)
elastic clause (p. 29)
writ of mandamus (p. 33)
Marbury v. *Madison* (p. 33)
original jurisdiction (p. 33)
appellate jurisdiction (p. 33)
judicial review (p. 34)
Kentucky and Virginia Resolutions (p. 34)

Readings For Further Study

A Machine That Would Go of Itself, by Michael Kammen (New York: Knopf, 1986), explores the role of constitutionalism in American life. Decisions of the Supreme Court interpreting the constitution are readily found in edited form in casebooks such as Alpheus T. Mason and D. Grier Stephenson, Jr., *American Constitutional Law,* 10th ed. (Englewood Cliffs, N.J.: Prentice-Hall, 1993). An explanation of the Constitution, section by section, appears in J. W. Peltason, *Corwin and Peltason's Understanding the Constitution,* 12th ed. (San Diego: Harcourt Brace Jovanovich, 1991). Useful insight into American political thought in the founding era can be gleaned from Alpheus T. Mason and Richard H. Leach, *In Quest of Freedom,* 2d ed. (Englewood Cliffs, N.J.: Prentice-Hall, 1973). *The Federalist* essays are widely available in several editions. The best collection of Antifederalist literature is Herbert J. Storing, ed., *The Complete Anti-Federalist,* 7 vols. (Chicago: University of Chicago Press, 1981). Constitutional development since colonial days is the subject of Alfred H. Kelly, Winfred A. Harbison, and Herman Belz, *The American Constitution,* 7th ed., 2 vols. (New York: Norton, 1991).

2 Federalism: States in the Union

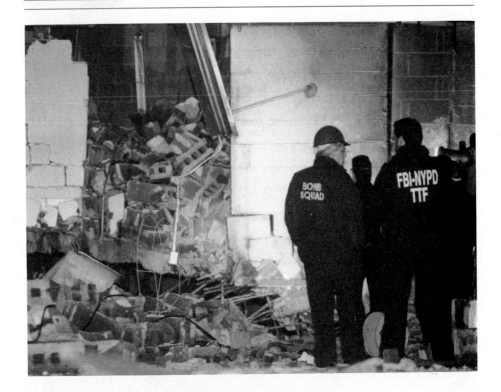

The Constitution established a national government with power dispersed among separate branches. The document also created a second kind of power diffusion: the sharing of power between the national government and individual states. This sharing of power is the principal characteristic of a "federal" system. At root, federalism is the product and symbol of the continuing struggle between the value of unity and the value of diversity as they compete for dominance in the political system.

This chapter considers what federalism is and why comprehending it is crucial to a full understanding of American government. Continuing tension between national and state governments requires a look at the place of state governments in the Constitution and their role in American politics. The chapter discusses the legal, fiscal, and political relationships among national, state, and local governments. The national government has progressively become more dominant, but the chapter concludes by reviewing federalism as a complex, adaptable system of relationships in which states have begun to assume a more energetic and vigorous role in domestic policy.

The Idea of Federalism

Federalism is a system of government in which a national government *and* state governments share governmental power within the same political system. As the bombing of the World Trade Center in New York City in 1993 demonstrated, a single event may trigger action by officials of both levels of government.

In a federal system, *both* the national and state governments have jurisdiction over individuals. For example, in preparation for the tax-filing deadline each year, individual citizens perform tasks resulting directly from the existence of a federal system. Taxpayers must file returns with the national government, and in most states (those that choose to have income taxes) they must file returns with state governments as well. The duty of filing national and state tax returns illustrates an important point about federalism: Individuals receive services from Washington *and* their state capitals, and they must consequently send money to two different levels of governments.

The federal system is a compromise between a strong central government and a league of separate states. Because the states ultimately had to approve any change to a new constitution, the challenge for the framers of our Constitution was clear: How could a stronger national government be created without, at the same time, instilling so much fear in the states that the proposed new structure would be rejected? The states, after all, were already in place. The framers pressed for change, but not so much change that their efforts would fail. The result was a federal system.

Confederate, Unitary, and Federal Forms of Government

As Figure 2.1 illustrates, the powers of states and the powers of a central or national government can assume different combinations in different political systems. A **confederation** is a loose collection of states in which principal power lies at the level of the individual state rather than at the level of the central or national government. Individual states, not the central government, have jurisdiction over individuals. As Chapter 1 made clear, the Articles of Confederation comprised such a system when it was in force during the decade before the Philadelphia Convention of 1787. Under the Articles, the states retained many important powers.

In contrast to a confederation, a **unitary system** of government is one in

FIGURE 2.1
Unitary, Federal, and Confederate Systems

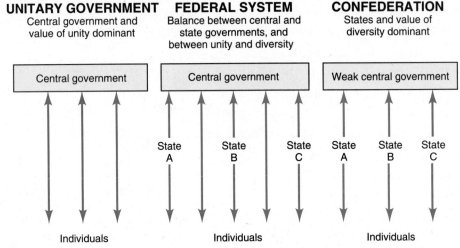

The central government has jurisdiction over individuals in a unitary government. If states or provinces exist, they are symbolic or administrative units with no real power. In a confederation, states are dominant and have jurisdiction over individuals. In a federal system, the central *and* state governments have jurisdiction over individuals.

which principal power within the political system lies at the level of a national or central government rather than at the level of some smaller unit, such as a state or province. Individual citizens have direct allegiance to the national or central government, which possesses ultimate power to make all political choices and determine public policy. The government of France is an example. The 50 American states are themselves unitary governments with respect to their own local governments. As later discussion in the chapter will make clear, principal power *within* each state lies with the state government rather than with local governments.

Confederations are founded on the political idea of diversity and local control. Such structures allow individual states to pursue diverse approaches to policy matters. On the matter of voting rights, for example, one state might allow every citizen over the age of 18 to vote, another might require that voters own property, and a third might make the right to vote contingent on passing a literacy test. According to the idea of diversity, individual states know best their own people and their own needs. Consequently, individual states ought to have their own powers to pursue individual approaches to the problems they face.

Unitary structures rest on the value of unity. Such structures assume that there is a national interest in meeting needs and problems in a particular way. Individuals are citizens of the nation (not separate states), and procedures and approaches to policy problems ought to be uniform rather than individualized and disparate. In the voting rights example, voter qualifications would be determined at the central level in the interest of a unified voting rights policy for all citizens of the nation.

In creating a federal system, the framers of the Constitution sought to change the political structure of a loose collection of states so that the value of unity might be more easily achieved. Although they were moved by a mix of considerations, the most important in the move to a national government were probably economic, foreign policy, and military.[1] Foreign and military policies are areas in which centralized approaches are essential to success. Diverse approaches in these areas (e.g., if North Carolina and Massachusetts were to conduct their own foreign policies) would surely make any kind of union among the states impossible. Indeed, this was a major fault with the Articles of Confederation. The weak central government had no real way to prevent the states from going in separate directions. At the same time, however, the framers had to acknowledge the continuing existence of diverse states and their diverse approaches in some areas of public policy.

Unity and Diversity in the Federal System

Diversity among the states can be measured in numerous dimensions. States differ in historical traditions, unemployment rates, economic development, ethnic composition, social welfare spending, federal funding, age distributions, religious affiliations, voter turnout rates, degrees of political party competitiveness, and even physical environments.[2] That states differ in physical size and population is readily evident from several examples. Rhode Island is a state of just over 1000 square miles. Alaska, by far the largest state, comprises more than 570,000 square miles. About 541 Rhode Islands could fit into Alaska. California, a state with 30 million people, has 65 times the number of people living in Wyoming.

Per capita income is another measure of state differences. Illustrating the great disparities of income among the states, Connecticut and New Jersey in 1991 each had per capita incomes almost double the per capita income of Mississippi.[3] Such basic factors of wealth help to determine how much individual states can tax and how much they can spend on programs such as education and public assistance.

To what degree should physical, economic, and social differences among the states allow diverse public policies, and when should national values prevail? The minimum drinking age and highway speed limits are contemporary issues that illustrate the search for an appropriate balance between state and national approaches to public policy two centuries after the framers originally wrestled with

---

[1] John P. Roche, "The Founding Fathers: A Reform Caucus in Action," *American Political Science Review* 55 (1961): 804; William H. Riker, *Federalism: Origin, Operation, Significance* (Boston: Little, Brown, 1964).

[2] For a seminal discussion of different political cultures among the states, see Daniel J. Elazar, *American Federalism: A View from the States,* 3d ed. (New York: Harper & Row, 1984), pp. 114–142.

[3] Bureau of Economic Analysis, U.S. Department of Commerce, *Survey of Current Business* 72 (August 1992): 48.

The 50 American states illustrate both the unity and the diversity federalism allows. Some of the states individually have economies larger than many nations in the world. While each state has problems and characteristics unique to itself, common needs and problems also exist, and governors frequently look to Washington for help. In this photograph, President Clinton meets with state governors in the East Room of the White House. Of the presidents since World War II, only three had previously been governors: Carter of Georgia, Reagan of California, and Clinton of Arkansas.

the problem. The repeal of Prohibition in 1933 granted to the states the power to regulate alcohol in whatever ways they saw fit. States had various minimum drinking ages ranging from 18 to 21. By the early 1980s, the problem of drunk driving had received national attention. People under the age of 21 were found to be responsible for a disproportionate number of alcohol-related traffic fatalities and injuries. In response to growing pressure from groups like Mothers Against Drunk Driving (MADD), Congress enacted a measure withholding from individual states some portion of national highway funds unless the states raised their minimum drinking age to 21. Whether there should be a national minimum drinking age or whether the individual states ought to decide their own minimum age is a classic problem in federalism. Is the value of unity of national approach more or less important than the value of diversity of individual state approaches in a matter that has been the states' own prerogative for more than half a century?

Debate over highway speed limits illustrates the same question. To conserve fuel in a time of oil shortages, Congress in 1973 mandated a 55-mile-per-hour speed limit throughout the nation. As concern over energy supplies dissipated, opponents of the law argued that a single national speed limit could not accommodate differences in highway conditions among the states. Some states, especially those in the West, have long stretches of straight, flat highways on which slower speeds contribute to driver boredom. In 1987 Congress passed a law allowing states to raise the speed to 65 miles per hour on interstate highways in rural areas. Should there be a national speed limit, or should states decide for themselves speed limits within their borders? Highway speed limits pose the kind of question in federalism that the framers confronted two hundred years ago.

A Comparative Perspective on Federalism

Federalism is not unique to the United States. Other countries having federal constitutional systems include Australia, Brazil, India, Malaysia, Nigeria, Pakistan, Switzerland, and Venezuela. Although such countries may differ in size, wealth, and military power, what is common to them is the attempt to pull together disparate groups while acknowledging in some way the groups' separate identities. The search for the appropriate balance in power between the states and the national government in the United States resonates in other federal systems as well.

Daniel Elazar, the renowned federalism scholar, has written that "[f]ederalism has to do with the need of people and polities to unite for common purposes yet remain separate to preserve their respective integrities. It is rather like wanting to have one's cake and eat it too."[4] Groups in federal systems might be cultural or language minorities, people living in geographical units whose history predates the creation of the federal system, or different religious denominations in which no single one is dominant. Federal systems have pulled together, or tried to, French and English speakers, Lithuanians and Ukrainians, and Pennsylvanians and New Yorkers. Such groups get together for purposes such as a common defense or a common currency, but they retain their separate identities for other purposes, such as education or law enforcement.

The relative power of the central government and constituent groups will vary among countries. But federal systems generally have a dynamic quality in which there is a continuing search for the appropriate balance between national purposes and group needs. Some of the world's great political conflicts are essentially struggles to define this balance. For example, debate over the political status of French-speaking Quebec, the only one of Canada's 10 provinces with a French majority, has strained Canadian politics. Whether Quebec can or will go it alone remains a troubling issue for Canada.

The dissolution of the Soviet Union is an illustration of how changes in a federal system can have momentous implications for world politics. A military superpower, the Soviet Union was comprised of 15 republics held together by the Communist Party backed by the threat of military force. Unchallenged central control made the system federal in name only. Worsening economic conditions,

---

[4] Daniel J. Elazar, *Exploring Federalism* (Tuscaloosa: University of Alabama Press, 1987), p. 33.

the emergence of ethnic demands, and attempts at liberal reforms showed cracks in the system. After an attempted coup by Communist Party hardliners failed in 1991, the central government's power over the 15 Soviet republics dwindled sharply. Individual republics declared their independence, and what was left of the Soviet Union quickly unravelled. The Soviet government officially disbanded several months after the failed coup and was replaced by a Commonwealth of Independent States in which the republics retained their independent status.[5] With the crumbling of central control, the republics are now confronting the problem of deciding how much their own self-interests, especially in economic and military matters, require recognition of their interdependence.

States in the Constitutional System

That there are 50 states is a historical accident. If wars had been lost instead of won, if treaties and land purchases had not been made, if rivers coursed through different areas, the number, names, and sizes of states would be different. States are integral parts of our social and political consciousness. State boundaries are superimposed on satellite pictures of weather patterns. State universities enjoy great attention through the exploits of their athletic teams, and children in elementary schools throughout the land spend time trying to memorize the names of state capitals. The existence of states is simply assumed.

States play a crucial role in the American political system, including administering social welfare policies, grappling with regional problems, amending the Constitution, and shaping electoral contests at the national level. States, for example, act in some measure as administrative units to help carry out national social welfare programs substantially funded by Congress, such as food stamps, Medicaid, and Aid to Families with Dependent Children. Through the device of the **interstate compact,** states can enter into formal agreements with other states to deal with policy problems that cross state lines. An example is the agreement between New York and New Jersey to establish the New York Port Authority to regulate transportation in the New York City area. States also play a role in the process of formally amending the Constitution. Controversy has swirled about a variety of proposed amendments, including issues involving abortion, flag burning, and a balanced budget. But no formal change to the Constitution can be made without the states considering, debating, and voting on the issue.

With the exception of the president and vice-president of the United States, *every* elected official in the country is chosen either by the voters in a particular state (the governor or a U.S. senator) or by voters in part of a state (U.S. representatives or state legislators). Every elected official, except for the president and vice-president, has a geographic constituency that is either a state or part of a state, such as a county or a congressional district. This simple but crucial fact helps to

---

[5] See Gregory Gleason, *Federalism and Nationalism: The Struggle for Republican Rights in the USSR* (Boulder, Colo.: Westview Press, 1990) for a discussion of Soviet federalism prior to the creation of the Commonwealth of Independent States.

explain much legislative behavior at the national level when, for example, members of Congress press for national legislation that helps industries in their home states or oppose the closing of military bases in their districts.

Another illustration of the role of the states is the **electoral college,** a political institution that, following the mandate in the Constitution, determines the winner in presidential elections. Presidents are elected not by a plurality (the highest number) of votes cast by voters throughout the United States but by a majority of electoral college votes. Each state has a number of electoral votes equal to the number of its members in the House and Senate combined. Because the number of representatives is determined by population, the states with larger numbers of people have a larger number of electoral votes. California, for example, has 54 electoral votes, whereas Delaware has only 3. In every state but two, the presidential candidate receiving the largest number of popular votes in the state receives *all* that state's electoral votes.[6]

In effect, on the day of the presidential election, 51 separate elections are taking place (in the 50 states and the District of Columbia). Voters choose among slates of electors committed to one or another of the candidates. When the popular votes in each state are counted, state-by-state electoral college vote totals are combined to determine the presidential victor. After the election, victorious electors officially cast their presidential votes in their respective state capitals. From the perspective of federalism, the important point is that *states as states* play a crucial role in electing the person who holds the most important political office in the land. Presidential candidates must appeal not to an amorphous mass of citizens but to Texans, North Carolinians, Californians, and Virginians.

The center of the U.S. population changes as more and more people follow the sun in their moves to the South and the West. Florida, California, and Texas have gained population. New York, Ohio, Pennsylvania, Illinois, and Michigan have suffered relative losses of residents, with implications for power shifts in the U.S. House and in the electoral college. Figure 2.2 shows the shifts in regional power between 1942 and 1992. After the 1990 census, almost one out of four members of the U.S. House is from California, Texas, or Florida, and the presidential candidate winning California receives 20 percent of the electoral votes needed to win the presidency.

The Rise of the National Government

As Chapter 1 made clear, the states were clearly dominant under the Articles of Confederation. The national government quite literally started out from nothing, yet we have today a national government whose actions, from delivering Social Security checks to regulating the safety of toys and nuclear power plants, pervades the daily lives of citizens. How did this change come about? Massive technological, communications, and economic changes have transformed the nation over the

---

[6] The two exceptions are Maine and Nebraska, which allocate electoral votes on the basis of candidate victories in congressional districts.

FIGURE 2.2

Shifts in Regional Power, 1942 and 1992, as Measured by the Size of State Delegations in the U.S. House of Representatives

Shifts and changes in population between 1942 and 1992 meant that over the past half-century parts of the East and the Midwest lost seats in the House of Representatives and the West and South gained. The apportionment of the 435 House seats is calculated for each state following the census every 10 years. A state may increase its population but lose a seat if the *rate* of gain in other states is much greater.   SOURCE: U.S. Bureau of the Census.

past two centuries. War and depression have made their own contributions to the shift in focus of demands and expectations.

The conflict between unity and diversity, which gave birth to the federal system, also shaped the relationships between the national and state governments in the early decades of the new nation. The national government cooperated with the states in a variety of areas. With economic development among the highest priorities of the new nation, the national government provided funds and technical assistance to the states for construction of roads and canals. Land grants to states in the West for educational purposes signaled greater cooperation to come.[7]

Despite the cooperation, however, sharp conflicts also occurred between the national government and the states in the early decades of the Republic. The **Kentucky and Virginia Resolutions,** adopted by the legislatures of those states in 1798, held that the Constitution created a compact among the states and that the power of the national government was sharply limited by the states. In 1819 the state of Maryland contested the right of the national government to establish a national bank. And in 1832 the South Carolina legislature declared a national tariff law null and void. The very existence of national power was at issue in these instances of national-state conflict. The federal system was ultimately tested in war.

The early skirmishes between the national government and the states paled in significance compared to the Civil War. At one level the war was about the question of slavery. But at another level the war was a question in federalism. Could a state (or several states) leave the Union and, in effect, unravel the work of the Constitutional Convention of 1787? From the perspective of federalism, the most important consequence of the war was preservation of the Union. President Lincoln is best known as emancipator of the slaves, but his sharp and unyielding refusal to allow dissolution of the Union was crucial in the evolution of federalism. The significance of Lincoln's stance cannot be overstated. Here was the chief executive in a national government that did not even exist a century earlier using *national* resources in a major war effort to resist by brute force the claims of the seceding states, four of which predated the national government itself.

The end of the Civil War marked the beginning of a rapid change in the character of the nation's economy. Transcontinental railroads pulled the nation together and brought farmers, producers, and sellers closer to buyers and consumers. Major new industries like steel, oil, and later, the automobile, began to emerge. With them came new forms of economic organization. Corporations crossed state boundaries in their activities and their consequences. Control and regulation of economic matters increasingly eluded the grasp of any single state, with political demands that the national government confront the problems that economic monopolies left in their trail.

Later in the twentieth century, the economy plunged into the Great Depression of the 1930s. Farm and industrial prices collapsed, factories closed, banks failed, homes were foreclosed, and unemployment rates shot up. State and local govern-

---

[7] See Daniel J. Elazar, "Federal-State Cooperation in the Nineteenth-Century United States," *Political Science Quarterly* 79 (1964): 248–265.

ments were simply overwhelmed by the needs and demands of millions of Americans who clearly needed help to survive. National problems seemed to require national solutions. As never before, the national government embarked on a series of social welfare policies that both improved the economic conditions of many and generated expectations that the national government could solve a variety of social problems in the future. Today many domestic programs administered by the states or their localities are funded by the national government.

Finally, the national government has responsibility for national security and relations with other nations. In the twentieth century, the Cold War and the increasing interdependence of the world economy combined to make the national government's conduct of foreign affairs important on a continuing basis. The end of the Cold War may mean a smaller national military establishment, but the need for national government policies to enhance the nation's competitiveness in the global economy promises to become more acute.

The seemingly inexorable rise in the power of the national government has been accompanied by political demands that state and local governments assume a larger presence in the making of policy decisions affecting them. For example, **New Federalism,** a term most closely associated with the Republican administrations of Richard Nixon (1969–1974) and Ronald Reagan (1981–1989), calls for state and local governments to assume a much greater role than they traditionally had during the explosions of national policy initiatives in the Democratic administrations of Franklin Roosevelt (1933–1945) in the New Deal and Lyndon Johnson (1963-1969) in the Great Society.[8] New Federalism holds that state and local governments should not only be entrusted with greater responsibilities, but that they should also be allowed to follow their own best judgment in deciding what to do. Giving state and local governments more discretion in how they spend national grant money is an illustration. This view of federalism dovetails with the traditional Republican party "grass-roots" philosophy that the government in the best position to make good policy choices is the government "closest" to the people. But whether nationally defined policy goals, such as the amelioration of poverty, can (or should) accommodate state and local policies that may diverge from those goals is an old question in federalism.

Express and Implied Powers

The search for the right balance between state and national power remains an enduring issue in the federal system. What powers do the states have in their relationships to each other and to the national government? What powers does the national government have over the states? The Republic has struggled with these questions since 1787. The Constitution prohibits the exercise of some powers by one or both levels of national and state governments; for example, states may not coin money. In addition, national and state governments share some *concur-*

---

[8] For an examination of the differences between the Nixon and Reagan approaches to New Federalism, see Timothy Conlan, *New Federalism: Intergovernmental Reform from Nixon to Reagan* (Washington, D.C.: Brookings Institution, 1988).

rent powers, such as the power each has to tax the same individual's income. However, the most important point about national and state powers is the distinction between *delegated* and *reserved* powers.

In accepting the Constitution, the people in the states through the ratification process *delegated* important new powers to the new national government. The statement of these powers is contained in Article 1, Section 8, of the Constitution (see the appendix). **Delegated powers** are ordinarily divided into two types: express powers and implied powers. **Express powers** are specifically enumerated as belonging to Congress. Among these are the power to levy and collect taxes, to borrow money, to regulate interstate commerce, to coin money, to declare war, and to raise and support armies.

However, the last statement of power listed in Article 1, Section 8, also delegates to the national government **implied powers,** which by their very nature have been subject to intense dispute. This provision is also known as the "elastic" or "necessary and proper" clause, and delegates to Congress the power "to make all Laws which shall be necessary and proper for carrying into Execution the foregoing Powers, and all other Powers vested by this Constitution in the Government of the United States, or in any Department or Officer thereof." Obviously, what is "necessary and proper" in a particular circumstance is a matter open to varying interpretations. A narrow interpretation would constrict the powers of the national government, whereas a broad interpretation would enlarge them.

The first time the clause was specifically interpreted was in *McCulloch* v. *Maryland*, one of the most famous and consequential Supreme Court decisions ever made.[9] The case represented an ideological division over the powers of the national government and the place of the states in the Union. Conflicting political objectives were sought in terms of opposing theories of federalism. Congress had chartered a national bank. Some states opposed the bank because it competed with state-chartered banks. Hoping to put the national bank out of business, Maryland imposed a tax on the new bank. McCulloch, its cashier, refused to pay. As part of its case, Maryland argued not only that a state could tax a nationally chartered bank but also that Congress had no authority to charter a bank in the first place because banking was not a power delegated to Congress. Instead, banking was a subject the Constitution reserved for the states.

Contrary to Maryland's claims, Chief Justice John Marshall (1801–1835) declared that Congress possessed ample constitutional authority to charter a bank even though such a power was not expressly listed in the Constitution. In Marshall's view, the power to establish a bank was implied in the express powers, such as the powers to tax and to coin money. A bank was a means to achieving the ends spelled out in the Constitution. Marshall's interpretation of the "necessary and proper" clause clearly allowed expansive power to the national government. In his memorable words,

> Let the end be legitimate, let it be within the scope of the constitution, and all means which are appropriate, which are plainly adapted to that end,

---

[9] 17 U.S. (4 Wheaton) 316 (1819).

which are not prohibited, but consistent with the letter and spirit of the constitution, are constitutional.

Furthermore, Marshall held that Maryland could not tax the bank because it was an instrument of the national government. In a conflict between an act of Congress and a state law, the former would prevail. No single part of the political community could be allowed to subvert a policy undertaken by the whole community represented in Congress.

Because of the brevity of the Constitution, many of its clauses and phrases are ambiguous and give little or no direction to what is "legitimate" in a particular circumstance. The framers could not address every problem or clarify every uncertainty. According to Marshall's decision in *McCulloch,* the Constitution created a stronger national government by delegating to it express and implied powers. But exactly how strong it was to be or how it would evolve was left for later generations to decide.

Reserved Powers: What Do the States Do?

If the new government was to be more powerful and the states were nonetheless to continue to exist, what powers were left to the states? Although simpler in theory than in practice, the principle is that states can do all things not specifically prohibited to them and not delegated exclusively to the national government. These remaining powers are known as **reserved powers**. State and local governments are responsible for delivering the vast majority of public services. Working for the national government are about 3 million civilian employees, a number that has remained relatively constant for more than two decades. However, growth in government employment has occurred at the state and local levels. In 1992, state and local governments employed 15.7 million people, more than five times the number of civilian employees working for the national government.[10] This number of employees indicates that states and localities play a large role in providing public services.

The **Tenth Amendment** states that "the powers not delegated to the United States by the Constitution, nor prohibited to the States, are reserved to the States respectively, or to the people." Politicians and groups whose political ideas are served by advocating "states' rights" have frequently pointed to the Tenth Amendment as support for their claims. However, that amendment, unlike the Articles of Confederation, does not contain the word *expressly* in citing powers delegated to the national government. Such delegated powers *include* the implied powers cited by Chief Justice Marshall in *McCulloch* v. *Maryland.*

Among powers reserved for the states are "police" responsibilities for the health, safety, and welfare of citizens. For civilized life to be possible, people must be able to carry on their day-to-day activities with the reasonable assurance that

---

[10] U.S. Office of Management and Budget, *Budget of the United States Government, Fiscal Year 1994* (Washington, D.C.: GPO, 1993), Appendix One, p. 42.

physical threats to their health and well-being are kept to an absolute minimum. For example, among the health responsibilities of states are dealing with outbreaks of contagious diseases, the disposal of wastes, the need for cleanliness in public eating establishments, and the administration of networks of state hospitals and mental institutions.

In one of their most visible roles, the states also have primary responsibility for preventing and prosecuting criminal activities. Most of this work occurs at the level of local governments whose organization, powers, and functions are constitutionally subject to control by state governments. Some crimes, such as airline hijacking, kidnapping, tampering with the mails, and counterfeiting money, are violations of national law enforced by national government personnel. However, most law enforcement officers in the country are state agents and local personnel who act as agents of the state. From state police officers to county sheriffs who track down suspected criminals, to the local police who deal with matters like burglary and domestic violence, most law enforcement responsibilities lie at the state and local levels. Most suspected rapists, murderers, thieves, burglars, muggers, and assorted swindlers are pursued only by state and local law enforcement personnel, prosecuted only in state courts, and incarcerated only in state prisons.

Practically all individuals encounter state power in a direct and personal way many times in their lives. A variety of inoculations and vaccinations may be required by the state before entrance into elementary school systems. The right to drive a car requires application for a state driver's license and the passing of a driver's test administered by a state officer. Individuals who wish to marry must apply for a (state) marriage license, and the ceremony is performed either by a public (state) official such as a justice of the peace or by a minister, priest, or rabbi who acts as an agent of the state in performing the ceremony. In divorce, the contesting parties must go through some (state) judicial proceeding to legally dissolve the relationship. And when the custody of children is at issue, state courts are called on to make the decisions.

States also play a regulatory role in a variety of matters having to do with business and commerce within the state. From laws on safety to zoning practices to requirements for filing periodic tax and information reports, practically no enterprise can escape the touch of the state. Entrance into many professions is controlled by state licensing boards, which set rules, regulations, and standards that are supposed to ensure the quality of services delivered to citizens but which also serve to limit entry into the profession. Such licensing procedures touch barbers, lawyers, medical specialists, dieticians, cosmotologists, real estate agents, and even taxidermists.

Perhaps the most visible and pervasive role of the state is in the area of public education. State policies of universal education have emerged from the belief in the importance of schools for improving literacy, inculcating civic and cultural values, and generally enhancing the capabilities of citizens. In administering educational systems, local school districts are agencies of the state. Curricula, certification of teachers, the length of the school year, and policy on truancy are all matters of state power and concern. Some of the great policy debates of the past generation have focused on the role of the states in education. Should prayers be

Law enforcement is primarily the responsibility of state and local governments in the American federal system. Occasionally, however, civil disorders strain the resources of local police departments and require deployment of federal troops, as happened in the riots in Los Angeles, California, in late April 1992, following the acquittal in *state* court of police officers charged in the beating of motorist Rodney King. Although local in nature, such events can have an impact on national politics too. (Conviction of two of the officers occurred in *federal* court in April 1993.)

said aloud in the schools, or should a moment of silence for "meditation" be allowed at the beginning of each school day? Should schools be desegregated and, if so, how? Should the busing of schoolchildren be required to achieve integration? Should states be required to equalize expenditures among wealthier and poorer school districts? The *national* government can pursue *national* approaches, but its stress on unity can limit or threaten diversity among the states. Educational policy debates illustrate the vitality of the federal system. When shall the national government have its way, and when shall the states be allowed to go their separate ways?

Local Government: A Political Landscape of Contrasts

One of the reserved powers of the states is their control over the structure and powers of local governments. The Constitution makes no mention of cities or other local governments, except for the nation's capital, the "Seat of Government." This fact makes local governments "creatures of the state." The relationships between state legislatures, traditionally with a rural bias, and local governments, especially those of larger cities, have been frequently stormy. Through much of the nineteenth century, state legislatures kept local governments on a tight rein by determining with great specificity their powers, functions, and procedures. In the late nineteenth century and the first half of the twentieth, however, many local governments—particularly those of larger cities—were granted **home rule,** the power to determine, within broad limits, their powers and functions. In the 1960s local governments (again, those of larger cities in particular) increasingly developed relationships—generally created by flows of cash—directly with the national government. Nonetheless, all local governments are, according to the Constitution, agents of the state performing what are constitutionally state functions.

Table 2.1 shows that there are more than 83,000 local governments in the United States. These local governments perform many of the unglamorous services essential to civilized life, such as collecting trash, pursuing criminals, putting out fires, and providing drinking water. Local governments range in size from huge cities like New York with more than 7 million people (more than in 41 states) to small villages and hamlets with fewer than 100 inhabitants. Governments at the local level differ in their structure. Some have a **mayor-council**

TABLE 2.1
Governmental Units in the Federal System

1	National government
50	States
83,186	Local governments
3,042	Counties (called parishes in Louisiana)
19,200	Municipalities
16,691	Towns and townships
14,721	School districts
29,532	Special districts

SOURCE: U. S. Bureau of the Census, *Statistical Abstract of the United States, 1992 (Washington, D.C.: GPO, 1992), p. 278. Data are for 1987.*

The federal system contains many governments, but they all do not do the same things. The national government, all state governments, and many local governments are general-purpose governments; that is, they perform a wide variety of functions. A city government, for example, will typically provide police protection and numerous social services. School districts and special districts geographically overlap with general-purpose governments and perform only a single function, such as education, water distribution, fire protection, or sewage treatment. The largest growth in number of governmental units in recent years has occurred in special districts because they enable local areas to provide collectively services that they could not afford individually. Moreover, the particular tasks of special districts often stretch beyond the boundaries of local general-purpose governments. Finally, some local governments, such as towns or townships, have not been given power by their state constitutions and governments to perform such functions.

form of government, which mirrors the executive-legislative structure at the state and national levels. Others have a **council-manager** form in which appointed managers look after the day-to-day operations of the government. Still others have a **commission** form of government in which power is diffused, and no single individual is in charge. Some local governments are "general purpose." That is, they are responsible for a wide variety of functions including police protection, housing, social services, and parks administration. School districts and special districts overlap these general-purpose governments and are limited to a single function, such as education, mosquito control, fire protection, or transportation.

Although residents do not usually pay much attention to local government, they can and do get intensely interested during a local crisis or controversy. For example, when the water supply becomes polluted with toxic wastes, citizens get involved. School board meetings can be drab affairs, but they can become arenas of excitement and drama when matters like AIDS education programs or higher taxes for a new school are at issue. Similarly, most local zoning board hearings are routine and sparsely attended. But a proposal by a hamburger chain to locate near a predominantly residential area or the effort of a chemical company to place a toxic waste facility in or near a town are issues that practically guarantee action by affected residents. In terms of size, structure, functions, and degrees of citizen interest, local governments are a mosaic of contrasts.

Government Relationships in the Federal System

The existence of different levels of government within a federal system means that federalism is about *relationships* among governments.[11] Because these governmental relationships are intangible and constantly shifting and changing, trying to understand them is not an easy task. Unlike the presidency, for example, federalism is not an institution with a physical place where its work is done. But one way to understand federalism is to picture it as a series of *legal, fiscal,* and *political* relationships among levels of government.

Models of Federalism

The federal system can at first appear to be a jumble of intangible relationships without order or obvious meaning. The effort to create models is an attempt to create pictures or portraits that bring some order to the complexity and chaos. Two models are particularly important.

---

[11] For a comprehensive view of government relationships in the federal system on which this section draws, see Deil S. Wright, *Understanding Intergovernmental Relations,* 3d ed. (Pacific Grove, Calif.: Brooks/Cole, 1988), especially Chap. 2.

The first is **dual federalism,** a model positing the view that national and state governments are separate and independent from each other, with each level exercising its own powers in its own jurisdiction. This model, supporting the rights of the states, was important as a judicial theory of federalism in the nineteenth and early twentieth centuries. In *Hammer* v. *Dagenhart,*[12] a decision the justices later overturned, the Supreme Court ruled that Congress could not ban shipment across state lines of products made with child labor because labor regulation was a state power only.

Dual federalism was never a completely realistic description of the relationship between the nation and the states. For example, in the nineteenth century the national government gave land to the states to use for educational purposes. Indeed, some of the nation's great universities today are among the "land grant" institutions that resulted from this policy. But the model does reflect the fact that the state and national governments in much of the nineteenth and early twentieth centuries did not interact with each other with the regularity taken for granted today. Dual federalism is also known as the "layer cake" model because the separate levels of government in the model are likened to distinct layers of a cake.

The second model is **marble cake federalism,** a view of federalism that likens intertwining relationships between the national and state and local governments to the intertwining flavors in a marble cake.[13] Across a wide range of public policies, despite occasional conflict, all levels of government work closely with one another. Minnesotans and Georgians are also Americans, and that fact helps to explain the intermingling of governmental functions. Interstate highways are largely funded by federal grants, but the highways are built and patrolled by the states. Medical care for the poor is jointly funded by national and state governments. National, state, and local law enforcement authorities regularly combine forces in pursuit of criminals, such as drug smugglers, bank robbers, or suspected murderers whose escape routes take them across state lines. State and local health authorities call on the expert services of the national Centers for Disease Control when outbreaks of contagious or mysterious diseases threaten communities. State environmental and health agencies work with national units, such as the Environmental Protection Agency or the Nuclear Regulatory Commission, when problems with toxic or radioactive wastes arise.

The relationships are not always smooth and free of conflict. State and local officials criticize the national government for cuts in funding. FBI agents may run up against local police policies that in the agents' view hinder efficient law enforcement work. State and local officials may confront national regulations that they see as either pointless or unnecessarily encumbering. Nonetheless, marble cake federalism is a portrait of the federal system in which officials from different levels of government work together regularly.

---

[12] 247 U.S. 251 (1918).
[13] The classic statement of the model can be found in Morton Grodzins, "The Federal System," in *President's Commission on National Goals, Goals for Americans* (Englewood Cliffs, N.J.: Prentice-Hall, 1960), pp. 265–282.

Legal Relationships

One consequence of having different levels of government in the same political system is the likelihood of conflict over who has the power to do what. Legal conflicts between the national and state governments have both a rich past and a continuing vibrancy. The Supreme Court has played a major role in answering the questions such conflicts raise.

The Court has interpreted the Constitution to mean that diverse approaches among the states in some matters is constitutionally unacceptable. It has generally supported the national government and national constitutional values in conflicts with the states, for example, in its interpretation of the interstate commerce clause. The "regulation of interstate commerce" is one of the most important powers that the Constitution grants to Congress. This provision has allowed Congress to shape national economic and even social policy. States do have a role to play. They can enact legislation affecting commerce to protect the health and safety of citizens. States can also act in the absence of congressional action or when not prohibited by Congress. But when Congress does act, the Supreme Court has generally allowed wide latitude to national legislation that limits state power in interstate commerce. For example, upholding the reach of congressional power in the Civil Rights Act of 1964, the Court in 1964 held that hotels and local restaurants could not discriminate on the basis of race in their services because travelers and food served were in interstate commerce.[14]

Through its interpretation of the due process clause of the Fourteenth Amendment, the Court has also applied most of the limitations on the power of the national government contained in the first eight amendments to the activities of the states themselves. These amendments were added to the Constitution in the early years of the new government to assuage fears that the new national government might be a powerful threat to individual liberties. Ironically, the Court has applied these limitations to the states themselves. For example, states must now provide counsel for people accused of crimes and may not sponsor prayers in the public schools.[15]

The Court's interpretation of the Fourteenth Amendment's *equal protection clause* has also limited state power. For example, by requiring equal populations in state legislative districts, the Court's reapportionment decisions shifted political power from rural to urban areas.[16] The Court has even shaped the structure of local government. As an example, the Court found in violation of its "one person, one vote" rulings New York City's Board of Estimate, a local government body with substantial powers over land use, the city's budget, and other matters.[17] The five boroughs of New York had equal representation on the Board, despite great population differences among the boroughs. The Court's decision was the impetus

---

[14] See *Heart of Atlanta Motel* v. *United States,* 379 U.S. 241 (1964), and *Katzenbach* v. *McClung,* 379 U.S. 294 (1964).

[15] *Gideon* v. *Wainwright,* 372 U.S. 335 (1963); *Engel* v. *Vitale,* 370 U.S. 421 (1962).

[16] *Baker* v. *Carr,* 369 U.S. 186 (1962); *Reynolds* v. *Sims,* 377 U.S. 533 (1964).

[17] *Morris* v. *Board of Estimate,* 489 U.S. 103 (1989).

for elimination of the Board of Estimate and a major restructuring of New York City's government.

Using the equal protection clause the Court has also held that the states cannot exclusively determine for and by themselves the shape of their own school systems, even though public education has been traditionally among the reserved powers of the states. In *Brown* v. *Board of Education*[18] the Court unanimously declared that racially segregated school systems are unconstitutional. Some constitutional values are so important that they must be nationally determined and, if necessary, enforced by national power.

Despite the support the Court has generally given the national government, the constitutional power of the states in conflicts with the national government is not a settled issue. In some recent cases the Court has weakened the power of the states and slighted the principle of federalism. But in others the Court has asserted a constitutional role for the states protecting them from incursions of congressional power. For example, may Congress set minimum wages and maximum hours for the employees of state governments and their political subdivisions? Although the Court upheld such standards for private employers a half-century ago, the Court declared in 1976 that states were immune to such requirements. But the Court reversed itself in 1985 by ruling in *Garcia* v. *San Antonio Metropolitan Transit Authority* that Congress *may* apply minimum-wage and maximum-hour legislation to state employees.[19] Three years later, in *South Carolina* v. *Baker, Secretary of the Treasury,* the Court ruled that Congress could tax state and local government bearer bonds,[20] a decision that limits the tax immunity of state and local governments. The *Garcia* and *South Carolina* decisions made state and local officials wonder whether the Court had "abandoned" Tenth Amendment protection of state powers.[21]

However, assuaging such fears, the Court ruled in 1991 that a congressional statute banning age discrimination does *not* overrule a provision in the Missouri Constitution requiring state judges to retire at age 70. In other words, the state of Missouri can reasonably determine for itself mandatory retirement policies for state officials.[22] The Court also ruled in 1992 that Congress cannot require a state to "take title" to radioactive waste produced within its borders if the state does not make provision for its disposal.[23] These cases indicate that states continue to draw on powers reserved to them in the Constitution.[24] The search for the proper legal balance between state and national power continues. The line between them has not disappeared.

---

[18] 347 U.S. 483 (1954).

[19] *National League of Cities* v. *Usery,* 426 U.S. 833 (1976); *Garcia* v. *San Antonio Metropolitan Transit Authority,* 469 U.S. 528 (1985).

[20] 485 U.S. 505 (1988).

[21] See, for example, David E. Nething, "States Must Regain Their Powers," *State Government* 63 (January–March 1990): 6–7.

[22] *Gregory* v. *Ashcroft,* 59 U.S.L.W. 4687 (1991).

[23] *New York* v. *United States,* 60 U.S.L.W. 4603 (1992).

[24] See Charles Wise and Rosemary O'Leary, "Is Federalism Dead or Alive in the Supreme Court? Implications for Public Administrators," *Public Administration Review* 52 (November–December 1992): 559–572.

Fiscal Relationships

Federalism is more than just legal relationships. Cooperative *fiscal* relationships have become the single most important characteristic of federalism in the twentieth century, for money is a kind of glue that binds the different levels of government. It is now commonplace to cite ratification in 1913 of the **Sixteenth Amendment,** which granted Congress the power to tax incomes, as a significant event contributing to the national government's unparalleled capacity to raise revenue. This capacity to raise funds reinforced the unprecedented emergence of public expectations for national government action in the Great Depression. The national government was cast in the role of a banker, doling out money to deal with social and economic ills that states had either ignored or found too large for local solutions.

The terms and conditions of specific programs vary enormously from one program to another, but cash grants from the national government to state and local governments are usually divided into two groups: categorical grants-in-aid and block grants. A **categorical grant-in-aid,** the predominant form of national aid, is a transfer of cash from the national government to state or local governments for some specific purpose, usually with the accompanying requirement that state and local governments match the national money with some funds of their own. The purposes of these grants are determined by the national government; and state and local governments have little or no discretion or flexibility in how the funds can be spent. If the money is given for highways, it cannot be spent on libraries or airports. Some of these grants are given to state and local governments on the basis of some formula that takes into account factors like population and poverty and income levels. Others distribute money for specific projects in response to applications from state or local governments.

Categorical grants are available in practically every policy area, including highways, health, education, and nutrition assistance. The Advisory Commission on Intergovernmental Relations reported that there were 478 categorical grant programs in 1989.[25] However, a small number of grants comprise a large proportion of total grant dollars. For example, the president's budget office estimated that the three largest programs, Medicaid (medical benefits for the poor), aid for highways, and family support (welfare) payments, together made up 56 percent of the grant total in 1994. Medicaid, the largest single grant program, *alone* accounted for more than 40 percent of the total.[26]

A **block grant** is a transfer of cash from the national government to state and local governments that allows the recipients greater discretion in its use. Instead of defining with great specificity how the money ought to be spent, the national government permits expenditures in some broad policy area, such as community development, social services, or criminal justice. An increase in this type of grant was a major federalism priority of the Reagan Administration because block grants

---

[25] *A Catalog of Federal Grant-in-Aid Programs to State and Local Governments: Grants Funded in 1989* (Washington, D.C.: GPO, 1989), p. 1.
[26] Calculated from program estimates in Office of Management and Budget, *Budget of the United States Government, Fiscal Year 1994* (Washington, D.C.: GPO, 1993), Part One, pp. 81–85.

The familiar and ubiquitous interstate highway system, such as this complex configuration in California, is a classic illustration of fiscal relationships in the federal system. Dollars from the national government blended with smaller amounts of revenue from the states have helped pull together the trilogy of automobiles, highways, and the American people.

allow greater discretion at the state and local levels. In 1989 there were 14 block grants, which together accounted for almost 11 percent of the national aid total.[27] State and local governments prefer the flexibility allowed by block grants to the more rigid procedural requirements that accompany categorical grants.

In 1922 the national government granted to the states the paltry sum of $122 million, the major proportion of which was spent on highway construction.[28] Figure 2.3 shows the sharp increase in such aid over the past four decades. Reflecting the explosion of Great Society grant programs in the 1960s, national aid in current dollars almost quintupled between 1965 and 1975, from $11 billion to $50 billion, and almost tripled again in the decade and a half after 1975.

---

[27] *A Catalog of Federal Grant-in-Aid Programs,* p. 2.
[28] Advisory Commission on Intergovernmental Relations, *Categorical Grants: Their Role and Design* (Washington, D.C.: GPO, 1978), p. 16.

FIGURE 2.3

National Aid to State and Local Governments Since 1950, in Current and Constant Dollars, in Billions

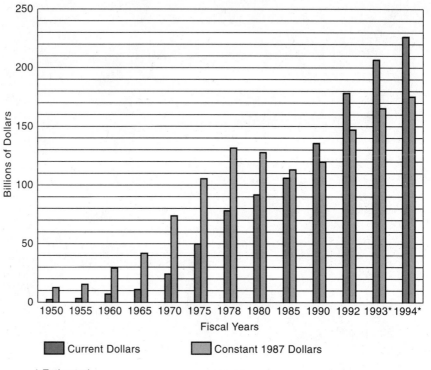

Fiscal Years

■ Current Dollars   ▢ Constant 1987 Dollars

* Estimated

National aid to state and local governments rose sharply after 1965 to a high point in 1978 of $131 billion in constant 1987 dollars, then fell in constant dollars through the 1980s. In the early 1990s, aid began to rise again, in both current and constant dollars. In 1994, the amount in constant dollars was 14 times the amount of aid in 1950.

SOURCE: Office of Management and Budget.

However, as Figure 2.3 also shows, in constant dollars, that is, with the effects of inflation taken into account, through the 1980s national aid to state and local governments *declined* after 1978. In 1980 15 percent of the national budget was spent on grants, a proportion that fell to 11 percent in 1990.[29]

Figure 2.3 shows that national aid is projected to rise in the early 1990s, but the growth area in national government dollars is in programs providing payments for individuals, such as Medicaid. In 1960, 35 percent of federal grant dollars were spent on payments for individuals. By 1994 that proportion increased to about 63

---

[29] Office of Management and Budget, *Budget, Baselines, Historical Data, and Alternatives for the Future* (Washington, D.C.: GPO, 1993), p. 428.

percent.[30] The proportional drop in grant programs that allow state and local *governments* to spend money, such as funding for capital projects and the discretionary dollars provided by the now defunct revenue-sharing program, forced those governments to depend increasingly on their own resources to support programs that had previously been aided by Congress. President Clinton's first budget proposal projected into the late 1990s the continuing trend of proportionally more dollars for individuals and proportionally less money for other programs.[31]

Political Relationships

The federal system can be viewed as a series of legal and fiscal relationships. However, a third way to look at the federal system is to see it as an arena for *political* relationships among officials at all levels of government who lobby and cajole one another, and who bargain and negotiate with one another. The cast of political players includes members of Congress representing states and local districts, the president, governors, state legislators, mayors, county and township commissioners, and national, state, and local bureaucrats. These officials band together into groups, such as the National Governors' Association, the National Conference of State Legislatures, and the United States Conference of Mayors, all of which are among the participants in federal system politics.

The range and variety of political relationships are enormous because officials at all levels in the federal system press for their own interests as they see them. Scarce resources, the search for the appropriate balance between state and national power, and social and economic differences among the states all drive these political relationships. Sometimes local or state officeholders as a group will make demands on the national government. In the competition for dollars, for example, mayors want more federal money. In the battle over which level of government has the power to do what, governors want fewer federal regulations and more state flexibility in deciding regulatory policy.

But many of the political relationships in the federal system derive from economic differences among regions and states and their localities as they compete with each other to press their individual interests. Economic development and the creation of new jobs are always among the highest priorities of state officials. New businesses and jobs can bolster tax collections, help political incumbents keep their posts, and make the state more attractive to outsiders. Understandably, states are in constant competition with each other to attract new industry and to retain the industry they have. Domestic and foreign corporations that are planning new plant sites are wooed by governors, economic development staffs, and local officials, all of whom cite favorable tax provisions, excellent physical facilities, and a skilled and dependable work force as reasons why the new plant should be located in their state.

Given the huge budget expenditures of the national government, state officials

---

[30] *Budget of the United States Government, Fiscal Year 1994*, p. 79.
[31] Ibid.

Politics and Economics

Fiscal Stress in the States

The fiscal woes of state governments in the early 1990s show that debates over money dominate the policy agendas of states. Whether taxes should be raised, and who should pay them, whether program cuts should be imposed, and which program beneficiaries should suffer the costs of the cuts are old questions in state politics. But conflicts over state taxing and spending took on a new intensity as state budgets were squeezed by the pressures of a lagging economy, changes in national government aid, and increases in national government mandates.

A major issue in the 1992 presidential campaign, the budget deficit of the national government is like an ominous storm cloud hovering over practically all policy deliberations in Washington. Political demands to reduce the deficit may grow, but the national government is not constitutionally or statutorily required to have a balanced budget. Most states, however, do not enjoy the luxury of being able to carry a deficit. Most states are bound by their constitutions or statutes to produce a balanced budget every year.

Although the degree of pain varied among regions, most states faced acute budget problems in the early 1990s. To balance their budgets in 1992, 35 states were forced to cut spending in budgets that had already been enacted. The cuts totaled almost $4.5 billion and ranged from $2 million in Idaho to $558 million in Florida. Because of a weak economy, state revenues simply had not kept pace with program demands.

For their revenues, states in large measure rely on some combination of sales, income, and corporate taxes. But the number of tax dollars going into state treasuries is dependent on conditions in the economy over which state governments have little control. If the rate of unemployment in the state increases or remains high, fewer people pay income taxes. If people who lose higher-paying jobs are forced into lower-paying ones, they pay fewer dollars in taxes. If consumers are worried about their jobs and have little confidence in the future, they buy less, producing lower sales tax collections. If corporations lose money or close plants, they pay less in taxes. A persistent recession in the early 1990s, with unemployment rates exceeding 7 percent and fragile consumer confidence, produced a bleak economic picture for most states. In 1992, 31 states found that incoming revenues were below projections on which budget plans had been based. These shortfalls forced some states to eliminate programs, lay off workers, and reduce funding aid to local governments, among other strategies.

Early in 1993, the Center for the Study of States reported an increase in state tax collections, reflecting in state treasuries the consequences of a stronger economy. Although economic re-

lobby to get what they see as their fair share of national funding. Associations of state and city officials and organizations such as the Northeast-Midwest Institute and the Sun Belt Institute promote the economic interests of the regions they represent. Thirty-eight states even have offices in Washington, D.C., to facilitate their own lobbying efforts to get federal grants and contracts. Illustrating the global reach of state competition, 39 states have offices in Japan to press their interests in the search for international trade and investment.[32]

---

[32] Numbers on state offices in Washington and Japan are taken from General Accounting Office, *Federal-State-Local Relations* (GPO: Washington, D.C., 1990), p. 32.

covery began to ease the financial woes of most states, other pressures continued to constrain state budgets.

The fiscal problems that states face have been exacerbated by changes in national government aid. States now receive from the national government less discretionary funding and a smaller proportion of direct aid. The termination in 1981 of **general revenue sharing** for the states, a program through which Washington gave every state money that the state could use with practically no strings attached, eliminated a major source of national funding. General revenue sharing for cities was abolished in 1986, forcing city governments to dig more deeply into their own revenue sources, or convince their state governments to help fill the gap, or do without. In addition, an increasing proportion of federal grant dollars are funding payments for individuals (e.g., welfare payments) with a smaller proportion of federal aid funding capital projects (like sewage treatment plants) and state training and education programs.

The largest payment-for-individuals program is Medicaid, a joint federal-state effort providing health care for the poor. The explosive growth of Medicaid has made that program the second largest item in state budgets, after elementary and secondary education. Rising health care costs are partly responsible, but Congress in 1990 mandated wider coverage for poor children under the program, adding to pressures on state budgets. Such mandates from Washington, which require additional spending of scarce state resources, add to the fiscal stress of the states.

That economic recovery leads to higher state tax collections underlines the sensitivity of state budgets to the vagaries of a changing economy. Improving economic conditions ameliorate state fiscal problems, but economic uncertainty, changes in national aid, and mandates from Washington conspire to present states with tough budgetary choices. In light of its own budget deficit, can the national government be reasonably expected to substantially increase national aid to the states? Given the pressures on budgets on all levels of government, who should pay the costs of an expanded Medicaid program and other policy mandates?

Notes: Data on 1992 budget cuts in the states were taken from *The Fiscal Survey of the States* (Washington, D.C.: National Governors Association and National Association of State Budget Officers, October 1992). Data on Medicaid were taken from *The Book of the States, 1992–93 Edition* (Lexington, Kentucky, 1992), pp. 347 and 605. Data on state tax collections from the Center for the Study of States report are cited in Sylvian Nasar, "National Recovery Fattening Tax Revenues in Many States," *The New York Times,* February 17, 1993, pp. A1, D18.

Members of Congress want for their states and districts the "plums" of national policy, like military contracts, but not the undesirable consequences of national policy, like nuclear waste dumps. Competition among the states for national defense dollars is especially keen. Military installations and work on new weapons systems may bring millions of dollars into a state each year, and efforts to close facilities or cut weapons development meet with predictable opposition from state officials and congressional representatives. Understandably, Mississippi's members of Congress think that naval ships built in Mississippi are better than ships built in Virginia. With the end of the Cold War, states and localities that depend on defense spending scramble to limit the economic damage of a smaller military pie.

Other policy examples beyond the struggle for money illustrate the conflicts among states and between states and the national government. The long history of slavery and discrimination against blacks in the South created epic battles between the southern states and the national government. Fights over school integration over the past generation illustrate the durability of the struggle. The issue did not reach the same intensity in states with different traditions and different avenues of economic development. Some of the great battles in Congress over environmental policy are conflicts between members of Congress trying to represent the interests of their states. Californians want stricter auto emissions standards to ameliorate their problem of dirty air, but autoworkers in Michigan fear the economic consequences of stricter standards for their industry. As these illustrations suggest, political relationships in the federal system shape many public policies.

Federalism in the 1990s

In the last decade of the twentieth century, the federal system appears to be a curious blend of contrasts as each level of government asserts its role. The states are now innovators in a variety of public policy areas, including education, welfare, and the environment. But policy innovation is not a new role for the states, for, like "laboratories" they have in the past experimented with new ideas that were later accepted as national policy. For example, a variety of states enacted old-aged pension laws several years before Congress mandated Social Security as a national policy in 1935. Similarly, the state of Wisconsin had a program of unemployment compensation that predated national policy on the matter.[33]

Some states are now experimenting with marketlike approaches in public education by allowing parents to choose the schools their children will attend, and in others state courts are mandating more equal educational expenditures across school districts. The latest round of welfare reform, requiring welfare recipients to get into job or training programs, was actually presaged by states that had already begun to experiment with such programs.[34] And across a range of environmental policies, including auto and power plant emissions, recycling, and water quality, some states have set more stringent standards than the national government. Federal budget cuts help to explain this increased vigor of the states. As the national government has wrestled with its own budget deficit, the states have expanded their policy role.

The states are doing more. But the national government has proportionally cut funding going to state and local *governments,* even though it has increased the amount of money going to grant programs for individuals (like Medicaid). At the same time, the national government has increased the number of regulations

---

[33] Arthur M. Schlesinger, Jr., *The Coming of the New Deal* (Boston: Houghton Mifflin, 1965), pp. 301–303.

[34] Julie Rovner, "Welfare Reform: The Issue That Bubbled Up from the States to Capitol Hill," *Governing* (December 1988): 17–21.

applying to state and local governments.[35] Examples of these regulations, which result in higher costs that state and local governments must pay, include the federal mandate that local school districts remove asbestos materials from school buildings and the requirement that municipalities monitor a large list of pollutants in drinking water.[36] Protecting water supplies and the health of schoolchildren are worthwhile objectives, but which level of government should pay to meet the costs of national policy mandates?[37] States are being asked to do more to achieve policy objectives set by the national government but with fewer federal resources. The box on pages 62–63 entitled "Politics and Economics: Fiscal Stress in the States" addresses the variety of pressures that shape state budgets.

Governors, state legislators, and mayors are more active, but many of them believe that the national government is curtailing their powers and responsibilities and denying them sufficient resources to perform the tasks they are asked to do. The national government has increasingly preempted state and local action in a variety of areas. For example, the national government has told the states to stay out of the economic regulation of buses, trucks, and airlines.[38] The rise in federal demands and the scarcity of dollars at all levels have increased tensions among governments in the federal system. State and local governments have assumed a prominent policy role, but the lively debate over which level of government should have the power to do what, whether national or state action is more appropriate, and who should pay the costs in light of budget deficits, illustrates the continuing vitality of the federal system.

Summary

1. Federalism is a system of government in which a central or national government and regional or state government exercise governmental power within the same political system. Federalism is a compromise between a confederation, in which states hold principal power, and a unitary form of government, in which a central government is dominant. Countries throughout the world have federal systems, and some of the most bitter and consequential conflicts in other countries are battles to redefine the shape of federal systems.

2. In policy, the amendment process, and elections, states play an important role, but the national government has become more dominant in the federal system over the past two centuries. The Constitution delegates express powers to the national government, and the Supreme Court has given expansive

---

[35] See General Accounting Office, *Federal-State-Local Relations*. David R. Beam discusses legal, fiscal, political, and administrative approaches to the regulatory relationships between levels of governments in the federal system in "On the Origins of the Mandate Issue," in *Coping with Mandates: What Are the Alternatives?* eds. Michael Fix and Daphne Kenyon (Washington, D.C: Urban Institute, 1990), pp. 23–31.

[36] Ibid., pp. 28–29.

[37] Timothy J. Conlon, "And the Beat Goes On: Intergovernmental Mandates and Preemption in an Era of Deregulation," *Publius* 21 (Summer 1991): 50–53.

[38] *Federal-State-Local Relations*, pp. 30–31.

interpretation to the implied powers clause in the document. Powers not delegated to the national government are reserved for the states and include police powers ensuring the health, safety, and education of citizens. Among state powers is control over local governments, which vary greatly in size, structure, and functions.

3. Two models of the federal system are dual federalism and marble cake federalism. The federal system can be seen as a series of legal, fiscal, and political relationships among governments. Through its interpretation of the Constitution, the Supreme Court has generally supported national constitutional values and the national government. At the expense of support for capital and other programs, an increasingly greater proportion of national aid to state and local governments goes to payments for individuals. Officials at all levels press for the interests of their governments in political relationships with other officials in the federal system.

4. States are now vigorous policy innovators, but budget deficits and the rise in national regulations have increased tensions in the federal system.

Key Terms

federalism (p. 39)
confederation (p. 39)
unitary system (p. 39)
interstate compact (p. 44)
electoral college (p. 45)
Kentucky and Virginia Resolutions (p. 47)
New Federalism (p. 48)
delegated powers (p. 49)
express powers (p. 49)
implied powers (p. 49)
reserved powers (p. 50)

Tenth Amendment (p. 50)
home rule (p. 53)
mayor-council (p. 53)
council-manager (p. 53)
commission (p. 54)
dual federalism (p. 54)
marble cake federalism (p. 55)
Sixteenth Amendment (p. 58)
categorical grant-in-aid (p. 58)
block grant (p. 58)
general revenue sharing (p. 63)

Readings for Further Study

K. C. Wheare's *Federal Government,* 4th ed. (New York: Oxford University Press, 1964) is a classic comparative exposition of the principles of federalism. Thomas J. Anton's *American Federalism and Public Policy: How the System Works* (Philadelphia: Temple University Press, 1989) offers a contemporary view of federalism in which coalitions seek policy benefits. The Council of State Governments (Lexington,

Kentucky) publishes biennially *The Book of the States,* a compendium of demographic, structural, and policy data about the states. Articles describing and analyzing state and local governments in the federal system can be found in the journals *Publius* and *National Civic Review.* The Advisory Commission on Intergovernmental Relations, a bipartisan group created by Congress to study the federal system, compiles data and publishes reports on a variety of issues in American federalism. David Osborne provides case studies of policy vigor in the states in *Laboratories of Democracy: A New Breed of Governor Creates Models for National Growth* (Boston: Harvard Business School Press, 1990). Carl E. Van Horn, ed., *The State of the States* (Washington, D.C.: Congressional Quarterly, Inc., 1989) provides a series of informative essays on the significance of contemporary changes in state government. Alice Rivlin's *Reviving the American Dream: The Economy, the States and the Federal Government* (Washington, D.C.: The Brookings Institution, 1992) presents provocative proposals to reorder policy responsibilities between the national and state governments.

3 Civil Liberties and Civil Rights

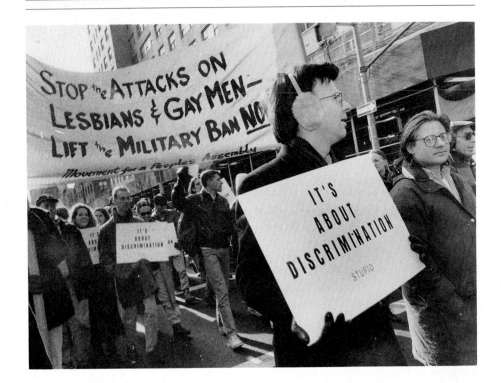

Chapter 1 explained that a constitution can be a mainstay of rights. Beyond organizing and granting authority, constitutions place limits on what governments may do. Collectively, these limits are known as civil liberties and civil rights. **Civil liberties** are legally enforceable freedoms to act or not to act and to be free from unwarranted official intrusion into one's life. They include (but are not limited to) the First Amendment's guarantees of free expression and religious freedom and the Fourth, Fifth, Sixth, and Eighth Amendments' strictures governing police and courts in fighting crime. **Civil rights** encompass participation—citizens' rights under the law to take part in society on an equal footing with others. They embrace the guarantees of the three Civil War amendments to the Constitution (the Thirteenth, Fourteenth, and Fifteenth), as well as laws passed to give those amendments meaning and force. They are assurances that people are not penalized because of criteria (such as race or gender) that society decides should be irrelevant in making public policy. Yet, even after more than 200 years' experience as a nation, we continue to disagree over what liberty and equality mean in practice.

The Bill of Rights: Securing the Blessings of Liberty

As explained in Chapter 1, when the Constitution left the hands of the framers in 1787, there appeared to be too few restrictions on what the national government could do, leaving individual liberty without sufficient protection. Several of the state conventions that ratified the proposed Constitution did so on the promise that a "bill of rights" would soon be added. And it was, with ratification of the first 10 amendments completed in 1791 (see Table 3.1).

Applying the Bill of Rights to the States

Nearly 180 years elapsed before most of the rights spelled out in the Bill of Rights applied fully to state governments. This was because, as Chief Justice John Marshall (1801–1835) held for the Supreme Court, the Bill of Rights was not intended to apply to the states.[1] As a result, only to a small degree at first were disputes between states and their citizens controlled by the federal constitution. For most abuses of power, citizens had recourse only to their state constitutions and state courts. But ratification of the **Fourteenth Amendment** in 1868 laid the groundwork for a drastic change in the nature of the Union. First, its language is directed to *state* governments, so aggrieved persons have the federal constitution as an additional shield between themselves and their state governments. Second, the words of the amendment are ambiguous. What, for instance, is the "liberty" the amendment protects?

The Supreme Court was initially hesitant to use the Fourteenth Amendment as a vehicle by which to make the Bill of Rights applicable to the states. Within a century, however, the Court did just that. Without additional formal amendment of the Constitution, the Court "incorporated" or absorbed the Bill of Rights into the Fourteenth Amendment in a series of about two dozen cases beginning in 1897 and concluding in 1969. Today almost all the provisions of the first eight amendments, whether involving free speech or the rights thought necessary for a fair trial, apply with equal rigor to both state and national officials and the laws they make. Only the Sixth Amendment stipulation on a trial's location, the Seventh's stipulation for a jury trial in most civil suits, the Eighth's ban on excessive bail and fines, and the Second and Third Amendments still apply only to the

---

[1] *Barron* v. *Baltimore*, 32 U.S. (7 Peters) 243 (1833).

TABLE 3.1
Content of the Bill of Rights

Amendment 1	Nonestablishment of religion; free exercise of religion; freedoms of speech, press, petition, and peaceable assembly
Amendment 2	Keep and bear arms
Amendment 3	No quartering of troops
Amendment 4	No unreasonable searches and seizures; standards for search warrants
Amendment 5	Indictment by grand jury; no double jeopardy or self-incrimination; no deprivation of life, liberty, or property without due process of law; compensation for taking of private property
Amendment 6	Speedy and public trial by impartial jury in state and district where crime was committed; nature and cause of accusation; confrontation of accusers; compulsory process for witnesses; assistance of counsel
Amendment 7	Jury trial in certain civil cases
Amendment 8	No excessive bail or fines; no cruel and unusual punishments
Amendment 9	Recognition of the existence of rights not enumerated
Amendment 10	Reserved powers of the states

Consisting of barely 450 words, the Bill of Rights (Amendments 1 through 10) was intended to remedy a defect critics found in the Constitution of 1787. In September 1789 Congress proposed 12 amendments for approval by the states. As the eleventh state (three-fourths of 14), Virginia's ratification in December 1791 made the Bill of Rights officially part of the Constitution. The remaining 3 states—Connecticut, Georgia, and Massachusetts—did not ratify until the 150th anniversary of the Bill of Rights in 1941. One amendment was never ratified. It dealt with apportionment of the House of Representatives and is now obsolete. The other amendment was not ratified until 1992—203 years after it was proposed! The Twenty-seventh Amendment—called the "lost amendment"—delays any increase in congressional salaries until a congressional election has intervened.

national government. Of these, only the Second and Eighth are substantively important. (The Ninth and Tenth Amendments, although part of the Bill of Rights, do not lend themselves to absorption into the Fourteenth Amendment.)

The Fragility of Civil Liberties

Charters of liberty, like a bill of rights, are commonplace today in the constitutions of many governments. Yet even a casual observer of world affairs knows that civil liberties are more likely to be preserved (or suspended) in some countries than in others. Even in the United States, the liberties enshrined in the Bill of Rights have meant more in some years than in others because of changing interpretations by the Supreme Court. For example, the Fourth Amendment's ban on "unreasonable searches and seizures" did not apply for a long time to electronic surveillance unless police physically trespassed on the suspect's property. This meant that state and federal agents could eavesdrop electronically in many situations without fear of violating the Constitution. Then in 1967 the Court ruled that the Fourth Amendment covered most electronic searches too, as long as there was a "reasonable expectation of privacy."[2] The words in the Bill of Rights have not changed, but the meaning attributed to those words has changed in the context of Supreme Court decisions.

Exactly why civil liberties thrive in one place or time and not another is a complex phenomenon. But this much is certain: Civil liberties are fragile. The most frequent and sometimes the most serious threats to civil liberties have come not from people intent on throwing the Bill of Rights away but from well-meaning and overzealous people who find the Bill of Rights a temporary bother, standing in the way of objectives, often laudatory ones, they want to reach. Put another way, constitutional protections are sometimes worth the least when they are needed most. When public opinion calls for a "crack down" on certain rights, those demands are felt in judicial chambers just as they are heard in legislative halls. Unsupported, courts and the Bill of Rights alone cannot defend civil liberties.

Free Expression: Speech, Press, and Assembly

The place of the **First Amendment** in the Bill of Rights is symbolic. Its liberties are fundamental because they are essential to the kind of nation the framers envisioned.

The Value of Free Expression

Free expression serves several important objectives. First, *free expression is necessary to the political process set up by the Constitution.* It is difficult to imagine government being responsive to a majority of the political community if the members of that community are afraid of saying what they think. It is even more difficult to imagine members of a political minority trying to persuade the majority without the right to criticize political officeholders. For democratic politics to work, free speech must prevail.

Second, in politics, as in education, *free expression allows the dominant wisdom of the day to be challenged.* Open discussion and debate aid the search for truth and thus foster intelligent policymaking. Whether the question is safeguarding the environment or probing the causes of birth defects, free speech encourages both investigation of the problem and examination of possible solutions.

Third, *free expression aids self-development.* Intellectual and artistic expression

---

[2] *Katz* v. *United States,* 389 U.S. 347 (1967), overruling *Olmstead* v. *United States,* 277 U.S. 438 (1928).

may contribute to realizing one's full potential as a human being. If government has the authority to define what kind of art is "acceptable," other kinds will be discouraged or suppressed altogether. Freedom of expression does not guarantee success as a poet, artist, or composer, but it does guarantee each person's right to try.

Free expression has its risks, however. There is no assurance that open debate and discussion will produce the correct answer or the wisest policy. Letting people speak their minds freely will surely stretch out the time it takes for a political community to decide what to do. Free speech can also threaten social and political stability. If there are risks in silencing dissent, risks exist in permitting it too. Nations in upheaval rarely tolerate vocal dissent against official policy. But on balance, the American people, through their public officials and judges, seem willing to accept these risks most of the time.

The Tests of Freedom

Even though the First Amendment has been part of the Constitution from almost the beginning, freedom's record has not been free of blemishes. The ink had hardly dried on the Bill of Rights when Congress passed the Sedition Act of 1798, making it a crime to publish "false, scandalous, and malicious" statements about government officials. The law was not challenged in the Supreme Court even though at least 10 individuals were convicted before it expired in 1801. Scattered instances of suppression occurred on both sides during the Civil War, but the next major nationwide attack on speech came on virtually anyone or anything pro-German during World War I and on socialist ideas during the "red scare" that followed.

Only then did the Supreme Court first interpret the free speech clause of the Constitution. During World War I, Charles Schenck was found guilty of violating the Espionage Act by printing and circulating materials designed to protest and obstruct the draft. Announcing the **clear and present danger test,** Justice Holmes (1902–1932) ruled that the First Amendment provided no shield for Schenck's words. "The question . . . is whether the words are used in such circumstances and are of such a nature as to create a clear and present danger that they will bring about the substantive evils that Congress has a right to prevent. It is a question of proximity and degree."[3]

Although Schenck lost his case, Holmes's reasoning remained important. Only when harmful consequences of speech were imminent could government act. As Justice Brandeis (1916–1939) later declared, "If there be time to expose through discussion the falsehood and fallacies, to avert the evil by the processes of education, the remedy to be applied is more speech, not enforced silence."[4]

For a while, however, the Holmes-Brandeis view of free speech was rejected by most justices on the Supreme Court, who preferred to apply the **bad tendency**

---

[3] *Schenck* v. *United States,* 249 U.S. 47 (1919).
[4] *Whitney* v. *California,* 274 U.S. 357, 377 (1927), Justice Brandeis concurring.

test. Under this rule, government could silence unpopular speech, even if harmful consequences were not immediate.[5] Fortunately for the vitality of free speech, the bad tendency test was replaced in later cases by the clear and present danger test. The major exception since World War II occurred in cases involving suspected communists, mainly in the 1950s,[6] although as late as 1961 the Court maintained that someone who vigorously advocated actions to overthrow the United States government by force could be sent to jail.[7] Otherwise, the Supreme Court has been highly suspicious of restrictions on the *content* of speech. With few exceptions, such restrictions are now presumed to be at odds with the First Amendment. Since 1969 the clear and present danger test has evolved into the **incitement test,** stressing the Court's insistence that harmful consequences (such as a riot) be exceedingly imminent.[8]

Gags

Of the possible restrictions on speech today, the Court is least likely to approve a **prior restraint.** This is official censorship *before* something is said or published, or censorship that halts publication already under way. Prior restraints are especially dangerous to free expression because government does not have to go to the trouble of launching a prosecution and convicting someone at a trial. Even when *The New York Times* and *The Washington Post* reprinted verbatim parts of a purloined classified study of Defense Department decision making on Vietnam, the Supreme Court, in the "Pentagon Papers case," refused to ban further publication.[9] Most of the justices admitted that the government could make it a crime to publish such materials but concluded that there could be no restraints in advance. Likewise, the justices will only rarely approve a pretrial gag on newspaper and television reports about a crime, even if that would help protect another constitutional right, the right to a fair trial.

Obscenity and Libel

Descriptions and depictions of various sexual acts have presented a special problem. Unlike cases involving other types of speech, the Court has required no evidence that obscene materials are in fact harmful. Yet the Court steadfastly regards **obscenity** as unprotected speech because of the widespread public view that exposure to obscenity is deleterious. But the justices have had a hard time writing a clearly understood definition of what is obscene. Justice Stewart (1958–

---

[5] *Pierce* v. *United States,* 252 U.S. 239 (1920).
[6] For example, see *Dennis* v. *United States,* 341 U.S. 494 (1951), and *Yates* v. *United States,* 354 U.S. 298 (1957).
[7] *Scales* v. *United States,* 367 U.S. 203 (1961).
[8] *Brandenburg* v. *Ohio,* 395 U.S. 444 (1969).
[9] *New York Times Co.* v. *United States,* 403 U.S. 713 (1971).

1981) once admitted, "I know it when I see it." Under the current standard, the Court will uphold an obscenity conviction if

> (a) "the average person, applying contemporary community standards," would find that the work, taken as a whole, appeals to the prurient interest, (b) . . . the work depicts or describes, in a patently offensive way, sexual conduct specifically defined by the applicable state law, and (c) . . . the work, taken as a whole, lacks serious literary, artistic, political, or scientific value.[10]

The target seems to be "hardcore" pornography. Within limits the "community" to which the Court refers is local and not national, making the definition of obscenity variable. The policy thus allows one locale to suppress sexually explicit materials while another tolerates them. Obscenity continues to trouble the nation. Films, videotapes, and magazines portraying explicit sex are big business. Many think the Supreme Court's definition is both too lax and insufficiently enforced. Although reluctant to advocate censorship, some feminists object to obscenity because it degrades women and may even contribute to sexual crimes against them.

Like obscenity, **libel** is not protected by the First Amendment. Involving published defamation of a person's character or reputation, libel may subject a publisher or television network to damage suits involving thousands or even millions of dollars. Beginning in 1964, however, the Supreme Court made it very difficult for public figures and public officials to bring successful libel suits against their critics. The reason is that the democratic process needs robust and spirited debate, which might be muted by threat of legal action. In such situations, public figures and officials initiating libel suits must be able to prove "actual malice"— that is, that the author published information knowing it was false or not caring whether it was true or false.[11]

Freedom of Assembly and Symbolic Speech

People often convey ideas and attempt to build support for a cause by holding a meeting or a rally. This is an example of the freedom of assembly that the First Amendment protects. Sometimes assembly involves **symbolic speech** where words, pictures, and ideas are not at issue but action is. A person may *do* something to send a message, usually in a dramatic, attention-getting manner. It might be a sit-in at the mayor's office to protest a budget cut or a sit-down on a public road leading to a nuclear power plant under construction. In some instances, demonstrators may be constitutionally punished for such nontraditional forms of expression, not because of the ideas expressed but because of the harm that results from the *mode* of expression. It is not the message but the medium that can be the basis of a legitimate arrest.

---

[10] *Miller* v. *California*, 413 U.S. 5, 8 (1973).
[11] *New York Times Co.* v. *Sullivan*, 376 U.S. 254 (1964).

Yet in a 1989 decision that generated a storm of controversy, the Supreme Court overturned the conviction of Gregory Lee Johnson for burning the American flag in violation of a Texas law.[12] In a demonstration at the Dallas City Hall during the Republican National Convention in 1984, protestors chanted, "America, the red, white, and blue, we spit on you," as Johnson doused the flag with kerosene and set it ablaze. Short of a protest that sparks a breach of the peace or causes some other kind of serious harm, the Court held (5 to 4) that a state may not criminalize the symbolic act of flag burning. The reasoning is that government protects the physical integrity of the flag because the flag is a symbol of the nation. Just as people may verbally speak out against what they believe the nation "stands for," they may also express the same thought by defacing or destroying the symbol of the nation. The following year, the Court held that the First Amendment also barred Congress from criminalizing flag burning, a decision that sparked a renewed drive to amend the Constitution.[13] The drive failed in 1990 when Congress failed to pass a constitutional amendment by the required two-thirds vote in both houses.

The Court has also invalidated a city ordinance which outlawed cross burning and other forms of symbolic hate speech directed against certain minorities.[14] The ordinance was defective because it was content-based: Some, not all, hate-messages were banned. The decision may be far-reaching because it calls into question the constitutionality of similar bans at public universities.

Religious Freedom

Guarantees of religious freedom form the first lines of the First Amendment. Ahead of other protections are an assurance of free exercise and a prohibition of an establishment of religion. Removing religion from the reach of political majorities reflected practical needs in 1791. The United States was already one of the world's most religiously diverse countries.

Religion and the Constitution

The Constitution is intentionally a non-sectarian document. It had to be if the framers were to secure ratification after 1787 and if the new government was to avoid the religious divisiveness that had plagued Europe before and after the Reformation as well as the American colonies. Even though a few states still maintained established (state-supported) churches in 1791, the First Amendment said that the nation could not have one.

The United States is even more religiously diverse today. About three-fifths of the population are members of churches, synagogues, and mosques. More than

---

[12] *Texas* v. *Johnson*, 491 U.S. 397 (1989).
[13] *United States* v. *Eichman*, 496 U.S. 310 (1990).
[14] *R.A.V.* v. *City of St. Paul*, 60 U.S.L.W. 4667 (1992).

90 distinct religious groups claim more than 50,000 members each. Within this context, the religion clauses have the same objectives but work in different ways. The **free exercise clause** preserves a sphere of religious practice free of interference by government. The idea is that people should be left to follow their own dictates of belief or nonbelief. The **establishment clause** keeps government from becoming the tool of one religious group against others. Government may not be a prize in a nation of competing faiths.

Even though both religion clauses work to guard religious freedom, they concern different threats and so seem at times to pull in opposite directions. Rigorous protection of free exercise may appear to create an establishment of religion. Rigorous enforcement of the ban on establishment may seem to deny free exercise.[15]

Aid to Sectarian Schools

The Supreme Court has never limited the First Amendment's ban to the literal establishment of an official state church. But how much involvement between church and state is too much? Coins, for example, display the motto "In God We Trust." A troublesome area for almost a half century has been public financial support for sectarian schools. The current standard for determining when government has violated the establishment clause in this context dates from a 1971 decision by the Supreme Court.[16] To pass scrutiny under the **Lemon test,** a law must have, first of all, a *secular purpose.* Second, the primary effect of the law must be *neutral,* neither hindering nor advancing religion. Third, the law must not promote *excessive entanglement* between church and state by requiring government to become too closely involved in the affairs of a religious institution. Using these criteria, the Court has upheld some, but not most, forms of state aid that have been challenged. Generally, direct grants of money from a government agency to a religious institution are the least likely to be found acceptable under the Constitution.

Prayer in the Public Schools

Whether religious observances can take place in public schools is another thorny issue. Because of strong emotions on both sides, the Court's decisions have stirred up controversy. In 1962 the justices outlawed a nondenominational prayer prescribed by the Board of Regents for opening daily exercises in the public schools of New York State. The following year a Pennsylvania statute mandating daily Bible readings in public schools met a similar fate.[17] Reaction to these decisions in Congress and the nation was anything but dispassionate. After the New York prayer case, the U.S. House of Representatives unanimously passed a resolution to have

---

[15] For example, see *Westside Community Schools* v. *Mergens,* 496 U.S. 226 (1990).
[16] *Lemon* v. *Kurtzman,* 403 U.S. 602 (1971).
[17] *Engel* v. *Vitale,* 370 U.S. 421 (1962); *School District of Abington Township* v. *Schempp,* 374 U.S. 203 (1963).

the motto "In God We Trust" placed behind the Speaker's desk in the House chamber. The motto is still there for all to see during televised sessions of Congress.

Of course, the Supreme Court has never said that students cannot pray in school. Students have been doing that before exams for years. But the Court has remained firm in its opposition to state-sponsored religious activities in public schools. For example, an Alabama statute authorizing a period of silence at the start of the school day for "meditation or voluntary prayer" was seen by most justices as constitutionally defective because the law endorsed religion as a preferred activity.[18] A bare majority of the Court even found constitutionally objectionable an invocation offered by a rabbi at a public middle school commencement. Although student attendance at the ceremony was optional, the prayer nonetheless carried "a particular risk of indirect coercion" of religious belief, according to Justice Anthony Kennedy.[19] For the four dissenters, Justice Antonin Scalia asserted that the nation's long tradition of prayer at public ceremonies was a compelling argument that the school had not violated the establishment clause.

Religious Observances in Official Settings

Because of the impressionable nature of children, the Court has been quickest to strike down religious influences in elementary and secondary schools. Elsewhere, the justices sometimes wink. In 1983 the Court approved Nebraska's practice of paying the state legislature's chaplain out of public funds.[20] (Both houses of the United States Congress also have chaplains who pray at the beginning of each day's session.) The following year, a bare majority allowed city officials in Pawtucket, Rhode Island, to erect a municipally owned Christmas display, including a crèche, in a private park. However, the Court has placed some limits on official observances of religious holidays, finding unacceptable a privately owned crèche displayed in the county courthouse in Pittsburgh, Pennsylvania. Above the crèche was a banner proclaiming "Gloria in excelsis Deo" (Latin for "Glory to God in the highest"). Yet in the same case, the Court found acceptable a nearby display that combined an 18-foot menorah and a 45-foot tree decorated with holiday ornaments. The justices explained that the crèche and banner impermissibly "endorsed" religion, but that the menorah and tree only "recognized" the religious nature of the winter holidays.[21] Such decisions point to the difficulty in deciding how much separation the establishment clause commands between government and religion.

Free Exercise of Religion

Contemporary free exercise problems typically arise from application of a law that by its own words has nothing to do with religion, yet works a hardship on some religious groups by commanding them to do something that their faith forbids or

---

[18] *Wallace* v. *Jaffree,* 472 U.S. 38 (1985).
[19] *Lee* v. *Weisman,* 60 U.S.L.W. 4723 (1992).
[20] *Marsh* v. *Chambers,* 463 U.S. 783 (1983).
[21] *Allegheny County* v. *American Civil Liberties Union,* 492 U.S. 573 (1989).

by forbidding them to do something that their faith commands. This kind of conflict often occurs with small separatist groups whose interests are overlooked when laws are made. Relying on the free exercise clause, they ask to be exempted on religious grounds from obeying the law. For example, a nearly unanimous bench in 1972 exempted members of the Old Order Amish and the Conservative Amish Mennonite churches from Wisconsin's compulsory school attendance law.[22] Like most states, Wisconsin required school attendance until age 16. The Amish were religiously opposed to formal schooling beyond the eighth grade. The justices found a close connection between the faith of the Amish and their simple, separatist way of life. The law not only compelled them to do something at odds with their religious tenets but also threatened to undermine the Amish community. On balance, in the Court's view, the danger to religious freedom outweighed the state's interest in compulsory attendance.

Recently, however, the Court has become less hospitable to free exercise claims. In 1990, the justices ruled against two members of the Native American Church who were fired from their jobs as drug counselors in a clinic in Oregon after they ingested peyote (a hallucinogen) as part of a religious ritual. Oregon officials then denied them unemployment compensation because their loss of employment resulted from "misconduct." Under state law, peyote was a "controlled substance" and its use was forbidden. The two ex-counselors cited scientific and anthropological evidence that the sacramental use of peyote was an ancient practice and was not harmful. The Court, however, decided that Oregon had not violated the First Amendment. When action based on religious belief runs afoul of the criminal law, the latter prevails.[23]

Fundamentals of American Criminal Justice

The American system of criminal justice insists not simply that a person be proved guilty but that the guilt be proved in the legally prescribed way. This is the concept of **legal guilt,** inherent in the idea of "a government of laws and not of men."[24] Courts sit not just to make sure that wrongdoers are punished but to see that law enforcement personnel obey the commands of the Bill of Rights. The precise meaning of these commands at a given time represents the prevailing judgment on the balance to be struck between two values: the liberty and the safety of each citizen. The first emphasizes fairness to persons accused of crimes and teaches that preservation of liberty necessitates tight controls on law enforcement officers, even if some guilty persons go unpunished. The second emphasizes crime control,

---

[22] *Wisconsin* v. *Yoder,* 406 U.S. 205 (1972).

[23] *Oregon Employment Division* v. *Smith,* 494 U.S. 872 (1990).

[24] This phrase was popularized by John Adams shortly before the Revolutionary War and was later incorporated into the Massachusetts constitution, the oldest of the American state constitutions still in force.

teaching that too many rules hamstring police and judges, give lawbreakers the upper hand, and disserve honest citizens. Tension between the two values persists.

Inconvenient as they may be, the strictures of the Bill of Rights deliberately make government's crimefighting tasks harder to perform. Yet, holding police to standards of behavior set by the Constitution protects the liberty of everyone. Otherwise, officials would have the power to do whatever they wanted, to whomever they wanted, whenever they wanted. Without limits to authority, America would be a far different place in which to live.

Presumption of Innocence and Notice of Charges

Often misunderstood, the idea that a person is "innocent until proved guilty" does not mean that the police and prosecuting attorney think that the accused person is innocent. It would be a gross injustice if obviously innocent people were put through the torment of a criminal trial. Instead, the **presumption of innocence** lays the burden of proof on the government. It is up to the state to prove the suspect's guilt "beyond a reasonable doubt." Along with a convincing case of factual guilt, the prosecution must also demonstrate criminal intent, or *mens rea*.

A suspect is entitled to know what the state intends to prove and, therefore, what he or she must defend against. The state must go beyond saying merely that someone is a thief. The charge must explain, among other things, (1) what was stolen, (2) approximately when it was stolen, (3) by whom, and (4) from whom it was stolen. This principle also means that criminal laws must be as specific as possible so that citizens can have fair notice of what conduct is prohibited. The greater the vagueness in a law, the greater the danger of arbitrary arrests and convictions.

The basic fairness component of advance notice is why the Constitution prohibits **ex post facto laws,** criminal laws that apply retroactively. The Constitution also forbids a bill of attainder for a similar reason. A **bill of attainder** is a law that imposes punishment but bypasses the procedural safeguards of the legal process. A person might not have the opportunity for even a simple defense in that situation.

Limits on Searches and Arrests

The **Fourth Amendment** denies police unbounded discretion to arrest and search people and their possessions. Many searches and some arrests cannot take place at all until a judge has issued a **warrant,** or official authorization. To obtain a warrant, the police must persuade a judge that they have very good reason (called **probable cause**) for believing that someone has committed a crime or that evidence is in a particular location. Warrantless searches of arrested suspects or automobiles are permitted in certain circumstances, but police officers who have made a warrantless search must still convince a judge afterward that they had probable cause to act.

Electronic surveillance is also usually a search in the constitutional sense.

Under current law, practically all such "bugging" must be done on a warrant's authority, except for exceptional situations involving agents of foreign powers.[25] Tests to detect use of illegal drugs may also raise Fourth Amendment concerns (see "Contemporary Controversies: Drug Testing" on page 81).

What happens when a judge concludes that the police have acted improperly when making an arrest or conducting a search? The **exclusionary rule** may come into play. This judge-made rule puts teeth into the Fourth Amendment by denying government in many situations the use of evidence gained as a result of violation of the suspect's rights. The rule lies at the heart of the clash between the values of fairness and crime control.[26]

Assistance of Counsel and Protection Against Self-Incrimination

Other constitutional restraints are at work in the police station and in the court-room. As interpreted by the Supreme Court, the Fifth Amendment denies govern-ment the authority to coerce confessions from suspects or to require suspects to testify at their own trials. These restraints conform with the presumption of inno-cence. The state makes its case. It may not compel the suspect to do its work. Under *Miranda* v. *Arizona,*[27] judges exclude almost all confessions, even if no physical coercion is present, unless police have first performed the following actions:

1. Advised the suspect of a right to remain silent (that is, a right not to answer questions)
2. Warned the suspect that statements he or she might make may be used as evidence at a trial
3. Informed the suspect of a right to have a lawyer present during the interrogation
4. Offered the services of a lawyer free of charge during the interrogation to suspects financially unable to retain one

If a suspect refuses to talk to the police, the police may not continue the interrogation. If a suspect waives these *Miranda* **rights** and agrees to talk, the state must be prepared to show to a judge's satisfaction that the waiver was done "voluntarily, knowingly, and intelligently." As it is, many "streetwise" suspects decide that it is in their interest to talk as part of a **plea bargain**—a deal with the prosecutor to obtain a lighter sentence in exchange for a guilty plea. Guilty pleas allow most criminal cases to be settled without going to trial, so the legal use of confessions continues.

For a long time, the **Sixth Amendment's** assurance of counsel, or legal assistance, remained more promise than substance. Many defendants simply could not afford to hire an attorney, and some courts provided free counsel for the poor

---

[25] *United States* v. *U.S. District Court,* 407 U.S. 297 (1972).
[26] See *Mapp* v. *Ohio,* 367 U.S. 643 (1961), and *United States* v. *Leon,* 468 U.S. 897 (1984).
[27] 384 U.S. 436 (1966).

Contemporary Controversies

Drug Testing

Widespread use of illegal drugs has prompted a variety of countermeasures, including stepped-up law enforcement and education programs. A third device, however, has sparked almost as much concern as drug use itself: drug testing. Advocates of tests argue that they will deter drug use. Persons subject to testing will avoid using drugs in order to avoid detection, especially if positive test results might lead to loss of one's job. Opponents maintain that benefits of decreased drug use will be far outweighed by the loss of individual liberty. A better solution, they say, is to reserve testing for people suspected of illegal drug use. Besides, the tests may prove inaccurate. People who are adept at using drugs illegally without generating suspicion may be just as adept at foiling tests. Advocates note, however, that subjecting everyone to tests means that suspicion is cast on no one. If testing can be done only on the basis of suspicion, even negative test results may leave a shadow on a person's reputation. Moreover, requiring tests for drugs as a condition of employment is no greater threat to privacy and liberty than general physical examinations, chest X rays, and family medical histories. Drug testing involves the Constitution. If drug tests are "searches" within the meaning of the Fourth Amendment, may government authorities conduct the tests only on the basis of individualized suspicion? Individualized

suspicion is normally required before police may lawfully stop and search someone. However, in two important rulings the Supreme Court held that suspicion of drug usage is not always necessary. In one case the Court approved a Department of Transportation policy requiring blood and urine tests of all members of a train crew following an accident, even if no one appeared to be impaired by illegal drugs.[a] In another case the Court upheld a policy of the Customs Service requiring drug tests of all employees applying for transfer to certain drug-sensitive positions.[b] The reasoning was that individualized suspicion is not needed when government's interest is something other than law enforcement. In the railroad case, the testing was designed to promote safety. In the Customs case, the tests were intended to maintain public confidence in a drug-free work force. Where such special needs exist, government infringement on individual liberty must only be "reasonable." What do these decisions say about the protection afforded by the Fourth Amendment? Might the Court's rationale in the drug testing cases be extended to weaken other constitutional guarantees?

[a] *Skinner* v. *Railway Labor Executives Association,* 489 U.S. 602 (1989).

[b] *Treasury Employees* v. *Von Raab,* 489 U.S. 656 (1989).

---

only in **capital cases** (cases in which the death penalty might be imposed). Until the 1970s, for example, 75 percent of people accused of **misdemeanors** (less serious offenses, punishable by a jail term of less than one year) went legally unrepresented. Since the 1930s the Supreme Court has greatly expanded the Sixth Amendment right. Today all persons accused of **felonies** (serious offenses, punishable by more than one year in jail) and all accused of misdemeanors for which a jail term is imposed must be offered counsel, at the government's expense if necessary.[28]

---

[28] *Powell* v. *Alabama,* 287 U.S. 45 (1932); *Gideon* v. *Wainwright,* 372 U.S. 335 (1963); and *Scott* v. *Illinois,* 440 U.S. 367 (1979).

Still, none of the right-to-counsel rulings creates full equality in access to legal assistance. The Constitution, after all, does not guarantee a "perfect" trial, only a "fair" one. Indigents must be content with public defenders and court-appointed attorneys paid from public funds. Public defenders carry heavy case loads, their time is spread thin, and compared to others in their profession, they are underpaid. In federal courts they are now responsible for over half of all defense work. They can cope with their case loads only with the help of plea bargains. Defendants retaining counsel at their own expense also fare differently. Only a few can "afford the best."

Limits on Punishment

Guilty verdicts by juries or guilty pleas usually result in punishment for the accused. Generally, the Constitution leaves the particular sentence to legislators and judges, subject to the **Eighth Amendment's** prohibition of "**cruel and unusual punishment**." In the Supreme Court's view this means, first, that certain kinds of penalties (torture, for example) may not be imposed at all; second, that certain acts or conditions (such as alcoholism) may not be made criminal;[29] third, that penalties may not be imposed capriciously; and fourth, that death may be a punishment only for murder. Indeed, the Eighth Amendment comes into play most frequently when someone has been sentenced to death. In only two noncapital cases has the Court overturned a sentence because it was too extreme.[30]

Between 1930 and 1993 there were approximately 4005 legal executions in the United States, with 95 percent of these occurring before 1972. Today, 37 of the 50 states, plus the federal government, allow capital punishment, but the states vary widely in terms of the number of executions carried out, as Figure 3.1 shows. Nationally more than 2600 persons were on "death row" as of early 1993. Opponents of the death penalty would like the Supreme Court to impose more restrictions on the states. Even if executions are not inherently "cruel and unusual," many believe that they are racially discriminatory because blacks are more likely than whites to be sentenced to die, as are killers of whites as opposed to killers of blacks.[31] Others conclude that the sentencing process is fundamentally flawed because it results in caprice. One study found little or no difference between the facts of murder cases where the death penalty was imposed and where it was not.[32]

---

[29] *Robinson* v. *California,* 370 U.S. 660 (1962).
[30] *Weems* v. *United States,* 217 U.S. 349 (1910), and *Solem* v. *Helm,* 463 U.S. 277 (1983). *Harmelin* v. *Michigan,* 59 U.S.L.W. 4839 (1991), which upheld a mandatory sentence of life imprisonment without the possibility of parole for possession of more than 650 grams of a substance containing cocaine, means that legislatures have almost complete discretion in setting punishments for noncapital offenses.
[31] David C. Baldus, George Woodworth, and Charles Pulanski, "Comparative Review of Death Sentences: An Empirical Study of the Georgia Experience," *Journal of Criminal Law and Criminology* 74 (1983): 661; see *McCleskey* v. *Kemp,* 481 U.S. 279 (1987).
[32] Victor L. Streib, "Executions under the Post-*Furman* Capital Punishment Statutes," *Rutgers Law Journal* 15 (1984): 443.

FIGURE 3.1

Executions by State, 1976–1992

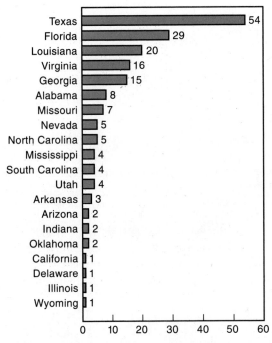

In *Furman* v. *Georgia,* 408 U.S. 238 (1972), the Supreme Court ruled 5 to 4 that the death penalty, as then administered, was cruel and unusual punishment in violation of the Eighth Amendment. Too much discretion in the hands of juries and judges had made application of the death penalty capricious. Most states then reinstated capital punishment (as did Congress for aircraft hijacking) with more carefully drawn statutes to meet the Court's objections in *Furman.* In *Gregg* v. *Georgia,* 428 U.S. 152 (1976), a majority of the Supreme Court concluded that the death penalty was not inherently cruel and unusual and upheld a two-step sentencing scheme designed to set strict standards for trial courts. A jury would first decide the question of guilt and then in a separate proceeding impose punishment.

Of the 37 states that now permit capital punishment, three (South Dakota, Vermont, and New Hampshire) sentenced no one to death between 1976 and 1992. Of the 34 states where death sentences have been imposed, executions were carried out in only 20 states during this period. The states of Texas, Florida, Louisiana, and Virginia accounted for 65 percent of the executions. Thirteen states executed 30 convicted murderers in 1992, the largest number of executions in a single year since 1962 when 47 persons were put to death. Of the 30 executions in 1992, 12 occurred in Texas.   SOURCE: U.S. Department of Justice.

A Right to Privacy

Some liberties Americans enjoy are not specifically mentioned in the Constitution, as the **Ninth Amendment** cautions. One such judicially discovered civil liberty is the right to privacy, announced in 1965.[33] With far-reaching implications, this decision invalidated a Connecticut statute that prohibited the use of birth control devices.

The Abortion Controversy

Several decisions that followed led to ***Roe v. Wade,***[34] the landmark abortion case. Throwing out the abortion laws of almost all the states, the Court recognized a woman's interest in terminating her pregnancy, the state's interest in protecting her health, and the state's interest in protecting "pre-natal life." According to the seven-justice majority, the Constitution prohibited virtually all restrictions on abortions during the first trimester of pregnancy, allowed reasonable medical regulations to guard the woman's health in the second trimester (but no outright prohibitions of abortion), and permitted the state to ban abortions only in the third trimester after the point of fetal "viability" (except when the pregnancy endangered the woman's life). For 15 years after *Roe,* Congress and some state legislatures tried to limit the availability of abortion and to discourage its use, but the Supreme Court invalidated most restrictions. The reasoning was that because the right to an abortion was a fundamental right, the government had to show compelling reasons when the right was curtailed.

In 1989 opponents of abortion won a significant victory in the Supreme Court. In a case from Missouri five justices upheld, among other things, a requirement for fetal viability testing prior to the twenty-fourth week of pregnancy, something which the Court previously would have doubtless struck down.[35] Moreover, the Court discarded *Roe's* trimester-based analysis of the abortion right, but stopped short of overruling *Roe.* In 1992 the Court upheld parts of a Pennsylvania statute which imposed several conditions before a woman could obtain an abortion.[36] These included informed consent provisions, a 24-hour waiting period, parental consent for minors, and record-keeping regulations for medical personnel. However, the Court refused to accept a requirement for spousal notification because it imposed an "undue burden" on the abortion right.

The decisions in the Missouri and Pennsylvania cases have led to four conclusions. First, as of early 1993, abortion is no longer a fundamental right, but it does enjoy modest constitutional protection. Second, and as a consequence of the first, total or near-total bans on abortion are almost certainly unconstitutional. Third, it remains to be seen what additional abortion regulations the Court is prepared to accept. Fourth, except for outright bans, a woman's freedom to terminate a preg-

---

[33] *Griswold* v. *Connecticut,* 381 U.S. 479 (1965).
[34] 410 U.S. 113 (1973).
[35] *Webster* v. *Reproductive Health Services,* 492 U.S. 490 (1989).
[36] *Planned Parenthood of Southeastern Pennsylvania* v. *Casey,* 60 U.S.L.W. 4795 (1992).

nancy now depends largely on what her state legislature, Congress, and the executive branch allow. For example, in 1993 as one of his first actions as president, Bill Clinton lifted a ban imposed by President Reagan in 1988 that banned abortion counseling in federally funded family planning programs.

Personal Autonomy and Sexual Orientation

For many people, the principle of personal autonomy, which lies at the heart of the privacy cases, suggests that government should leave people alone in their choices about sexual relations, including a gay life-style. Nonetheless, all states today have laws regulating private behavior and personal relations to some extent. Homosexual marriages, for example, are not officially recognized by any state although some cities have accorded them semi-official status. In many locales, homosexual couples may not adopt or have legal custody of children. Although a few cities and states have banned discrimination against homosexuals in housing and the workplace, it remains legal in most places for landlords to

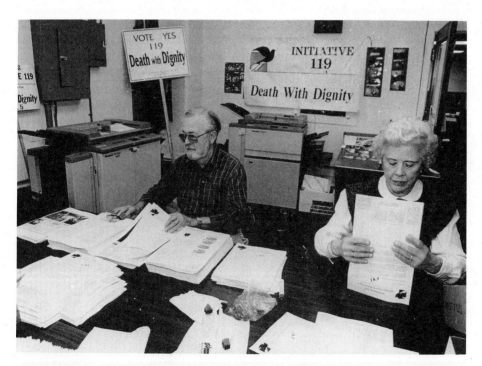

One of the most contentious civil liberties issues of the 1990s promises to be physician-assisted suicide. On November 5, 1992, voters in the state of Washington rejected a proposal that had never before appeared on a ballot in the United States: should doctors be allowed by law to kill terminally ill patients who have asked to die?

refuse to rent and for employers to fire or to refuse to hire because of someone's sexual orientation. Nearly half the states outlaw sodomy (oral or anal sex) between persons of the same gender, a policy the Supreme Court found acceptable under the Constitution in 1986.[37]

Gay rights were a factor in the 1992 election. According to exit polls conducted by the television networks, 72 percent of gay and lesbian voters supported Bill Clinton. After his victory on November 3, leaders of the Gay and Lesbian Task Force called on the president-elect to make good on his campaign promise to abolish the Defense Department's ban on homosexuals serving in the military. The task force also announced plans to push for the inclusion of gay-rights protections in the nation's civil rights laws.[38]

In the same election, gay rights were the subject of initiatives in two states. In Oregon voters defeated a measure that would have declared homosexuality "abnormal" and "perverse" and which would have barred the spending of public funds to "promote, encourage or facilitate" homosexuality. In Colorado, by contrast, voters approved an initiative that blocked both the state and local governments from enacting gay-rights protections, but a judge promptly blocked enforcement of the initiative, pending review by the state supreme court. Thus, the debate in the nation continues over the legal status of a homosexual lifestyle.

Racial Equality

The United States is racially and ethnically wealthy because of centuries of immigration from virtually every part of the globe. The nation's motto (*E Pluribus Unum*—"out of many, one") symbolizes this coming together of peoples as much as it does the union of the states. Some groups have encountered massive discrimination, however. Racial, religious, and ethnic stigmas have been real barriers for many. Perhaps because of color and certainly because of centuries of slavery, blacks have had the hardest time overcoming discrimination in America. Hispanics, whose numbers in this nation have increased in recent years, have faced some of the same obstacles to equality.

Equality: A Concept in Dispute

A word like *equality* can mean different things to different people. For believers in **equality of opportunity,** it is enough if government removes barriers of discrimination that have existed in the past. If life is like a marathon, all people should be allowed to participate by having a number and a place at the starting line. Others think government should promote **equality of condition.** To do this,

---

[37] *Bowers* v. *Hardwick,* 478 U.S. 186 (1986).
[38] Bill McAllister, "Gay Rights Groups Applaud Clinton's Win," *Washington Post,* November 5, 1992, p. A30.

policies should seek to reduce or even eliminate handicaps the runners face because of the lingering effects of past discriminations. The marathon can hardly be fair, they say, if some runners start out with their shoelaces tied together or have to wear ill-fitting shoes. Accordingly, the government will have to redistribute income and resources, collecting from those who have more and giving to those who have less. Head Start programs for preschool children and need-based scholarships for college students are obvious devices intended to further equality of condition. Some find such policies inadequate. The effects of inequality, whether of wealth or race or gender, are too strong and pervasive. Government must therefore pursue **equality of result.** In the marathon, government may have to carry some runners to the finish line if they are to get there at all. Some affirmative action programs are aimed at results.

The Legacy: Slavery and Third-Class Citizenship

Shortly after the Civil War ended, ratification of the **Thirteenth Amendment** in 1865 banished slavery and "involuntary servitude" from the land. Following quickly were ratification of the Fourteenth and Fifteenth amendments in 1868 and 1870 and passage of several civil rights acts. Collectively these conferred rights of citizenship on the newly freed slaves and officially removed race as a criterion for voting. Especially significant was the **equal protection clause** of the Fourteenth Amendment: ". . . nor shall any State deny to any person within its jurisdiction the equal protection of the laws" (see Table 3.2).

By the end of the nineteenth century, however, it was clear that the nation had abandoned the promises of full citizenship for the former slaves. Enforcement of civil rights laws became lax, and the Supreme Court made it clear that the Constitution would not stand in the way of racially discriminatory policies. In *Plessy* v. *Ferguson,* for example, the Court announced the **separate-but-equal doctrine** in upholding a Louisiana law that required racial segregation on trains.[39] As long as racially separate facilities were "equal," the Constitution had not been violated.

Three kinds of policies then developed that denied many black Americans their rights until after the middle of the twentieth century. First, virtually every aspect of life in the South (the region of the nation where most blacks lived) became racially segregated by law. Elsewhere, segregation existed too, but it was enforced more by custom than by law. No section of the nation was immune to racist attitudes and racially motivated violence, including riots and lynchings. Segregated neighborhoods became fixtures in the North and South alike.

Second, Southern politicians systematically excluded blacks from the political process. To get around the Fifteenth Amendment, legislatures turned to devices such as poll taxes, good character tests, and literacy tests to keep blacks away from the ballot box. Until its use was declared unconstitutional by the Supreme Court,[40] the "grandfather clause" allowed whites to vote who would otherwise

---

[39] 163 U.S. 537 (1896).
[40] *Guinn* v. *United States,* 238 U.S. 347 (1915).

TABLE 3.2
Chronology of Major Civil Rights Decisions, Laws, and Amendments

1865	Thirteenth Amendment abolishes slavery and "involuntary servitude."
1868	Fourteenth Amendment prohibits state action denying any person "the equal protection of the laws."
1870	Fifteenth Amendment removes race as a qualification for voting.
1875	Civil Rights Act bans racial discrimination in places of public accommodation.
1883	Civil Rights Cases hold 1875 statute unconstitutional.
1896	*Plessy* v. *Ferguson* upholds constitutionality of state law requiring racial segregation on trains in "separate but equal" facilities.
1920	Nineteenth Amendment extends franchise to women.
1954	*Brown* v. *Board of Education* declares unconstitutional racially segregated public schools; *Plessy* v. *Ferguson* reversed.
1957	Congress establishes the Civil Rights Commission.
1963	Congress passes the Equal Pay Act.
1964	Congress passes the Civil Rights Act: Title II outlaws racial discrimination in places of public accommodation; Title IV allows the Justice Department to sue school districts on behalf of black students seeking integrated education; Title VI bans racial discrimination in federally funded programs; Title VII prohibits most forms of discrimination (as on the basis of race or gender) in employment and creates the Equal Employment Opportunity Commission. Twenty-fourth Amendment eliminates poll taxes in federal elections.
1965	Congress passes the Voting Rights Act. President Johnson bans racial discrimination by federal contractors.
1968	Civil Rights Act's Title VIII prohibits most forms of discrimination in sale or rental of housing.
1971	Twenty-sixth Amendment lowers national voting age to 18.
1972	Congress submits Equal Rights Amendment to states for ratification.
1978	*Regents* v. *Bakke* invalidates a medical school admissions program that reserved a specific number of seats for minority applicants.
1979	*Steelworkers* v. *Weber* upholds legality of a voluntary affirmative-action plan for industrial apprenticeships that gives preference to black workers over white workers with greater seniority.
1982	Ratification of Equal Rights Amendment fails. Congress extends and amends Voting Rights Act. Title IX of Educational Amendments bars sex discrimination in "any education program or activity receiving Federal financial assistance."
1989	*Richmond* v. *J. A. Croson Co.* invalidates a municipally mandated 30 percent set-aside quota for racial minorities.
1990	Congress enacts the National Hate Crimes Statistics Act which requires the Justice Department to gather data on crimes motivated by prejudice about race, religion, ethnicity, or sexual orientation. The Americans with Disabilities Act becomes law.

TABLE 3.2 continued

| 1991 | Congress enacts a civil rights bill designed to modify several 1989 Supreme Court decisions that had made on-the-job discrimination more difficult to prove and which had made affirmative-action plans easier to challenge in court. |

The drive for political equality for all Americans has been a long process and remains incomplete. Important in achieving equality thus far are congressional statutes and Supreme Court decisions since the Civil War.

have been disfranchised by those same barriers. Of all the discriminatory devices, the **white primary** was probably the most effective. Because one party, the Democratic, was dominant in the region after 1900, the real electoral choices in state, local, and congressional races were made in the primary, not in the general election. White Democrats thus excluded blacks from meaningful political participation by adopting party rules that allowed only whites to vote in the Democratic primaries. Even though the white primary seems an affront to the Fifteenth Amendment, it was not until 1944 that the Supreme Court ruled that such deception violated the Constitution.[41] Still, for two decades afterwards most blacks were kept from voting in many places.

Third, without the vote blacks were shortchanged across the board in the delivery of public services such as education. Favors are rarely extended to entire groups that are permanently disfranchised, especially when they bear racial or religious stigmas as well. So the spirit of *Plessy* was honored only in part. Although separate, services and facilities were only rarely equal.

The Counterattack

Opponents of racism saw little hope of victory through the legislative process. At the local level, blacks were politically powerless in the areas where segregation was most pervasive. At the national level, Congress operated racially segregated schools in Washington, D.C., and provided separate eating and working places for black civil servants. Even Uncle Sam's toilets were marked "Whites Only" and "Colored." The armed forces remained racially segregated until President Truman (1945–1953) ordered an end to the practice in 1948.

So the counterattack against racism looked to the federal judiciary and was led principally by the National Association for the Advancement of Colored People. Known by its initials, the **NAACP** was founded in 1909 to improve the social, economic, and political condition of blacks. A separate division for litigation, called the Legal Defense Fund (LDF), began work in 1939 and had the primary responsibility for pressing the desegregation drive in courtrooms in the 1940s, 1950s, and 1960s. One prominent black attorney in the LDF was Thurgood Marshall, later the first black justice on the Supreme Court (1967–1991).

---

[41] *Smith* v. *Allwright,* 321 U.S. 649 (1944).

The assault on racial segregation reached a climax in the landmark decision of May 17, 1954: ***Brown v. Board of Education of Topeka***.[42] "Does segregation of children in public schools solely on the basis of race, even though the physical facilities and other 'tangible' factors may be equal, deprive the children of the minority group of equal educational opportunities?" asked Chief Justice Earl Warren (1953–1969). "We believe that it does. . . . In the field of public education," he concluded, "the doctrine of 'separate but equal' has no place. Separate educational facilities are inherently unequal." *Plessy* was overruled.

Putting *Brown* to Work: The Law and Politics of Integration

The Court had made its decision. What was to happen? Rather than order an immediate end to segregation, the justices announced that integration was to proceed "with all deliberate speed."[43] In most places "deliberate speed" proved to be a turtle's pace. A decade after the Court's historic pronouncement, less than one percent of the black children in the states of the old Confederacy were attending public school with white children. In six border states and the District of Columbia the figure was much higher: 52 percent.

Several factors severely hampered quick implementation of *Brown,* making the 1954 decision a test case of the Supreme Court's power. First, some federal judges in the South were themselves opposed to integration. They did little to press for *Brown*'s speedy implementation. Second, state legislatures and local school boards usually reflected strong white opposition to *Brown*'s enforcement. Third, fear of hostile reaction by the local white community discouraged litigation. It was economically and physically risky for parents of black children to sue local officials. Fourth, the Court received little initial support from Congress, the White House, and a large part of the organized legal community.

Significant enforcement of *Brown* and the lowering of other racial barriers did not come until civil rights activists like Martin Luther King, Jr., riveted the nation's attention on injustices that persisted and called for action. Congress then enacted two important pieces of legislation: the **Civil Rights Act of 1964** and the Elementary and Secondary Education Act of 1965. The importance of the first for *Brown* came in Title VI: Every federal agency that funded local programs through grants, loans, or contracts was required to press for an end to racial discrimination. The 1965 school aid act was the first massive federal appropriation for local school systems. But to keep the money, school systems had to move swiftly on integration. The 1964 act was the hook, and the 1965 act was the bait. Ironically, public schools in the South are now among the most integrated in the nation, whereas schools in the Northeast are among the most segregated.

---

[42] 347 U.S. 483 (1954).
[43] *Brown* v. *Board of Education of Topeka* (II), 349 U.S. 294 (1955).

The Continuing Effects of *Brown*

Supreme Court decisions on school integration since 1971 have come largely from states outside the South. Nonsouthern school systems had segregated schools, but rarely had they been recently segregated by law. The racial composition of these schools reflected decades of residential segregation that had resulted from economic inequities and private discrimination. This kind of "unofficial" segregation was called **de facto segregation.** But in a pair of decisions from Ohio,[44] the Supreme Court decided that "racially identifiable schools" in any district probably resulted from school board policy. What many had thought to be de facto segregation was now considered **de jure segregation:** racial separation caused by government policy. Local officials now have the affirmative duty of redrawing attendance zones and busing pupils from one part of town to another.

Large metropolitan areas present a special problem. Typically, a city will have a single school district where racial minorities are already a majority or well on their way to becoming a majority of the school population. Around the city are heavily white suburban school districts. Segregation is commonly between districts, not merely within a single district. In a Michigan case,[45] the Court (by a vote of 5 to 4) rejected a metropolitan integration plan involving busing among more than 50 school districts spread over the city of Detroit and three suburban counties. Only when there is evidence that school boards have caused the segregation between districts will the Court find a constitutional violation.

Busing itself remains controversial. Many parents, black and white alike, object to having their children transported farther than seems necessary. Many prefer neighborhood schools. Aside from achieving integration, scholars disagree on the effects of busing and similar measures on the schoolchildren involved, debating whether integration improves the educational performance of black students. Although integrated schools often mean that black parents lose control over schools in black neighborhoods, integrated education probably prepares all students better for living in a racially diverse society. Moreover, many believe that "green follows white"—that the presence of white students assures more generous economic support of a school by local officials. Nonetheless, the Supreme Court has now taken the position that once a school district has eliminated segregation, the district may cease to be under a constitutional obligation to continue the policies that produced the integrated system, even if "re-segregation" might result.[46]

Whatever the progress with school integration, social segregation remains a fact in many areas of the nation. Even though the Civil Rights Acts of 1964 and 1968, respectively, prohibit racial discrimination in employment and the sale or rental of housing (as do the laws in most states and hundreds of

---

[44] *Columbus Board of Education* v. *Penick,* 443 U.S. 449 (1979); *Dayton Board of Education* v. *Brinkman,* 443 U.S. 526 (1979).
[46] *Freeman* v. *Pitts,* 60 U.S.L.W. 4286 (1992).
[45] *Milliken* v. *Bradley,* 418 U.S. 717 (1974).

municipalities), black Americans remain the most segregated minority group, the group most isolated from whites.

Affirmative Action

Many people believe that ending discrimination is not enough. Positive steps called **affirmative action** are also needed to overcome the residual effects of generations of racial bias. Others oppose affirmative action if it involves preferential treatment for minorities. They argue that jobs and university scholarships, for example, are finite. To give to one means to withhold from someone else. The nonminority applicant who loses out because of race has been hurt just as much as a minority applicant in earlier years who was kept out because of race. One side says that two wrongs make right; the other side answers that they do not.

If a national consensus has developed against racial discrimination in its old forms, no firm consensus exists on affirmative action. Even the Supreme Court has been divided, as *Regents of the University of California* v. *Bakke*[47] illustrates. In this landmark affirmative action case, the Supreme Court invalidated the use of a racial quota for medical school admissions at the Davis campus of the University of California but said that race could still be taken into account. Admissions officers may use race as one of several criteria in evaluating the record of an applicant but may not admit or exclude solely on the basis of race. In other cases, the Court has allowed governments and private businesses wide latitude in personnel decisions. Title VII of the Civil Rights Act of 1964 bans job discrimination on the basis of "race, color, religion, sex, or national origin." Even with such sweeping language, the Court has reasoned that a law intended to end discrimination against racial minorities and women should not be used to prohibit programs designed to help those groups.[48]

What, then, are the limits under the law to affirmative action? There is no clear answer to this question. Generally, policies by an employer to overcome the effects of its own past discrimination are permissible; indeed, they may be required. Even some policies by an employer to alleviate general "societal discrimination" for which the employer is not responsible are permissible. Policies that look like "quotas" have the best chance of being struck down.[49]

Voting Rights

Two centuries ago most Americans were denied the right to vote. The Constitution left voting qualifications to the states, with the result that women, blacks, and some white adult males were left out. Since the 1820s the national trend has been

---

[47] 438 U.S. 265 (1978).
[48] For example, see *United Steelworkers of America* v. *Weber,* 443 U.S. 193 (1979) and *Johnson* v. *Transportation Agency,* 480 U.S. 616 (1987).
[49] *Richmond* v. *J.A. Croson Co.,* 488 U.S. 469 (1989).

to chip away at these restrictions so that today almost all adult citizens in the United States have the right to vote.

As late as 1964, however, blacks in particular were systemically denied the right to vote in most parts of the South. The response to this situation was the **Voting Rights Act of 1965,** the most important voting legislation ever enacted by Congress. Besides removing many barriers to voting, the act requires that any change in a "standard, practice, or procedure with respect to voting" in certain parts of the United States (most of them being in the South) can take effect only after being cleared by the attorney general of the United States or by the United States District Court for the District of Columbia. The Supreme Court has interpreted "standard, practice, or procedure" to include any change in a locale's electoral system. This advance clearance requirement is satisfied only if the proposed change has neither the *purpose* nor the *effect* of "denying or abridging the right to vote on account of race or color." This means that black voting power can in no way be weakened or diluted by any change in local election practices.

Congress made an important change in the law in 1982, banning *existing* electoral arrangements anywhere in the United States with a racially discriminatory effect. Conceivably, this addition to the law may produce a realignment of political

A march led by Reverend Martin Luther King, Jr., in March 1965 from Selma to Montgomery, Alabama, sparked violent protests by whites who opposed voting by blacks. As a result Congress passed the far-reaching Voting Rights Act. In this photograph, King officially starts the last leg of the march to the Alabama state capitol building. Next to King is his wife, Coretta. Those on his right include Dr. Ralph Bunche and Reverend Ralph Abernathy.

power in any section of the country where blacks and Hispanics amount at least to a sizable minority of the population and where local political practices dilute the political influence of these minorities.

The Voting Rights Act has had a far-reaching impact. Blacks in the southern states now vote at a rate approximating that for whites. In the 1992 election for the U.S. House of Representatives, voters nationally chose 39 black and 19 Hispanic members, a record number that amounts to nearly 14 percent of the chamber. In the same year, Illinois voters sent the first black woman, Carol Moseley Braun, to the U.S. Senate.

Sexual Equality

Because the political system has been the battleground for so many years in the fight for racial equality, it is easy to suppose that sexual equality has occupied the attention of Congress and the courts for just as long. It has not. Making the nation free of discrimination based on gender has been a national priority for barely three decades.

The Legacy

Until recently the legal status of women in the United States was one of substantial inequality. Legally a wife had no existence apart from her husband. Without his consent, she could make no contracts binding either of them. In response to such attitudes, the first convention on women's rights was held in 1848 at Seneca Falls, New York. Change in attitudes came slowly. Even the Fourteenth Amendment spoke of "male inhabitants." The Nineteenth Amendment, extending the franchise to women, was not ratified until 1920 after a long and turbulent suffrage movement. Not until 1971 did the Supreme Court first invalidate a law because it discriminated against women.[50] As late as 1973 there were 900 sex-based federal laws still on the books.

Gender to the Forefront

Attacks on racial discrimination during the 1950s helped to turn attention to laws that penalized women because they were women. Sex discrimination became a political issue few politicians could ignore after publication of books like Betty Friedan's *Feminine Mystique* in 1963 and Kate Millett's *Sexual Politics* in 1971 and after formation of the National Organization for Women (NOW) in 1966. At about the same time the female half of the postwar "baby boom" entered college, graduate schools, and the work force. There were more women than ever before

---

[50] *Reed* v. *Reed,* 404 U.S. 71 (1971).

at an age and place in their lives and careers for whom questions of gender discrimination were very important.

Responding to inequities that had become obvious, Congress passed the Equal Pay Act in 1963, which commanded "equal pay for equal work." Title VII of the 1964 Civil Rights Act outlawed sexual (as well as racial) bias in employment and promotion practices. Title IX of the 1972 Educational Amendments banned sex discrimination in education programs and activities at colleges receiving federal financial aid. (Title IX remains contentious because of its applicability to how universities allocate dollars between male and female athletic teams.)

As a result of changes in both laws and attitudes, sex-based retirement plans, for example, may no longer require women to make higher contributions or to receive lower monthly benefits than men just because women as a group live longer than men as a group.[51] States may no longer operate single-sex schools of nursing (and probably any other kind), even if coeducational public nursing schools also exist.[52] In the workplace, not only has sexual harassment been judged to be a violation of Title VII, but the Supreme Court holds employers responsible under the law for not taking steps to prevent it.[53] Despite such remedies, sexual harassment continues to be a problem in many settings, as the reaction to Anita Hill's accusations against Supreme Court nominee Clarence Thomas in 1991 revealed (see Chapter 11).

Many people believe that real economic equality between the sexes will not be achieved without **comparable worth** (equal pay for jobs of equal value), a policy not required by federal law. Otherwise, they say, full-time female workers will continue to earn on average no more than about two-thirds the pay of full-time male workers.

Other Americans and Civil Rights

Discrimination against women and blacks has occupied a prominent place on the public agenda in recent years, but discrimination has claimed other victims as well. Native Americans, Hispanics, immigrants, and the disabled have all demanded, with varying degrees of success, that public officials take steps to remedy years of neglect and unequal treatment. (Sexual orientation has also been the basis for discrimination by governments, businesses, and individuals, and has been discussed as an aspect of privacy earlier in this chapter.)

Native Americans

From an estimated sixteenth-century population of perhaps two million or more[54] (no one knows for sure), Native Americans (also called American Indians) numbered barely a half million in 1900 as war, disease, and systematic slaughter took

---

[51] *Los Angeles* v. *Manhart,* 435 U.S. 702 (1978); *Arizona* v. *Norris,* 463 U.S. 1073 (1983).
[52] *Mississippi University for Women* v. *Hogan,* 458 U.S. 718 (1982).
[53] *Meritor Savings Bank* v. *Vinson,* 477 U.S. 57 (1986).
[54] *Historical Atlas of the United States* (Washington, D.C.: National Geographic Society, 1988), p. 34.

their toll. Today, there are 1.5 million, less than one percent of the total U.S. population. As a group, Native Americans suffer disproportionately high rates of sickness, poverty, illiteracy, and unemployment. Not until 1924 did Congress recognize them as citizens.

Many Native Americans have understandably resisted assimilation into the rest of the population, insisting instead on preserving their culture and heritage. Approximately half live on 285 semiautonomous reservations and, in Alaska, in 200 native villages under the supervision of the Bureau of Indian Affairs in the Department of the Interior. The Indian Self-Determination and Education Assistance Act of 1975 granted Native Americans greater control over their own affairs, and the Indian Bill of Rights of 1968 gave Native Americans living on reservations protections similar to those found in the Constitution.

Recent policy reflects resurgent ethnic pride and new political awareness asserted by activist groups such as the National Indian Youth Council and the American Indian Movement. Not only have such groups protested inadequate national assistance and the plight of the reservation population, but they have also attempted, with some success, to recover through litigation ancient tribal fishing and land rights, sometimes worth millions of dollars.

Hispanics

Numbering more than 18 million, making up about 8 percent of the population, Hispanics are the nation's fastest-growing minority. By the year 2000 Hispanics will probably outnumber blacks. A majority originally came from Mexico; most of the others came from Puerto Rico, South America, and parts of Central America. Mexican-Americans reside mainly in the Southwest, Cuban-Americans in Florida, and Puerto Ricans in the Northeast.

For decades, Hispanics have encountered the same discriminations in voting, education, housing, and employment that have confronted blacks, compounded by a language barrier. Amendments to the Voting Rights Act of 1965 require ballots to be printed in Spanish as well as in English in areas where Spanish-speaking people number more than 5 percent of the population. (Partly as a result, between 1972 and 1984 Hispanic voter registration jumped 52 percent nationwide, yet Hispanics are still less likely than blacks and whites to register to vote.) Moreover, Title VI of the Civil Rights Act of 1964 requires public schools to provide bilingual instruction to students deficient in English. Both education and political participation are important to any group seeking to maintain ethnic identity in a diverse culture. Policies to lower language barriers have sparked a backlash among those who see non-English-speaking (especially Spanish-speaking) persons as a threat to an American cultural identity.

Immigrants

The Statue of Liberty signifies that America is a land of immigrants, but some have been more welcome than others. Until 1921 entry into the United States was virtually unlimited, but in that year Congress established the first of a series of

During the 1992 campaign, candidate Bill Clinton promised a cabinet that "looks like America," meaning one that reflected the nation's diversity. In fact, Clinton appointed more women and nonwhites to his cabinet than any previous president, but also more millionaires than the preceding Bush presidency. Here, President Clinton presides over his first cabinet meeting in the Cabinet Room of the White House, January 22, 1993. By this date, only the post of attorney general had not been filled. (Janet Reno was subsequently confirmed as attorney general, the first time a woman held the post.)

ceilings on immigration that discriminated against persons from Eastern Europe and Asia, a bias not eliminated until 1965. Today the law sets a ceiling of 700,000 (a number that is scheduled to drop to 675,000 after 1994), including those admitted because of job skills and family relationships. Exceptions to the ceiling for refugees (approximately 131,000 in 1992) and others mean that the total annually admitted easily exceeds 800,000.

Thousands more—no one knows the exact number—successfully enter the country illegally, putting pressure on public services and, many people believe, taking jobs from citizens and others legally present. In response, Congress passed the Immigration Reform and Control Act in 1986. Among other things, the law requires employers to verify the American citizenship or legal status of all job applicants and provides stiff penalties for employers who hire illegal aliens. The 1986 law has had an unintended consequence: discrimination against persons of Hispanic or Asian descent. A study by the General Accounting Office (an investigatory agency of Congress) found that one in five of the 4.6

million employers surveyed admitted that the law encouraged them to discriminate against job applicants who were "foreign-appearing" or "foreign-
sounding."[55]

It was the 1986 immigration act that complicated President Clinton's search
for an attorney general early in 1993, prior to Janet Reno's nomination on February
11. Zoe Baird, Clinton's first choice and an Aetna insurance executive, asked that
her nomination be withdrawn after she admitted having employed a Peruvian
couple in violation of the act. U.S. District Judge Kimba Wood, Clinton's second
choice, also withdrew her name even though her employment of an illegal alien
occurred before the effective date of the 1986 act.

The Disabled

The nation's largest minority group consists of the more than 43 million Americans
with a physical or mental disability. Long victims of bias in both the public and
private sectors, the disabled were not covered by the Civil Rights Act of 1964, the
most comprehensive antidiscrimination legislation ever enacted by Congress.

In 1990 Congress passed the Americans with Disabilities Act, which bans
discrimination in employment (in businesses with more than 15 employees) and
in places of public accommodation (including not only restaurants and hotels but
establishments as varied as physicians' offices, zoos, sports arenas, and dry clean-
ers). Called a bill of rights for the disabled, the law also stipulates that newly
manufactured buses and railroad cars be accessible to persons in wheelchairs and
that telephone companies provide service for those with hearing and speech
impairments. The law's definition of the disabled goes beyond those who rely on
wheelchairs or who have difficulty seeing or hearing. It includes people with
mental disorders and those with AIDS (Acquired Immune Deficiency Syndrome)
and HIV (the virus that causes AIDS), but not those who use illegal drugs or who
abuse legal drugs such as alcohol.

Liberties and Rights in the Constitutional Framework

Civil rights and liberties, the subjects of this chapter, are part of the framework of
American constitutional government. Freedoms of political and religious expression, limits on the police, protection of privacy—all examples of civil liberties—
are not only essential components of the political process but help to define the
quality of life Americans enjoy. Civil rights in turn are inspired by the bold assertion
of the Declaration of Independence that "all men are created equal." Against a
legacy of toleration of inequality, much of what government and private citizens
have done in recent decades has been driven by an intoleration of inequality.

[55] Paul M. Barrett, "Immigration Law Found to Promote Bias by Employers," *Wall Street Journal,* March 30, 1990, p. A18.

Through application of constitutional provisions, laws, and policies, many people have tried to make the Declaration's words a reality, for women as well as men, for blacks as well as whites. Their efforts employ the tools of politics and the major institutions of government, described in the chapters that follow.

Summary

1. Civil liberties are freedoms, protected by law, to act or not to act and to be free from unwarranted governmental intrusion in one's life. Civil rights encompass participation in society on an equal footing with others.
2. Initially the Bill of Rights restrained only the national government, but, using the Fourteenth Amendment, the Supreme Court has applied most of the protections of the Bill of Rights to the states.
3. Free expression is necessary to the democratic political process. Only in rare instances today will the Court approve restrictions on the content of what a person says.
4. The free exercise and establishment clauses have two main objectives: separation of church and state and toleration of different religious faiths.
5. Other parts of the Bill of Rights guard liberty by placing limits on what officials may do in the process of fighting crime.
6. By interpretation, the Constitution includes a right of privacy, protecting basic decisions about procreation from undue interference by government. Abortion continues to be a divisive national issue.
7. Only since the landmark case of *Brown* v. *Board of Education of Topeka* in 1954 has the nation made significant progress toward removing discrimination on the basis of race from American life. The Voting Rights Act of 1965 has enabled black Americans especially to participate more equally in the political process.
8. Most discriminations based on sex are generally forbidden by statute and by the Supreme Court's interpretation of the Fourteenth Amendment.
9. Native Americans, Hispanics, immigrants, and the disabled are other groups who face discrimination and present special needs.

Key Terms

civil liberties (p. 68)
civil rights (p. 68)
Fourteenth Amendment (p. 69)
First Amendment (p. 71)
clear and present danger test (p. 72)
bad tendency test (p. 72)
incitement test (p. 73)
prior restraint (p. 73)

obscenity (p. 73)
libel (p. 74)
symbolic speech (p. 74)
free exercise clause (p. 76)
establishment clause (p. 76)
Lemon test (p. 76)
legal guilt (p. 78)
presumption of innocence (p. 79)

ex post facto laws (p. 79)
bill of attainder (p. 79)
Fourth Amendment (p. 79)
warrant (p. 79)
probable cause (p. 79)
exclusionary rule (p. 80)
Miranda rights (p. 80)
plea bargain (p. 80)
Sixth Amendment (p. 80)
capital cases (p. 81)
misdemeanors (p. 81)
felonies (p. 81)
Eighth Amendment (p. 82)
cruel and unusual punishment (p. 82)
Ninth Amendment (p. 84)
Roe v. *Wade* (p. 84)

equality of opportunity (p. 86)
equality of condition (p. 86)
equality of result (p. 87)
Thirteenth Amendment (p. 87)
equal protection clause (p. 87)
separate-but-equal doctrine (p. 87)
white primary (p. 89)
NAACP (p. 89)
Brown v. *Board of Education of Topeka* (p. 90)
Civil Rights Act of 1964 (p. 90)
de facto segregation (p. 91)
de jure segregation (p. 91)
affirmative action (p. 92)
Voting Rights Act of 1965 (p. 93)
comparable worth (p. 95)

Readings for Further Study

The Bill of Rights by Irving Brant (Indianapolis: Bobbs-Merrill, 1965) remains one of the best treatments of the origins of the liberties protected in the Constitution. The rapidly changing field of criminal procedure can be followed in George Cole, *Criminal Justice: Law and Politics,* 6th ed. (Pacific Grove, Calif.: Brooks-Cole, 1992). Efforts to achieve racial equality are fully described in Richard Kluger's *Simple Justice* (New York: Knopf, 1976). Abigail M. Thernstrone's *Whose Votes Count?* (Cambridge, Mass.: Harvard University Press, 1987), discusses reform in voting rights. *Gender Politics* by Ethel Klein (Cambridge, Mass.: Harvard University Press, 1984) looks at the political concerns of women.

4 Political Ideologies

P olitics is about power and influence—who gets what, when, and how. But politics is also about ideas. **Political ideology** is an integrated set of political ideas about what constitutes the most equitable and just political order. Political ideologies are concerned with the proper function of government, the issues of liberty and equality, and the distribution of goods and services.

All of the ideological perspectives discussed in this chapter and given any serious attention by Americans accept the basic ideas of democracy—representative government and individual liberty. They do not question the fundamental precepts of American political life. They differ on matters of emphasis and degree. Although most Americans do not think in rigid ideological terms, ideology does influence how Americans think about political leaders. Politicians and policies tend to be labeled liberal, conservative, radical, or reactionary, and with some frequency we hear the terms *neoconservative* and *neoliberal* (*neo* being Greek for "new"). This chapter is intended to introduce the landscape of contemporary American political ideas and movements—liberal, conservative, neoliberal, neoconservative, socialist, and libertarian.

American Political Ideologies

Ideology "spells out what is valued and what is not, what must be maintained and what must be changed."[1] Most political leaders and most Americans share elements of or identify with mainstream ideologies. Generally identified as *liberal* or *conservative*, these ideological positions do not challenge the existing political order. For example, neither liberals nor conservatives want to make major changes in our political and social order. They accept capitalism American-style as a successful economic system, and the economic marketplace as the chief instrument for the distribution of economic goods. At the same time, liberals and conservatives accept most of the economic reforms of the New Deal (explained later in this chapter)—Social Security, unemployment insurance, and farm price supports—as a permanent part of our political system. Their differences are over matters of emphasis and degree. By contrast, radical ideologies, such as *democratic socialism* and *libertarianism,* challenge much of the existing social and political order. Democratic socialists do not accept the capitalist system or what they consider the inordinate power of the big corporations. Socialists want to remove most of the major economic decisions on investments, wages, and prices from the private sector and place them in the hands of government. Libertarians seek to establish an economic system free of governmental interference and regulation and to dismantle most of the existing welfare state programs. These ideologies challenge many of the existing arrangements in our political system.

Exotic as socialism or libertarianism may seem to most Americans, these ideologies and movements operate within the framework of our democratic system. Democratic socialists and libertarians believe in peaceful change and accept the rules of the game. They frequently enter candidates in elections, although they rarely win and only then at the state and local levels. But because their ideas challenge the dominant ideologies of our time, it is important to understand their criticisms and their prescriptions for the future just as it is important to understand beliefs that are more widely held.

---

[1] Roy C. Macridis, *Contemporary Political Ideologies* (Boston: Little, Brown, 1983), p. 9.

Liberalism

One influential American ideology is liberalism. **Liberalism** begins with the assumption that individuals are, in the main, rational beings capable of overcoming obstacles to progress without resorting to violence. The roots of liberalism can be traced to the great English philosopher John Locke (1632–1704). Locke, who believed in the natural goodness of man, developed the **contract theory of the state**. According to Locke's theory, the state gains its legitimacy from the consent of the governed and is formed primarily to protect individuals' rights to life, liberty, and property. Locke's ideas of limited government, resting on the consent of the governed, became the textbook of the American Revolution. Locke was an inspiration to Thomas Jefferson, one of the most important early American liberal thinkers.

Classical Liberalism: Thomas Jefferson and Andrew Jackson

Contemporary American liberalism is vastly different from what was known in the nineteenth century as **classical liberalism** (see Table 4.1). Liberals of that time, going back to Thomas Jefferson and Andrew Jackson, believed that the government that governed least governed best. Those nineteenth-century liberals felt that government should step out of the way so that the new entrepreneurs of the young Republic—the small business owners and farmers—could have an opportunity to compete in the economic system. Jefferson shared Locke's view that government must treat property rights with particular care. Jefferson had high praise for Adam Smith's *Wealth of Nations* (1776), the bible of capitalism. In his first inaugural address Jefferson stated:

> A wise and frugal government, which shall restrain men from injuring one another, shall leave them otherwise free to regulate their own pursuits of industry and improvement and shall not take from the mouth of labor the bread it has earned. This is the sum of good government.[2]

President Andrew Jackson's struggle against the wealth and power of a national bank (see Chapter 2) was a classic example of the nineteenth-century liberal creed in action. Jackson also opposed extensive government expenditures on roads and canals. He believed that such expenditures "would make the federal government a partner with business in the financial prosperity of the upper class."[3] Speaking for the liberal reformers of his day, Jackson declared that a strong central government "is calculated to raise around the administration a moneyed aristocracy dangerous to the liberties of the country."[4]

---

[2] Quoted in Walter E. Volkomer, ed., *The Liberal Tradition in American Thought* (New York: Capricorn Books, 1969), p. 104.
[3] Robert V. Remini, *Andrew Jackson and the Course of American Freedom, 1822–1832,* vol. 2 (New York: Harper & Row, 1981), p. 116.
[4] Ibid., p. 33.

TABLE 4.1
Key Ideas of American Ideologies

Ideology	Key Ideas and Policies
Liberalism	
Classical Liberalism	Minimal government; protection of property rights
Populism	Democratization of government; economic reforms
Progressivism	Social programs to cope with problems caused by industrialization; public limits on private corporate power
Contemporary Liberalism	The positive state; faith in solving problems collectively through government; programs to provide for the economic well-being of the nation, including the basic material needs of each individual; tolerance of various life-styles
Neoliberalism	Creation, not redistribution, of wealth; free trade; reform of entitlement programs; a strong but economical defense
Conservatism	
Early American Conservatism	Sanctity of private property; distrust of unchecked popular rule; duty of government to promote a healthy economic environment and a virtuous citizenry
Industrial Age Conservatism	Laissez-faire economics; individualism; social Darwinism
Contemporary Conservatism	Reduced spending on social programs; revamping tax policies to encourage economic growth; strong military defense; little positive action to redress racial and gender discrimination; duty of government to promote a virtuous citizenry
Neoconservatism	Skepticism of government's ability to solve social and economic problems; acceptance of a modest welfare state; opposition to racial and gender quotas to redress discrimination; creation, not redistribution, of wealth; assertive foreign policy
Challenges to the Status Quo	
New Right	Critical of big government, big corporations; distrustful of national media; social ills seen as the product of liberal policies; radical steps needed to return the nation to traditional cultural values
Democratic Socialism	Public ownership of basic industries, banks, agricultural enterprises, and communications systems; wage and price controls; redistribution of wealth to achieve true economic equality; expanded welfare programs
Libertarianism	Minimal government; protection of property rights and freedom of individuals; no governmental regulation of the economy; noninterventionist foreign policy; drastic reduction in defense spending

Different forms of liberalism and conservatism have defined much of the ideological debate in American politics; other ideologies challenged and influenced mainstream ideas.

Like Jefferson, Jackson believed that liberty was the absence of government interference with the rights of all citizens to enjoy the fruits of their labor and prosperity.

Populism and Progressivism: The Repudiation of Classical Liberalism

In the latter part of the nineteenth century, liberal attitudes toward government began to change. In the decades following the Civil War, American farmers, the backbone of support for Jeffersonian and Jacksonian liberalism, suffered through a perpetual economic crisis. Agricultural prices fell and interest rates rose. The target of liberal reform became the railroads and the banks, not the government. Out of this turmoil evolved a new liberal movement, known as **populism**. The populists, who formed their own political party in the 1880s, called for further democratization of government through the secret ballot, direct election of senators, and voter initiatives and referenda. They also advocated fundamental economic reforms that would strengthen government's role, including nationalization of the railroads and the telegraph, a graduated income tax, free coinage of silver, and a vastly expanded supply of paper money. The Populist party did not supplant either of the two major parties but its ideas, particularly with the nomination of William Jennings Bryan as the Democratic presidential candidate in 1896, profoundly affected the Democratic party in the twentieth century.

In urban America, among the middle classes, there was also a growing movement for social and economic reform, known as **progressivism**. Progressives supported government programs to ease the problems of industrialization, including worker's compensation, a ban on child labor, regulation of corporations, and a minimum wage.

Progressives achieved their major successes during the presidential administrations of Theodore Roosevelt (1901–1909) and Woodrow Wilson (1913–1921). During Roosevelt's years, Congress passed the Hepburn Act, which regulated the railroads, and the Pure Food and Drug Act and the Meat Inspection Act, which eliminated many of the unhealthy practices of those industries. Woodrow Wilson signed into law bills regulating the banking industry, restricting unfair business competition, and establishing an eight-hour day for railroad workers. The populist and progressive belief that government could remedy the economic ills of the nation by limiting the power and wealth of private corporations and banks had a profound effect on American liberalism. The rise of populism and progressivism signaled a decline in the faith of liberalism in laissez-faire (minimal government regulation of economic affairs) and began a new era of belief in the power and virtues of a strong central government.

Wilson felt that Jefferson would have understood the need for more activist government. He said:

> If Jefferson were living in our day, he would see what we see: that the individual is caught in a great confused nexus of all sorts of complicated circumstances, and that to let him alone is to leave him helpless.[5]

---

[5] Quoted in Arthur A. Ekrich, Jr., *Progressivism in America* (New York: New Viewpoints, 1974), p. 170.

Contemporary Liberalism: The Welfare State and Beyond

The administration of President Franklin D. Roosevelt (1933–1945) took the concerns of the populists and progressives a step further. Roosevelt's New Deal program reflected the change in the constituency of liberalism. In contrast to the nineteenth-century liberal, who addressed the needs of the entrepreneurial class, New Deal liberals were concerned about the farmers, the unemployed, and the labor union movement. Carrying on the populist and progressive tradition, liberals no longer saw government as a threat to liberty or as the inevitable partner of the rich and powerful. In a complex industrial age, particularly one racked by the Great Depression of the 1930s, liberals believed that government action should ensure the economic well-being of the nation and should provide basic material guarantees (food, shelter, health care, and education) for every individual. The New Deal included programs to ensure protection for the unemployed, pensions for the elderly, and guaranteed prices for the farmers. The New Deal symbolized the idea of the positive or interventionist state. This became the hallmark of contemporary liberalism.

At the behest of President Franklin Roosevelt (1933–1945), Congress in 1933 created the Civilian Conservation Corps, an agency which provided work for unemployed men in a variety of natural resource and conservation projects. Shown here are several members of the corps on their way to a work site in 1940. The CCC is one of the inspirations for the national service program President Clinton proposed to Congress in 1993.

In the 1960s, President Lyndon Johnson's Great Society moved beyond the New Deal. Civil rights laws protected the rights of minorities, Medicare and Medicaid laws provided health insurance for the elderly and the poor, and funds aided impoverished elementary and secondary school districts. In the 1970s, liberals proposed a broad range of programs to protect the environment, to assist consumers, and to expand welfare benefits through the food stamp program.

Liberals today believe that a strong central government is necessary to protect individuals from the inequities of a modern industrial and technological society and that the growth of government has enhanced, not diminished, individual freedom. Although the positive state is central in the contemporary liberal creed, liberals do not believe that government should displace private enterprise. Most liberals are capitalists, if not forthrightly so. In fact, many argue that American capitalism has survived because government has humanized the industrial order and that Franklin Roosevelt's New Deal saved capitalism from repudiation during the 1930s. Liberals argue that the positive state cushions the inequalities of power and wealth that arise in any capitalist system. They see government as correcting the injustices of the marketplace, not supplanting it. Liberals recognize that in any society there will be some inequalities of wealth and income. But they feel that government must intervene to redress the most excessive inequalities. Thus, frequently in debates over tax laws, liberals support shifting more of the burden to people in the upper income brackets.

The idea of a benevolent government that offered services to the disadvantaged (unemployment insurance) as well as to the middle class (Social Security) has been for generations the centerpiece of American liberalism. Liberal ideas fueled the administrations of Presidents Franklin Roosevelt, Harry Truman, John Kennedy, and Lyndon Johnson. Johnson, for one, saw the United States as "an endless cornucopia." His Great Society began a virtual torrent of new government programs: rent supplements for the poor, scholarships for college students, aid to the arts and humanities, higher pensions for government workers and veterans, aid to handicapped children, and a massive food stamp program. These programs assisted the poor and the disadvantaged as well as many in the middle and upper income brackets.

But in the 1970s and early 1980s the growth rate of the economy declined while the demand for government services continued. Unlike his predecessors, President Carter (1977–1981) did not offer a new set of governmental programs and benefits. Hampered by the problems of inflation and an energy shortage, Carter could offer few initiatives. His administration stirred little enthusiasm among liberals.

Liberals remain wedded to the idea of affirmative government. In the early 1980s, some began to discuss the idea of an **industrial policy.** Championed by liberal economic thinkers such as Robert Reich and Felix Rohatyn, an industrial policy involves a partnership in economic decision making among government officials, labor unions, and public interest groups. President Bill Clinton (1933–   ) endorsed this approach in a slightly modified form in his 1992 election campaign, and later named Reich secretary of labor.

But in matters involving national security and personal morality, liberals seek to restrict the role of government. This tendency became more pronounced in the

President Lyndon Johnson (1963-1969) pushed many Great Society programs through Congress, including Medicare and Headstart. Along with other believers in contemporary liberalism, Johnson had an expansive vision of what government could do for people.

1970s and 1980s. Liberals extend broad tolerance to different life-styles and dispute government efforts to impose a single standard of religious practice or sexual morality. Consequently, liberals are at the forefront of opposition to constitutional amendments that might sanction prayer in schools or might limit the rights of women to obtain an abortion.

Since the Vietnam War, liberals have backed away from an interventionist, military-oriented foreign policy. In January 1991 most Congressional liberals voted against authorizing President Bush to use military force in the Persian Gulf and preferred the continuation of economic sanctions against Iraq. Liberals are also critical of large defense budgets and, with the end of the Cold War, advocate deep cuts in military spending.

In general, liberals favor government programs and budgeting priorities that put domestic social programs before those of the Pentagon. Their belief in a strong activist government concentrates primarily on domestic issues (see Table 4.2).

Who are the liberals? They are usually found in the Democratic party, although the Democrats do harbor some conservatives and the Republicans a handful of liberals. The association of liberals with Democrats is in part because the constituency of the Democratic party—minorities, the labor movement, feminists, the

TABLE 4.2
Milestones in American Liberalism

1690	John Locke's *Second Treatise on Government* published.
1776	Adam Smith's *Wealth of Nations,* Thomas Paine's *Common Sense,* and the Declaration of Independence published.
1832	President Andrew Jackson vetoes a bill to recharter the Bank of the United States.
1892	First Populist party convention held.
1896	William Jennings Bryan wins Democratic presidential nomination; the Democratic party adopts much of the Populist program.
1909	Herbert Croly's *Promise of American Life* published; a group of black leaders, including W. E. B. Du Bois, meets at Niagara Falls, Canada, and inaugurates the modern civil rights movement.
1913–1916	President Woodrow Wilson steers his New Freedom program through Congress.
1933–1936	President Franklin Roosevelt's New Deal reforms inaugurate the modern welfare state.
1954	The Supreme Court declares racial segregation unconstitutional in *Brown* v. *Board of Education of Topeka*.
1964	Congress passes the landmark Civil Rights Act of 1964.
1965	President Lyndon Johnson successfully pushes his Great Society programs through Congress.

poor—supports a wide range of liberal welfare programs. **Americans for Democratic Action** (ADA) is the best-known pressure group for contemporary liberalism. Founded in 1947, ADA presidents have included Senators Hubert Humphrey (D-Minn.)* and George McGovern (D-S.D.), both one-time nominees of the Democratic party for president. Headquartered in Washington, D.C., the ADA is an advocate of legislation designed to reduce economic inequality and defense spending and to protect consumers. It opposes laws that encroach on civil rights and civil liberties. Each year it rates members of Congress on a broad spectrum of liberal issues.

Neoliberalism: Adjusting Liberalism to the 1990s

During the administrations of Franklin Roosevelt, Harry Truman, and John Kennedy, liberalism focused on economic issues and emphasized government's obligation to assist those on the lower end of the income scale. In recent decades

---

* "D-Minn." is a journalistic designation for members of the U.S. Senate and House of Representatives. As used throughout this book, "D" or "R" indicates political party, followed by the member's home state.

TABLE 4.3
A Guide to Contemporary Political Ideas and Leaders

Ideology	Major Journal (Circulation)	Leading Spokesperson	Political Leaders
Liberalism	*New Republic* (95,000)	Arthur Schlesinger, Jr.	Mario Cuomo
Neoliberalism	*Washington Monthly* (30,000)	Charles Peters	Paul Tsongas
Conservatism	*National Review* (110,000)	William F. Buckley, Jr.	Newt Gingrich
Neoconservatism	*Public Interest* (11,000)	Irving Kristol	William Bennett
Paleoconservatism	*Chronicles* (13,000)	Paul Gottfried	Pat Buchanan
New Right	*Conservative Digest* (23,000)	Pat Robertson	Jesse Helms
Democratic Socialism	*Dissent* (8,500)	Irving Howe	Bernard Sanders
Libertarianism	*Reason* (32,000)	Murray Rothbard	André Marrau

American ideologies are expressed through a variety of journals, writers, and political leaders.

liberalism shifted its focus somewhat and reached into social and foreign policy issues. It did so at a political cost. The strong association of liberalism with the civil rights movement hurt liberals among southerners who identified with the old white-dominated political order and among northern white ethnics living in urban enclaves who also felt threatened by black advancement. Many voters also associated liberalism with controversial Supreme Court decisions legalizing abortion and banning school prayer. After the Vietnam War, liberals were highly critical of American military intervention and the level of defense spending, alienating some voters who considered them "soft" on defense. Although liberal candidates were quite successful in congressional and state elections, these negative associations dogged them at the presidential level.

Stunned by these successive presidential defeats, a group of young journalists and elected officials attempted to sharpen and modernize the focus of contemporary liberalism. The leader of the movement was Charles Peters, the editor of the *Washington Monthly* (see Table 4.3) who adopted the label "neoliberal." **Neoliberalism** calls for a shift in the emphasis of liberalism from the redistribution of wealth to the promotion of wealth, for a far less critical attitude toward American capitalism, and for policies that promote greater government and business cooperation.

Neoliberals do not repudiate the New Deal and Great Society legacies. They simply feel that the emphasis of liberal reform should be different. They argue that liberals must confront public distrust of government. As a writer for the *Washington Monthly* put it, "any time a liberal politician says the word 'program,' most voters hear 'bureaucracy' and right away get turned off."[6]

Neoliberals direct their attention not to the expansion of government services but to their effective delivery. Neoliberals criticize government unions and the size and costs of the government bureaucracy. Neoliberals also call for reform of entitlement spending programs such as Social Security that go to people who already are well protected by private pensions and their own investments. The

---

[6] Paul Glastris, "The Phillips Curve," *Washington Monthly,* June 1990, p. 54.

neoliberals criticize civil service and military retirement benefits for being far more generous than those in the private sector. They would gear the increases in these programs not to the cost of living but to the rate of real growth in the economy.

Traditional liberals take issue with the neoliberal emphasis on government efficiency. They would emphasize older liberal issues such as the problem of personal income inequality that became more pronounced in the 1980s. Traditional liberals would increase the top income tax rate, which was reduced to 28 percent during the Reagan years. They unapologetically champion the cause of affirmative government and the positive state. Arthur Schlesinger, Jr., a prominent liberal spokesperson for over a generation, argues for greater government investment in research and development and in education; in the rehabilitation of our bridges, dams, and highways; and in the protection against toxic waste, acid rain, and the greenhouse effect. "The markets," writes Schlesinger, "will solve none of these problems."[7]

Some traditional liberals feel that Michael Dukakis's emphasis on competency not ideology during the 1988 presidential campaign was in fact a neoliberal theme that failed to ignite the electorate. By contrast, Bill Clinton in 1992 was able to blend older, more populist ideas, such as raising taxes on the rich, with neoliberal themes, such as a partnership between government and business.

Conservatism

In contrast to liberalism's confidence in the capacity of individuals to overcome obstacles collectively, political **conservatism** reflects doubt and distrust. Conservatism emphasizes the value of tradition and established practices as guides for the future. It finds its origins in the writings of Edmund Burke (1729–1797), whose most famous work, *Reflections on the Revolution in France* (1790), is considered the first major statement of conservative principles. A leading figure in the British Parliament, Burke was appalled by the excesses of the French Revolution and by its rejection of tradition. Burke was suspicious of any generation's claim that it could remake society, believing that the experience of past generations was the most reliable guide to good government. Customs, traditions, and laws embodied the wisdom of the past and should not be carelessly discarded. Thus, argued Burke, people should act with deliberation, seeking change only when necessary. Burke believed that society grew slowly and with purpose; therefore, the past gave continuity to present and future generations. Burke was suspicious of the general public and its capacity to appreciate tradition and custom. He believed in government by the propertied class. People were not equal in ability or talent, according to Burke, and should not be so considered when it came to the governing of society. In Burke's view, a natural inequality among people meant that a ruling class of ability and property must control government.

---

[7] Arthur Schlesinger, Jr., "The Liberal Opportunity," in *The American Prospect,* Spring 1990, p. 15.

Early American Conservatism: John Adams

It was difficult to make Burkean conservatism relevant to the American experience, which had no landed aristocracy, no established church, and no royal tradition. American conservatism, although influenced by Burke, found its own voice in John Adams, the second president of the United States, who lived from 1735 to 1826. Like Burke, Adams was repelled by the excesses of the French Revolution, particularly its executions and confiscation of property. With Burke, Adams agreed unreservedly about the sanctity of private property (see Table 4.1). But unlike Burke, Adams did not associate property rights with a landed aristocracy. Adams believed that property should be widely held and that a propertied class would produce a natural aristocracy of talent. Although Adams was one of the architects of the American Revolution and a passionate defender of the right of every individual to life, liberty, and property, he distrusted unchecked democratic rule as much as he did excessive power in the hands of the aristocracy. Unlimited rule of the people led to clamor for dictatorship. Adams rejected the Jeffersonian notion of the natural goodness of humankind. People were neither totally innocent nor totally depraved. Laws and government, in Adams's view, were needed to promote public virtue and to curb private greed. By public virtue Adams meant "a positive passion for the public good, the public interest, honor, power, and glory established in the minds of the people."[8] A properly balanced government could serve to suppress the evils of ambition, selfishness, self-indulgence, and corruption.

John Adams found this balance in the American Constitution. A popularly elected House would represent the people, an indirectly elected Senate would protect the rights of property, and the president would represent the whole. Thus the poor could not confiscate the property of the rich, and the rich would not be able to exploit the poor. Society would retain its balance, and liberty would be safeguarded from both the excesses of democracy and the abuses of an aristocracy. After Adams had appointed John Marshall, a conservative Federalist, to the Supreme Court in 1801, Adams looked to the judicial branch as the ultimate guarantor of property rights against any attempts by legislatures to compromise them.

In the 1820s, long after he had left the presidency, Adams joined with other American conservatives, including Chief Justice Marshall and Senator Daniel Webster, in opposing the elimination of property qualifications for voting. These conservatives considered *universal suffrage* (and in that era they debated only universal *white manhood suffrage*) a threat to the Republic. Men without property lacked the independence, judgment, and virtue to be voting members of a free republic.[9]

Chancellor James Kent of New York, one of the most famous legal scholars and jurists of the early nineteenth century, argued that "there is a tendency in the majority to tyrannize over the minority and trample down their rights; and in the indolent and profligate to cast the whole burden of society upon the industrious and virtuous."[10] The victory of Jacksonian democracy in the states during the

---

[8] Quoted in James M. Burns, *The Vineyard of Liberty* (New York: Knopf, 1982), p. 225.

[9] Clinton Rossiter, *Conservatism in America,* 2d ed., rev. (Cambridge, Mass.: Harvard University Press, 1982), p. 118.

[10] Quoted in Jay Sigler, ed., *The Conservative Tradition in American Thought* (New York: Capricorn Books, 1969), p. 118.

1820s brought an end to antidemocratic conservatism. Conservatives seemed to realize the finality of their defeat on that issue and concentrated in the latter part of the nineteenth century on a defense of property rights and the system of economic laissez-faire.

Conservatism and the Industrial Age: Herbert Spencer and William Graham Sumner

Industrialization following the Civil War brought a major change in American conservatism. Although conservatives of the early Republic fervently believed in property rights, the belief that government should play a limited role in the economy did not necessarily follow. Conservatives like John Adams, John Marshall, and Alexander Hamilton supported a strong central government to defend the propertied classes from the encroachments of the more radical state governments. They defended the Bank of the United States against the attacks of the Jefferson-Jackson liberals.

But as America industrialized, conservatives embraced **laissez-faire economics**—an economic system that operated free of government control. Burke and Adams regarded the state as essential to the promotion of public virtue and the protection of property, but in the Industrial Age the state became the object of conservative scorn. In stressing individualism, economic growth, and the limited role of government, they seemed closer to Jefferson and Jackson in this regard than to Burke and Adams.

An English social scientist, Herbert Spencer (1820–1903), and an American sociologist, William Graham Sumner (1840–1910), developed the theory of economic individualism that became the keystone of late-nineteenth-century and early-twentieth-century conservatism. It was popularly known as **social Darwinism.** Sumner stated the case in a somewhat extreme form. People, Sumner argued, should be free to compete with each other for survival. From this economic competition, the fit would survive and the weak would perish. The result would be the betterment of humankind through the survival of superior individuals. Sumner opposed governmental aid to the needy as inconsistent with his views on social and economic evolution. Government was inefficient by nature, Sumner argued, and should be limited to fundamental concerns. Sumner wrote, "At bottom there are two chief things with which government has to deal. They are, the property of men and the honor of women. These it has to defend against crime."[11]

Although these views were far too extreme even for the nineteenth century, Spencer and Sumner made a great impact on conservative thinking. Conservatives of the Industrial Age did not emphasize the individual's obligation to the state or the state's obligation to promote public virtue. The emphasis was almost entirely on the individual. If people worked hard, the argument went, they could become successful, and economic growth would ensue. The government need only stand out of the way. Many business leaders were attracted to this philosophy, although it did not prevent them from helping themselves to governmental favors (tariff

---

[11] Quoted in Rossiter, *Conservatism in America*, p. 138.

protection or direct subsidies) when the occasion arose. They invoked conservatism to justify opposition to antitrust laws, bills regulating hours and wages, and a progressive income tax.

In short, conservatism became the ideology of America's business class. So long as most Americans shared somewhat in the growth of the American economy, they were willing to accept most of the tenets of conservatism. From the end of Reconstruction to the New Deal, Americans elected presidents (with the exceptions of Theodore Roosevelt and Woodrow Wilson) who reflected those values.

Contemporary Conservatism: A Response to the Welfare State

The Great Depression ended America's romance with conservatism. It brought about the election of Franklin Roosevelt and the beginning of the New Deal with its numerous welfare state programs. The general popular acceptance of these programs placed American conservatism on the defensive for the next several generations. During the period 1933–1981, conservatism could be better measured by what it was against than what it was for. Conservatives opposed most major liberal domestic reforms, from the Social Security Bill of 1935 to the Medicare Bill of 1965.

Conservatism in the 1980s took on a more positive cast, with an agenda of its own—reducing social spending, reshaping the tax code, and rebuilding national defense. In economic matters, conservatives draw on many of the ideas of nineteenth-century individualism. Conservatism still remains at its core a defense of economic individualism against the growth of the welfare state. Conservatives oppose any increase in the role of the federal government over the general direction of the economy and contend that a vibrant private-sector economy can best create jobs for the poor, immigrants, and minorities. Welfare state programs, conservatives argue, only create a permanent class of the poor who are dependent on the state and without genuine incentives to enter the world of work.

Although many conservatives opposed the major civil rights laws of the 1960s on the grounds that they represented a serious encroachment on states' rights, most now accept these laws as a permanent part of our political landscape. But they do challenge the idea of quotas and other affirmative-action policies as a means of enforcing civil rights laws in the areas of jobs, educational opportunities, and access to federal contracts. They argue that civil rights should mean equality of treatment and not equality of results.

On social and cultural issues they remain close to Burkean ideals. Contemporary conservatives believe that the state must promote virtue and social responsibility and take appropriate measures to improve the moral climate of society. They support constitutional amendments restricting abortion and permitting prayers in public schools. They oppose the concept of civil rights for homosexuals in jobs, the military, and housing. Speaking as a modern-day Burkean, conservative philosopher and syndicated columnist George Will wrote, "Traditional conservatism has not been, and proper conservatism cannot be, merely a defense of

Although he spoke in favor of President Bush's renomination in August 1992, Pat Buchanan had vigorously and articulately opposed Bush in some of the Republican primaries earlier that year. In his campaign, Buchanan preached some of the themes of contemporary conservatism, but combined them with appeals to nativism, protectionism, isolationism, and the New Right. Buchanan has never held elective office, but he has worked in the White House press office and as a journalist on CNN.

industrialism and individualist 'free market' economics. Conservatism is about the cultivation and conservation of certain values, or it is nothing."[12]

As conservative causes have gained broader public support, conservatives no longer invoke the suspicion of the masses, as they did in John Adams's day (see Table 4.4). Nor do they talk very much about the independence of the judicial branch as a check on the excesses of legislative power. In fact, conservatives have been particularly critical of Supreme Court decisions outlawing prayers in school and legalizing abortion.[13]

They support efforts to have them overturned by constitutional amendment

---

[12] George Will, *Statecraft as Soulcraft: What Government Does* (New York: Simon & Schuster, 1983), pp. 119–120.
[13] *Engel* v. *Vitale,* 370 U.S. 421 (1962); *Roe* v. *Wade,* 410 U.S. 113 (1973); *Wallace* v. *Jaffree,* 472 U.S. 38 (1985).

TABLE 4.4
Milestones in American Conservatism

1790	Edmund Burke's *Reflections on the French Revolution* published; Alexander Hamilton, first U.S. Treasury secretary, introduces a report recommending a national bank.
1883	William Graham Sumner's *What Social Classes Owe to Each Other* published.
1890	Herbert Spencer's *Social Statics* published.
1905	Supreme Court in *Lochner* v. *New York* strikes down New York law limiting working hours of bakers as a violation of freedom of contract under the Fourteenth Amendment.
1920	Warren Harding elected president, marking the beginning of a new era of conservative dominance lasting until 1932.
1955	*National Review* founded, marking the beginning of the intellectual revitalization of post–World War II conservatism.
1964	Barry Goldwater receives the Republican presidential nomination, beginning the conservative ascendancy in the party.
1981	President Ronald Reagan begins his program of tax reductions, domestic spending cuts, and defense buildup.

---

or weakened by legislative action. Direct democracy, so feared by the conservatives of the eighteenth and nineteenth centuries, has become an important tool of contemporary conservatives. Conservatives have successfully employed the popular referendum (a device that permits people to vote on policy questions as well as for candidates) in California and Massachusetts as a check on the power of state legislatures to tax their own citizens.

Some conservative causes have generated intense (although not broad) rank-and-file support. In part because of conservative support for reduced taxes, prayer in school, and restrictions on abortion, conservatism has been transformed from an elitist philosophy of the propertied class to a more populist cause of the working and middle classes.

Who are the conservatives? In most cases their political home is in the Republican party. Ronald Reagan was the first president since the Great Depression to identify himself openly with conservatism and conservative causes. Previous Republican presidents—Eisenhower, Nixon, and Ford—were men of the center who shunned ideology and ideological labels. Perhaps the best-known conservative journal is *National Review,* founded by William Buckley, himself one of the most prominent spokespersons for modern conservatism.

Neoconservatism versus Paleoconservatism: Conservative Splits in the 1990s

In the 1970s a number of leading American intellectuals, many of them longtime liberals, became openly critical of the drift of contemporary liberalism. Labeled **neoconservatives** in the popular press, they felt that liberals had overestimated the ability of government to solve social problems such as industrial pollution, economic inequality, and racial discrimination. Neoconservatives argue that liberals have gone beyond the initial New Deal concept that government need only provide a "safety net" for the subsistence needs for society's victims—the unemployed, the disabled, and the elderly. Contemporary liberalism, the neoconservatives claim, transformed the New Deal's modest welfare state into a more intrusive paternalistic state. Neoconservatives disagree with such liberal ideas as the use of racial or gender quotas as a means of assuring fairness in hiring, promotion, or acceptance to professional schools. They also reject the idea of forced school busing as a means of achieving racial balance in enrollments. They consider these ideas elitist liberal schemes not supported by the vast majority of Americans.

Neoconservatives feel that liberals no longer speak for the "average person" but rather for a "new class" of relatively affluent reformers—lawyers, social workers, educators, city planners—with careers in the expanding public sector. This liberal new class intends "to propel the nation from that modified version of capitalism we call 'the welfare state' toward an economic system so regulated in detail as to fulfill many of the traditional anticapitalist aspirations of the left."[14]

Neoconservatives also argue that liberals emphasized policies such as higher taxes on the upper middle class that were aimed not at creating wealth but only at redistributing it. Skeptical about government's ability to erase economic inequalities, neoconservatives stress policies such as lower taxes on large incomes and less regulation of business to promote economic growth. Such growth, they feel, would more likely broaden economic opportunity and create greater social stability. Likewise, they are suspicious of policies that polarize one class or group against another: racial busing that pits the white working-class communities in the large cities against the poor black community and gender and racial quotas that place the interests of women and minorities against those of white males.

In short, neoconservatives feel that modern liberals have promised too much to too many groups, and that a government that promises too much cannot deliver and becomes "overloaded." As a result, their argument goes, government loses its authority and cannot govern effectively. But neoconservatives differ from traditional conservatives in that neoconservatives support, in principle and practice, a modest welfare state (Social Security, unemployment insurance, and Medicare). In fact, neoconservatives argue that a properly constructed welfare state strengthens citizens' loyalty to the existing capitalist system and is thus a stabilizing force.

Neoconservatives have engendered some resentment among many members of the Old Right, now dubbed **paleoconservatives** (*paleo* from the Greek meaning "ancient"). They decry the neoconservative accommodation to the welfare state and remain hostile to government efforts to establish social and economic equality. The paleoconservatives believe that religious traditions embodied in the

---

[14] Irving Kristol, *Reflections of a Neoconservative: Looking Back, Looking Ahead* (New York: Basic Books, 1983), p. 212.

church and family should be the basis of a stable and ordered society. The welfare state philosophy of the New Deal and Great Society is, according to them, an effort to create a secular moral order. By defending the New Deal legacy, the paleoconservatives charge the neoconservatives with defending not only a misguided political idea but a religious heresy.

The sudden collapse of communism in 1989 opened up new fissures in contemporary conservatism. With the unraveling of the Soviet Union, some paleoconservative leaders such as journalist Patrick Buchanan, who challenged President George Bush in the 1992 primaries, sounded older conservative themes of isolationism and America first. Neoconservatives, in turn, strongly supported the continued American leadership in world affairs.

Yet, the neoconservative belief in a limited form of welfarism has influenced a new generation of conservative political leaders. Rep. Newt Gingrich (R-Ga.) and former Housing and Urban Development Secretary Jack Kemp have developed a new conservative "empowerment" agenda to assist the poor with an emphasis upon antibureaucratic market-oriented programs. For example, Kemp proposes allowing the poor to manage their own public housing residences or to have housing vouchers to buy their own homes and providing them with tuition tax credits to select their own schools. Kemp also favors additional tax relief for the working poor and more community-based mental health facilities for the homeless.

Neoconservatism has emerged as an influential intellectual and political force. Its ideas influenced the Reagan administration and brought a more respectful hearing for conservatism in general among academics and intellectuals. Nonetheless, the resentment of neoconservatism by the paleoconservatives could be played out in the 1996 Republican contest for the presidential nomination.

Ideological Challenges to the Status Quo

Not all American ideologies fit comfortably under the rubrics *liberal* and *conservative*. Some challenge dominant opinion and propose policies that are outside today's mainstream. Yet the fact that they represent a minority point of view does not make them unimportant. The history of American political thought is full of examples of "extreme" ideas that gained acceptability and entered the mainstream.

The New Right: Populist Conservatism

In the late 1970s and 1980s a new political movement combined the elements of traditional conservatism and the populist belief that government was run by narrow, selfish interests. Known as the **New Right,** it included Christian evangelicals, antiabortionists, and anti-gun control advocates. It also included many members of the working and middle class who were alienated from contemporary liberalism and who never felt comfortable with pro-business conservatism (see Table 4.1).

The New Right feels that permissive liberal values are responsible for a broad range of social ills, including high levels of premarital sex, adultery, abortion, income tax cheating, excessive personal and government debt, and large numbers of middle-class and wealthy people (farmers, businesspeople, and bankers) expecting government subsidies.

The movement may be conservative only in the sense that its cultural values are traditional because the New Right, unlike most conservative movements, does not defend established institutions. The New Right believes that the major institutions of contemporary America—the bureaucracy, the media, the managerial hierarchies of the unions and corporations—should not be defended but exposed.

The political strategy of the New Right is to gain control of the presidency and perhaps Congress as the means of transforming the values and the nature of these institutions. One New Right political leader does not even adopt the label *conservative*. "We are radicals who want to change the existing power structure. We are not conservatives in the sense that conservative means accepting the status quo."[15]

In the late 1980s and early 1990s, New Right political organizations atrophied. The end of the Cold War removed communism as a powerful political issue. The retirement of President Ronald Reagan and a series of sex scandals that implicated evangelical television ministers Jim Bakker and Jimmy Swaggart disheartened the movement. The Reverend Jerry Falwell disbanded his Moral Majority organization; Pat Robertson's 1988 presidential campaign gained little support, and his Christian Broadcasting Network focused more on entertainment than politics. Nor did the New Right political leaders consider Yale-educated George Bush someone whose heart was genuinely with them.

Democratic Socialism: A Radical Challenge to American Capitalism

Democratic socialism is an economic system in which the basic industries, banks, agricultural systems, and communication networks are owned and controlled by the government at either the local or national level. While a private sector of the economy may continue to exist under socialism, major industries and corporations are owned by the state, and thus the government is responsible for planning and directing the economy. Key decisions concerning investments, prices, and wages would be placed in the hands of public institutions. What separates democratic socialists from communists, who also believe in the principle of public ownership, is that democratic socialists reject the idea of violent revolution. Instead, democratic socialists advocate the adoption of socialism through peaceful and constitutional means, and they support the basic democratic rights embodied in our Constitution.

Economic equality is an essential idea in socialism. Socialists argue that capitalism in America, despite its success in creating wealth, has failed to solve the fundamental problem of poverty. Equality of opportunity is not enough, socialists

---

[15] Richard A. Viguerie, *The New Right: We're Ready to Lead* (Falls Church, Va., Viguerie, 1981), p. 56.

argue. A genuinely democratic society must produce equality of results. Socialists wish to replace a society based on competition with a society based on cooperation. The socialist ideal sees individuals motivated not by profit and personal gain but by a sense of social responsibility.

In short, democratic socialism requires:

1. Government ownership and control of the major industries, utilities, and transportation systems
2. A limit on individual wealth and property
3. A welfare system that guarantees all persons decent health care, an education, and adequate food and shelter
4. Extensive governmental regulation of the economy

Democratic socialism has been a powerful force in Western Europe throughout the twentieth century. But in the United States socialism and social democratic parties have had little or no success. In the early years of the twentieth century the Socialist party, headed by Eugene V. Debs and later by Norman Thomas, gained some influence and support. During the Great Depression the millions of unemployed provided the socialists with a major opportunity. In 1932, their last significant showing in a presidential election, Norman Thomas gained about 2 percent of the popular vote. But the election of Franklin Roosevelt and acceptance of his New Deal welfare measures stole much of the socialists' thunder. Irving Howe, co-chair of the Democratic Socialists of America, admitted in 1984 that "the Socialist Party fell apart because it could not come to terms with Roosevelt."[16]

The Democratic Socialists of America, the successor to the Socialist party of Debs and Thomas, no longer expects to galvanize broad mass support behind its banners. Instead, it operates within a number of liberal organizations, including the Democratic party, to influence their ideas and direction.

The issues that faced the socialist movement in the pre–New Deal days were relatively simple and dramatic. The elderly needed a guaranteed pension. The unions needed government guarantees of their rights to organize and bargain. The unemployed needed some form of protection. The New Deal established these programs, and the subsequent questions of their financing and administration were no longer dramatic. What then is the social democratic program in the post–New Deal, post–welfare state era?

Full employment, guaranteed by the government, has become a major demand of contemporary socialists. This requires a reduction of the work week from 40 to 35 hours so that more people can work fewer hours, with the government compensating workers with tax credits for any wages they lose by a reduction of their hours. Socialists call for a massive public works program for rebuilding America's *infrastructure* (roads, bridges, sewage systems) in order to create millions of new jobs for the currently unemployed. Because full employment can

---

[16] "Voices from the Left: A Conversation Between Michael Harrington and Irving Howe," *New York Times Magazine,* June 17, 1984, p. 28.

stimulate inflation, the socialists would also employ controls on wages, prices, incomes, rents, and dividends.

Sensitive to the issue that socialism spawns bureaucracy and centralization, American socialists support a system of public ownership characterized by worker-owned or community-controlled businesses and factories. Nevertheless, Americans remain resistant to the idea of socialism, associating it with either the authoritarian communism that plagued Eastern Europe or, in its democratic form, with the sluggish economy that characterized pre-Thatcherite Great Britain. In the present era, socialism presents more of an intellectual challenge to American capitalism than a serious political threat. Nonetheless, in 1990 longtime socialist Bernard Sanders, not running under the Democratic banner, was elected to the House of Representatives from Vermont. He was the first independent socialist elected to Congress in over half a century.

Libertarianism: A Revival of Classical Liberalism

Although the Libertarian party remains on the fringe of American politics, its ideas have stimulated considerable interest. The intellectual roots of libertarianism can be traced to the classical liberal movement of the eighteenth and nineteenth centuries and the ideas of Thomas Jefferson and Andrew Jackson. In the 1980 presidential election, the Libertarian party candidate, Ed Clark, polled almost 1 million votes, a considerable accomplishment for an unknown candidate from a minor party.

Like classical liberalism, **libertarianism** holds that the state must be kept extremely small. The essential role of government should be only the protection of human rights:

1. The right to life, by which libertarians mean protection against the use of force by others
2. The right to liberty, meaning the freedoms of speech, press, and assembly and protection against any government restrictions on ideas, books, films, or any other means of communication
3. The right to property; libertarians support legislation that protects the property rights of individuals against confiscation, robbery, trespass, libel, fraud, and copyright violations.[17]

Libertarians also oppose the interference of government in the private lives of citizens. They seek, for example, the repeal of all laws that involve so-called victimless crimes (prostitution, pornography, gambling). They seek an unfettered, free market economy and oppose laws regulating the price of milk as well as those that prohibit the use of marijuana. Unlike the liberals, who support laws expanding the role of government in the economy, and the New Right, which supports legislation outlawing abortion and pornography, the libertarians oppose

---

[17] John Hospers, "What Libertarianism Is," in Tibor Machan, ed., *The Libertarian Alternative: Essays in Social and Political Philosophy* (Chicago: Nelson-Hall, 1974), p. 13.

with equal fervor laws that regulate either the moral or the economic life of individuals.

Libertarians favor nonintervention in the affairs of other nations. They believe that military alliances and arms aid only lead to war, and that wars and war preparation bring about a vast increase in the power of government. One leading libertarian theorist argues that the United States should revoke all its military and political commitments to other countries.[18]

Libertarians call for a drastic reduction in the defense budget and a defense policy designed solely to defend the territory of the United States. Accordingly, the military draft is considered a form of involuntary servitude. Because the Libertarian movement and the Libertarian party have no immediate prospect of coming into power, their positions remain free of the need to compromise. In the 1980 campaign, candidate Ed Clark called for a 30 percent cut in federal expenditures during his first year in office, the reduction of taxes by almost 50 percent, the abolition of the Departments of Energy and Education (a pledge that President Reagan made and later withdrew), the phasing out of Social Security, and the elimination of federal support for education and the substitution of a tuition tax credit for each child attending a school or university.

Although the Libertarian party remains a minor party, its ideas have influenced both major parties. The Republican party has taken a much more aggressive stand against the social programs of the 1960s and 1970s. It has also championed the reduction of income tax rates and the deregulation of business and industry. The Democratic party has supported broader freedom from government interference in the areas of abortion, school prayer, and gay rights. Nevertheless, Americans have generally been reluctant to follow radical or revolutionary movements. Perhaps they perceive libertarianism as an interesting criticism, but they are not yet prepared to accept its far-reaching solutions.

Summary

1. People do not simply fight over their own self-interest. They also differ, at times sharply, over what constitutes a good society. Since the American and the French revolutions, disputes between liberals and conservatives have occupied center stage in the Western democracies and in the United States especially. But liberalism and conservatism have often changed colors and even exchanged attitudes.

2. Nineteenth-century liberals Thomas Jefferson and Andrew Jackson equated the idea of a powerful state with the protection of the wealthy merchant classes. But liberalism changed in the Industrial Age. Deeply affected by the Populist and Progressive movements, liberalism saw government as an important vehicle for the protection of the many from the exploitation of the few. Liberals and neoliberals in the 1980s still regard governmental programs

---

[18] Murray Rothbard, *For a New Liberty: The Libertarian Manifesto,* rev. ed. (New York: Collier, 1978), p. 291.

and intervention as the key to solving our economic problems. But in matters of personal morality, liberals hark back to an earlier age. Their opposition to governmental interference in matters of abortion and school prayer is reminiscent of Jefferson's concerns.

3. Conservatives in the early days of the American republic were the supporters of a strong government. They believed that only a government of a talented and propertied elite could preserve the sacred rights of all people. As the voting franchise extended to more and more people, conservatives lost their faith in central government and focused on the rights of property, independent of the state, and rights of individuals to be free of governmental interference. But by their opposition to abortion, pornography, and gay rights, conservatives remain true in matters of moral and social policy to the old Burkean belief that the state can promote social virtue. The central difference between liberals and conservatives today is not over whether government should be strong or weak but when it should be strong or weak.

4. The New Right, libertarianism, and democratic socialism advocate fundamental alterations in the status quo. The New Right wants to use government to curb the power of the big banks, the media, the unions, and the big corporations. Their programs may not be welfarist in that they oppose most social programs, but by their opposition to people in positions of power and influence, their tone and temperament are clearly populist.

5. Social democrats, by contrast, focus on the good of the whole society and envision a system under which all people will be equal economically and politically. They support a broad program of governmental control including ownership of the major corporations and industries. Unlike the libertarians, who see the state as the greatest threat to human liberty, the social democrats see the state as the greatest hope for human equality.

6. Libertarians, in their opposition to the very idea of big government, hark back to the nineteenth-century liberals. They are opposed to government interference in the setting of agricultural price supports as well as in the prohibition of so-called illegal drugs. Government exists primarily to defend the rights to life, liberty, and property and to defend the homeland from attack.

Key Terms

political ideology (p. 101)
liberalism (p. 103)
contract theory of the state (p. 103)
classical liberalism (p. 103)
populism (p. 105)
progressivism (p. 105)
industrial policy (p. 107)
Americans for Democratic Action (p. 109)
neoliberalism (p. 110)

conservatism (p. 111)
laissez-faire economics (p. 113)
social Darwinism (p. 113)
neoconservatives (p. 116)
paleoconservatives (p. 117)
New Right (p. 118)
democratic socialism (p. 119)
libertarianism (p. 121)

Readings for Further Study

A broad overview of political ideologies can be found in Roy C. Macridis, *Contemporary Political Ideologies,* 2d ed. (Boston: Little, Brown, 1983). Both Walter E. Volkomer, ed., *The Liberal Tradition in American Thought* (New York: Capricorn Books, 1969) and Jay Sigler, ed., *The Conservative Tradition in American Thought* (New York: Capricorn Books, 1969) provide a valuable collection of important historical readings. Alpheus T. Mason and Gordon E. Baker, *Free Government in the Making,* 4th ed. (New York: Oxford University Press, 1985) supplements readings on American political thought with helpful essays. Readers interested in exploring socialist thought should consult Michael Harrington, *Socialism* (New York: Saturday Review Press, 1970). Those interested in a greater understanding of libertarianism should see Murray Rothbard, *For a New Liberty: The Libertarian Manifesto,* rev. ed. (New York: Collier, 1978). For a discussion of neoliberal and neoconservative thought, readers should consult Charles Peters and Phillip Keisling, eds., *The Neoliberal Movement* (Lanham, Md.: Madison Books, 1985) and Irving Kristol, *Reflections of a Neoconservative* (New York: Basic Books, 1983). For an overview of the impact of the contemporary ideological debate on American politics, see E. J. Dionne, Jr., *Why Americans Hate Politics* (New York: Simon & Schuster, 1991).

5 Public Opinion, the Mass Media, and Political Participation

This chapter examines what the American people actually think about politics, how they come to think what they do, and how they translate their thoughts into politically relevant actions. Chapter 4 described the major patterns of American political beliefs in philosophical and historical terms. Here the concern is with the extent to which the general public actually subscribes to those beliefs. This leads into an examination of how people learn to think about politics. What are the influences that encourage people to become Democrats, independents, or Republicans, as well as determine their opinions on political issues? These topics are discussed in the sections on political socialization and the mass media. Because of its effects on behavior, political thinking matters, so the chapter concludes with a discussion of how ideas are translated into political action ranging from voting to protest demonstrations and civil disobedience.

Public Opinion: What Americans Think About Politics

What Americans *think* about politics is important because it determines, in part, how they *act* politically. The diverse but predominantly moderate character of Americans' political views and the relatively modest intensity with which most people advance their views set the tone for the whole political process. To understand how people think about politics is to understand an essential element of the environment within which the political process functions.

The Character of Public Opinion

Public opinion sounds like a simple and stable concept, but the reality it describes is far from that. **Public opinion** is a combination of the views, attitudes, and ideas held by individuals in the community. There is no single public opinion; there is, rather, a wide variety of viewpoints. Different publics or groups of people think differently about political questions. Some people hold very sophisticated views about politics; others do not. Some people devote their entire lives to politics; others hardly ever think about politics.

Some facets of public opinion are remarkably *constant:* Love of country and pride in the nation's accomplishments, for instance, are attitudes that are almost always present and widely shared. Other facets of public opinion are *dynamic,* fluctuating considerably in response to social, political, and economic events. Some opinions are held *intensely;* others seem to be little more than *casual preferences.* An opinion that is intensely held is more likely to influence what a person thinks about political candidates and how that person might get involved politically.

The politically sophisticated and the general public observe the same political world. However, much of the public sees it, to borrow an expression from the Bible, "through a glass darkly." Politicians and political commentators can argue at length about what they see as the major political issues of the time, but much of this seems to pass by most of the public. As explained in the following sections, a substantial share of the American public does not care much about politics, knows relatively little about it, and does not think about it in very sophisticated terms. Still, few would admit that public opinion is unimportant. Indeed, political analysts and politicians are very concerned about what the public thinks.

How Much Americans Care and Know About Politics

The first public opinion pollsters assumed that the public cared and was reasonably well informed about politics, but were startled to find that many Americans cared little and knew less about what went on in the political arena. More recent surveys have done little to contradict these early findings or show any recent increase in public interest and information—a surprising finding given the rising level of education and the proliferation of the media, particularly television news, over the last few decades.

This is not to say that the public as a whole is not at all interested in politics; indeed, a substantial proportion of them indicates a considerable degree of interest. For example, in mid-1987 one survey found 41 percent of the public saying that they followed government and public affairs "most of the time," but 35 percent saying only "some of the time," 15 percent saying "only now and then," and 7 percent saying "hardly at all."[1] These results fall short of the democratic ideal of a keenly interested electorate, but are reasonably reassuring in that most people do seem to be at least somewhat interested in politics.

But the meaningfulness of those expressions of interest is called into question by the public's level of information on politics. A 1989 study found that 25 percent of Americans did not know the name of the vice-president (Dan Quayle), 31 percent did not know which party controlled the House of Representatives (the Democrats), 54 percent did not know what the first 10 amendments to the Constitution are called (the Bill of Rights), and 75 percent did not know the names of the two U. S. senators from their state (the reader can fill in the parentheses here, we hope!).[2]

What Americans Hold in Common

On many fundamental political matters, the vast majority of Americans are in substantial agreement. First of all, Americans are proud of their country and emotionally attached to it and its symbols. In a 1988 study, 94 percent of Americans said they were either extremely proud or very proud to be Americans—less than 1 percent said they were not very proud to be Americans; 92 percent of Americans said they felt extremely strong or very strong love for their country; and 85 percent said they felt extremely good or very good when they see the flag flying.[3] Studies consistently show that the percentages of people expressing enthusiasm and pride for their country are, in fact, higher in the United States than in any other country.

Americans are also positive about their country's political, social, and economic institutions. Asked how much confidence they had in their country's public and private institutions, Americans consistently responded more favorably than

---

[1] Special survey conducted by the Gallup Organization for the Times Mirror Company, April–May 1987, reported in Norman Ornstein, Andrew Kohut, and Larry McCarthy, *The People, the Press, and Politics* (Reading, Mass.: Addison-Wesley, 1988), pp. 53–55.

[2] Michael X. Delli Carpini and Scott Keeter, paper presented at the meeting of the American Association for Public Opinion Research, St. Petersburg, Florida, May 1989.

[3] American National Election Survey, 1988.

Contemporary Controversies

The Rise of the "Don't-Care Generation"?

Younger people have always been less politically involved than older people—less interested, less informed, less likely to vote. But in recent years that gap has grown substantially. For example, in 1965 Americans under 30 were only 7 percent less likely to get information from a newspaper each day than those over 50, and only 10 percent less likely to get information from television. But by 1990 the newspaper gap had grown to 25 percent and the TV gap to 28 percent.[a] Similarly, in the 1972 Presidential election 21 percent fewer 18-to-24 year-olds voted than 45-to-64 year-olds, while in the 1988 election 32 percent fewer young people than old people did.[b]

Younger people's lower level of political participation has always been understood in terms of their preoccupation with getting an education, starting a career, and beginning a family. But the current generation's indifference to politics and public affairs is so pronounced that it has some political observers worried. One study concluded that the current generation of young people "knows less, cares less, votes less and is less critical of its leaders and institutions than young people in the past."[c] Another study warned that America was confronting a "citizenship crisis" in which its "youth are alarmingly ill-prepared to keep democracy alive in the 1990s and beyond."[d]

Past generations have started out slowly politically but have become more politically involved as they got their careers and families established. Perhaps the current generation will do the same. Unlike the sixties and seventies, when desegregation in the schools and the draft for the Vietnam War hit young Americans the hardest, the eighties was a decade reasonably devoid of issues that directly affected younger people. So perhaps the "Don't-Care Generation's" indifference is not surprising. But no matter what the reason, it is clear that the current generation of young people will start from a lower level of political participation than their parents and grandparents. And the consequences for the future if they do not rebound from their apathy are considerable: A society in which such low levels of interest and information are the norm may have difficulty functioning democratically.

What signs of political indifference do you see in your generation? Do you think it is really any greater than in the past? Why do you think young people are indifferent? Do you think the "Don't-Care Generation" will outgrow its indifference or is it a more permanent problem? How serious of a problem do you think it is? What, if anything, can or should be done about it?

[a] Times Mirror Center for The People and The Press, 1990.

[b] U.S. Bureau of the Census, *Current Population Reports.*

[c] "The Age of Indifference," a report of The Times Mirror Center for The People and The Press, June 1990.

[d] People for the American Way, 1989.

citizens from four other European democracies (Figure 5.1). Although some Americans are critical of their nation's institutions, what is most striking is that Americans are clearly less critical than people in other countries. Even for institutions that are sometimes singled out as objects of public disdain in the United States, such as the media, labor unions, and Congress, Americans consistently have more confidence in them than do their European counterparts.[4]

[4] Laurence Parisot, "Attitudes About the Media," *Public Opinion* (January–February 1988): 18.

FIGURE 5.1
Confidence in Public Institutions: A Comparative Perspective

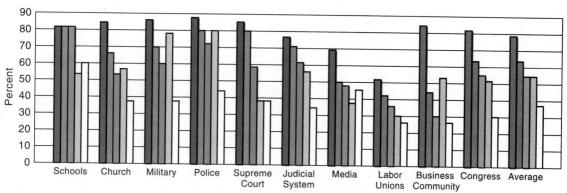

Question: How would you rate your confidence in the following institutions?
Percentage answering "a great deal" or "some" in five Western democracies in 1987.

■ United States   ■ Germany   ■ France   ■ Britain   □ Spain

Americans consistently express greater confidence in their country's political, social, and economic institutions than do citizens of other democratic countries. *SOURCE:* Louis Harris & international affiliates, 1987, cited in Laurence Parisot, "Attitudes about the Media: A Five Country Comparison," *Public Opinion* (January/February 1988): 18.

Why are Americans generally so proud of their country and positive about its institutions? One reason is that they have been taught all their lives to think of America as the best (as will be discussed in the section on political socialization). But the roots run deeper than that. Americans also take pride in their country because they are generally raised to hold certain basic values and to believe that the United States, among all nations, is particularly dedicated to the fulfillment of those values. The Declaration of Independence, discussed in Chapter 1, provides a good start on a list.

> We hold these truths to be self-evident, that all men are created *equal*, that they are endowed by their Creator with certain unalienable *Rights*, that among these are *Life, Liberty, and the pursuit of Happiness*. That to secure these rights, Governments are instituted among Men, deriving their just powers from the *consent of the governed*. [italics added]

To these three basic values of democracy —equality, freedom, and consent of the governed—can be added most Americans' commitment to capitalism and the free enterprise system.

- *Equality.* Surveys suggest that roughly 80 percent of Americans genuinely believe in equality and that, whether or not they really think people are

FIGURE 5.2
Fundamental Freedoms: A Comparative Perspective

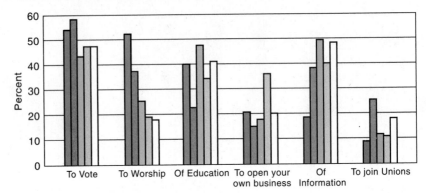

Question: Of the following freedoms, which two do you consider the most fundamental?

■ United States   ■ Germany   ▨ Spain   ▨ France   ▢ Britain

Like the citizens of other democratic countries, Americans believe in the importance of the freedom to vote and the freedom to get an education. They see freedom of religion as particularly important, but care relatively less about freedom of information and the freedom to join a union.   SOURCE: Louis Harris & international affiliates, 1987, cited in Laurence Parisot, "Attitudes about the Media: A Five Country Comparison," *Public Opinion* (January/February 1988): 19.

equal, more than 90 percent believe that the government should treat everyone as if they were equal.[5]

■ *Freedom.* Americans believe in their capacity to do what is best for themselves. Hence, they think that individuals should be free to act as they please, with minimal government interference, as long as they do not interfere with other people's freedom. Surveys have long shown a strong commitment to freedom of speech, press, religion, and association.[6] A better perspective on Americans' views of freedom can be gained by comparing those views with the views of people from other countries. One cross-national survey asked Americans and Western Europeans which was more important, freedom or equality. Americans chose freedom over equality, 72 percent to 20 percent, while Western Europeans chose freedom over equality by a much smaller margin, only 49 percent to 35 percent.[7] The importance that Americans place on the different types of freedom also varies somewhat from citizens in other democracies (Figure 5.2).

---

[5] ABC News/*Washington Post* Poll, Survey 77.
[6] Herbert McClosky and Alida Brill, *Dimensions of Tolerance: What Americans Believe About Civil Liberties* (New York: Russell Sage Foundation, 1983), pp. 48–135.
[7] Gallup Poll press release, May 21, 1982.

- *Consent of the governed.* Americans see their acceptance of government as voluntary. About four-fifths believe that "the government gets its power and authority from the people of this country" and that "the American people have the right to change the form and system of government we have in this country."[8] Americans also believe firmly in the idea that the majority (more than half) of the people should rule in political affairs. At the same time, though, they believe that majorities should not possess unlimited power and that the rights of a minority (less than half) of the people should be protected against the whims of the majority.

- *Capitalism and the free enterprise system.* Americans believe in the value of hard work, in private property, in economic competition, and in profit. In contrast to some other societies, most Americans tend to view hard work as a virtue and laziness as a vice—the so-called Protestant ethic. They see private property as an essential element of economic progress. They believe that competition brings out the best in people and that the most successful competitors deserve the greatest rewards. Americans' preference for freedom over equality manifests itself in the economic as well as the political sphere. This particular combination of values fits well with a free-market, entrepreneurial economy. Americans like the idea of a fair competition in which everybody starts out equally, but in which they all have the freedom to pursue their self-interest and people end up unequally well-off according to how well they have pursued their self-interest. Perhaps most important, Americans see a free economic system as an important contributor to a free political system. A 1978 survey found 80 percent endorsing the idea that the free enterprise system was necessary for the survival of free government, compared to 6 percent who thought it was not. The survey also found 87 percent of respondents saying that private property was as important to a good society as freedom. Thus Americans have little interest in moving toward a communist or socialist system.

Although Americans are proud of their country and its system of government and believe in the fundamental values on which it rests, they are not beyond finding fault with it. In fact, since the 1960s the American political system has struggled with a widespread undercurrent of dissatisfaction with the way in which the system is working, fired by the urban disorders of the 1960s, the Vietnam War, the Watergate scandal, and the nation's ongoing economic problems. Between 1964 and 1990 the percentage of Americans who said they trusted the government in Washington to do what is right all or most of the time fell from 76 percent to 28 percent, and the percentage who said that public officials care what "people like me" think declined from 62 percent to 23 percent.[9] This growing sense of disaffection and alienation from the political process played a significant role in the 1992 presidential campaign and is discussed in greater detail in the section on voter turnout in Chapter 7.

---

[8] ABC News/*Washington Post* Poll, Survey 77.
[9] Warren E. Miller and Santa Traugott, *American National Elections Studies Data Sourcebook, 1952–1986* and *American National Elections Study, 1990.*

Where Americans Differ

Citizens of the United States manifest considerable agreement on the general principles of democracy just described, but consensus is far from complete. The American people differ on the implications of these general principles when applied to particular cases. They also differ in their political ideologies.

The Meaning of Equality   Although Americans profess a belief in equality in the abstract, just what this means and to whom it applies are matters for disagreement. First, as discussed in Chapter 3, does equality mean equality of opportunity or equality of result? That is, should everybody have an equal chance to pursue an education and earn a high income, or should everybody get the same education and earn the same income? Americans seem to lean away from equality of result. Nearly 80 percent disapprove of putting a cap on personal income.[10] And 73 percent disapprove of introducing socialism (one element of which is equality of income) in the United States, as opposed to only 12 percent who approve.[11]

Second, just which "men" are equal? Some Americans do not believe that men and women are equal. According to a 1988 survey, 15 percent think that "women's place is in the home rather than business, industry, or government."[12] A substantial percentage of Americans do not regard blacks and whites as equals. In a 1990 survey, 78 percent of whites thought that blacks were more likely to prefer living on welfare than whites, 62 percent thought blacks less likely to be hardworking, 56 percent thought blacks more prone to violence, and 53 percent thought blacks less intelligent.[13] Blacks see this sense of racial inequality from a different perspective. In a 1992 survey taken in the aftermath of the Los Angeles riots, 51 percent of blacks agreed that "our nation is moving toward two societies, one black, one white—separate and unequal,"[14] and 40 percent of blacks attributed at least one of the African-American community's problems to a racist conspiracy by whites against them.[15]

Limits of Freedom   Although Americans believe in freedom as a general principle, they do see it as having definite limits. More than 95 percent endorse the principle of freedom of expression in the abstract, but percentages drop sharply with the possibility that "bad" or "dangerous" ideas will be expressed.[16] For many Americans, freedom of expression does not extend to speaking, writing, or teaching when the ideas are unpopular ones—antireligious themes, racism, communism, or homosexuality (see Chapter 3).[17] Further, some Americans do

---

[10] Civic Service survey, March 1981.
[11] Ibid.
[12] American National Election Study, 1988.
[13] National Opinion Research Center, General Social Survey, 1990, cited in "Whites Retain Negative View of Minorities, a Survey Finds," *New York Times*, January 10, 1991, p. B10.
[14] *Gallup Poll Monthly*, Number 321 (June 1992), pp. 7–9.
[15] *Gallup Poll Monthly*, Number 319 (April 1992), p. 29.
[16] For perhaps the most thorough analysis of the gap between support for freedom of speech in the abstract and support for it in particular situations, see McClosky and Brill, *Dimensions of Tolerance*, pp. 48–58.
[17] National Opinion Research Center, General Social Survey, 1988.

not agree that people should be able to express their views any way they want. The Supreme Court's decisions in 1989 and 1990 upholding the rights of protesters to burn the American flag set off a bitter national debate on this form of expression.

Majority Rule Versus Minority Rights   The American people's adherence to the ideals of majority rule and minority rights sometimes loses something in the translation to everyday political questions. Slightly more than half of the respondents in one survey held that only people who were well informed about issues should be allowed to vote in elections where questions relating to "tax-supported undertakings" are at issue, and four out of five held that only taxpayers should be allowed to do so.[18] The idea that any citizen should be able to grow up to be president is endorsed in the abstract but rejected by some in practice. One out of eight Americans would not vote for a qualified woman for president and one out of six white Americans would not vote for a qualified black for President.[19]

Free Enterprise in Practice.   As enamored of the free enterprise system as Americans are, their affection for it still has some limits. Whereas only about 35 percent of Americans think "business has too much power in American life," 82 percent think that "big business" has too much power.[20] And, although Americans are against government regulation of business in the abstract, they actually support its current level or favor increasing it in many particular instances. Americans fault business for not paying enough attention to the quality of goods, making excessive profits, neglecting the environment, and dishonesty.[21] A particular concern as America has faced tougher economic competition from abroad has been business's focus on short-term profits rather than long-term growth and prosperity.[22]

Political Ideology   Perhaps the most important matter on which Americans differ is political ideology. American politics is often portrayed as a controversy between "liberals" and "conservatives." As discussed in Chapter 4, with the rise of neoconservatism, neoliberalism, the populist conservatism of the New Right, and the return to classical liberal principles in libertarianism, particularly in recent years, the reality has become much more complicated than that. Commentators have also distinguished among the different dimensions of liberalism and conservatism: economic, social, and cultural. Such debates have certainly occupied the attention of the intellectual elites, but what is striking is how far removed they are from the concerns of most Americans. Even the most basic notions of liberalism and conservatism meet with limited recognition. Only about half of U.S. citizens

---

[18] James W. Prothro and Charles M. Grigg, "Fundamental Principles of Democracy," *Journal of Politics* 22 (1960): 276–294.

[19] National Opinion Research Center, General Social Survey, 1988.

[20] American National Election Survey, 1976.

[21] Roper Survey Report, June 1982.

[22] Seymour Martin Lipset and William Schneider, *The Confidence Gap* (New York: Free Press, 1983), pp. 166–168.

FIGURE 5.3

Americans Rate Themselves on the Liberal-Conservative Scale, 1973–1990

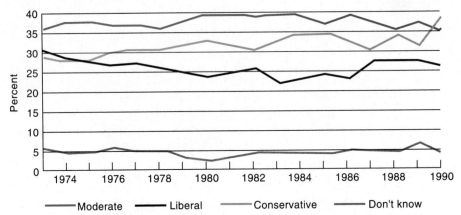

Throughout recent history, moderates have predominated in the American electorate. Since the mid-1970s conservatives and, more recently, moderates have gained at the expense of liberals.   *SOURCE:* National Opinion Research Center, General Social Surveys, 1974–1990.

recognize the terms *liberalism* and *conservatism* and have some general sense of what they mean.[23] In a 1988 national survey, fully 30 percent of the respondents declined to place themselves on a liberal-conservative scale when asked to do so because they said they did not know or had not thought that much about it.[24] Studies of people's answers to questions raising liberal-conservative issues have long shown little consistency between answers, suggesting that many people do not think about politics in ideologically coherent terms.[25] This is important because, first of all, it suggests that a good share of the population does not really have a grasp on the debate between liberals and conservatives. It also raises questions about the meaningfulness of the American public's responses to questions about their political ideology. When people are unsure what they are being asked, a safe response is often in the middle.

Figure 5.3 shows how over the last 20 years more Americans have characterized themselves as moderates than as liberals or conservatives. Over this period, between 35 and 40 percent said they were moderate. Between 25 and 30 percent (though decreasing somewhat) said they were liberal, and between 30 and 36

---

[23] Eric R. A. N. Smith, *The Unchanging American Voter* (Berkeley: University of California Press, 1989), pp. 56–58.

[24] American National Election Study, 1988.

[25] The path-breaking study on attitude consistency in particular and mass political ideology more generally is Philip Converse's "The Nature of Belief Systems in Mass Publics," in David Apter (ed.), *Ideology and Discontent* (New York: Free Press, 1964). For perhaps the best overview of the long and complicated series of challenges and counter-challenges to Converse's work over the last 25 years, see again Smith, *The Unchanging American Voter.*

percent (but increasing somewhat) said they were conservative. Thus the American public can best be described as centrist in that more people see themselves as being in the center than anywhere else.[26] Further, the public is centrist in that roughly equal numbers of people align themselves on the right and on the left, so that the overall balance of opinion does lie roughly in the center.

But if the center of American public opinion lies in the middle, there is nevertheless some unmistakable evidence of a shift to the right. Whereas in the early 1970s liberal and conservative responses were given in approximately equal numbers, more recently conservative responses have come to outstrip liberal ones by a ratio of about four to three. Analysts attribute this primarily to public disenchantment with high taxes and ineffective government programs, as well as public attraction to the conservative philosophy and programs so effectively advocated by Ronald Reagan.

What this really means is difficult to interpret without some sense of what the American public means when it uses the words *liberal* and *conservative*. Different people appear to mean different things by them. A national election survey in 1988 asked people what they had in mind when they said that someone's political views were liberal or conservative. Setting aside the substantial number of people who said they did not know, as mentioned already, the most common responses described liberals as people who are open to change and new ideas, for government action to help solve social problems, allied with working people, inclined to spend government money, and somewhat rash. In contrast, conservatives were viewed as resistant to change, for free enterprise solutions, allied with big business and the rich, against government spending, and cautious.[27]

And what about the people who don't think in terms of or even recognize *liberal* and *conservative?* Political scientists have tried to plumb political thinking to get at the mental images of these people. What they have found does not paint an encouraging portrait. Many Americans seem to respond to political issues on an essentially individual basis, without any broad or overarching political philosophy to guide them. Instead, their responses are shaped by their sense of identification with one or another political party or group, by their feelings about whether "it's good times" or "it's hard times," or by their feelings about a particular candidate or public figure.[28]

However, there may be an important qualification to all this. The level of coherence in public thinking may be at least partially responsive to how politicians handle issues in campaign and policy-making discussions. When candidates and public figures address the public on issues, the public does seem to respond by becoming more conscious of and concerned about those issues. For example, in the relatively placid 1950s, candidates and parties did little to bring issue differences to the attention of the public, and the public showed little awareness of issues or coherence in its thinking about them. But from the mid-1960s on into

---

[26] See Richard M. Scammon and Ben J. Wattenberg, *The Real Majority* (New York: Berkley, 1970).

[27] American National Election Survey, 1988.

[28] Angus Campbell, Philip E. Converse, Warren E. Miller, and Donald E. Stokes, *The American Voter* (New York: Wiley, 1960); Norman H. Nie, Sidney Verba, and John R. Petrocik, *The Changing American Voter*, enlarged ed. (Cambridge, Mass.: Harvard University Press, 1979).

Politics and Economics

Economic Status and Ideology

Conventional wisdom has it that political ideology is closely tied to economic status, with the less well-off holding liberal beliefs and the better-off aligning themselves with a conservative viewpoint. But how well does this relationship hold up in America? Figure 5A shows the relationship between the respondent's professed political ideology and the income of the respondent's family. The poorest Americans manifest comparatively the most liberal views; but even among their ranks, conservatives dominate and moderates are almost as numerous. In every other income category, liberals are clearly the smallest contingent. Conservative and moderate views outnumber liberal views in all of the higher income categories. One striking feature of these data is the relative weakness of the ideological differences between the income groups. More than 35 percent of the poorest Americans describe themselves as conservative. Almost 20 percent of the wealthiest Americans describe themselves as liberal. Surprisingly, then, not everybody who pays, through taxes, for liberal government programs opposes them, and not everybody who might benefit from them supports them. Clearly, economic standing alone does not determine the ideological views of the American public.

What other factors might determine how liberal or conservative a person is? How do you think the neoliberal and neoconservative viewpoints discussed in Chapter 4 might relate to economic status?

FIGURE 5A
Political Ideology and Income

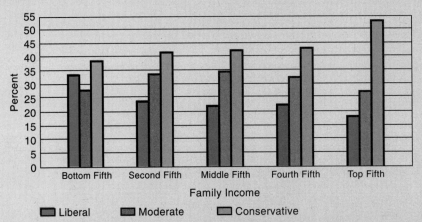

Poor people tend to be more liberal and rich people more conservative, but all income levels have substantial numbers of conservatives, and some rich people are liberal.
SOURCE: American National Election Study, 1988.

the 1970s, candidates began to discuss compelling issues such as the Vietnam War and urban disorder, and the public seemed to respond with increased awareness and coherence.[29]

More recent research has called into question the degree and meaningfulness of the changes observed in the 1960s and 1970s, suggesting that they may result from changes in the way questions were asked and that much of the research into this area may be fatally flawed. It may be that the public's level of sophistication about politics has always been low and that it has changed little over the last 40 years. Whatever apparent increases in liberal-conservative thinking there have been may result from the public merely parroting the heightened liberal-conservative rhetoric of candidates without really understanding it.[30]

The political beliefs of the American public establish patterns that help to fix the shape of politics. The general agreement on principles such as freedom and majority rule defines the boundaries within which the game of American politics is played. These limits help to blunt any potential for political instability or violence. Commitments to ideas such as equal opportunity tend to define the basic objectives of the political system. The relatively low level of ideological thinking provides political leaders with room to maneuver and thereby fosters political stability.

Nevertheless, differences in ideological perspective determine some of the most fundamental conflicts that the political process must resolve. For instance, how actively should the government promote the interests of disadvantaged or oppressed groups? Where should the government strike the balance between promoting social change and maintaining social stability? How the public thinks about politics defines, in part, some of the most fundamental principles and problems of American democracy.

The Sources of Public Opinion: Political Socialization

Given the importance of public opinion, it is useful to comprehend why the public thinks as it does about politics. The origins of public opinion lie in history and philosophy, as discussed in Chapter 4. But knowing where ideas come from does not explain how people come to hold certain beliefs. Understanding that phenomenon requires a discussion of political socialization and of one of its most important agents, the mass media.

Political socialization is the process by which citizens come to think what they think about politics. Through political socialization, citizens internalize, or incorporate into their own thinking, beliefs, feelings, and evaluations (judgments on whether something is good or bad) about the political world in which they live. Think of the tremendous range of knowledge, feelings, and evaluations that

---

[29] Nie, Verba, and Petrocik, *The Changing American Voter*.

[30] The best summary of, and most substantial contribution to, this recent research is Smith, *The Unchanging American Voter*. On the role of political rhetoric, see especially pp. 45–104.

people have about politics. And think of the many sources from which they all come. Political socialization is obviously a long and complicated process.

Most of what people think and feel about politics has been learned from somebody else. But to leave it at that would deny the dynamic nature of the process and ultimately the possibility of any political change. That is, if all people simply stuck with what they had been taught about politics, nobody would ever think of anything new, and nothing would ever change. Clearly, then, some people break away from rigid adherence to old ideas and put thoughts together in new ways. But even those people start somewhere, building upon what already exists. Thus political socialization is important to both stability and change in American politics.

The Processes of Political Socialization

How do people learn about politics? Psychologists say that people tend to repeat behavior patterns that are rewarded and not to repeat patterns that are not rewarded or are punished. Much of what people know about politics they learn through **explicit teaching.** Information is presented to them, and they are either rewarded for learning it (by a higher grade or the praise of teachers or parents, for example) or punished for not learning it (by a lower grade or the criticism of teachers or parents). The mechanisms of learning are really the domain of psychology. Here it will suffice simply to identify some of the basic **processes** that political scientists have identified as important in political socialization.

- ■ *Social learning theory.* People experience subtle rewards and punishments from the psychological attachments they form to some of the people around them. People may admire others or dislike them. Because people like to have favorable images of themselves, they may attempt to boost their self-images by acting like people they admire or by avoiding the behavior of those they do not like. Thus a little boy may parrot his mother's views about the president, or a rebellious teenager may criticize a candidate whom her disliked father holds dear.

- ■ *Transfer theory.* People may carry over attitudes developed in a narrower setting such as the family or school to the broader political setting. A boy who dislikes his father may rebel against political authority more generally.

- ■ *Cognitive development theory.* What people can learn about politics depends on the stage of their mental development. There are some things that can be learned only early in life and other things that can be learned only later on. An adult immigrant newly arrived in America may never develop the deep emotional attachment to the nation felt by a person who has grown up in this country from birth. By contrast, a first grader lacks the intellectual capacity to master the intricacies of federalism.[31]

---

[31] Robert D. Hess and Judith V. Torney, *The Development of Political Attitudes in Children* (Garden City, N.Y.: Doubleday/Anchor Books, 1967), pp. 24–26, offers a good overview of various psychological theories of socialization.

These different accounts of how people learn about politics are not competing alternatives but complementary ones. Social learning sometimes occurs through explicit teaching. The possibilities of transference, social learning, and explicit teaching probably all vary, depending on the intellectual development of the learner. Political socialization is too complex to be accounted for by any one theory or explanation.

The Agents of Political Socialization

Agents are the people and institutions from which we learn. A person growing up in the United States learns about politics from many teachers. A comprehensive list would be too long to include here, but it is possible to identify a few of the most important ones. (Another of the most important agents, the mass media, is discussed in the next section.)

The Family   Under almost any realistic theory of political socialization, the family is uniquely situated to be a potent agent. The young individual who, according to developmental theory, is most vulnerable to socialization, spends much time with the family. So the family has the first chance at the developing political being. Psychological attachments are often strong and therefore conducive to the transference of attitudes toward authority. This opens up the way for imitation of attitudes and behavior relating to participation and partisanship. Although much learning takes place in the family, how much of it is political is difficult to pinpoint. Politics is not of paramount interest to most Americans, so it is not usually at the top of the typical family's agenda for discussion. Thus it is not surprising that children sometimes grow up to be politically different from their parents. Research indicates that the transmission of political attitudes from parents to their children is substantial only when the attitudes relate to topics that regularly come up for discussion in the family.[32]

The School   The school is also a prime agent of political socialization. Education can be related to many political orientations—political participation, political knowledgeability, and political tolerance, among others. Certainly the school is the primary explicit teacher of information about politics: how the president is chosen, how many senators and members of Congress there are, and so on. A good share of this fades away, as every student well knows, unless it is periodically reinforced by additional education, exposure to the media, political discussion, or repeated use.

However, school is more than the presentation of facts. It is a complicated and diverse bundle of experiences and impressions. Students encounter teachers, books, authority figures and role models such as principals and coaches, and their fellow students or peers. Some of these people are very much like themselves, and some may be very different, giving many students their first real encounter

---

[32] M. Kent Jennings and Richard Niemi, *Generations and Politics* (Princeton, N.J.: Princeton University Press, 1981), pp. 76–114.

with social diversity. Students may involve themselves in low-level political activities: class and club elections, student government, protests against school policies, and so on. They acquire not just facts but subtle impressions of the way things are and the way things ought to be. They develop feelings about social and political involvement and what they can hope to accomplish through the political process.[33]

Peer Groups   **Peer groups** are groups of people, roughly equal in social position, who interact with one another. Students who go to school together, people who work together in an office or factory or bowl on the same team, the neighbors on the block—all are peer groups. Social pressures on group members to conform can be quite powerful. Group members adopt "proper" attitudes and behavior because they seek the boost to their self-image that comes with the approval of others or because they fear that nonconformity will lead to ostracism. Because other things are usually more important, peer groups do not always set norms relating to politics. However, when they do, the political consequences can be significant.[34]

The Development of the Political Self

How does political learning actually take place? How do politically blank infants develop into full-blown political beings? Probably the first political thought to blossom in the mind of a small child in the United States is a psychological attachment to America. This is by no means a sense of what America is, just a feeling of belonging to it. In families where partisanship is important, a primitive sense of "I'm a Republican" or "I'm a Democrat" may appear. A sense of external authority above the authority of the parents that must be obeyed also emerges. This is most often attached to two specific figures: the president and the police officer. The president is the focal point of the American political system, so it is not surprising that this focused attention influences even very small children. The police officer gains attention as a less remote figure of considerable authority who moves about in the children's world. Perhaps the most striking feature of these early images is their positive character. Small children tend to idealize political authorities, attributing to them all possible virtues.[35]

As children grow, their political orientations evolve. In school they begin to acquire substantial new knowledge pertinent to politics. Much of this they soon forget, but some becomes part of their lasting store of information. Their conceptions of politics become less personal and more institutional. For example, the president is important not so much as a person but as a position. Idealization of political authority fades to realism: Public figures have flaws, they make mistakes,

---

[33] David C. Bricker, *Classroom Life as Civic Education* (New York: Teachers College Press, 1989), is one recent discussion of some of these issues.

[34] Theodore M. Newcomb, "Persistence and Regression of Changed Attitudes: Long-Range Studies," *Journal of Social Issues* 19 (1963): 3–14.

[35] Fred I. Greenstein, *Children and Politics* (New Haven, Conn.: Yale University Press, 1965).

and people criticize them. Once in school, where teachers may try to minimize classroom conflict by downplaying partisan differences, children tend to become less partisan.

As partisanship declines, the ability to deal with the political world on a more abstract level increases. Children develop intellectually and morally to the extent that they can begin to look at politics in a more sophisticated and structured way. The critical age at which political thinking really starts to blossom seems to be about 12. Within a couple of years children's thinking becomes nearly as abstract and sophisticated as adults'. Also, with increasing exposure to the sometimes unattractive facets of political life, realism often fades into cynicism. By the late teens, most individuals have established a political identity.

Political socialization does not end at the age of 21. Learning about politics continues through adulthood. As people age, their needs and concerns evolve from, for example, their own education to their children's education to, in later life, their own health care. People's social environment changes, as their family role shifts from child to parent to grandparent, as the school years recede into the past, and as peer groups switch from fellow students to fellow workers to fellow retirees. Broader social change affects political learning too, as such large-scale social transformations as the civil rights movement and the women's movement alter the expectations that people have of themselves and of society. Major unresolved issues are how much childhood socialization persists into adulthood and how much adult political learning is constrained by what has been learned before.[36]

Diversity in Socialization

Socialization is not an identical process nationwide. American society includes many subsocieties, some with their own distinctive political subcultures or shared patterns of political attitudes and behavior. Some of the most important are racially and ethnically based. Blacks constitute the largest distinctive subculture. Although the youngest black children share an idealized image of authority with their white counterparts, their positive views seem to erode more quickly and they develop less of a sense of political efficacy or effectiveness.[37] Harder to characterize are the Hispanic and Asian subcultures. One reason is that each is not a single subculture, but a collection of them. The rapidly growing Hispanic subculture encompasses the Mexican-oriented culture of the Southwest, as well as the Cuban-oriented culture of south Florida and the Puerto Rican and Jamaican-oriented culture of New York City and other large cities. Similarly, the Asian subculture includes the long-established Chinese communities of San Francisco, Los Angeles,

---

[36] Roberta S. Sigel, ed., *Political Learning in Adulthood* (Chicago: University of Chicago Press, 1989) provides a good overview of adult political socialization and recent research on the topic.

[37] Edward Greenberg, "Orientations of Black and White Children to Political Authority," *Social Science Quarterly* 51 (1970): 934–943; Paul Abramson, *The Political Socialization of Black Americans* (New York: Free Press, 1977).

and New York City, and the more recently established communities of immigrants from Vietnam and other southeast Asian countries.

The different regions of the United States also constitute, to some degree, distinctive subcultures with unique patterns of political thought and behavior. The South is perhaps the most distinct from the others, owing to the continuing legacy of slavery and subsequent racial strife, as well as its more rural, agricultural subculture. Earlier studies of socialization found children in the South to differ from those in the North, but these differences seem to be fading.

In fact, the general trend seems to be away from clear-cut differentiation and toward greater homogeneity. Some attribute this to the "nationalization" of American culture and politics, which tends to blur regional differences. Americans in all parts of the country eat the same fast food and buy the same national-brand products. Most important politically, they read the same wire-service news stories and national news magazines and watch the same network news broadcasts. As a result, public opinion in the United States is becoming more and more uniform from region to region.

One other aspect of diversity involves not a subculture but a segment of society: gender differences in political socialization. The thrust of much early research on political socialization was to portray females as less political than males and to trace those differences back to the childhood years.[38] But the changing social and economic role of women from the eighteenth century to today is both a cause and a result of changes in the political interest, competence, and involvement of women.[39] The move toward more equal roles for men and women fostered by the feminist movement is likely to manifest itself in, and benefit from, less political difference between young males and females.

The Sources of Public Opinion: The Mass Media

The mass media play a profound role in shaping American political thinking, making them important and certainly the most visible agents of political socialization. Much of what people know and think about politics comes to them through the mass media. The **mass media** encompass all the forms and content of mass communication—newspapers, magazines, radio and television, political news, nonpolitical news, fact and fiction, entertainment and enlightenment. That particular part of the mass media that deals with news is the press, so named because of the machines (printing presses) that produce newspapers.

The press is sometimes called the **fifth branch** of government, after Congress, the president, the Supreme Court, and the bureaucracy. This characterization reflects the fact that the press is an important part of the political process and can even serve as an additional check on the powers of public officials through

[38] See, for example, Fred I. Greenstein, "Sex-Related Political Differences in Childhood," *Journal of Politics* 23 (1961): 353–371.
[39] Ethel Klein, *Gender Politics* (Cambridge, Mass.: Harvard University Press, 1984), pp. 117–119.

discovery and coverage of news and commentary on events. The fundamental role that the press plays in the political process is recognized formally in the Constitution, in the First Amendment. However, it is important to keep in mind that the media are not a formal part of the government. In fact, they are mainly businesses that exist to make money.

The Media as an Institution

The media are not a single institution but a set of institutions. The oldest, and still very important, mass medium is the newspaper. In 1990, more than 1600 newspapers were published in the United States every day, with a circulation of more than 60 million and readership in 67 percent of American households. Magazines are another important form of print journalism. Counting scholarly journals, nearly 11,000 periodicals other than newspapers are published in the United States. Although most are small or have little to do with public affairs, political news and opinion are the main content of many. Mass circulation news weeklies include *Time, Newsweek,* and *U.S. News and World Report.* Others, such as *Washington Monthly, The New Republic,* and *National Review* (described in Chapter 4), are journals of opinion and are targeted at different political audiences.

Neither newspapers nor magazines figure as prominently as mass media as they used to. This is because of the extraordinary explosion of mass electronic communication, which began with Marconi's invention of wireless communication in the early twentieth century and erupted into a major industry after the first commercial radio broadcasts began from KDKA in Pittsburgh in 1920. Not far behind was television. Its astonishing growth since 1950 now permits almost every household to be served by at least several stations. Through its first 30 years, the television industry was dominated by the three major networks, ABC, CBS, and NBC, and television journalism was dominated by their three network news departments. But thanks to the rapid growth of cable television, which now reaches nearly 60 percent of all households in the United States, television has changed dramatically. Most homes now receive 11 or more broadcast stations and a variety of channels available only over cable. This proliferation of alternatives has weakened the major networks and threatened the dominance of their news operations.

One source available only by cable, Cable News Network (CNN), has become the main alternative to broadcast network news operations and, in the process, a worldwide source of news. Many world leaders, including the president of the United States, watch CNN, especially to follow critical events as they unfold at almost any point on the globe. In the first hours of Iraq's invasion of Kuwait on August 2, 1990, for example, President Bush and his closest advisers in the White House turned to CNN for information as much as they did to the Central Intelligence Agency.

As a result of the phenomenal growth of the video industry, television has surpassed the newspaper and radio as the primary source of national news for most Americans, although newspapers remain the main source for local news.

Average household television usage in the United States is more than six hours every day. Americans listen to the radio for over three hours and spend about 20 minutes with newspapers and 10 minutes with magazines each day. Seen a different way, over four-fifths of the population come in contact with a television program or a periodical on any given day. On Sunday nights, for example, it is a safe bet that over 115 million Americans will watch at least one television program. So the print and electronic media seem to provide most of the people with a variety of entertainment and information sources.

Although the printed word has almost unrestricted freedom under the First Amendment, electronic journalism operates under some restrictions imposed by an important governmental institution, the **Federal Communications Commission** (FCC). The FCC has broad rule-making authority, which it has employed to require radio and television stations to operate "in the public interest." For instance, stations are limited in the number of commercials that may be broadcast per hour, a certain amount of time must be set aside for public service and public affairs programming, and obscenity and "filthy words" are prohibited.[40] The justification for such governmental intrusion has been that frequencies (and therefore the number of stations) are finite and that the airwaves are public property.[41] The FCC is composed of five commissioners who are appointed by the president and confirmed by the Senate for seven-year terms. Since the 1970s the FCC has moved toward less regulation of radio and television, adopting the view that the marketplace and not the commissioners should dictate development of the industry, with the commission confining itself to licensing stations, assigning frequencies, and policing their use.

Nevertheless, two FCC regulations have been very significant for news reporting. The first is the **equal-time rule,** which requires stations to give or sell time to a political candidate if the station has already given or sold time to another candidate for the same office. To ensure fairness, the time must not only be equal in length but it must also be at a similar time of day. In 1984 the FCC decided that the equal-time rule does not apply to televised debates among political candidates, thus allowing a station to invite some candidates and not others.

The second is the **fairness doctrine,** an FCC regulation that applied throughout the year, not just during political campaigns. Stations had to devote a "reasonable" percentage of airtime to a discussion of public issues and had to ensure fair coverage for each side. If a station presented only one side of an issue or supported a political candidate, advocates for the other side had a legal right to be heard. Given the trend toward deregulation of the broadcast industry, it was not surprising that the FCC repealed the fairness doctrine in 1987. The FCC concluded that the doctrine was unconstitutional and that expansion of cable television had largely undercut the original rationale for treating radio and television stations differently from newspapers. Most communities now have access to more television channels than newspapers, meaning that the potential for competition among viewpoints is now greater in electronic than in print journalism.

---

[40] *Federal Communications Commission* v. *Pacifica Foundation,* 438 U.S. 726 (1976).

[41] *Red Lion Broadcasting Co.* v. *Federal Communications Commission,* 395 U.S. 367 (1969).

Politics and the Press

Understanding why the press is so important in the political process requires a look at several roles the media play in American politics. The media serve as vehicles of direct communication, as gatekeepers of political knowledge and attitudes, as spotlights on issues, and as talent scouts in campaigns.

- *Direct communication: the media as vehicles.* Radio and television have become *vehicles*, making it possible for a president or other national political leader to speak simultaneously and directly to virtually everyone in the land. Recent president George Bush was less inclined to use television to communicate directly with the American people. During his first year in office Ronald Reagan gave nine prime-time television addresses. In the same period Bush delivered only three. Instead, Bush preferred informal sessions with reporters, and thereby relied on them to convey his message

Coverage of presidential candidates has long been a staple of network newscasts, but one distinguishing feature of the 1992 presidential race, which will probably be repeated in 1996, was the extent to which candidates reached out to the public through talk shows on radio and television. Shown here is Democratic nominee Bill Clinton as the guest on "Larry King Live" on CNN, telecast from Louisville, Kentucky, on October 28, 1992.

to the public. In the first months of his administration, Bill Clinton avoided formal news conferences with the aggressive White House press corps in favor of controlled televised addresses and direct interaction with carefully selected citizens in "town meeting" settings.

■ *Political knowledge and attitudes: the media as gatekeepers.* As gatekeepers, editors and journalists in newsrooms across the land decide in large measure what the American people will know. News stories contribute to emotions and impressions that can matter politically, apart from whatever facts are transferred from the tube or page to the brain. Feelings of outrage, sadness, pride, trust, or distrust can linger long after the specific content of a news story has been forgotten.

■ *Issue making and issue reporting: the media as spotlights.* The media help to identify and define the issues people regard as important. Moreover, prominent coverage of a topic (for example, drunk driving) day after day may heighten the importance people assign to it, just as an absence of coverage can lead people to believe that a problem (such as hunger) is no longer serious. When news stories and "op-ed" pieces highlight events and conditions, government officials and other politicians will frequently regard them as important too. Extensive video footage of drug sales on street corners in broad daylight, for instance, is almost certain to produce some kind of response from the mayor or police chief. As a result there is more media attention because officials are now considering the problem and deciding what action, if any, to take. So the media do not tell the people what to think. Rather the American media are significant because they tell the people about what (and about whom) to think.

■ *Candidates and campaigns: the media as talent scouts.* Just as every aspiring singer and shortstop wants to be noticed and taken seriously, candidates for political office want "good press." The media are the voters' primary source of information about political candidates. More voters can see a presidential candidate simultaneously in a single appearance on television today than during a three-week whistle-stop train tour of the nation 50 years ago. Good reporting can help voters understand a candidate's stand on the issues. This is a significant change from the past, when the political parties were the major identifiers and publicizers of candidates for public office.

All these ways in which the media play a direct role in the political process are important. But the media's role is amplified far beyond that. What it transmits directly to just some people is then transmitted indirectly to many others. One woman reads about problems with health care policy in *Newsweek* and tells her friends at work who do not follow politics about what she read. This is what social scientists call a **two-step flow** of political information and evaluation. A more sophisticated **opinion leader** who pays closer attention to politics acquires information from the media, forms an opinion, and then passes it on to less sophisticated "followers" who pay less attention.[42]

---

[42] Paul F. Lazarsfeld, Bernard Berelson, and Hazel Gaudet, *The People's Choice*, 2d ed. (New York: Columbia University Press, 1948), pp. 49–51.

Are the Media Biased?

Politicians, including most American presidents, have long complained about news coverage. Most Americans apparently agree. No less than 76 percent of the public report that they see a "great deal" or a "fair amount" of political bias in news coverage.[43] Some bias is probably unavoidable in reporting the news. The bias is both personal and structural. That is, it results from the political attitudes of reporters and editors as well as from the nature of the news-reporting business itself.

The Personal Biases of Journalists   Of course, news is influenced by the people who write it. The attitudes and outlooks of reporters and commentators are bound to affect what they write and say and what Americans read and see, even if journalists make every effort to be accurate.

What are the political attitudes of the journalists who staff the major newspapers and network news bureaus? Few have been politically active in the sense of strongly identifying with and working for a party and its candidates. Yet when they vote, journalists overwhelmingly favor Democratic or otherwise liberal candidates.[44] Moreover, they tend to be suspicious of most politicians, whether Democratic or Republican, liberal or conservative. This is, one scholar has concluded, because politicians have to compromise.[45] Suspicion of politicians in turn leads to suspicion of "the establishment," the people in power. In a campaign, the underdog may be more appealing than the supposed front-runner. And with numerous exposés to their credit that have uncovered corruption and shady deals by public officials, it is only natural that journalists see themselves as a permanent "loyal opposition" or "watchdog" beyond that provided by the two-party system.

However, other forces tend to compensate for a liberal bias, to the extent it exists in the national press. Editorial endorsements from the "front office" usually go to conservatives, and reporters in towns and small cities may have a more conservative outlook too. Because journalists rely on officials for access to information, journalists may put favorable slants on the stories they write. Conservative officials and causes, therefore, may get more balanced treatment than they would otherwise receive.

Structural Biases in Reporting the News   One source of structural bias arises in decisions about what constitutes news. Because literally thousands of events occur in the world every day, space and time constraints mean that most of them go unreported. Selecting what becomes news is especially critical in television. Approximately 22 minutes are available for news during a 30-minute news show, allowing for 10 to 15 stories at most. This means that even the major stories are usually allotted only two to three minutes each. If a "big story" is in the news, other stories are crowded out.

What factors seem to guide this inevitable selection? Some events are destined

---

[43] The People and The Press; Part 5 (Los Angeles: Times Mirror, Inc., 1989), p. 13.

[44] A 1992 study for the Freedom Forum by David Weaver and G. Cleveland Wilhoit, reported in William Glaberson, "More Reporters Leaning Democratic, Study Says," *New York Times,* November 18, 1992, p. A20.

[45] Austin Ranney, "The Cook Lectures: Politics in the Television Age," *Law Quadrangle Notes* 26 (1982): 19. See also Austin Ranney, *Channels of Power* (New York: Basic Books, 1983), pp. 55–63.

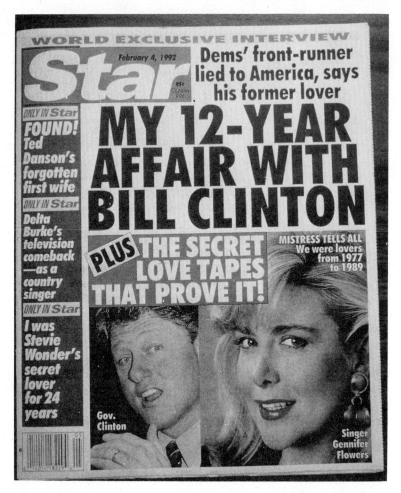

A dilemma for journalists is whether and to what extent a candidate's or an official's private life should be subject to public scrutiny. Early in the 1992 presidential race, Bill Clinton's campaign survived potentially ruinous charges of marital infidelity which the media widely reported after the *Star*, a supermarket tabloid, published an interview with Gennifer Flowers about her alleged 12-year affair with Clinton. Lending credibility to Clinton's denial of the affair was knowledge that the *Star* had paid Flowers for the interview and that Clinton's wife Hillary publicly came to the support of her husband.

to become news: natural disasters and political "turning points" such as elections, revolutions, and military invasions. Other events or circumstances will become news if they happen to appeal to the people responsible for selecting stories or if they have a high interest among the reading and viewing audience. Still others qualify as news because they are "scoops"—attention-getting stories made public by a single newspaper or station.

Economics also plays a part in news selection. Especially for television, operating costs are high. For every story viewers see, there is not only a reporter but also a camera operator, a technician, and a producer involved directly on the scene. Equipment is expensive and broadcast circuits must be paid for. Network news editors, therefore, do not casually send reporters, crews, and equipment to all potentially newsworthy locations. This is one reason why about half the network news stories originate from, or focus on, Washington.[46] Even within Washington, news coverage is not equally dispersed. About half the stories deal primarily with the "golden triangle" of the White House and the Departments of Defense and State. Congress receives somewhat less coverage, with the Senate drawing more attention than the House. Regulatory agencies and the Supreme Court receive the least. This disparate treatment is partly a function of the stories journalists think are most important. Also, the executive branch, though many times larger than Congress, is more easily personified in the president.

Another source of structural bias arises in decisions about how the news should appear. Journalists have some discretion in emphasizing the favorable or unfavorable aspects of a story. As a result, public officials and candidates today are reluctant to leave interpretation of events solely to journalists. After the debates in the 1992 presidential campaign, for example, candidates Bush, Clinton, and Perot had hardly uttered their closing statements when the "spin doctors" went to work. Reporters and viewers were presented with instant analyses from officeholders and campaign officials eager to explain what "really happened."

Because news reporting is a business, stations sell time on news programs just as they do during weekend football games and afternoon soap operas. Newspapers sell space. Understandably, media executives are acutely conscious of TV ratings and circulation figures. Such numbers largely determine commercial revenue and, therefore, profits. The pressure to attract as many viewers and readers as possible impels broadcast and print editors to highlight action, conflict, and drama in the news.

Particularly important to the question about how the news appears is the **impact of the visual.** Television gives a special meaning to the old saying that a picture is worth a thousand words. A news article about a plane crash will not have the same effect as color videotape of the same scene. The visual also becomes a factor in the selection of stories and in the way those stories are presented. Television news editors prefer stories that can be easily visualized and that display action. Televised reports on political campaigns, for instance, typically emphasize rallies, parades, flag waving, and handshaking rather than substantive issues.[47] Candidates know this and conduct their campaigns accordingly, as will be discussed further in Chapter 7.

Does Media Bias Betray a Trust?   Charges of bias in news reporting sometimes cast journalists as betraying a trust. The implication is often that journalists are not worthy of the protections afforded them by the Bill of Rights. The First Amendment does not assume a bias-free press any more than the Constitution assumes pure and ambition-free politicians. Recall the constitutional system of checks and bal-

---

[46] Dom Bonafede, "The Washington Press," *National Journal,* April 17, 1982, p. 664.
[47] Thomas E. Patterson and Robert D. McClure, *The Unseeing Eye: The Myth of Television Power in National Politics* (New York: Putnam, 1976), pp. 22–23; "The Age of Indifference," p. 28.

ances discussed in Chapter 1. At the heart of this arrangement, the media amount to another kind of check and balance. Just as the Constitution allows ambition to counter ambition, so the First Amendment allows one opinion to combat another—one claim of truth, perspective, and opinion to compete with another. In this way, the media best serve democratic politics.

Political Participation

So far we have examined what Americans think about politics and why they think what they do. The issue now is what they do about what they think. In other words, how is public opinion translated into political participation? Of course, putting it in those terms suggests that **political participation** stems from exclusively political considerations such as concern about issues and ideology. But that is only part of the story.

Motives for Political Participation

The conventional image of political participation has concerned citizens trying to advance their views by engaging in political activity. This is no doubt an accurate picture for some people. However, substantial numbers of people who are relatively unconcerned about politics nevertheless participate, and substantial numbers of people who are concerned about politics do not participate. Obviously, other factors must also motivate political participation.

Some participation is sparked by *political motivations*. **Political efficacy** is a person's sense of being able to accomplish something politically. It involves judgments both about one's own competence in the political arena (sometimes called *internal efficacy*) and about the responsiveness of the political system to one's efforts (*external efficacy*). People with a very strong sense of efficacy are more likely to be politically active than those with a weak sense of efficacy. Other citizens are motivated to become involved by a **sense of duty.** They may care less about the issues or be put off by politics, but they have been socialized to think that good citizens get involved in politics. People with a strong sense of duty are more likely to participate politically than those without it.

Party identification, the psychological attachment that many Americans feel toward a particular political party, also provides a strong impetus to political action. The highest rates of political activity are observed among people with a strong commitment to one or another of the political parties. A person who strongly supports programs advocated by the Democratic party, for example, will probably work to promote a Democratic victory. Yet someone who sees little difference between the parties and who cares little about issues may not even vote.

Other factors spurring people on to political involvement are essentially non-political or *social motivations*. Many people engage in political activity for its social rewards. It is a good way to meet people, make friends, develop new relationships. People low in self-esteem or lacking in confidence may attempt to bolster their self-image by taking on the social opportunities and challenges that political activity offers. In other cases, concern about an issue initially mobilizes a citizen into political involvement and then fades away, but the social connection keeps the person going.[48] This is not to say that political activity so inspired is of no political consequence; the labor, the money, or the vote of such a person counts the same as that of the most ideological partisan. Rather, it is to say that not all politics can be understood simply in terms of political motives.

Forms of Participation

Any American who wants to become politically involved has a broad range of options, from doing nothing at all or merely glancing at the TV news occasionally all the way up to being president of the United States. Some of these forms of participation are the focus of other chapters in this book. Participation related to campaigns and elections will be discussed in greater detail in Chapter 7. Much political activity occurs within the framework of interest groups and political parties. These facets of participation will be examined more closely in Chapter 6. The rest of this section focuses on some of the most important other ways in which Americans can participate politically.

Following Politics   Just paying attention to politics constitutes a simple form of political participation. And for many Americans, politics is, if nothing more, an entertaining spectator sport. As noted earlier in this chapter, about three-fourths of Americans say they follow government and public affairs "most" or "some" of the time. How active their pursuit of public affairs is suggested by this: 66 percent of the American people say they read a newspaper "just about every day" and a slightly higher percentage (71 percent) say that they regularly watch the nightly network news broadcasts.[49]

Contacting Public Officials   One of the most direct ways to convey a political message is to deliver it straight to a politician or governmental authority. Not many Americans do this very often. One recent study found that only 30 percent of Americans had phoned or sent a letter or a telegram to a public official in the last four years.[50] So where does all that mail to public officials come from? First, an occasional letter from even a small proportion of a large number of constituents can generate a lot of mail, as the caseworker in almost any congressional office can confirm. Beyond that, it appears that a small group of letter writers writes a large number of letters. Another study estimated that two-thirds of all mail to public officials comes from just 3 percent of the population.[51]

---

[48] Samuel J. Eldersveld, *Political Parties: A Behavioral Analysis* (Chicago: Rand McNally, 1964), pp. 290–292.
[49] Ornstein, Kohut, and McCarthy, p. 133.
[50] Ibid.
[51] Philip E. Converse, Aage R. Clausen, and Warren E. Miller, "Electoral Myth and Reality: The 1964 Election," *American Political Science Review* 59 (June 1965): 321–336.

Direct face-to-face contact with members of Congress and other public officials is harder to assess. One estimate is that about 20 percent of Americans directly contact public officials about an issue or problem.[52] Another standard strategy for contacting public officials is the petition, a right protected by the First Amendment. A petition is a written statement requesting that the government follow some course of action, circulated among and signed by a group of citizens. More than half (55 percent) of Americans claim that they have signed petitions, although only 10 percent claimed to have circulated them.[53]

Protests Within and Beyond the Law   Abstract theories of representative democracy and, indeed, the original Constitution itself focus on the election of representatives as the principal means of communication between citizens and government. But the First Amendment to the Constitution, in its guarantees of freedom of speech, assembly, and petition, reminds us of other forms of political expression. These guarantees reflect a political tradition in which political protest sometimes assumes an important role and embody a view of at least some such actions as legitimate.

Political protest can assume many different forms. A reasonably comprehensive listing of forms of protest includes:

- *Marches and rallies.* Marches and demonstrations have a long-standing tradition in American politics. Perhaps the most famous example was the great march on Washington in August of 1963. This landmark event in the civil rights movement, which brought more than 250,000 peaceful demonstrators to the Mall, culminated with Dr. Martin Luther King's historic "I have a dream" speech from the steps of the Lincoln Memorial. The Vietnam War brought numerous marchers to Washington in the late 1960s and early 1970s. In the 1980s and early 1990s, the abortion issue drew many pro-choice and pro-life marchers to the streets of the nation's capital and some state capitals, as has the issue of gay rights.
- *Boycotts.* Boycotts, the refusal of citizens to buy some product or use some service, are another important tool of protest. In the late 1950s, the refusal of blacks in the South to ride in the rear of buses exerted economic pressure on municipalities and attracted public attention to their cause. Some 15 percent of the American people say that they have participated in a boycott.[54]
- *Picketing.* Groups of protesters trudging back and forth or huddled around a fire in an empty metal barrel, angry placards in hand, are a common sight on the American political scene. One of the most frequent uses of picketing in the late 1980s was by the anti-abortion movement, which picketed doctors' offices and clinics where abortions were being performed.

---

[52] Sidney Verba and Norman Nie, *Political Participation in America: Political Democracy and Social Equality* (New York: Harper & Row, 1972), p. 31.
[53] Ornstein, Kohut, and McCarthy, p. 133.
[54] Ibid.

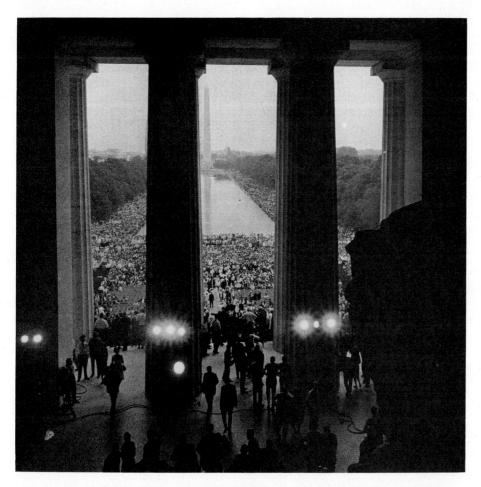

One of the most famous and influential mass gatherings in American history was the March on Washington on August 28, 1963. More than 250,000 people assembled on the Mall between the Washington Monument and the Lincoln Memorial to show their support for equal rights for blacks and to listen to leaders of the civil rights movement. Among them was the Reverend Martin Luther King, Jr., who ended the day with his "I have a dream" oration. The view in this photograph looks east from inside the Memorial across the reflecting pool. Lincoln's statue is on the right.

Protest demonstrations are one of the most visible, though certainly not the most common, forms of political participation in America. Accurate estimates of the extent of protest are notoriously difficult to obtain because people are sometimes reluctant to admit their participation to researchers. A study spanning a four-year period in the mid-1980s found 6 percent of Americans saying that they had participated in at least one public demonstration over that period.

Estimates of participation are even more difficult when it comes to actions that involve violence and crime.

- *Political violence.* On some occasions, American citizens have engaged in violent outbursts with political connotations. At the very founding of the United States, Massachusetts farmers led by Daniel Shays forced the closing of local and state courts before they were themselves forcibly put down by the state militia. The antidraft riots of the Civil War, the urban ghetto riots of the 1960s, and the antiwar violence of the Vietnam War era resulted in widespread personal injury and destruction of property for political ends. In the last few years, perhaps the most visible recurring instances of political violence have involved anti-abortion protesters forcibly blocking and even burning abortion clinics. An even more dramatic event occurred in the spring of 1992: the large-scale riot in Los Angeles, which followed the announcement of not guilty verdicts in the cases of four police officers accused of brutally beating a young black motorist, Rodney King. The riot resulted in the destruction of more than $500 million in property and the loss of more than 90 lives.

- *Politically motivated crimes.* Although riots and other violent outbursts have at least the appearance of spontaneous actions, other politically relevant acts are clearly premeditated criminal violence. The civil rights movement in particular has spawned a number of violent reactions: the death of four black children in a fire-bombed church, the murder of three young civil rights workers—Goodman, Chaney, and Schwerner—in Mississippi in 1963, and the assassination of Dr. Martin Luther King in Memphis in 1968.

Many types of political protest are perfectly legal, particularly as long as they do not endanger the well-being of others. Peaceful marches and demonstrations certainly fall into this category. Others are clearly illegal: Most people would probably agree that rioting and assassination fall into this category because they destroy both life and property. Nevertheless the line between legitimate and illegitimate political protest is sometimes hard to define. Further, some acts of political protest are undertaken, even if illegal, on the basis of a moral justification. These are acts of **civil disobedience,** a deliberate violation of the law as a means of asserting the illegitimacy of the law or calling attention to a higher moral principle. Civil rights activists in the South in the 1950s and 1960s organized sit-ins at lunch counters and other facilities designated for whites only with the explicit intention of being arrested. They saw this as a way of calling attention to unjust laws and to their treatment more generally. A related strategy was the practice of **passive resistance**—one form of which was not struggling with angry white citizens or police, but simply lying down in the face of attack or arrest and forcing the police to drag the protesters off to the police van and jail. In recent years, anti-abortion activists have adopted some of these tactics in their efforts to shut down abortion clinics.

Dr. Martin Luther King, Jr., provided a good explanation of the moral legitimacy of an illegal action in a famous letter that he wrote from a Birmingham jail:

> I submit that an individual who breaks a law that conscience tells him is unjust, and willingly accepts the penalty by staying in jail to arouse the conscience of the community over its injustice is in reality expressing the very highest respect for law.

Civil disobedience is thus characterized by a moral justification, a willingness to accept whatever penalty the action incurs, and, some would add as a critical element, an intention to avoid physical harm to others. Only a small proportion of Americans, 2 percent, say that they have themselves broken the law in a protest for a political or social cause.[55] However, civil disobedience is widely recognized as an acceptable strategy in extreme circumstances: Asked whether people should obey the law without exception or if there are exceptional occasions on which people should follow their consciences even if it means breaking the law, 40 percent of a national sample supported obeying the law, whereas 52 percent opted for following one's conscience.[56]

Differences in Participation

What determines the forms of political participation in which citizens tend to engage? In probably the most thorough study yet done of political participation in America, Sidney Verba and Norman Nie identified six categories of citizen participation and determined the kinds of people who fell into each.[57]

1. ***Inactives.*** These people, comprising about 22 percent of the population, take virtually no part in political life. Lower-status social and economic groups, blacks, women, the youngest, the oldest, and the least concerned about politics are particularly likely to fall into this category.

2. ***Voting specialists.*** About 21 percent of the population do little more politically than vote regularly. This group is distinctive primarily in its strong sense of partisanship. It seems that some inactives get firmly attached to a party and that connection is enough to bring them to the polls at most elections.

3. ***Parochial participants.*** About 4 percent of the population contacts public officials when they have a particular personal problem and seek governmental assistance in solving it. This is more common among lower-status groups, Catholics, and urban dwellers than among higher-status, Protestant, and rural citizens. Such people show little partisan or ideological involvement, but they can sometimes make a difference in what government does.

4. ***Communalists.*** Another 20 percent of the population have little involvement in electoral politics apart from voting, but they do engage in group and community activities with the aim of solving social problems. This group is highly involved in politics, but decidedly nonpartisan and non-conflictual in its orientation. It is very much an upper-status group socially and economically, predominantly white, Protestant, and more small-town and rural than urban.

---

[55] Ibid.
[56] National Opinion Research Center, *General Social Surveys,* 1983–1987.
[57] Verba and Nie, *Political Participation in America,* pp. 56–81. If a particular characteristic is not mentioned, the group is about average in that respect.

5. ***Campaigners.*** In sharp contrast to the preceding group, this 15 percent of the population engages in little group activity but much campaign activity. This pattern stems in part from a highly partisan and more conflictual orientation to politics. The group tends to be of higher status, but blacks and Catholics are also campaigners, as are urban and suburban dwellers.

6. ***Complete activists.*** About 11 percent of the population do it all: voting, contacting, group activities, and campaigning. This is a group highly attuned to politics, predominantly upper-status and middle-aged.

What difference does it make that different groups tend to participate in different ways? Public officials are bombarded with messages from the public and people claiming to represent the public. Public officials have preconceptions and make judgments about the forms of political participation they need to be most attentive to. Because different kinds of people tend to participate in numerous ways, officials get varying impressions of public opinion depending on the forms of participation to which they pay attention. A senator who

During the 1992 presidential campaign, Ross Perot inspired thousands of people to work at the local level on his behalf. His supporters were successful in collecting enough signatures on petitions to place his name on the ballot as an independent candidate in all 50 states. Shown here are Perot volunteers about to deliver boxes of signed petitions to one state's election officials on May 11, 1992.

focuses on constituency service by reading all the mail from parochial participants will get a different sense of the public's mind than one who hobnobs
with campaign workers and financial supporters. The people staging a sit-in in
front of a congressional representative's district office have very different things
on their minds from those who pulled the lever in the voting booth a couple
of Novembers earlier. For politicians assessing public opinion, the medium of
participation in large measure determines the message. What is distinctive about
political participation in America becomes clearer when compared with participation in other countries (see Figure 5.4).

The Impact of Political Participation

Does political activity really make any difference? The stereotypical notion of
democracy is that the people's wishes become the law of the land. However, the
democratic process cannot be that simple. On some issues, many people do not

FIGURE 5.4
Differences in Participation: A Comparative Perspective

Question: Of the following freedoms, which two do you consider the most
fundamental?

■ Vote in national elections   ■ Contact extra local official   ☐ Ever worked
                                  on personal matter   for party

■ Vote in local elections   ■ Active member of group   ☐ Attend political
                                                                     meetings or rallies

■ Contact local official   ☐ Work through
  on personal matter   community group   * Question not asked

As in most democracies, voting is the predominant form of participation in the United
States, even if it is not as common as in some other democracies. Americans are particu-
larly inclined to try to solve community problems by joining or working through groups.
They also get involved in political campaign activities, but they tend not to use contact
with public officials as a way of resolving difficulties in their personal matters.   *SOURCE:*
Sidney Verba, Norman H. Nie, and Jae-on Kim, *Participation and Political Equality: A Seven-Nation
Comparison* (Cambridge, England: Cambridge University Press, 1978), pp. 58–59.

know what they want. Even if they do, they may not be moved to express their preferences via the political process. Politicians, whether they are presidents, Senate or House members, or Supreme Court justices, may be attentive to what the "public" wants, but that is rarely the only factor they take into account. First of all, there are many publics, not just one. Further, there are constitutional constraints, legal constraints, budgetary constraints, foreign policy constraints on domestic policy, and domestic policy constraints on foreign policy, to name just a few.

Little wonder, then, that most studies of the relationship between public opinion and public policy have found the connection to be a relatively loose one.[58] Public opinion is usually sufficiently amorphous, officials' perceptions of it sufficiently cloudy, and more tangible pressures sufficiently strong that officials are not severely constrained by it. But when there is a clearly expressed body of opinion on a salient issue, the relationship between public opinion and public policy can be substantial.[59] For one example, growing public concern over drugs in the late 1980s led politicians to move antidrug legislation to the top of the agenda. For another example, the much-publicized oil spill from the tanker *Exxon Valdez* into Prince William Sound on the Alaska coast in 1989 re-energized the flagging environmental movement and sparked a flurry of environmental legislation in the early 1990s.

The Rationality of Political Participation

Does it make sense to participate politically? Thirty-five years ago, Anthony Downs pioneered a new field of political analysis in an important and influential book called *An Economic Theory of Democracy*.[60] He examined political activity in terms of the so-called **rational actor model:** The citizen rationally weighs the costs and the benefits of participating. If the benefits exceed the costs, the citizen participates; if not, the citizen does not. Focusing on voting, Downs pointed out that getting registered, keeping informed, and going to the polls all take a substantial amount of time. The benefits, by contrast, are actually quite low: What politicians from one party or the other actually do after an election may not be very different from what their opponents would have done. Even more important, one individual's vote is very unlikely to determine whether his or her favored candidate wins. These factors make the expected benefit of voting relatively small.

A similar analysis could be made of most other individual political actions. The costs weighed against the low probability of any benefit make individual political actions appear to be of dubious rationality. One possible exception is Verba and Nie's "parochial participation." With a narrow personal objective and

---

[58] Perhaps the most famous study is Warren E. Miller and Donald E. Stokes, "Constituency Influence in Congress," *American Political Science Review* 57 (1963): 45–56.

[59] Benjamin I. Page and Robert Y. Shapiro, "Effects of Public Opinion on Policy," *American Political Science Review* 77 (1983): 175–190, show how changes in public policy between 1935 and 1979 in the United States related to changes in public opinion, particularly when there were large and enduring changes in public opinion on salient issues.

[60] New York: Harper & Row, 1957.

the expenditure of a fair amount of effort directed toward a particular decision maker, the individual may stand a fair chance of achieving success.[61] Collective activities may also be more effective. Joining together allows costs to be shared and resources to be pooled. All other things being equal, many citizens will probably be more influential than one.

Finally, even political protest may prove to be a rational strategy. Minority and dissident groups often lack political clout because they lack resources and thus cannot afford the costs of participation. One political scientist has called this "the **problem of the powerless**."[62] One rational strategy is to attract the attention of those with resources and draw them into the cause. A minimal expenditure of resources is required to engage in unusual or dramatic activities, such as sit-ins and demonstrations, that call public attention to the plight of the protesters. It is, to borrow one apt description, the use of "protest as a political resource."[63]

Summary

1. Public opinion is complicated because there is not one public, but many, and because it varies over time and in intensity and sophistication. Americans differ widely in their interest in and information and sophistication about politics; most of them have relatively little day-to-day concern, knowledge, or real understanding about what goes on in the political world. Americans do agree on certain basic values. However, they disagree about exactly what many of these values mean in particular circumstances and about political ideology.

2. Political socialization is the process by which young Americans are taught about political life in the United States. Through various processes of socialization, young people acquire the information and the ability to reason about politics. The values that they draw on as political actors are learned from their parents, schools, peers, and the mass media.

3. The mass media are an important agent of political socialization. Newspapers, magazines, radio, and, most of all, television influence people's political attitudes and actions, primarily by focusing public attention on particular issues. A major concern is bias in the media, owing to both journalists' personal biases and structural biases inherent in the reporting process.

4. Americans involve themselves in politics in many ways for a variety of reasons. Involvement can range from simply following politics and voting to intense immersion in campaigns, community activities, or more dramatic forms of participation such as protest marches, sit-ins, and demonstrations. But the impact of participation on policy is often weak, and much political participation is hard to justify in purely rational terms.

---

[61] Verba and Nie, *Political Participation in America*, pp. 104–106.
[62] James Q. Wilson, "The Strategy of Protest: Problems of Negro Civic Action," *Journal of Conflict Resolution* 3 (September 1961): 291.
[63] Michael Lipsky, "Protest as a Political Resource," *American Political Science Review* 62 (1968): 1144.

Key Terms

public opinion (p. 126)
political socialization (p. 137)
explicit teaching (p. 138)
process (of socialization) (p. 138)
social learning theory (p. 138)
transfer theory (p. 138)
cognitive development theory
    (p. 138)
agent (of socialization) (p. 139)
peer group (p. 140)
political self (p. 140)
mass media (p. 142)
fifth branch (p. 142)
Federal Communications Commission
    (p. 144)
equal-time rule (p. 144)
fairness doctrine (p. 144)

two-step flow (p. 146)
opinion leader (p. 146)
impact of the visual (p. 149)
political participation (p. 150)
political efficacy (p. 150)
sense of duty (p. 150)
party identification (p. 150)
civil disobedience (p. 154)
passive resistance (p. 154)
inactives (p. 155)
voting specialists (p. 155)
parochial participants (p. 155)
communalists (p. 155)
campaigners (p. 156)
complete activists (p. 156)
rational actor model (p. 158)
problem of the powerless (p. 159)

Readings for Further Study

Classic works on public opinion include Walter Lippmann's *Public Opinion* (New York: Macmillan, 1960) and one of the first major reports on survey research into public opinion, *Voting: A Study of Opinion Formation in a Presidential Campaign,* by Bernard R. Berelson, Paul F. Lazarsfeld, and William N. McPhee (Chicago: University of Chicago Press, 1954). Paul Abramson's *Political Attitudes in America* (San Francisco: Freeman, 1983) provides a more recent overview. Perhaps the major contributor to our understanding of basic American political values is Herbert McClosky, who has written (with Alida Brill) *Dimensions of Tolerance* (New York: Russell Sage, 1983) and (with John Zaller) *The American Ethos* (Cambridge, Mass.: Harvard University Press, 1984). Although oriented more toward comparative than American politics, *Political Socialization,* 2d ed. (Boston: Little, Brown, 1977), by Richard E. Dawson, Kenneth Prewitt, and Karen S. Dawson, provides a good overview of the topic of political socialization.

Journalists and their work in the political area are the subjects of Edward Jay Epstein's *Between Fact and Fiction: The Problems of Journalism* (New York: Random House/Vintage Books, 1975). Timothy Crouse, *The Boys on the Bus* (New York: Random House, 1972), is a case study of journalists in the 1972 presidential contest. A broader treatment is Ronald Berkman and Laura W. Kitch, *Politics in the Media Age* (New York: McGraw-Hill, 1986). For the role of television particularly, consult Austin Ranney, *Channels of Power: The Impact of Television on American Politics* (New York: Basic Books, 1983), and Shanto Iyengar and Donald R. Kinder, *News That Matters* (Chicago: University of Chicago Press, 1987). Perhaps the best overall empirical study of political participation in all its facets is *Political Participation in America: Political Democracy and Social Equality* (New York: Harper & Row, 1972), by Sidney Verba and Norman Nie.

6 Interest Groups and Political Parties

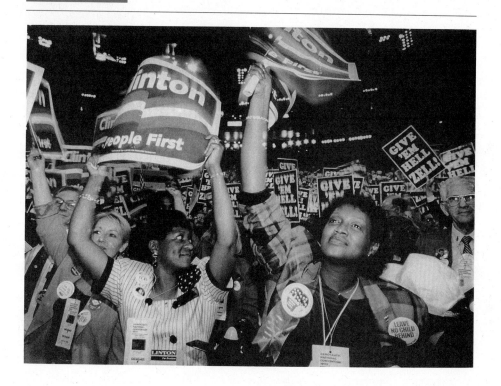

People get involved in politics not just as individuals but also in groups. This chapter examines the uniquely important role that two kinds of groups, interest groups and political parties, play in the American political system. The first part focuses on interest groups, their activities, and the reasons behind differences in their effectiveness. These ideas set the stage for a discussion of some of the major interest groups on the American political scene today and an evaluation of the role that interest groups play. The second part focuses on parties, which differ from interest groups in that political parties run candidates for public office. By trying to elect members to office, the party serves a variety of important political functions, for example, channeling and clarifying political consensus and conflict, training political leaders, and organizing elections and government. The American parties form a loosely organized two-party system. And it is a system in transition. Are the parties in trouble? What does the future hold for them? These questions are considered in this chapter.

Interest Groups in American Politics

Interest groups are associations of people who hold common views and who work together to influence what government does. Their interest is in a position, benefit, or advantage (such as favorable treatment under the tax laws) that they want to protect and perhaps enlarge. Interest groups look out for their members' political interests by campaigning for policies that promote their goals and by opposing policies that work against those goals. The American Federation of Labor–Congress of Industrial Organizations (AFL–CIO), one of the largest groups of unionized labor in the nation, obviously seeks to win favorable wage and job benefits from companies employing its members, but it also exists to ensure that government protects its unionizing activities and adopts policies on issues such as trade, interest rates, and education that promote the well-being of its members.

Interest groups have been a prominent feature of American politics since the earliest years of the Republic. During the thick of the public debate over the adoption of a new constitution in 1787, James Madison wrote in *Federalist* No. 10 about the divisions he saw as naturally developing in a society:

> A zeal for different opinions concerning religion, concerning government, and many other points. . . . have, in turn, divided mankind into parties, inflamed them with mutual animosity, and rendered them much more disposed to vex and oppress each other than to cooperate for the common good . . . . The regulation of these various and interfering interests forms the principal task of modern legislation and involves the spirit of party and faction in the necessary and ordinary operations of government.

Compared to other countries, interest groups in the United States play a particularly prominent role in political life. Chapter 5 reported Verba and Nie's finding that roughly 30 percent of Americans (communalists and complete activists) engage in group activities and that joining and working through groups to solve community problems is more common in the United States than in other democracies. It is not surprising, therefore, that scholars studying the American social and political system have focused on interest groups as a uniquely important element in American life. As noted in "Politics and Ideas: Pluralism and Elitism," many see the group as the basic building block of American political life. Perhaps the dominant view is of America as a **pluralist democracy:** American society is made up of many different groups, each looking to secure its members' interests.

Politics and Ideas

Pluralism and Elitism

Pluralism is one of the fundamental ideas of American politics. But it is hard to appreciate this unique American contribution to political thought without understanding a little about the political perspective with which it so sharply contrasts. **Elitism** holds that power in a society is concentrated in the hands of a small group of powerful people, a ruling class. This "elite" is often seen as exercising its power in ways that work to its own benefit and to the disadvantage of those whom it rules, the "masses." Other commentators portray elites as more benevolent, using their power to improve the lot of the less fortunate and to promote democratic values. The major American contributor to elitist theory was C. Wright Mills.[a] He saw real power in the United States as concentrated in the hands of the highest political, military, and corporate leaders. Mills did not argue for malevolent conspiracy. Rather, he saw the leaders of these institutions as coming from similar backgrounds, sometimes trading positions, interacting with one another, and therefore tending to hold similar values. Foremost among them was a belief in a strong and stable society.

Pluralism, in contrast, sees power as dispersed among many different centers of power, the leaders of various groups that make up society: labor organizations, professional associations, veterans, industries, and the like. Sometimes these centers of power are in agreement, but other times they are not. In any case, collective action is difficult without a reasonable amount of consensus among the groups about what should be done. This need for consensus compels politics to be moderate and stable. For example, laws passed since the early 1970s to reduce harmful automobile emissions were not imposed on the nation by a single small elite. The standards represent not a "perfect" solution but a compromise among many groups: environmentalists, health care specialists, the elderly, automobile manufacturers and dealers, labor unions, and petroleum companies.

What evidence of a power elite do you see in American society? Who is in it? To what ends does it use its power? What evidence do you see of pluralism in American society? What are the dominant groups? How do they use their power?

[a] *The Power Elite* (Oxford: Oxford University Press, 1956).

The principal task of government is therefore one of managing the interplay of group interests.

Why American society and politics should be so group-conscious is hard to say. Probably the best explanation is that America is the coming together of so many diverse groups—the "**melting pot**" of different races, nationalities, religions, cultures, and languages—that the variety itself constantly calls attention to the existence and the activities of groups. Beyond being one of the most universally identified features of American politics and society, interest groups are also among the most controversial. Interest groups have long been praised as one of the most important contributors to the success of American democracy. Yet, particularly as they have become more visible, sophisticated in their tactics, and powerful, interest groups are now sometimes condemned as one of the greatest threats to the continuing viability of the American political system. These are concerns to which we will return later.

Characteristics of Interest Groups

A stunning variety of organizations fits under the general definition of *interest group.* The different forms and features that interest groups assume can have an impact on a group's political effectiveness. Of course, no determinant of effectiveness is absolute. A group's influence must be measured relative to the groups with which it contends. Several major characteristics distinguish interest groups and affect their influence.

One of the most obvious is size. Interest groups vary dramatically in size. All other things being equal, the bigger the group, the more effective it is likely to be. Large groups can mobilize more members, raise more money to support lobbying activities and favored political candidates, and swing more votes in an election. As will be seen shortly, being big is not an unequivocal advantage for an interest group. But given a democracy's reliance on plurality and majority decision making, it is generally better than being small. Sometimes, when an interest group is large or a number of interest groups band together in a common cause, the result is referred to as a **movement,** as in the civil rights movement, the environmental movement, or the feminist movement.

Interest groups vary in membership procedures. Some groups enroll members formally, as when labor unions ask workers to join and pay dues. Other groups rest on a more informal notion of membership in which people just think of themselves as belonging. People may never go to church but nevertheless think of themselves as Catholics. Even this informal sense of membership can vary: Some groups evoke in their membership a very strong sense of identification with the group, whereas others do so only weakly. For still other groups, membership is not even a choice of the individual involved—people belong by the fact of having a particular characteristic. Blacks and women are often identified as important interest groups, but most blacks and most women belong to no race- or gender-based organization. They may not even think of themselves as belonging to some large group. Rather, they are labeled as a member of the group simply because they possess a particular biological characteristic. Generally speaking, the stronger the bonds of the individual members to the group, the more effective the group will be.[1]

Groups also differ in how well they are organized. The success of an interest group in advancing its interests depends in some measure on how well it is organized. A strong network of communication and control can amplify the power of one group, whereas poor internal organization and an inability to coordinate common efforts can dissipate the influence of another. Groups also differ in how democratic they are. Some groups are run as virtual autocracies, with the leadership exerting almost dictatorial control over the group, and others are very democratic. The relationship between how democratic a group is and its effectiveness is an uncertain one. Groups run democratically may gain in effectiveness from the additional commitment that broad membership participation engenders as long as

---

[1] The ideas in this section and the next are drawn in part from the seminal discussion of group influences in politics in Angus Campbell, Philip E. Converse, Warren E. Miller, and Donald E. Stokes, *The American Voter* (New York: Wiley, 1960), pp. 295–332.

there is substantial consensus in the group. But when a lack of consensus hinders decision making in the group, the group may suffer from a lack of common purpose. Conversely, groups run by narrow elites may benefit from singleness of purpose but suffer a lack of support if members feel estranged from the leadership.

How connected a group is to politics can also affect its influence. Some interest groups have little if any connection to politics. They are generally not concerned with political issues or involved in political activity. The town bowling league rarely has anything to do with politics. Indeed, it would probably suffer as an organization if it became embroiled in partisan political struggles. Its political significance lies in its potential to become politically active should its interests somehow be threatened in the political arena. Legislation to outlaw bowling as an immoral pastime would undoubtedly inspire it to take up the cudgels of politics. However, under normal circumstances it stands completely aside from the political fray. Other interest groups exist solely to pursue political ends. A political action committee, about which more will be said later, exists in most cases solely for the purpose of channeling money to political candidates sympathetic to the interests of the group. Between these two extremes reside many organizations that are involved in politics to a greater or lesser degree. The more closely a group is tied to political issues, personalities, and organizations, the more likely it is to be effective politically.

Finally, groups differ in terms of their agreement with what seem to be mainstream views of society. Some groups pursue a course outside the American mainstream—for example, the American Nazi party to the right of it and the Communist party to the left of it. Where a group stands in relation to the consensus of American politics has considerable effect on how influential it will be. The most passionate, best-organized interest group in the country will make little headway if it pursues policies that are far off the beaten track of American politics. Groups that argue for complete nationalization of health care, for example, are likely to make less headway than those that argue for modest reform in the current system.

What Interest Groups Do

Interest groups engage in a broad range of activities to protect and advance the well-being of their members. Foremost among them is their attempt to influence public opinion. Many interest groups try to create public support or sympathy for their political goals. The major channel for accomplishing this is the mass media. When a group's political interests are threatened, representatives of the group use the media to make the group's views known. Interviews on radio and television news broadcasts, quotations in newspaper and magazine articles, letters to the editor, and essays for newspaper op-ed pages are all tools of influence for interest groups. In recent years interest groups have developed the use of an individual (as opposed to mass) medium to influence public opinion. This is the **direct mail** method, in which modern computer technology is used to generate thousands of personally addressed letters soliciting support and financial contributions from potentially sympathetic citizens.

Interest groups, of course, are involved in the electoral process through the

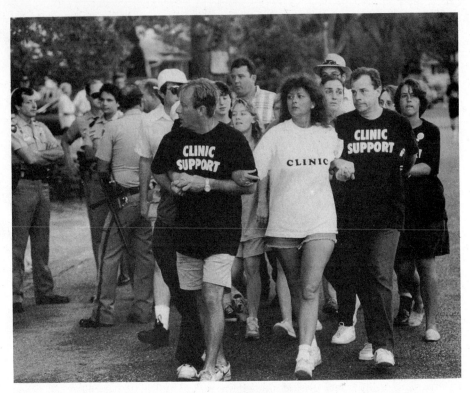

Some activists hope to influence public policy through dramatic, attention-grabbing events, such as this protest at an abortion clinic in Wichita, Kansas, in August 1991. Supporters of the clinic lead a woman past demonstrators from Operation Rescue, a pro-life group.

votes their members cast. More important, interest group members can work in the campaigns of their favored candidates. In recent years interest groups have been deeply involved in the financing of political campaigns, usually through **political action committees** or PACs. These are organizations devoted to channeling money from members of interest groups to political candidates sympathetic to the groups' policy preferences. By law, PACs must register with the Federal Election Commission (FEC), have at least 50 contributors, and make contributions to at least five candidates for federal office. No contributor can give any one PAC more than $5000, and no PAC can give any one candidate more than $5000 per election. Individuals are limited in their total contributions to candidates and committees to $25,000, but there is no limit on how much PACs may raise or give in total. Nor is there any limit on the total amount that a candidate can accept from different PACs. In addition to making direct contributions to candidates, PACs may also spend as much money as they want on independent activities in behalf of one or more candidates, usually purchasing advertising in the broadcast or print media.

PACs blossomed as a result of the **Federal Election Campaign Act of 1974,** which was an attempt to prevent the misuse of campaign funds brought to light in the Watergate scandal. A few PACs existed previously, but the 1974 act, by setting limits of $1000 on individual contributions and $5000 on group contributions, made group contributions more attractive and led to a proliferation of PACs. From 1974 to 1991, the number of PACs increased from 100 to about 4200 (see Figure 6.1). During the same period the amount of money contributed to federal candidates by PACs rose from about $10 million to over $150 million. PACs have become a controversial issue in American politics, with many questioning whether the post-Watergate reforms have not been a cure worse than the disease.

Lobbying, the attempt to influence the shape of legislation emanating from the U.S. Congress and other political decision-making bodies, has traditionally been a mainstay of interest group activity. Lobbying involves more than just hobnobbing with legislators. In many cases, lobbyists are a major source of reliable information for them. Lobbyists provide published materials and advisory letters and testify before congressional committees. They sometimes become deeply involved in the actual process of writing legislation by collaborating with members of Congress

FIGURE 6.1
The Proliferation of PACs, 1974–1991

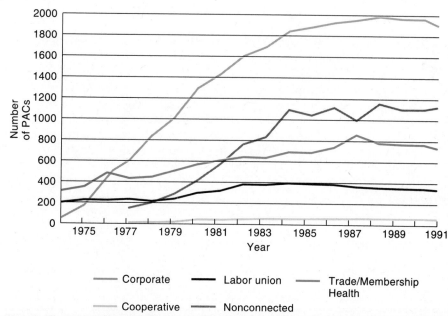

The number of political action committees has soared since the post–Watergate campaign reforms made them the preferred vehicle for channeling money from interest group members to political candidates. *SOURCE:* Federal Election Commission Press Release, January 20, 1992.

and their staffs on the drafting of bills or amendments. In some cases, they may even draft legislation themselves and pass it on to a senator or representative willing to introduce it on the floor. Modern lobbyists are a far cry from the shady figures of folklore. Some are among the most highly paid, respected, and influential figures in Washington.

The idea of lobbying extends beyond the corridors and offices of Capitol Hill. The effect of a law depends not just on how the legislation is written but also on how it is translated into action. Therefore, interest group representatives keep close watch on the rules and regulations set by the many agencies of the executive branch of government and the various independent regulatory commissions. When group interests appear to be threatened, representatives swing into action: They publicize the potential threat, mobilize group and public opinion, meet with agency officials, and ask legislators sympathetic to the "true intent" of the original legislation to intercede with the erring bureaucrats. Interest group representatives are so closely involved with legislators and administrators in the making and implementation of public policy that this threesome has come to be called the **iron triangle** of American politics.

Traditionally, the American judiciary has been seen as isolated from external political pressures. However, a more realistic appraisal is that the courts, like the other branches of government, are susceptible to the influence of interest groups in several ways. First, interest groups can affect the selection of judges who sit on state and federal benches. Most prominently, when the president nominates someone to fill a vacancy on the Supreme Court, interest groups line up to express their views to the Senate Judiciary Committee. For example, pro- and anti-abortion rights groups and women's groups angered by Anita Hill's charges of sexual harassment lobbied vigorously after Clarence Thomas was nominated for the high court in 1991 (see Chapter 11). Second, interest groups can play a role in the judicial process as parties in cases brought before the courts, either as litigants themselves or in **class action suits.** These allow litigation to be brought on behalf of a large number of individuals without any formal connection other than their sharing a grievance against another party. Third, interest groups can encourage individuals to bring legal action and provide the financial, legal, and moral support they need to do so. Fourth, interest groups can formally make their views known to the courts even in cases in which they are not themselves parties. This is done by filing an *amicus curiae* ("friend of the court") **brief,** in which a group offers "friendly" advice about how to decide a case.

Major Interest Groups

Americans belong to a myriad of interest groups. As noted, some are members of more than one group. *The Encyclopedia of Associations,* which confines itself to formal organizations, lists almost 22,000 different groups. There is even a lobby for lobbyists: the American League of Lobbyists. Taking into account all the un-counted formal groups and the multitude of informal groups, there are tens of thousands more. Interest groups can be categorized by their characteristics, goals, tactics, and degree of success. Major groups usually fit into economic, social, religious, ideological, or issue categories. Table 6.1 shows the major concerns of different types of interest groups and gives some examples of each.

Economic Groups   Interest groups frequently form around economic issues. In *Federalist* No. 10, Madison said, "The most common and durable source of factions has been the various and unequal distribution of property." The various ways in which people gain their livelihood lead to great diversity in the array of groups that form.

Business groups are among the most powerful of all interest groups. Perhaps business's most prominent advocate is the Chamber of Commerce of the United States, which pursues influence efforts on a broad front. It engages in extensive

TABLE 6.1
Types of Major Interest Groups

Type	Concerns	Examples
Economic	Business, labor, agriculture, and professions	National Association of Manufacturers; American Federation of State, County and Municipal Employees; American Bar Association; American Farm Bureau Federation
Social	Gender, race, and ethnic discrimination; economic advancement	National Organization for Women; National Association for the Advancement of Colored People; Mexican-American Legal Defense and Educational Fund; American Indian Movement
Religious	Religious freedom; values reflected in public policy	U.S. Catholic Conference; National Council of Churches; American Jewish Committee; Mennonite Central Committee
Ideological	Political impact of specific public policies	Americans for Democratic Action; People for the American Way; Heritage Foundation; National Committee for an Effective Congress
Single-Issue	Narrow agenda; limited political goals	Environmental Defense Fund; National Right-to-Life Committee; National Abortion Rights Action League
Public Interest	Broadly defined consumer and general welfare goals	Common Cause; Public Citizen; Consumers Union of the United States; Equal Justice Foundation; League of Women Voters

The table includes only a few of the thousands of groups that could be listed. A group may be of more than one type, as happens when economic groups make statements on social and ideological questions.

grass-roots lobbying by encouraging its members across the country to contact their elected officials about issues of concern. However, its effectiveness is sometimes diminished because the breadth of its membership makes it difficult to take stands that are satisfactory to all its members.

Depending on their special concerns, business interests have combined into all sorts of other organizations. Large manufacturing companies, for example, have come together in the National Association of Manufacturers. A vast array of industrywide trade associations, such as the American Iron and Steel Institute and the American Gas Association, represent more particular interests. At the other end of the spectrum is small business, the hundreds of thousands of small manufacturing concerns, neighborhood TV repair shops, and "mom and pop" grocery stores. The National Federation of Independent Business is one of the best-known small-business-oriented groups. Particular professions are represented by important organizations such as the American Medical Association (the leading organization of doctors), the National Association of Realtors, and the American Bar Association. Business groups do not always speak with one voice because political issues sometimes pit one business interest against another. For example, in the fall of 1992 the major television networks and their local affiliates won out over cable system operators when Congress passed a bill imposing new regulations on the cable TV industry.

When people think of labor as an interest group, they usually think first of its more visible side, labor as organized into unions. Individual unions themselves function as independent interest groups. The International Ladies Garment Workers Union, the Teamsters, and the American Federation of State, County and Municipal Employees are just a few of the many unions recognized as politically active. The American Federation of Labor–Congress of Industrial Organizations (AFL–CIO) is an umbrella organization of unions with a total membership of approximately 13.2 million that spearheads political activity on behalf of organized labor. Organized labor was once seen as a monolithic mainstay of the Democratic coalition. But in recent years its influence has diminished, primarily because the share of the labor force belonging to unions has dropped considerably in the last 40 years.

Labor has another side, less visible but numerically much larger than the unionized contingent. The majority of American working people do not belong to unions. In fact, workers in the new high-technology industries are much less likely to be unionized than workers in the old smokestack industries they are supplanting. The nonunion workers' lack of organization limits their political influence. Although some of their interests are advanced by their more organized counterparts, their opportunities for political representation are often limited to the actions of their individual members.

Farmers have long been a potent force in American politics. Even today agriculture is a huge industry. Long-standing organized groups include the American Farm Bureau Federation and the National Grange. They lobby furiously as Congress, once every five years, revises the rules governing agricultural subsidies. But dwindling numbers and hard economic times have conspired to reduce the political power of the agricultural interests. In 1930 more than 25 percent of all Americans lived on farms; by 1988 the number had fallen to only about 2 percent. Such pressures have spawned some more radical and aggressive farm groups, such as the National Farmers Organization (NFO) and the American Agricultural Movement (AAM). The heyday of the farm lobby is over, but agriculture remains a sector that cannot be ignored.

Social Groups Birth, not choice, determines membership in some interest groups. One of these groups, women, composes one of the largest potential interest groups in the United States. Slightly more than half of the American population are women, but relatively few belong to politically relevant women's organizations. The most prominent organization is the National Organization for Women (NOW), which presses for economic and political equality of women and, particularly, freedom of choice on abortion. NOW has only about 160,000 actual members, fewer than one out of every 750 American women. Within such a group, the sense of identification can run strong, although the feminist consciousness does not seem to run strong in the female population as a whole.

The women's movement is closely tied to politics in that many of its goals relate to political issues. Ties have also been strengthened by the increasing number of female candidates for public office. For many years the legitimacy of female

Lobbyists attempt to influence members of Congress in many ways. Here, Representative Patricia Schroeder (D-Colo.) shares a laugh on the Capitol steps with Nancy Zirkin of the American Association of University Women and Judith Litchman of the Women's Legal Defense Fund on September 30, 1992. Zirkin and Litchman were among the lobbyists for the family leave bill which President Bush later vetoed. Once Democrats reclaimed the White House in January 1993, Congress promptly passed the bill again, and President Clinton signed it into law.

involvement in politics was impugned by the old saying that "a woman's place is in the home," but recently women have increasingly been accepted as worthy participants in the American political process. Perhaps the best indication is the growing number of women who have been elected to public office in the past 20 years (see Figure 6.2). The nomination of the first major party female candidate for president or vice-president ever occurred in 1984, when Geraldine Ferraro was the Democratic candidate for vice-president. The 1992 elections saw unprecedented numbers of women running for and winning political office. Eleven women (including one incumbent) ran as major party candidates for the U.S. Senate and five (including the incumbent) won, increasing the number of women in the Senate from two to six. The number of women in the House jumped from 28 to 47, and the percentage of female state legislators increased from 18 percent to 20 percent, nearly double what it was 10 years earlier.

Certainly the most prominent of all biologically based interest groups in recent American history is the black population. Whereas blacks constitute only about one-tenth of the American population, they gain considerable influence from two sources: their strong sense of group identification and the close ties between the group and the world of politics. Shut out from the social and economic establishment, blacks had little recourse but to pursue advancement through the political system. That in itself has given their cause a special political legitimacy. Further, forceful black leaders like Dr. Martin Luther King, Jr., and the Reverend Jesse Jackson have not hesitated to spur blacks to political action. The *National Association for the Advancement of Colored People* (*NAACP*) remains perhaps the most visible black interest organization. Only a small percentage of blacks (less than 2 percent) belong to it. However, with a membership of about 400,000, it is the most widely recognized formal black organization in America.

FIGURE 6.2

Female, Black, and Hispanic National and State Legislators, 1969–1993

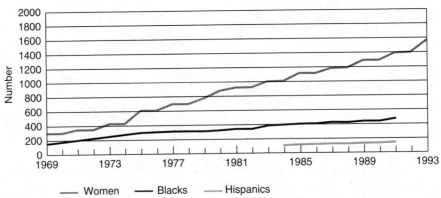

The increasing numbers of women, blacks, and Hispanics elected to public offices such as the U.S. Senate and House and state legislatures in the last 25 years demonstrate and result from the opening of the political process to members of these groups.   SOURCES: *Statistical Abstract of the United States,* 1992, pp. 267–8; and Center for the American Woman and Politics (CAWP), Eagleton Institute of Politics, Rutgers University. *Note:* Figures for blacks and Hispanics include some elected state officials.

Although the United States is far from a total resolution of its racial problems, the black civil rights movement has over the long term met with considerable success. This success is at least partly because the movement's goals are not an attack on fundamental values but, rather, a push for broader realization of traditional American social, political, and economic equality. In recent years, the major effort has been to get African-Americans to use their hard-won right to vote and get more blacks elected to public office. All told, the United States now has more than 7000 elected black officials[2] (see again Figure 6.2). After many years with no black U.S. senator, Carol Mosely Braun (D-Ill.) was elected in 1992. Moreover the number of blacks in the House rose significantly, from 25 to 38.

Another prominent ethnic group is the Hispanic segment of the American population: primarily Mexican-Americans, Cuban-Americans, and Puerto Ricans. Although Hispanics in the United States currently number about 20 million, they confront a situation similar to the one African-Americans faced 30 years ago. Like blacks, Hispanics lag in educational level and are only now developing a strong sense of collective political identity. Fewer Hispanic-Americans are registered to vote (only 36 percent of the 12.9 million Hispanics of voting age), and those who are registered do not always vote (29 percent, compared to the national average of 57 percent in 1988). Those who cast ballots do not necessarily vote for Hispanic candidates. Hispanics lack a cohesive national organization on the order of the NAACP. As a result, there are fewer elected Hispanic leaders (see Figure 6.2). Outside the Southwest and a few big cities, Hispanics are seldom recognized as a significant political bloc. However, the Hispanic people have considerable political potential. They are concentrated in a number of big states that can be critical to victory in a presidential election. Partly as a result, the number of Hispanics in the House jumped in 1992 from 10 to 17.

Religious Groups   Although the Constitution provides for separation of church and state, the religious freedom the Constitution also guarantees makes it virtually certain that religious groups will be active on a wide variety of political issues. This involvement has engendered some controversy. The **Christian Right,** as fundamentalist groups are also called, has worked for a constitutional amendment to allow prayer in the public schools, tax credits for private school tuition, and the teaching of creationism in public schools, and against the teaching of anything but abstinence in sex education and laws favoring the rights of women and homosexuals.

The religious right loomed as a major factor in American politics through the early 1980s, but its visibility receded in the late 1980s after revelations of sexual and financial misconduct by such well-known figures as Jim and Tammy Bakker and Jimmy Swaggart. However, since then conservative Christians have been working quietly but diligently around the country to elect their adherents to state and local offices and have virtually taken over the Republican party organization in several states. Perhaps the most prominent organization spearheading this ac-

---

[2] *Statistical Abstract of the United States,* 1990, pp. 257, 260.

tivity is television evangelist Pat Robertson's Christian Coalition. Other more socially liberal denominations such as the United Church of Christ—in effect, an emerging "Christian Left"—have involved themselves in controversies over arms control, human rights abroad (including apartheid in South Africa), and U.S. policy in central America, among others.

But no issue in recent years has drawn religious groups more into the political fray than abortion. The Catholic church and the Christian Right have both worked hard to make abortion a political issue through support of sympathetic candidates and demonstrations outside abortion clinics. A particularly dramatic example for the Roman Catholic church was its use of the threat of excommunication against Catholics who tolerate or even support abortion. Mobilized primarily around the issue of abortion, the Christian Right played a major role at the Republican convention in 1992, forcing an absolute ban on abortion into the party platform and casting Pat Robertson and the conservative political commentator Patrick Buchanan in prominent roles.

Ideological Groups   Some groups pursue an explicitly political agenda almost exclusively. When that agenda is broad, the group is characterized as an *ideological* one. Such groups typically have a clear philosophy of governmental action and evaluate public policy proposals in those terms. Perhaps the best example is the Americans for Democratic Action (ADA), a relatively small group with about 85,000 members that has long espoused a liberal perspective on American politics. It has thus become a beacon to those on the American left and a beast to those on the right. The ADA is perhaps best known for the ratings of members of the House and the Senate, which it publishes every year as a way of calling attention to individual legislators' fidelity to liberal values.

Single-Issue Groups   In contrast to the broad political agenda of the ideological groups, other groups have narrower agendas and more limited political goals. By far the most visible of all the narrow single-issue groups has been the anti-abortion or right-to-life movement. Groups such as the National Right-to-Life Committee, which claims some 7 million members, have been single-minded in their attempts to ban abortion. They regard it as the overriding issue of contemporary politics— a so-called litmus test of whether a candidate should be supported. The uncompromising position of anti-abortion groups has spawned some similarly uncompromising reactions from single-interest abortion rights groups. The most prominent among these groups is the National Abortion Rights Action League, which claims some 250,000 members.

Single-issue groups are a controversial political phenomenon. Advocates contend that there are indeed some overriding moral issues that people should rightly pursue to the exclusion of everything else. Others see single-issue groups as a threat to democracy because they refuse the compromise that helps to make a democratic system work.

Public Interest Groups   With so many interest groups vying for advantage in the political arena, it sometimes seems that everybody's political interests get served but the public's as a whole. Thus organizations have formed to represent broad-based notions of the public's interest. These groups focus on issues such as product safety and the effectiveness of government regulation of public utilities and industry. Perhaps the most prominent such group is Common Cause, the self-styled "citizens' lobby" founded in 1970. It has taken on a broad range of issues, including that of campaign financing.

Perspectives on Interest Groups

Given the visibility and the pervasiveness of interest groups in American democracy, it is not surprising that they evoke strong reactions from both the general public and political experts. Some citizens view interest groups in highly positive terms, as essential elements of a successful democracy. Others take a dimmer view, seeing them as a perpetual and inevitable danger to the common good.

Interest Groups as the Foundation of Democracy

Classical democratic theory demands that citizens be interested in politics, informed about politics, rational in their political judgments, and active in the political process. As Chapter 5 made clear, many people fall short of these expectations. The question is how American democracy can continue to function and even prosper in the face of this disparity.

Some observers see interest groups as the answer. As noted earlier, the United States is a pluralist society. Most Americans belong to at least one formal group as well as to a number of other groups. The leaders of these various interest groups act on behalf of their members to protect and advance their cause. Because there are so many groups, sheer force of competition prevents any single group or handful of groups from dominating the others. Thus every member of society has his or her interests protected without having to be politically active. Democracy functions via representation—not just formal representation via elected officials, but representation of individual citizens by the leaders of the interest groups.

Further, because most Americans belong to several groups, political disputes seldom run along the same lines. To illustrate, one woman may be a white Catholic homemaker, whereas her neighbor is a white Protestant public school teacher. The two will probably agree about property taxes and the Equal Rights Amendment but disagree about tuition tax credits for parents with children in private schools. Political scientists call this tendency for different coalitions to form on different issues **cross-cutting cleavage** and see it as a brake on polarizing conflict in society. These two elements, competition between interest groups and cross-cutting cleavages, contribute to an equitable and stable society. Indeed, some scholars laud the pluralistic character of American society as an essential factor in the success of its democratic system.[3]

---

[3] The leading advocate of this point of view is Robert A. Dahl. See, for example, his classic book *Who Governs?* (New Haven, Conn.: Yale University Press, 1961).

Not surprisingly, critics have found flaws in this flattering portrait of American politics. Not every citizen belongs in any meaningful way to a significant interest group. Leaders do not necessarily represent the best interests of all the group members. In fact, the structure of some interest groups may be very undemocratic. Also, pure competition cannot exist among all the interest groups in a society. Some groups are big and powerful and can dominate; others are small and weak and can be dominated. With what, after all, does a small and powerless interest group have to bargain? It is very hard for a group to enter into negotiations with nothing and emerge with something. So "pluralist democracy" may in reality turn out to be **interest group elitism.** The elites within interest groups pursue their own interests rather than their members' interests. Further, elite interest groups—the biggest and most powerful groups—pursue their interests at the expense of the small and powerless groups.

Interest Groups Versus the Public Interest

Interest groups are most widely reviled when they are seen as using the political process to achieve selfish objectives. A manufacturing group that resists regulation by the Consumer Product Safety Commission may claim that it is only defending the public's right to buy whatever it wants at the lowest possible price. The public may perceive the group instead as demanding a right to make money by producing shoddy and unsafe goods. This kind of spectacle is no doubt one of the greatest frustrations of democratic government and has caused many people to favor tighter regulation of lobbying and other interest group activities. But what is the "common good"? Who gets to define it? Should the common good never be impaired in the slightest, even to do a great good for a small number? Does a common good exist, in fact, apart from the outcome of the democratic process that defines it?

Interest group obstructionism of the majority will is something that looks indefensible until it is the observer's interests that the majority is about to trample on. A person might protest loudly when import quotas on automobiles make imported cars more expensive and push up prices of domestic models. Yet that same person would probably think differently if he or she worked in a Detroit auto assembly plant or owned a Ford dealership. The real quarrel of those who decry interest group activities may not be with interest groups but with the political processes that strike the balance between majority and minority interests.

Interest Group Gridlock

Pluralist theory envisions a myriad of interests doing battle in the political arena and the government emerging with policies that, although probably not ideal for any, are acceptable to all. But what if no consensus can be reached? Critics charge that a pluralistic system can arrive at a virtual state of paralysis, in which an overabundance of interest groups develops, each refusing to compromise. One commentator has called this situation **interest group gridlock,** analogous to the traffic gridlock that sometimes develops in large cities.[4] In an analogy to the clogged arteries that threaten many people's health, another commentator has characterized these problems as "demosclerosis," the political process clogged by the piling up of so many permanent commitments to interest groups that the government lacks the resources to deal with new problems that arise.[5] Interest group gridlock and demosclerosis may be stark warnings of the dangers of pluralism run amok. The hope of democracy is that good "traffic regulation" by public officials and a more moderate diet for interest groups can help to smooth the way for the successful development of public policy.

Political Parties

A **political party** is an organization that seeks to influence public policy by putting its own members into positions of governmental authority. In the United States and other democratic nations, where most important public officials are chosen by popular election, this means placing a party member's name on the ballot, identifying the candidate as a member of that party, and then working to elect the party member to the office. Parties and interest groups are alike in that their members may share common political views or objectives and may engage in collective political activities. They differ in that interest groups do not run their own candidates for public office. Further, there are many interest groups, each with narrower agendas, but there are just two major parties, each with a broader agenda.

What Parties Do

In the pursuit of elective office, parties can perform several important functions that help to bring order to the electoral process and coherence to government. First, by making themselves visible actors on the stage of politics and trying to gain public support, parties accomplish several important **socialization functions.** Because people tend to identify with political parties, parties provide a psychological hook that pulls people into the world of politics. Parties also help to structure people's perceptions of politics. They provide important cues to citizens as they perceive and try to make sense of the political world around them. Parties educate citizens about politics and mobilize them into political action. In their attempts to attract voters to their causes, parties tell voters about what is going on in politics, how it affects them, and why they should get involved. Finally, whereas candidates and issues come and go from one election to the next, parties tend to persist. By providing relatively fixed reference points in a changing political scene, parties help people keep their political bearings and thus help to maintain political and social stability.

---

[4] Robert J. Samuelson, "Interest Group Gridlock," *National Journal* (September 25, 1982): 1642.
[5] Jonathan Rauch, "Demosclerosis," *National Journal* (September 5, 1992): 1998–2003.

Winning elective office requires getting votes. Given the wide range of voters' interests, a single issue will probably not appeal to enough voters to win. The party, therefore, must put together a package of positions on a variety of issues that will attract sufficient numbers of voters. In doing so, parties accomplish four important **electoral functions.** The first is to integrate interests. It is unlikely that any one candidate will offer everything that every voter seeks. However, candidates who satisfy needs common to large numbers of voters will receive their support. In this way groups form, made up of people who agree on many but not all issues. Second, the set of alternatives voters can pick from is simplified. Because substantial numbers of voters find their views reflected by one or the other of the coalition candidates, fewer candidates are needed in the field. Third, the parties complement the legally established process for choosing public officials. By setting up procedures for determining who will represent a party in a campaign and for supporting these candidates in the election, parties fill important gaps in the selection process. Finally, parties are a prime means of recruiting and training political leaders. Parties provide many people with an entré into politics and opportunities to develop their political skills.

Once a political party achieves electoral victory, it confronts the task of governing. By trying to achieve what they have proposed during the campaign, parties accomplish two important **governmental functions.** They organize government and give coherence to governmental policy. Because the founders saw centralized political power as a threat to individual freedom, the Constitution dispersed power to avoid the tyranny of the majority. Power was broken up by function in the separation of powers and by geography in the federal system. Experience soon showed, however, that this fragmentation of power led to a lack of coordination, stagnation, and even paralysis in government. Political parties evolved as a new source of coordination in the political system. With like-minded individuals pursuing common objectives dispersed throughout the executive, legislative, and judicial branches of both the national and state governments, coherence and coordination were restored to policymaking.[6]

Further, parties help make government responsible to the people. Because parties are stable features on the American political scene, the electorate can reward a party that does a good job of governing and punish a party that does not. Thus, even though the public is not in a position to supervise every detail of governmental action, parties allow the public to exert some degree of oversight and control over what the government does.

Basic Characteristics of the American Party System

Political parties exist under almost every form of government. However, the particular shape a party system assumes varies from one country to another. In the United States, the party system is characterized by having just two major parties

---

[6] V. O. Key, *Politics, Parties, and Pressure Groups,* 5th ed. (New York: Crowell, 1964), p. 656.

Democrats in the 1992 campaign promised to reform the nation's health care system. Shortly after becoming president, Bill Clinton named his wife Hillary as the head of a task force to make recommendations to Congress on the delivery and financing of health care. Instantly the task force became the focus of dozens of interest groups representing virtually every aspect of health care in America.

and a loose relationship between the national, state, and local parties and the three components that make up the party: the formal party organization, the party in the electorate, and the party in the government.

A Two-Party System

From its beginnings, the United States has had a two-party system. Never have there been more than two large and enduring political organizations at the same time. Party fortunes, of course, have ebbed and flowed. At some times, minor parties have flourished. At other times, some people have feared that one party would rule the nation unchallenged. But always the minor parties have faded, the party with the overwhelming majority has faltered, or the opposition party has rebounded.

Why does this pattern consistently recur? One old saying is that "there are two political parties because there are two sides to every question." This explanation sounds good, but many political questions have more than two sides. Also, unless there are fewer sides to political questions in the United States than in other

Politics and Economics

Economic Status and Party Identification

Traditional wisdom portrays the Democrats as the party of the economically less well-off and the Republicans as the party of the more economically successful. How well does this image square with current reality? Figure 6A shows the relationship between party identification and family income in 1988. The most striking feature is the preponderance of independents at every income level. Regardless of income, a plurality of Americans see themselves as unaligned with either major party. Apart from that, the trends anticipated by the traditional image of the parties do appear. Far more of the poorest people are Democrats than Republicans, and considerably more of the

wealthiest people are Republicans than Democrats. However, a significant number of the poorest people are Republican, and an even larger number of the wealthiest people are Democrat. So economic status has some effect, but party choice in the United States is not made on grounds of economic self-interest alone.

Why is the Democratic party traditionally associated with the less well-off and the Republican party with the better-off? Why does party affiliation not divide more clearly along economic lines? That is, why are some poorer people Republicans and some richer people Democrats?

FIGURE 6A
Party Identification by Income, 1988

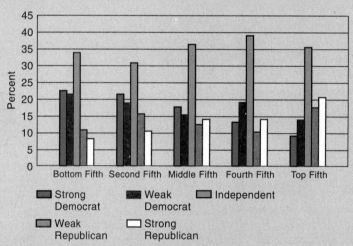

Independents have a plurality in every income category, but the balance tips in favor of the Democratic party in the lower income groups and in favor of the Republican party in the higher income groups. Nevertheless, a substantial percentage of poorer people identify with the Republican party and a substantial percentage of wealthier people identify with the Democratic party.   SOURCE: American National Education Study, 1988, Center for Political Studies, University of Michigan.

countries, every country should have a two-party system, and many of them do not.

Another old adage may come closer to the truth: "There are two political parties because there are two sides to every office—inside and outside." In the American system, where most offices are contested on an individual basis (i.e., one person wins a single office such as mayor or governor or congressional representative), winning usually requires simply getting more votes than anybody else. This is called **plurality election.** Plurality elections contrast with **majority elections,** where the victor must receive more than half of all the votes. A **runoff election** is required under a system of majority elections if more than two candidates run and none gets a majority. With plurality or majority elections, most electoral contests in the United States have a single winner and one or more losers—one "in" and one or more "outs." Because the only way for an outsider to displace an insider is to win more votes, the natural tendency is for political organizations to form around those in power and those out of power.

An alternative electoral system is **proportional representation,** whereby offices such as seats in a legislature are awarded in proportion to the percentage of votes a party receives. Proportional representation may encourage the growth of more than two parties because a party may place third or fourth in an election and still win seats. Proportional representation is relatively rare in the United States, but it is more common in other countries, such as France and Italy.

The plurality election system is not the only reason the United States has a two-party system. Undoubtedly other factors enter in as well, including the predominantly centrist distribution of opinion, the impact of history, and the absence of consistently intense ethnic and religious divisions that might lead to chronic political fragmentation. However, the electoral system has certainly played a significant role in shaping the basic structure of the American party system.

This discussion of the two-party system should not obscure the fact that **third parties** do have a place in the American political system. Figure 6.3 shows that they are not unusual. Although most third parties have been little more than temporary vehicles for a particular candidate or issue, they nevertheless have played an important role in influencing the actions of the major parties. They have raised issues that the major parties were eventually forced to address. For example, the abolitionist parties of the mid-nineteenth century forced slavery onto the agendas of the major political parties. Persistent advocacy of egalitarian ideas such as female suffrage, government regulation of big business, Social Security, and low-cost health care by the Populists, Progressives, and Socialists laid the groundwork for much of the New Freedom of Woodrow Wilson, the New Deal of Franklin Roosevelt, and the Great Society of Lyndon Johnson.

In a few cases, the presence of third parties in the field has tipped the balance from one of the major parties to the other. In 1912, in the middle of a long period of Republican dominance, former President Theodore Roosevelt's Bull Moose party garnered 27 percent of the popular vote and 88 electoral votes, siphoning off enough votes from the Republican incumbent William Howard Taft to give the Democrat Woodrow Wilson victory. (This was, by the way, the only time in American history that a third party actually outpolled one of the major parties in a presidential election.) In 1968 American Independent candidate George Wallace

FIGURE 6.3
American Political Parties Since 1789

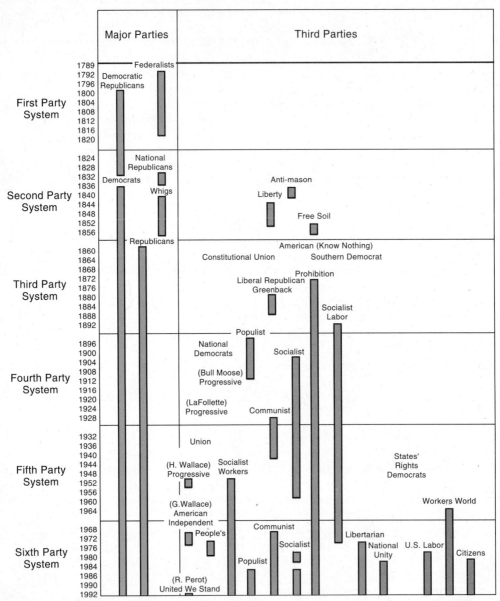

The chart indicates the years parties either ran presidential candidates or held national conventions. The life span for many political parties can only be approximated because parties existed at the state or local level before they ran candidates in presidential elections and continued to exist at local levels after they ceased running presidential candidates. For example 1992 saw nine other small parties running a candidate for president in at least one state. Only four candidates were on the ballot in all the states: Bill Clinton (Democratic), George Bush (Republican), Ross Perot (Independent), and André Marrou (Libertarian). SOURCES: *Congressional Quarterly's Guide to the U.S. Elections,* 2d ed. (Washington, D.C.: Congressional Quarterly, 1985), p. 224; *Congressional Quarterly Weekly Report,* November 5, 1988, p. 3184; Federal Election Commission, "1992 Official Presidential General Election Results," Press Release of January 14, 1993.

won 14 percent of the popular vote and 46 electoral votes, probably drawing off enough votes from Democrat Hubert Humphrey to give Republican Richard Nixon victory.

Finally, in 1992 independent presidential candidate Ross Perot, running under the banner of his United We Stand movement, garnered 19 percent of the popular vote, making his the most successful third-party movement in recent American history. Because Perot seemed to draw votes almost equally from Bush and Clinton, it is unlikely that he changed the outcome of the election. However, Perot participated in the three presidential debates and was instrumental in making deficit reduction and economic revival major issues in the campaign.

A Complex Party Structure

An American political party is not a single organization, but a broad family of related formal organizations and informal groupings. It is complex, not in the sense that it is particularly hard to understand, but in that it is made up of many different parts. Perhaps the most useful way to think about all these parts and the relationships between them is to imagine the party as being divided along two dimensions: a vertical dimension corresponding to the levels of government in the United States and a horizontal dimension corresponding to the different components that make up a party.

Parties and the Levels of Government: National, State, and Local Because party organizations tend to grow up and operate around institutions of government, it is only natural that their structure tends to parallel that of government. One of the most important divisions of government in the United States is the federal system. Just as the American government is divided into national, state, and local institutions, so also are parties divided into national, state, and local organizations and groupings. As in the government, the relationship among the levels is not a strictly hierarchical one. Each level retains some level of independence and autonomy from the others.

Parties and Their Components: Formal, Electoral, and Governmental Even at any one level of government, a political party is not just a single organization. Rather, it has at least three distinguishable sectors or components: the formal party organization, the party in the electorate, and the party in the government.[7] The **formal party organization** is the party narrowly construed, the part of the party that most people would think of if asked to say what a political party was. It consists of the people who actually work for the party as leaders or

---

[7] This distinction is another legacy of V. O. Key, Jr., originated in his *Politics, Parties, and Pressure Groups*, 5th ed. (New York: Crowell, 1964). It has now been widely adopted by students of the American party system. See, for example, Frank J. Sorauf and Paul Allen Beck, *Party Politics in America*, 6th ed. (Glenview, Ill.: Scott, Foresman, 1988).

followers, professionals or volunteers, members of committees or attenders of meetings.

The formal structure of American parties parallels the structure of federalism. Power is vested at both the national and state levels. Ultimate authority lies with the party's **national convention,** which meets prior to the presidential election every four years. Because political parties exist to contest elections, most of what the convention does is related to the upcoming presidential campaign: writing a **platform** (a statement of the party's proposed program) and selecting the party's candidates for president and vice-president. These activities are discussed in more detail in Chapter 7.

Some of the convention's activities have a more strictly organizational slant. It is the ultimate authority in setting the party's rules, and it formally designates the **national committee,** the permanent body that oversees the party's affairs on an ongoing basis. Each state's members on the national committee are usually picked by state party organizations in conventions or primaries. The national committee in turn formally elects the party chairperson. The national chairperson supervises the work of the headquarters staff, a role that has become more significant in recent years, for reasons to be seen shortly.

State and local parties for years were the bedrock of the American party system. In many areas this stemmed from the influence of state and local "political machines." A **political machine** is a political organization that recruits and controls its membership through the use of its governmental authority to bestow benefits on its supporters and withhold them from its opponents. This patronage included benefits such as government jobs, government contracts, and "favors." To gain benefits, people had to support the machine by voting for its candidates and campaigning for the machine. The great urban political machines, in large part, have faded from the American political scene, although the use of public power to perpetuate partisan dominance lives on in many municipalities and some states.

The structure of the state and local parties is in many respects similar to that of the national parties, with state party conventions and **state committees,** usually made up of representatives from the state's counties or congressional districts. The party typically elects a state chairperson, who is in charge of the day-to-day operations of the party. Underlying the statewide party organization is a hierarchy of county, city, ward (or district), and precinct committees and chairpersons. In some locales they constitute a formidable political force, while elsewhere the structure is moribund, with many of the positions not even filled.

There is more to a party than just its formal organization. A party includes, not in any formal sense, but psychologically and socially, the citizens out in the electorate who support it. This **party in the electorate** can be looked at in two different ways. At the individual level, the defining component of the connection of an individual to a party is **party identification,** "a psychological identification" or "sense of individual attachment to a party," independent of "legal recognition or even without a consistent [voting] record of party support."[8] Appropriate to the

---

[8] Campbell, et al., *The American Voter,* pp. 121–122.

definition, party identification has typically been measured simply by asking a person if "you think of yourself as a Republican, a Democrat, an Independent or what" and following up with questions on strength of feeling. Thus the party in the electorate is really defined by people saying whether or not they think of themselves as belonging to the party. Figure 6.4 shows how the distribution of party identification has varied over the last 40 years.

Individuals who identify with a party relate to it not just as individuals, but also as members of the various groups to which they belong. Parties, in other words, can be seen as coalitions of the various social, economic, regional, and religious groups. The Democratic party has traditionally been seen as the party of the working class, the rural areas, the South, and Catholics, whereas the Republican party has been seen as the party of the middle and upper classes, big business, and Protestants. The party in the electorate includes also these groups that are thought of as belonging to the **party's coalition.**

Finally, there is the **party in the government.** Once a party's candidates are elected, the elected officials (at least in theory) need to organize themselves and work together to implement the policies on the basis of which they campaigned. Thus the party in government consists of the elected candidates of a party— presidents, governors, mayors, senators, members of the House, state legislators, city council members. It also includes the organizations that they establish and leaders that they designate to help carry out their work. The most visible of these are the legislative party meetings (caucuses, as the Democrats call them, and conferences, as the Republicans call them), the congressional campaign committees, and the majority and minority leaders and whips. But the party in government

FIGURE 6.4
Party Identification of the American Electorate, 1952–1990

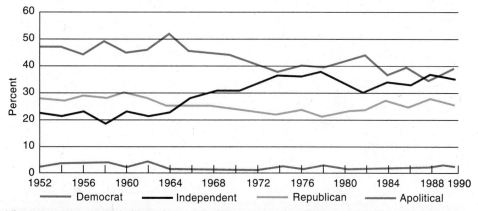

The Democratic party held a substantial edge in party identification from the 1950s into the 1970s, but this was eroded by an increasing percentage of independents in the 1960s and the beginning of a Republican resurgence in the 1980s. *SOURCE:* American National Election Studies, 1952–1990, Center for Political Studies, University of Michigan.

Congressional leaders are often leaders of their party as well. Robert Dole (R-Kan.) (as shown on the right) is the Minority Leader in the U.S. Senate and has used this highly visible position to advance the cause of the Republican party nationally. He has had experience in two presidential campaigns, having been the Republican candidate for vice president in 1976 and a contender for the Republican presidential nomination in 1988.

also includes the less visible and informal "executive party" created by presidents and governors who tend to appoint members of their own party to administrative positions and even the shadowy "judicial party" suggested by patterns of party-oriented bloc voting in some courts.[9]

American Political Parties: Past, Present, and Future

The health of the American party system has been one of the most talked-about political subjects over the last 25 years. To understand the current state of the American party system and what its future may be, it is necessary to understand a little about the history of the American party system.

---

[9] Sorauf and Beck, pp. 396–446.

Parties Past

Political parties emerged early in the history of the American republic and have existed ever since. American history up through 1968 can be divided into five major **party systems**[10] (see Figure 6.3). The **first party system** (1789–1824), which developed from the pre-revolutionary alignment of parties paralleling the British system of the period (conservative Tories and progressive Whigs), joined Federalists against Anti-Federalists. The two parties divided primarily on whether the new government should be relatively centralized and elite (the Federalist view) or decentralized and democratic (the Anti-Federalist view). The Federalist party faded away after 1800, but the Democratic Republicans, as the Anti-Federalists came to be called, continued on to govern through a period of comparatively little national political conflict between 1815 and 1825, called the Era of Good Feelings.

By the mid-1820s the weak framework of the Democratic Republican party began to fall apart. Andrew Jackson emerged from this factional conflict as the founder of the Democratic party, which continues as an active party today, making it the oldest party in the world. The Democrats confronted a new Whig party in the **second party system** (1824–1860). The Democrats were the party of lower-class rural and urban "working people" and old-fashioned machine politics, whereas the Whigs were the party of business and political reform. Slavery destroyed the Whig-Democratic party alignment; through the 1850s both parties split into northern and southern branches over the issue that would soon tear apart the nation as well.

Beginning in 1860, under the **third party system** (1860–1896), former Whigs, led by Abraham Lincoln of Illinois, combined with some progressive remnants of the northern Democrats to form the new Republican party, built on opposition to slavery, but also government as a promoter of commerce. The Democratic party receded into the Confederacy during the Civil War. After the war and the restoration of the union, the Democrats re-emerged on the national scene to compete vigorously with the Republicans for the favor of business. The pro-business tilt of the third party system fostered progressive and populist sentiment for more regulation of big business and protection of common people's interests.

These sentiments, fired by a series of disastrous recessions and depressions, came to a head in the election of 1896, when the populist Democrat William Jennings Bryan challenged the candidate of the business establishment, Republican William McKinley. The failure of the populist challenge marked the beginning of the **fourth party system** (1896–1932), throughout which the Republicans dominated the national political scene and allowed the capitalist system free reign. Only when former Republican president Teddy Roosevelt's progressive Bull Moose party split Republican ranks were the Democrats able to put their candidate, Woodrow Wilson, into the White House from 1912 to 1920.

---

[10] Walter Dean Burnham, "Party Systems and the Political Process," in *The American Party Systems*, eds. William Nisbet Chambers and Walter Dean Burnham (New York: Oxford University Press, 1967), p. 289.

The onset of the Great Depression in 1929, in part the result of the free hand allowed the free enterprise system, drove Republican president Herbert Hoover from office. Franklin Delano Roosevelt swept into the White House in 1932 on a flood tide of national discontent and despair. In a bold effort to use the power of the federal government to end the depression and restore economic prosperity, he ushered in a new era of governmental involvement in economic affairs and government responsibility for ensuring the people's basic well-being. He also initiated a period of Democratic dominance that constituted the **fifth party system** (1932–1968).

In each of these years—1824, 1860, 1896, 1932—a new party system evolved from an old one in a relatively short period of turmoil and change called "realignment." **Realignment** occurs when a reasonably stable pattern of party support based on a particular set of important political issues is replaced by a new pattern of party support based on a new set of issues. Because realignments are such landmark events in the American party system, scholars have devoted much effort to determining when and why they occur. They have identified a number of significant changes which seem to accompany realignment. Most notable among them is a period before each realignment in which the old party structure seems to fall apart, or **dealignment.** Why do realignments occur? As the preceding discussion suggests, the single most important factor may be the emergence of some new issue that cuts across the existing party lines and divides the electorate in some new way, for example, slavery in the third party system and the Great Depression and the role of the federal government in the economy in the fifth party system. Also, quite clearly, realignments have tended to come at approximately 36 year intervals.

Parties Present

Beginning in the mid-1960s, the fifth party system began to falter. This was most evident in the woes of the Democratic party, whose long-standing dominance began to unravel. Consistent with the pattern of a major partisan shift every 36 years, the Democratic party, which had won the White House in every election over the 36 years from 1932 to 1968 except 1952 and 1956—seven of nine elections—lost the 1968 election and over the next 20 years would win only one of five more. The only bright spot for the Democrats was that they did manage to hold on to their majorities in the House and Senate throughout the period, the one exception being that the Republicans gained a majority in the Senate from 1981 to 1987, primarily as a result of the Reagan victory in 1980.

That fact alone was sufficient to set political analysts abuzz. Dealignment was clearly underway. But while some saw realignment into a new Republican majority as in the offing, others worried that the party system was confronting an even more fundamental crisis—the possibility of complete collapse.

Certainly, beginning in the 1960s, both parties were beset by signs of deterioration. At the national level, the national party headquarters, the national chairperson, and the national committee seemed increasingly irrelevant to the course of American politics and, specifically, political campaigns. Their principal function seemed to be to organize the national party convention once every four years. The title of a study published in 1964 seemed to sum up their plight: *Politics Without Power: The National Party Committees.*[11]

The party in the electorate, the mass base of the political parties, also showed signs of weakening. Through the early 1960s more than 75 percent of the American people said that they identified strongly or weakly with one or the other of the parties and less than 25 percent described themselves as independents. But beginning about 1964 attachments to the party started to weaken substantially. By the late 1970s only about 60 percent said that they identified with a party and more than a third said they were independents. And it was not just that people were less likely to identify with the parties; voters were also less likely to see the parties in favorable terms and to vote according to their party identification.

Trouble loomed as well for the other aspect of the party in the electorate. The coalitions that had supported the major parties, particularly the Democratic coalition, seemed to be coming apart. At its peak in the Johnson landslide, the Democratic party had expanded to encompass not just the Roosevelt New Deal coalition of the working class, unions, the poor, urban areas, the South, Catholics, Jews, and liberals, but also blacks. The Republican party was left as the party of the upper class, big business, and the suburbs. But clearly through the 1970s and peaking in 1980, the Democratic coalition fell into disarray, as working class people, Catholics and some Jews, and white Southerners were drawn away in the Reagan landslide, leaving the Democratic party looking more and more like the party of liberals and blacks—two groups too small for the party to have much of a future as a winning coalition.

The parties in government also suffered their own difficulties through the 1970s and 1980s as party discipline and coordination seemed to deteriorate. Party discipline seemed to sag in the Congress, as members less dependent on the party for help in getting reelected increasingly broke party ranks when local needs or special interest groups dictated.[12] Party coordination between the executive and the legislature suffered as presidents and members of their own party in Congress were often at odds on legislation.

What caused the parties to go into **decline?** A number of governmental, electoral, and socialization changes seem to have contributed to the deteriorating condition of American political parties since the mid-1960s. As noted earlier, patronage was one of the traditional reservoirs of party strength. It provided party leaders with bargaining chips to use in the game of politics. But reformers intent on reducing the power of the bosses and increasing the competence and integrity of public employees pushed for the establishment of a system of civil service. As more public jobs fell under civil service, politicians found themselves with fewer "goodies" to give out and thus were less able to marshal political support.

Another governmental change that hurt the parties was the rise of the public

---

[11] Cornelius P. Cotter and Bernard C. Hennessy (New York: Atherton, 1964).

[12] William J. Keefe, *Parties, Politics, and Public Policy in America* (Hinsdale: Dryden Press, 1976), pp. 139–140; Barbara Sinclair Deckard, "Political Upheaval and Congressional Voting: The Effects of the 1960s on Voting Patterns in the House of Representatives," *Journal of Politics* 38 (1976): 326–345.

welfare system. The parties of earlier years built support by serving as a sort of informal welfare system for their supporters. A faithful party member in financial trouble could seek help in the form of money, food, or shelter from the neighborhood party organization. People came to owe the party. With the rise of the modern welfare system, the government itself began formally to ensure a minimal level of well-being among citizens. Consequently, the party lost its exclusive role as a source of help and its ability to put people in its debt.

Electoral changes played an important part too. In earlier years political parties were an essential part of the electoral apparatus of the United States. To get a message to the electorate, a candidate needed an army of workers to fan out over the constituency, buttonholing passersby, knocking on doors, handing out party literature, and twisting arms. Modern technology provides less labor-intensive alternatives. Nowadays, with a string of appearances on television news programs and in campaign advertisements, a candidate can make more frequent and seemingly more "personal" contact with far more voters than could an army of party workers on the streets. Computerized direct mailing techniques can yield large sums of money, which can be used to buy more television time and send out more mail, which can generate more money, and so on. Simply put, candidates no longer need to rely as much on parties and party workers to serve as their intermediaries with the public.

Parties have also traditionally been important sources of campaign funds for their candidates. Today, however, members of Congress benefit from the support of the PACs, and presidential candidates can rely on public financing. Access to these new sources of money has made candidates less dependent on parties for help and, consequently, has contributed to the weakening of the parties. Also, in an earlier era parties tightly controlled the process by which candidates for public office were selected. Party leaders got together in party **caucuses** (meetings) or conventions to pick the party's candidates. However, political reformers fought to open up the nomination process to represent a broader cross section of the population. This led to selection of convention delegates by open conventions or primary elections.

Parties long existed as standing armies of campaign workers, ready to step into political battle on behalf of the party candidates. Now more and more candidates are relying not on the party machinery but on their own personal organizations for campaign assistance. Although candidates obviously want to capitalize on their party's name, many run without the aid of the party machinery. Once in office, they are likely to feel little obligation to help the party. Single-issue groups also pose a challenge to the existing party system by threatening to siphon off precious campaign resources and public support. The anti-abortion movement is perhaps the most prominent recent example.

Finally, most people acquire their sense of party identification through socialization by their parents. But the process of transmission has appeared to break down in recent years. Between the 1950s and the 1970s the percentage of young people adopting the same party as their parents dropped by about 15 percent. Expansion of the Vietnam War tarnished both parties, the Republican party was scarred by the Watergate scandal, and the Democratic party suffered from the economically difficult Carter years. Party disenchantment in one generation sows party disenchantment in the next. Thus it is not hard to understand why the ranks of the party faithful dwindled and the ranks of the independents swelled.

Many of these changes were viewed with concern. Concern arose because it was not clear whether what was occurring was dealignment leading toward realignment or dealignment leading toward collapse. The deeper concern was that the functioning of our democratic system might be impaired by the weakening or disappearance of political parties. Think of all the valuable functions parties perform and then think about what might happen if the parties were not around to perform them.

Just as the idea that the parties were dead or dying began to gain widespread currency, a new group of commentators rose to argue that the parties were making a comeback. Led by Xandra Kayden and Eddie Mahe, Jr.'s *The Party Goes On: The Persistence of the Two-Party System in the United States*,[13] a number of new studies found evidence of the parties in **resurgence.** The major center of revitalization in the formal party organizations has been in the national party organizations, particularly the national party headquarters supervised by the national chairperson and operated on a day-to-day basis by an increasingly professional, sophisticated, and well-paid staff. These staff employ modern computerized systems to gather and analyze polling results, conduct direct mail campaigns, and raise money.

Although the American public has not flooded back to embrace the political parties, the trend against them has at least been arrested and perhaps slightly reversed. There is also some evidence that the party coalitions are reforming along somewhat different lines. The Democratic party has suffered from the loss of the white South and some working-class Catholic and union support, but it has gained a new constituency in female voters. The Republican party has gained substantially among working-class whites and in the South.

There is little concrete evidence that party discipline within the legislature or coordination between the president and his party in the legislature has improved. Indeed the budget crisis of 1990 suggested that it has not, as a majority of congress members broke with their leaders and the Republicans with their president, to defeat the budget deal worked out between the congressional leadership and the White House.

The primary reason for party resurgence is that the parties, instead of standing on the sidelines and allowing themselves to be kept out of the game, have at last recognized the changing environment of the American political system and adjusted their activities to it. For example, they have recognized that modern political campaigns depend less on armies of party volunteers tramping from door to door and more on money and the media. Thus they have moved to become a major source of political money, in effect not fighting the PACs but joining them. They have seen how candidates must rely on a modern media campaign and moved to provide candidates with the training and production services that they need to have to conduct such campaigns. They know that candidates want to use polling

---

[13] New York: Basic Books, 1985.

results and direct mail, so they share polling results and direct mail strategies and technologies.

Parties Future

Realignment, dealignment, resurgence—it is hard enough to say where the American party system is, much less where it is going. The Democrats' victory in the 1992 presidential election does not make the task any easier. Certainly some sort of realignment took place in the transition from the fifth party system's clear Democratic dominance to what seemed to be a sixth party system, starting in 1968, of divided government, with Republicans dominating presidential voting and Democrats dominating congressional voting. One possibility is that the 1992 election is just an aberration owing to the poor economy and that this mixed alignment will continue on for several years to come. Another possibility is that the current situation (again discounting 1992 as a deviating election) is simply a waystation on the road to a complete Republican realignment. Some observers, particularly Republicans, have hoped that the long-standing Republican dominance at the presidential level would solidify and "trickle down" into congressional, state, and local elections. But the 1992 election brought to the surface strains in the Republican coalition that have been growing over the last several years. The Republican party's presidential candidates went a long way with their conservative rhetoric, but the tough realities of the early 1990s forced them to shift their positions in ways that weakened their advantage. George Bush ran for president in 1988 on a strong pledge of "no new taxes," but within a year deteriorating economic conditions forced him to agree to some increases in taxes. A foreign and defense policy built around fending off the communist threat was a tenet of Republican philosophy for years, but the collapse of communism in Eastern Europe and the Soviet Union made that stance an anachronism. Finally, having firmly established itself as the anti-abortion party through much of the 1980s, pressure from women and party moderates split the party. George Bush was caught between losing female and moderate votes and alienating the party's hard-core conservative support.[14] These problems within the Republican party, combined with widespread public concern about the health of the economy, left open a door that a rejuvenated, more moderate Democratic party under Bill Clinton was able to walk through and into the presidency in 1992.

Is the recent resurgence of the parties just the last gasp of a dying system? Some critics think it is, that the two-party system is really on its last legs.[15] However, the parties' comeback probably represents a broader and more permanent change. Through much of American history, political parties were decentralized because political power in the United States was decentralized. But political power has become more centralized, and parties, although slow to react, have now adapted to that new reality with stronger central party organizations. It makes little sense

[14] William Schneider and Patrick Reddy, "Altered States: The Demographic Changes and Partisan Shifts of Four Decades," *The American Enterprise* (July–August 1990): 45–55.
[15] Theodore Lowi, "The Party Crasher," *New York Times Magazine* (August 23, 1992): 28–33.

to think that parties will move again toward decentralization unless the government does—and that does not appear to be in the offing. Similarly, the resurgence of the national party organizations occurred in response to the rise of the modern media campaign and the increased demand for campaign money. It would make sense to think that the organizations would again wither away only if the media and money somehow became less important. There is no sign that such changes are on the immediate horizon.

Of course, this analysis does not take into account the myriad of other factors that might change and affect the parties, either strengthening or weakening them. The recent episode of decline and resurgence, though, does teach us something about parties that is useful when contemplating their future: The parties have demonstrated an ability to adapt to changing circumstances, not always quickly, not always entirely successfully, but eventually and sufficiently. Unforeseen social and political changes involving circumstances hardly envisioned in this chapter may occur and lay the parties low again, but past experience suggests that parties—perhaps not exactly as we know them today, but parties nevertheless—will adapt again.

Summary

1. Groups are an essential element in the functioning of the American democratic system. A group's political effectiveness depends on its size, the strength of its members' identification, its proximity to politics, its internal organization, and its closeness to the broader societal consensus.
2. Interest groups engage in a wide array of politically relevant activities. They press their views on their own membership, the general public, and the political elites of the legislative, executive, and judicial branches. One of their most potent weapons of late has been the political action committee (PAC).
3. Some of the major group participants in the American political process are groups based on economic interests, for example, the Chamber of Commerce of the United States and the AFL–CIO; socially based groups such as the National Organization for Women (NOW) and the National Association for the Advancement of Colored People (NAACP); ideological groups like the liberal Americans for Democratic Action; single-issue groups such as the right-to-life and pro-choice movements; and public interest groups like Common Cause, the "citizens' lobby."
4. The role that interest groups play in a democratic society is as controversial as it is pervasive. Pluralistic theory sees interest groups as working to overcome the deficiencies of individual citizens and to perpetuate a functioning democracy. Other perspectives see interest groups as failing to serve their own members' interests, the public interest, or both.
5. In a democracy, political parties try to influence public policy by backing members as candidates in elections to public offices. In the course of getting their members elected to public office, political parties perform a number of important functions for the system of government: socializing citizens, pulling

together the diverse interests contending in a society, simplifying the alternatives confronting the voters, structuring campaigns and elections, recruiting and training political leaders, and organizing and coordinating government.

6. The American party system is a two-party system, probably due primarily to the plurality election system commonly used in the United States and the generally centrist distribution of political beliefs in America. The parties are characterized by a relatively loose relationship among their component parts: divided into national, state, and local levels and into formal party organization, the party in the electorate, and the party in the government.

7. Since 1789 the party system has gone through several major phases, from the Federalists and Anti-Federalists of the nation's infancy to the Republicans and Democrats of today, with the transition from each phase to the next called realignment. For much of the last 25 years, the parties have been in a state of decline, as formal party organizations weakened, citizens identified with parties less and less, the traditional party coalitions unraveled, and party discipline and coordination within government diminished. But in the past few years, some observers have traced a resurgence of the parties, with formal party organizations, particularly at the national level, becoming more active and effective, citizen attachment to parties increasing slightly, and perhaps new party coalitions forming. What the future holds for the parties is hard to predict. Solidification and expansion of Republican dominance and a permanent reversal in the favor of the Democrats, perhaps beginning with Bill Clinton's victory in 1992, are the two most obvious possibilities for realignment.

Key Terms

interest group (p. 162)
pluralist democracy (p. 162)
melting pot society (p. 163)
elitism (p. 163)
pluralism (p. 163)
movement (p. 164)
direct mail (p. 165)
political action committees (p. 166)
Federal Election Campaign Act of
　1974 (p. 167)
lobbying (p. 167)
iron triangle (p. 168)
class action suits (p. 168)
amicus curiae brief (p. 168)
grass-roots lobbying (p. 170)
Christian Right (p. 173)
cross-cutting cleavage (p. 175)
interest group elitism (p. 176)
interest group gridlock (p. 176)

political party (p. 177)
socialization functions (p. 177)
electoral functions (p. 178)
governmental functions (p. 178)
plurality election (p. 181)
majority election (p. 181)
runoff election (p. 181)
proportional representation (p. 181)
third parties (p. 181)
formal party organization (p. 183)
national convention (p. 184)
platform (p. 184)
national committee (p. 184)
political machine (p. 184)
state committees (p. 184)
party in the electorate (p. 184)
party identification (p. 184)
party coalition (p. 185)
party in the government (p. 185)

Readings for Further Study

James Madison's *Federalist* No. 10 remains mandatory reading for anyone interested in exploring the role of groups in American political life. A more modern, yet classic, study is *The Governmental Process* (New York: Knopf, 1951) by David Truman. For a fascinating, if highly critical, account of the interest groups' most potent tool, the political action committee, see Elizabeth Drew's *Politics and Money* (New York: Macmillan, 1983). Interest groups are important elements in the pluralist perspective on American democracy. Robert A. Dahl sets out that perspective most clearly in *Who Governs?* (New Haven, Conn.: Yale University Press, 1961). As a central feature of American politics, parties are one of the most written-about of all American political institutions. V. O. Key, Jr., provides a classic description of the role that parties play in the American political system in *Politics, Parties, and Pressure Groups*, 5th ed. (New York: Crowell, 1964). James L. Sundquist's *Dynamics of the Party System* (Washington, D.C.: Brookings Institution, 1973) offers a historical perspective on the parties, centering around the notion of realignment. Good overviews of the causes and consequences of the decline in American political parties are Everett Carll Ladd, *Where Have All the Voters Gone?* 2d ed. (New York: Norton, 1982) and Martin P. Wattenberg, *The Decline of American Political Parties* (Cambridge, Mass.: Harvard University Press, 1984). The best accounts of the parties in resurgence are Xandra Kayden and Eddie Mahe, Jr., *The Party Goes On* (New York: Basic Books, 1985), and Paul S. Herrnson, *Party Campaigning in the 1980s* (Cambridge, Mass.: Harvard University Press, 1988).

7 Campaigns and Elections

In a campaign and the election that concludes it, all the actors in the political process come into vigorous interplay. Parties begin selecting and promoting candidates. Interest groups mobilize their forces to ensure that their interests will be remembered. The mass media put politics more clearly and consistently at center stage. As a result, the public, whose interest in political affairs is generally limited, now turns its attention to the candidates vying for public office. This chapter examines the process from the perspectives of the two principal types of players in the drama: voters and candidates. For voters, the basic questions are whether to vote and how to vote. Candidates, whether presidential or congressional, must devise strategies that will bring voters to the polls and attract their votes. They must pull together the financial resources and organization needed for a credible campaign, obtain the nomination of their party, and compete against the other party's candidate in the general election campaign.

The Voter's Perspective: To Vote or Not to Vote

As discussed in Chapter 5, politics is not usually a matter of concern to most citizens. Their interest is most aroused around Election Day, when they begin to take note of the campaign, think about going to the polls to cast their ballots, and sometimes engage in activities related to the campaign. Many begin to follow it on television or in newspapers and talk about it with family and friends; some try to influence the way in which someone else will vote. A somewhat smaller number wear buttons, display stickers or signs on their cars or houses, and attend campaign meetings, rallies, speeches, or dinners. A few actually work for or give money to a candidate or party. But even with these other kinds of campaign-related activities, voting remains the most frequent act of political participation and the most meaningful act as well. In a representative democracy it is voting that forges the essential link between the citizens and their government. In the end, then, it comes down to two basic decisions: whether to vote and how to vote.

Voting Requirements and Eligibility

Not everyone is in a position to decide to vote. Some people are excluded by law. In fact, for more than 100 years after the founding of the United States, a majority of the American people were not eligible to vote. The states during that period controlled who could or could not vote, and they typically limited the electorate to white males over the age of 21. Since then the United States has made great strides in eliminating restrictions on voting.

Racial barriers to voting began to fall first. The **Fifteenth Amendment** (1870) outlawed denying the right of citizens to vote on grounds of "race, color, or previous condition of servitude." Nevertheless, after the Civil War the South created a new system of inferior status for blacks, which came to be called "Jim Crow." **Jim Crow** included several elements limiting black voting. These barriers were later swept aside by a series of constitutional amendments, Supreme Court decisions, and legislative acts. One element was the **white primary.** As discussed in Chapter 3, in the one-party South of the post-Reconstruction era, winning the Democratic primary was equivalent to an election because the general election was nearly always a rout of the disfavored Republicans. The Democratic party routinely excluded blacks from its primaries, which effectively barred them from any meaningful role in the electoral process. The white primary was struck down by the Supreme Court in *Smith* v. *Allwright* in 1944.

Another element was the **poll tax**: To vote, citizens had to pay a tax. This tax was often enforced cumulatively, meaning that people had to pay the tax for every previous election in which they had not voted. Because blacks had not been able to vote in many previous elections, they confronted large cumulated poll taxes, which they could not pay. Thus they were excluded from voting. Poll taxes were prohibited in federal elections by the **Twenty-fourth Amendment** and in state elections by the Supreme Court's decision in *Harper* v. *Virginia Board of Elections,* both in 1964. A third element of Jim Crow was the **literacy test**: to vote, a person had to demonstrate the ability to read. Many blacks at that time were illiterate, so they were thereby excluded. This was prohibited by the **Voting Rights Act of 1965,** which waived literacy tests for anyone with a sixth-grade education. The Voting Rights Act of 1965 and a subsequent amendment in 1982 took other important steps to protect black voting rights, as discussed in Chapter 3.

While black participation declined under Jim Crow, political pressures to grant **female suffrage,** the right of women to vote, increased. This movement stirred to life in the early nineteenth century and achieved its first major success when the territory of Wyoming granted suffrage to women in 1869. Activists first coalesced into two competing organizations with somewhat different styles—the more militant National Woman Suffrage Association led by Susan B. Anthony, and the more conservative American Woman Suffrage Association led by Lucy Stone. The two groups joined forces in 1890. Final success was not achieved on the national level until 1920, when the states ratified the **Nineteenth Amendment,** which gave women the right to vote.

Voting reforms in the 1960s, including the Twenty-fourth Amendment and the Voting Rights Act, set off an upsurge in voting by blacks. In this photograph, approximately 1000 black citizens wait in line to vote on May 3, 1966, in the Democratic primary in Birmingham, Alabama. It was the first time blacks in Alabama had been allowed to vote in large numbers since the late 1800s.

The last major broadening of the electorate occurred in 1971, when the **Twenty-sixth Amendment** reduced the voting age from 21 to 18. In the midst of the Vietnam War, the argument that people old enough to die for their country ought to be able to vote in their country's elections was very persuasive. In addition, both Republicans and Democrats hoped to capitalize on the large bloc of new voters. In combination with the coming of age of the post–World War II baby boom generation, the lowering of the voting age produced one of the greatest expansions of the electorate in American history.

The laws of the United States still exclude from voting people who are not citizens of this country. In most states, people who have been convicted of a felony or who are confined in prisons and mental institutions cannot vote. Most jurisdictions also typically exclude citizens who have not resided within their boundaries for a minimum amount of time. This law is intended to ensure that citizens are reasonably permanent residents of the community. Impediments to voting imposed by lengthy **residence requirements** were weakened substantially by the **Voting Rights Act of 1970,** which mandated that states require no more than 30 days' residency to establish eligibility to vote in presidential elections. Today the 30-day rule is standard for all elections.

Beyond meeting the basic qualifications, potential voters in most places in the United States are required to **register**—that is, to enter their names on the local government's list of those eligible to vote in a particular area, usually by visiting a government office. This requirement poses enough of an inconvenience that many people do not bother. Recent studies have shown, in fact, that the registration requirement may reduce electoral participation by as much as 10 to 15 percent.[1] Because registration reduces voting, it has long been the target of political reformers. Some places now permit registration by mail, and a few allow citizens to register on Election Day, even at the same time and place as they vote. Such arrangements seem to make a difference. In 1980 voter turnout in states with Election Day registration was 13 percent higher than the national average.[2]

The higher turnout rates in states with easier registration have inspired similar efforts at the federal level. Recent proposals include requiring states to allow eligible citizens to register at the same time they get their driver's licenses, to allow registration by mail, to allow registration at offices of state agencies, and prohibiting states from purging citizens from the rolls just because they have not voted in a recent election. Most recent proposals for changes in voting registration at the federal level have failed primarily because of Republican opposition. The historical pattern has been for Republicans to oppose such measures and for Democrats to support them. The Democrats generally emphasize the virtues of higher turnout, whereas the Republicans worry about opening the door to fraud.

---

[1] Steven Rosenstone and Raymond Wolfinger, "The Effect of Registration Laws on Voter Turnout," *American Political Science Review* 72 (1978): 22–45; G. Bingham Powell, Jr., "American Voter Turnout in Comparative Perspective," *American Political Science Review* 80 (1986): 35.
[2] David P. Glass, Peverill Squire, and Raymond E. Wolfinger, "Voter Turnout: An International Comparison," *Public Opinion* (December 1983–January 1984): 49–55.

Politics and Economics

Turnout, Choice, and Economic Status

Economic status influences voter turnout. For example, as Figure 7A shows, in 1988 the higher a citizen's income, the more likely the citizen was to vote. The same pattern has been observed in many previous elections. It emerges in part because higher income encourages many of the factors that promote voting, particularly education, political interest, and efficacy.

Voting choice is also influenced by economic status. As Figure 7B shows, in 1988 the higher a citizen's income, the more likely the citizen was to vote for George Bush. This tendency of higher-income people to favor Republican candidates has also been observed in many previous elections. It results primarily because higher-income people tend to identify with the Republican party,

FIGURE 7A
Voter Turnout by Family Income, 1988

The higher the income of a voter's family, the more likely that citizen is to vote.

SOURCE: American National Election Study, 1988, Center for Political Studies, University of Michigan.

Who Votes?

Voting turnout varies with people's social characteristics and psychological and political attitudes, as well as with the circumstances of voting. Voting participation used to vary dramatically across a wide variety of social groupings in the United States. Whites were much more likely to vote than blacks, men than women, and so on. In recent years there has been a general convergence in the voting rates among various types of citizens. This is due partly to the success of the long struggle to ensure equal access to the voting booth. Just as significant, the broader trend toward social and economic equality has tended to promote political equality.

Two social characteristics show the strongest relation to voting turnout: age and education. (A third important factor is discussed in "Politics and Economics:

as discussed in Chapter 6, and because Republican identifiers tend to vote for Republican candidates.

These two factors combine to hurt Democratic candidates and help Republican candidates. Democratic candidates have a greater following among lower-income people, but those people turn out less often. Republican candidates have a greater following among higher-income people, who vote more often. This is one reason why the Republicans, even as the minority party, have been so successful in getting their candidates elected to public office.

What other reasons are there for the Republicans' success in winning elections even though they have been in the minority for so long?

FIGURE 7B
Presidential Voting Choice by Income, 1988

The higher the income of the citizen's family, the more likely the citizen was to vote for Bush.
SOURCE: American National Election Study, 1988, Center for Political Studies, University of Michigan.

Turnout, Choice, and Economic Status.") The older a person is, the more likely that person is to vote. One reason is that older people move less often and, therefore, need to re-register less often. Young people are more likely to be away from their place of residence, for example, at college or in the military. Because voting by absentee ballot takes more forethought and is more difficult than voting in person, young people are more likely to be discouraged from voting. They are also more preoccupied with getting a start in life than with relatively remote political concerns. As people grow older, they have more time and inclination to participate in politics and consequently build a habit of voting.

The more educated a person is, the more likely he or she is to vote. About half of eligible voters with a grade school education or less voted in 1988, whereas more than 90 percent of those with a graduate school education voted. Education plays such a big role because it stimulates political interest and provides the information that people need to be effective participants in the political process. Differences in education have undoubtedly contributed to voting differences between social groups in the past. Blacks and women voted less often than white males in part because they did not enjoy the benefits of education that white males did. With the recent expansion of educational opportunities for minorities and women, levels of voting for these groups have approached those for white males.

Psychological influences play a role too. Not surprisingly, the greater a person's interest in politics, the more likely the person is to vote. The more a citizen thinks he or she can accomplish politically (i.e., the more political efficacy he or she has), the greater the likelihood the person will vote. Partisanship is a powerful motivating force. The stronger a person's attachment to a political party, the more inclined that person will be to vote. However, some psychological factors thought to have a major impact on turnout really do not. Conservatives and liberals are only slightly more likely to vote than moderates, probably because they tend to be more interested and partisan. Surprisingly, despite much attention in the late 1960s and early 1970s, trust—defined as reliance on the integrity of public officials—has little effect.

Finally, primarily as a result of differences in psychological factors, turnout varies substantially across the different types of elections. In elections that the public finds interesting and important, so-called **high-stimulus elections,** turnout is usually relatively high; in less interesting, **low-stimulus elections** it is usually low.[3] Presidential elections are generally higher-stimulus than congressional elections, and general elections are usually higher-stimulus than the primary elections that precede them. Turnout in recent presidential elections has averaged between 50 and 55 percent, while turnout in congressional elections has run between 35 and 40 percent. Voting rates in presidential general elections also typically far exceed the turnout rates of 30 percent and less observed in primary elections.

The 1992 presidential election vividly demonstrated the impact of the level of stimulus on turnout. Public concern over the weak economy, the saturation of the airwaves with political advertisements, campaign appearances in the debates and talk-television formats like "Today" and "Larry King Live," and Ross Perot's candidacy, with its strong appeal to those who had dropped out of or never joined in the electorate, combined to produce an unusually high level of interest in the campaign and a higher-than-usual rate of turnout. Voting turnout, which had hung in the low 50s in the early 1980s and sagged to 50 percent in 1988 rebounded to 56 percent in 1992.

Declining Turnout

Although the surge in turnout in 1992 was a promising sign, one good year cannot offset the troubling long-term trend toward lower voter turnout in the United States, shown in Figure 7.1. After an explosion in the early nineteenth century,

---

[3] Angus Campbell, "Surge and Decline: A Study of Electoral Change," in *Elections and the Political Order*, eds. Angus Campbell, Philip E. Converse, Warren E. Miller, and Donald E. Stokes (New York: Wiley, 1966), p. 41.

FIGURE 7.1

Turnout in Presidential and Congressional Elections, 1790–1992

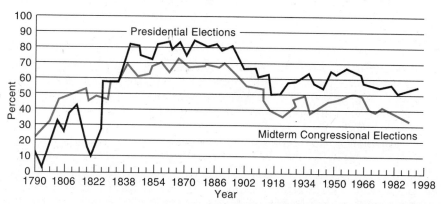

Since the end of the nineteenth century, the long-term historical trend has been downward. Turnout in midterm congressional elections is lower than in presidential elections.

SOURCES: Harold W. Stanley and Richard G. Niemi, *Vital Statistics on American Politics* (Washington, D.C.: CQ Press, 1990), p. 78; Federal Election Commission, "55.9 Percent Turnout in 1992 Presidential Election Highest Since 1968," Press Release of January 14, 1993.

owing to the expansion of the electorate discussed earlier in this chapter, voting turnout by 1988 had fallen to one of its lowest points in the last 150 years and had sagged substantially since its post–World War II peak in 1960. Although the long-term trend in turnout is striking, it is not necessarily ominous. The greatest part of the decline took place in the late-nineteenth and early-twentieth centuries. Some theorists attribute this to growing disaffection from the political system,[4] but other factors were probably involved. The widespread imposition of voter registration systems lowered turnout, both by excluding fraudulent votes and by discouraging some honest ones.[5] Moreover, Jim Crow laws in the South wiped out the gains made among black voters in the years after the Civil War.

The Nineteenth Amendment, which enlarged the electorate by giving women the right to vote, temporarily reduced turnout. Many women had never voted before and did not immediately begin to exercise the right. As women, particularly younger women, got used to the newly opened political world, turnout climbed steadily through the 1930s. World War II disrupted voting, but it bounced back in the 1950s. Demographic and institutional changes reduced voting in the 1960s and 1970s. The maturation of the postwar baby boom and the reduction of the voting age from 21 to 18 added millions of new voters. Because younger citizens are not as likely to vote as older people, this drove turnout down.

Yet many observers still believe that deep-seated psychological inclinations

---

[4] Walter Dean Burnham, "The Changing Shape of the American Political Universe," *American Political Science Review* 59 (1965): 7–28.

[5] Philip E. Converse, "Change in the American Electorate," in *The Human Meaning of Social Change*, eds. Angus Campbell and Philip E. Converse (New York: Russell Sage Foundation, 1972), pp. 281–286.

account for some of the contemporary decrease. Some blame **political alienation** or distrust. They argue that the American people are discouraged by what they see going on in politics and are therefore increasingly inclined not to vote. However, as noted earlier, trust does not seem to have much effect on voting, so an increase in distrust does not necessarily imply a decrease in voting. In fact, many of the new voters in 1992 seemed to be motivated more by anger at the system than anything else. On the other hand, decreasing partisanship and external political efficacy clearly relate to voting turnout.[6] Young people are less partisan, and less partisan people are less likely to vote. It may therefore be that weakening partisanship is due to the influx of young people into the electorate, resulting in a decline in voting.

Some commentators view the long-term decline in voting turnout with alarm. The success of democracy, they argue, depends on the enthusiastic participation of its citizens, so declining electoral involvement is not a good sign. However, other commentators believe that less than total participation may be desirable because it can give a democracy room for compromise and flexibility.[7] Nonvoting may not imply a lack of trust or support for the political system but is perhaps a passive nonvote of confidence. In other words, staying home on Election Day may just be a way of saying that everything is all right.

The Voter's Perspective: How to Vote

Just as various political, social, and psychological factors contribute to citizens' decisions to exercise their voting rights, different elements help determine for whom they cast their ballots. Analysts have identified three major factors that seem to influence how people vote: parties, candidates, and issues.

Parties

For many years, affiliation with a political party was regarded as the mainstay of voting decisions in the United States. For some people, all that mattered was that a candidate belonged to "their" party. However, this was not the only impact. In many instances party identification colored the way in which a voter looked at the pivotal elements of a presidential election. Party continues to play an important role in American electoral behavior. Ross Perot's presence in the 1992 presidential race complicated things, but how people voted still bore a strong relationship to their sense of partisanship. Thus 77 percent of Democrats voted for the candidate of their party, while only 10 percent crossed party lines to vote for Bush (13 percent voted for Perot). Moreover, 73 percent of Republicans voted for the candidate of their party, while again only 10 percent de-

[6] Paul Abramson, *Political Attitudes in America* (San Francisco: Freeman, 1983), pp. 291–306.
[7] This argument is most often associated with Bernard Berelson, *Voting* (Chicago: University of Chicago Press, 1954), pp. 305–323.

fected to Clinton (17 percent voted for Perot). As might be expected, independent candidate Ross Perot's greatest strength came from independents, among whom he captured 30 percent.[8]

Yet, as established in Chapter 6, there can be little doubt that party has weakened as a reference point for many American voters in recent years. As party has become less important to voters, it has become a less important determinant of their voting decisions. That has left more room for candidate characteristics and issues to have an influence.

Candidates

Opinions about the candidates themselves play a powerful role in influencing how voters ultimately vote. Because partisanship is fairly stable, assessments of the candidates are perhaps the major contributor to changes in presidential voting from one election to the next.[9] Voters seem to put the greatest weight on three factors:

- *Experience.* The public shows a marked preference for someone with substantial political experience, someone who seems to know what he or she is doing. Hence, the public leans very much toward incumbent presidents, vice-presidents, senators, and governors from large states. The only recent presidents without substantial national political experience prior to taking office were Dwight Eisenhower (1953–1961), who had extensive military experience, and Jimmy Carter (1977–1981), the governor of a smaller state, Georgia. Bill Clinton (1993–　), although the governor of a small southern state, had been active on the national scene for many years as a leader in the National Governors' Association and the Democratic Leadership Council.

- *Leadership.* The public inclines toward someone who seems able to take command of a situation, who does not wallow in pessimism or indecision but acts when the time is right. President Carter suffered in the 1980 campaign because, in the face of economic problems and the Iranian hostage crisis, he was not seen as taking decisive and effective action. Twelve years later in 1992 George Bush ran afoul of economic problems and a widespread public perception that he had no plan for addressing them.

- *Personal qualities.* At the same time that voters want someone who will be a strong leader, they are also inclined to want an attractive and "nice" person in the White House. Eisenhower, Kennedy (1961–1963), and Reagan (1981–1989) all benefited from attractive personalities. Bill Clinton's campaign in 1992 mounted a major effort to offset early perceptions of him as dishonest and untrustworthy—"Slick Willy"—with an image-rebuilding

---

[8] "Portrait of the Electorate" (results from November 3, 1992, exit polls conducted by Voter Research and Surveys), *New York Times,* November 5, 1992, p. B9.
[9] Donald Stokes, "Some Dynamic Elements of Contests for the Presidency," *American Political Science Review* 60 (1966): 19–28.

effort that campaign insiders dubbed the "Manhattan Project" after the World War II program to develop the atomic bomb.[10]

Candidate factors proved to be a major issue in the 1992 presidential campaign; the Republicans attacked Bill Clinton's lack of experience in national politics and his character for inconsistencies in his account of how he avoided the draft during the Vietnam War. The Democrats responded with attacks on Bush's character for violating his "read my lips" pledge not to increase taxes and for changing his story on his role in the Iranian arms-for-hostages deal while he was vice-president.

Issues

Today more than before, issues seem to drive the public toward a particular electoral choice. Even observers who have previously minimized the importance of issues now concede that they can make a difference when the public knows and cares about them and when the candidates differentiate themselves on them. Single-issue groups, described in Chapter 6, play a big role in emphasizing particular concerns. Opponents of gun control or abortion, for example, can "target" an official for defeat. But even without the participation of single-issue groups, social issues such as crime and foreign policy issues such as nuclear arms reduction usually receive considerable attention in a campaign.

More often, though, the voter's focus is on economic issues. Year in and year out, the mainspring issue driving most electoral decisions seems to be the economy. Even the earliest voting studies that discovered issues to be relatively unimportant found that bread-and-butter economic issues did make a difference. Personal economic well-being seems to influence how Americans vote. Figure 7.2 relates the percentage of the popular vote for president received by the incumbent party to an indicator of how much a citizen's disposable income had increased during the election year. Clearly, the better off people are during an election year, the more likely they are to vote for the party holding the White House. Some political commentators pointed to Ronald Reagan's celebrated question near the end of his 1980 election debate with Jimmy Carter—"Are you better off now than you were four years ago?"—as the symbolic turning point of that campaign. The statistical evidence suggests that the Reagan campaign may have been right in emphasizing the role of the economy. The same is true for the 1992 presidential election; exit polls showed Bush running far ahead of Clinton (62 percent to 24 percent) among voters who thought their family's financial situation had improved over the preceding four years, and the two candidates dead even (at 41 percent each) among those who thought things had stayed the same. But Clinton outpolled Bush 61 percent to 14 percent among those felt they were worse off and, fortunately for Clinton, those voters

---

[10] "'Manhattan Project,' 1992," *Newsweek*, special election edition (November/December 1992): 40–56.

FIGURE 7.2
The Economy and Presidential Voting

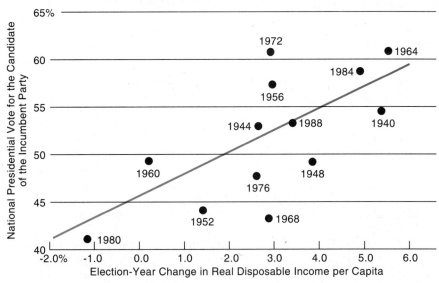

The better the economy, the better the candidate of the incumbent party does in the presidential election. The diagonal line shows the basic trend in the relationships—that is, how much, on average, voting is related to improvements in the economy.   *SOURCE:* Updated from Edward Tufte, *Political Control of the Economy* (Princeton, N.J.: Princeton University Press, 1978), p. 123.

outnumbered by a margin of 4 to 3 voters who felt they were better off—which was enough to give Clinton the victory.[11]

This is not to say that economics is the only issue that sways voters. Other issues have some impact. No doubt the candidates' differences on abortion, health care, and foreign policy influenced some voters to opt for Bush, Clinton, or Perot in 1992. However, 1992 was a year in which the economy again dominated the campaign and the electoral outcome.

In talking about parties, candidates, and issues separately, this discussion runs the risk of oversimplification—an impression that people vote only according to how much they like the parties or candidates or how they feel about the issues. The relation among parties, issues, and candidates as influences on the vote is complex. Voters may take a position on an issue because it is the position of their party—or choose their party on the basis of its position on issues. Voters may tend to prefer certain candidates because they are the candidates of their party and reject other candidates because they are candidates of the other party—or judge a party according to how much they like its candidates. And voters may like

---

[11] "Portrait of the Electorate," *New York Times*, op. cit.

candidates because they agree with their positions on certain issues—or adopt certain positions on issues because they like the candidates who advocate them. People and politics can sometimes get very complicated.

The Candidate's Perspective: Running for President

Voters need to decide whether and how to vote; candidates confront a more complicated set of choices. Their basic decisions are whether to run and how to attract enough votes to win. To do this they must make scores of strategic decisions. For a contemporary presidential candidate, these include carving out a clear position as a serious contender early on, raising large amounts of money, choosing the right campaign consultant, deciding which issues to raise, selecting the primaries and caucuses on which to concentrate, garnering enough delegates in the national convention to secure the nomination, choosing a running mate, and winning states with enough electoral votes to win the electoral college. The task is compounded by the fact that, in doing all this, a candidate must also outmaneuver opponents who are working equally hard to attract voters.

Who Runs for President?

In American political folklore, anyone can grow up to be president, whether from humble beginnings, like Abraham Lincoln, or high social and economic status, like Franklin Roosevelt. But is it true? In fact, the Constitution lays down few requirements: The person must be a natural-born citizen of the United States, a resident of the United States for at least 14 years, and at least 35 years of age. The **Twenty-second Amendment** (1951), ratified in the aftermath of Franklin Roosevelt's unprecedented four elections to the presidency, imposes one more restriction. A person cannot be elected to the presidency more than twice, or more than once if filling out more than two years of another person's term.

Despite the relatively small set of formal qualifications, however, the evidence suggests that the path to power is fairly steep and narrow. The key to attaining the highest political office in the United States is having held other reasonably high political offices. Consider the 17 individuals who have run under the banner of the major parties for the presidency in the last 12 elections. Six of them had been governor of their state. Seven had previously served as vice-president. Eight of them had served in the U.S. Senate. Only one had held no elective office: Dwight Eisenhower. One other factor is important too. The best assurance of being elected president is already to be president. In the 28 elections in which an incumbent president sought reelection, the incumbent was successful in 19, or 68 percent of the time. This probably stems in part from the incumbent president's unique ability to manipulate events in his favor and the high visibility and name recognition a president enjoys.

What other qualities put an individual in line to be considered for the highest office in the land? Recent history suggests some. For one, the presidency has so far been a white male preserve. Most presidents in recent times have been from at least reasonably well-off Protestant backgrounds and have been reasonably well-educated. Not until 1960, with the election of John F. Kennedy, did a Catholic become president. No Jew has ever been elected president. Harry Truman, elected in 1948, was the last president without a college degree.

In this age of media politics, an attractive image is clearly an important asset. But perhaps the most important quality of all is determination. Securing a major party's presidential nomination nowadays typically takes months, even years, of grinding work. That has meant in some cases starting in January of the year before the presidential election year and campaigning nonstop for almost the next two years. Presidential hopeful Gary Hart vividly illustrated the kind of ordeal that a modern presidential candidate has to endure when he revealed that some mornings during the 1984 campaign, he would awaken in a strange hotel room and have to reach for the phone book to find out what city he was in.

The Media Campaign

The primary determinant of the shape of the modern political campaign is the mass media. Candidates used to be concerned primarily with mobilizing the party organization behind their efforts. Now their principal concern is mobilizing the media, particularly television, to bring their name and "image" before the public. This effort assumes three principal forms. One is the expenditure of most of the campaign treasury on political advertisements. Precious paid television time is generally devoted to short advertisements that focus on simple images and issues, rather than longer speeches that focus on in-depth discussions of public policy. Campaign debates waged in 1-minute, 30-second, and even 15-second spots have drawn considerable criticism for oversimplifying campaign issues. Ross Perot's 1992 independent campaign defied traditional practice by spending millions of dollars on half-hour blocks devoted to detailed discussions of economic problems and solutions—and defied conventional wisdom by drawing large viewing audiences.

A second method is the structuring of traditional campaign events, such as speeches, rallies, and news conferences, to get media attention. These activities, once the core of the traditional political campaign, are now used mainly as "media events," or opportunities to attract coverage by the news media.

A third element is getting as much free television time as possible on regular news and interview broadcasts. Extended nationally televised appearances on the nightly network news broadcasts, traditional news interview programs such as "Nightline," and, new in 1992, "softer" interview shows like "Larry King Live" and "Donahue" are the candidate's dream, but hard to come by.

The bread and butter of free television time comes in two forms: the "sound bite" on the national network news broadcasts and the daily stream of interviews on local TV stations as candidates travel around the country. Sound bites are short taped excerpts from statements that a candidate makes. Candidates hope to get at least one sound bite on the network news broadcasts every night during the course

Contemporary Controversies

The Private Lives of Public People

The relevance of a candidate's private life to the candidate's suitability for public office has long been an issue in American politics, but has loomed as a particularly prominent issue in recent years. In 1988 two major contenders for the presidency were knocked from the race by charges of personal improprieties. One, Gary Hart, the former Democratic senator from Colorado, was driven from the race by charges of "womanizing," particularly with an attractive young model and actress named Donna Rice. Democratic senator Joseph Biden of Delaware dropped out after the discovery that he had plagiarized a campaign speech led to revelations that he had committed plagiarism in law school and misstated his academic record. In 1992 governor Bill Clinton was dogged by reports of extramarital affairs and public accusations of sexual involvement by a woman named Gennifer Flowers. Clinton responded in an unprecedented television appearance with his wife, in which he admitted that they had suffered marital difficulties in the past but had since overcome them.

These cases raise some difficult questions about the role of the media and the standards against which candidates for public office should be measured. How relevant is a candidate's personal conduct to his or her fitness for public office? A startling aspect of the Hart, Biden, and Clinton affairs was the degree to which the press became consumed by the charges swirling around the candidates. Once the charges were raised, coverage of their campaigns focused on little else. Even conceding that personal conduct is a legitimate issue for the press to cover, is it fair or right for the media to make it the only issue? Can and should the media's tendency to go into a "feeding frenzy" on such issues be controlled? How?

of the campaign and work to say things in ways that are "sound bite–able" to the TV crews covering them.

Another major development of recent years has been the rise of the professional **media consultant**. In the past candidates tended to rely on party leaders or a personal coterie to plan and execute their campaign strategy, but the current trend is toward reliance on professional campaign consultants. Such individuals, while certainly oriented more toward one party or philosophy than another, make themselves available for hire to candidates able to pay for their services. Perhaps the best known and most successful media consultant of the 1992 campaign was James Carville, who became a key figure in Bill Clinton's inner circle.

A focus of the media throughout the presidential campaign is the opinion polls. The media typically concentrate not on the issues of the campaign, but on the strategies, tactics, and likely outcome of the campaign. Politicians and commentators call all this the **horse race.** Poll results are tracked throughout the campaign to see who is in the lead and to test the potential effect of various moves by the candidates. Some critics have argued that the emphasis placed on the polls in the mass media serves to make polls the makers, rather than the measurers, of public opinion. Poll results showing a candidate doing better than expected tend to increase that candidate's credibility and thereby contribute to further gains in the polls. Polling results showing a candidate lagging far behind may lead the public to write off that candidate as a wasted vote. Also, a poor showing in the polls can cause potential contributors to cut the flow of money to the candidate. Politicians, particularly those trailing in the polls, like to say that "the only poll that counts is the one on Election Day." Yet preelection polls may encourage shifts in opinion that are translated into shifts in voting on Election Day. In 1992 interest in the election was heightened as public opinion polls showed the race between Bush and Clinton tightening in the last two weeks of the campaign, only to have the drama diminish as the apparent Bush surge fell back in the last few days before the voting.

In recent years, the media and the polls have become controversial even on Election Day itself. Modern sampling techniques and **exit polls** (interviews with voters leaving the polls) often enable analysts to predict the winner long before polls everywhere have closed. For example, in 1988 CBS and ABC projected George Bush as the victor over Michael Dukakis at 9:20 P.M. Eastern Standard Time, well before many voters in western states had voted. Do early predictions about who is winning or losing dissuade those who have not yet voted from doing so, or create a "bandwagon" effect for the projected winner, or a sympathy vote for the projected loser? The evidence on these questions is mixed, but there are some signs that early projections do reduce turnout. In 1992, to forestall criticism, the major networks avoided projecting winners in a state until the polls in that state had closed, and both candidates Clinton and Bush held off on their victory and concession speeches until polls on the West Coast had closed.

As the media have come more and more to shape the modern presidential campaign, and as dissatisfaction with modern campaigns has grown, the media have become the object of blame for the problems and the target of reform. As reasonable and laudable as the proposed media reforms sound, many of them collide with the First Amendment principles of freedom of the press and speech, potentially infringing on broadcasters' rights as journalists and candidates' rights to express themselves freely. Here are some of the specific proposals that have been advanced in recent years:

- Requiring broadcasters to give more free time to candidates. This would reduce the candidates' need for money to spend on advertising.
- Establishing rules for political advertising on television. Broadcasters and candidates might be forced to present only spots of one minute or more, and any unfair or negative elements could be prohibited.
- Conditioning federal campaign funding for presidential candidates on their agreement to participate in at least four televised debates.
- Challenging television news organizations to devote more time to the substance of the campaign and less to the horse race. (The major networks began to do this to a greater degree in the 1992 presidential campaign.)
- Prohibiting television news organizations from projecting winners before all polls have closed. An alternative is a uniform national poll-closing time.

Campaign Finance

Financing campaigns has always been an issue for presidential candidates. The rate at which modern media-based, jet-borne, poll-addicted campaigns consume money has made the problem even greater. One estimate is that total spending in all the 1992 political campaigns exceeded $800 million. With the demands for more money have come growing public concern and increased legislative action to prevent political money from tainting the electoral and governmental processes.

In 1971 Congress passed the **Federal Election Campaign Act** (FECA). The unfolding of the Watergate scandal in 1974 and other subsequent developments have led to amendments to FECA. Current campaign finance law requires full disclosure of the sources and uses of campaign funds on the theory that requiring candidates to disclose where their money came from will encourage them to behave more ethically. Candidates must thus file with the Federal Election Commission a complete accounting of where they get their money and how they spend it.

The law bans direct contributions to candidates by corporations and labor unions, although such organizations can set up political action committees (PACs) through which their employees or members can contribute. (For more on PACs, see Chapter 6.) The law also places limits on campaign contributions. Currently individuals may give up to $1000 per candidate in each primary and general election, but the total for each federal election year may not exceed $25,000. An individual cannot give more than $5000 to a PAC per election per year, and a PAC cannot give more than $5000 to a candidate in a federal election. However, there are no limits on the total a PAC can contribute to all federal candidates or on the total a candidate can receive from all PACs. National party committees can also spend about 6 cents per member of the voting population on the presidential election campaign.

The Revenue Act of 1971 created a system of public financing for presidential campaigns. Every taxpayer has the option of earmarking $1 of federal income tax for the **Presidential Election Campaign Fund.** This money is distributed directly to presidential candidates according to specific formulas that tie amounts that can be spent to the rate of inflation. Before the party conventions, candidates are eligible for federal matching funds. To receive these funds, candidates must raise at least $5000 in each of at least 20 states. Contributions are limited to $250 per contributor. Once a candidate has qualified, the federal government will match all individual contributions up to a specified amount if the candidate agrees to hold total spending under a limit. In 1992 individual contributions were matched up to $13.8 million if the candidate agreed to hold total preconvention spending to twice that, $27.6 million. After the party conventions, major-party candidates who give up the right to accept any contributions from the public whatsoever can opt for federal financing of their campaigns, up to limits set by the law. Since the law was passed, all major-party presidential candidates have opted for federal funding. In 1992 candidates Bush and Clinton each received about $55 million from the Presidential Election Campaign Fund. Two factors jeopardize the viability of the campaign financing fund. First, the percentage of taxpayers who check off a contribution on their tax forms has fallen to less than 20 percent. Second, although the amounts the fund must pay out increase with inflation, the amount that voters can

Contemporary Controversies

Negative Campaigning

Negative campaigning—candidates running for office by putting their opponents down rather than building themselves up—is nothing new in American politics. Candidates naturally make favorable comparisons between themselves and their opponents. But negative campaigning accentuates the defects of an opponent with little or no reference to the virtues of the candidate presenting the advertisement. Negative campaigning has become more of an issue as campaigns have become more television-based and ads have become shorter. Thirty seconds lends itself better to a quick shot at an opponent than to a reasoned argument in favor of oneself. Negative campaigning has also become more of an issue as it has spread from state and local to national campaigns.

Some candidates and political observers see negative campaigning as a valid way of getting opponents' political records out on the table for the public to see. Others see nothing wrong with it, but avoid negative campaigning because it may backfire: A negative ad from one candidate may provoke an even more damaging negative one from the opposition. Another issue is negative ads' effectiveness. Every indication so far is that they do work, perhaps because they are particularly good at penetrating to the uninvolved and impressionable voters who may tip an election one way or the other. However, although it may help a candidate, there is concern that negative campaigning may hurt the political process by fostering an attitude of cynicism about politics in general and by discouraging politicians from taking potentially unpopular stances or even getting involved in politics at all, for fear of being hammered by negative ads about some past action. As a result, some observers have called for a ban on negative advertising. One proposal is to require candidates themselves to appear in any negative ads they run about their opponents so that the origins of the allegations are clear to the public.

What exactly is a negative ad? Is it inappropriate or wrong to point out an unpopular action or position of an opponent, as long as what is said is true? Is there any way of controlling negative campaigning without infringing on freedom of speech and healthy political debate?

check off, set at $1 since 1971, has not. Thus income has sagged while expenditures have soared.

Direct individual, PAC, and party contributions, as well as federal funds, are not the only money that can be spent on a candidate's behalf. Independent of the official campaign, individuals and PACs can spend as much as they want on behalf of a presidential candidate on such things as their own political advertisements and direct mail. Also, candidates willing to forgo federal funding can spend as much of their own money as they want. In 1992 independent candidate Ross Perot was estimated to have spent at least $60 million of his own money in his bid to win the White House. Candidates who do opt for federal funding are limited to spending $50,000 of their own money.

The problems with PACs have led many recent candidates to reject financial support from PACs. Many critics now call for the abolition of PACs or tighter controls on them, but that raises serious questions of freedom of speech. As a result, PACs may be a permanent fixture of American politics, but how candidates manage their relationships with them is another, less predictable matter. Proposals for PAC reform include increasing the amounts that individuals can give to candidates to, for example, $5000 and restoring tax deductions for political contributions.

The major loophole in the controls on money that can be spent on a candidate's behalf was a seemingly innocuous amendment to the campaign finance laws passed by Congress in 1979—the so-called **soft money** loophole. The tight controls on party spending imposed by the FECA laws in the early 1970s had the effect of drastically reducing the money that the national party could give to state and local parties to help pay for grass-roots activities supporting the presidential campaign—handing out buttons and bumper stickers, for example. So in 1979 Congress moved to solve this problem by allowing the national parties to raise and spend money, without any restrictions, for state and local parties, routine operating expenses, and "party-building" activities, as long as they were not directly related to any federal campaign.

The parties soon began to exploit this exception to the hilt. Within the law, they moved to solicit unlimited contributions from individuals, corporations, and unions. Within the law, they cleverly spent the money in ways that were not technically directly associated with federal candidates, but clearly helped them and freed up other party funds to help federal candidates. Under the new law, parties have to report virtually nothing about how the money is raised or spent.

Many critics, led by such organizations as Common Cause, see in the parties' soft money exception an evasion of the entire structure of campaign finance law. They have prodded the Federal Election Commission to scrutinize more closely whether state and local expenditures are too closely tied to federal candidates and to rewrite the rules governing the raising and spending of soft money. The commission has been slow to make changes, but one reform that stands some chance is fuller disclosure of the sources and uses of soft money, partly because the parties have already begun to do this on a limited, voluntary basis in an attempt to head off more restrictive reforms. Some would like to see the 1979 amendment that opened the soft money loophole repealed, but that seems unlikely given that so many of the legislators voting on the issue benefit from the soft money system.

Getting Nominated

The modern-day orientation toward the media, supported by unending efforts to raise money, is superimposed over the traditional political events that in the heyday of political parties were the central mechanisms by which candidates were selected: primaries, caucuses, and conventions.

The most visible part of the presidential nominating process in recent years has been the long string of primary elections and party caucuses running from the Iowa caucuses and the New Hampshire primary in February and March to the big primaries in such populous states as California and New Jersey in June. **Primary elections** are intraparty elections in which a political party selects the candidates it will run for office in the final interparty **general election.** Primary elections differ from state to state in terms of who is allowed to vote. In an **open primary,** any voter regardless of party affiliation can participate in the selection of the party's candidates. In a **closed primary,** only voters registered as members of the party can participate in the selection process for that party. Some states express their presidential preferences in **caucuses,** or small party meetings. Caucuses typically include discussion before voting, thus giving them a more deliberative character than the simple voting of a primary election.

The earliest presidential primaries and caucuses are the most important because they quickly sort out the field into contenders and also-rans. Most important in this respect is New Hampshire, which provides the first real electoral test of the candidates' popular appeal. Candidates in the earliest contests run not so much against one another as against the expectations that the press and polls have created about how they should do. After the early contests shape the field, the political battles move out onto a broader plain. A special feature of recent primary seasons has been "Super Tuesday," when a number of southern states hold their primary elections simultaneously. The hope has been that this will lead the candidates to pay more attention to the South and perhaps produce nominees more palatable to the South. Bill Clinton's success in 1992 was partly attributable to his success as a "native son" southerner in dominating the Super Tuesday primaries.

The protracted series of primaries and caucuses leading up to the party conventions seems excessive to many observers. The crucial early events, which set the tone for the rest of the campaign, take place in relatively small and unrepresentative states. Some see this as a good thing. A long primary season with many of the early events centered in small states keeps the political process open by giving less well known candidates with limited resources a chance to break into the political arena. Others see this as a disadvantage. They say the American political process is served less well by the election of obscure outsiders than by that of better-known insiders who understand how to make the system work as soon as they take office.

One reform proposal is to compress in time and broaden in representation the primary process by instituting either a one-day national primary or a series of regional primaries. Advocates argue that such moves would speed up the nominating process and give the citizens of every state, not just those with early delegate selection procedures, the opportunity to play a meaningful role in the selection of presidential candidates. The one-day national primary strikes many as a radical change, giving only the best-known and most prosperous candidates a real chance at the nomination. A reasonable compromise between the current fragmented system and a single national primary has been suggested: a series of **regional primaries** in different areas of the country, perhaps spaced two weeks apart over two months. Lesser-known candidates would then have the opportunity to build from small beginnings in their home regions. The 1988 and 1992 "Super Tuesdays" in the South constituted a major experiment with this approach.

The state caucuses and primaries culminate in the selection of delegates to the national **party conventions** held in July and August of the presidential election year. It is here that the party nominees are finally selected. In the past, the outcome of the nominating contest was often in doubt as delegates wrangled over disputes about rules, credentials, and party platforms and as decisions were made in "smoke-filled rooms" by party elites. But in recent years conventions have become more sedate. The publicity surrounding the selection of delegates has made the convention process almost perfunctory. The parties have tried hard to settle differences in advance or off the convention floor, lest public bickering paint an inharmonious picture of the party on television screens across the country. As the parties have tried to control and exploit media coverage of their conventions, the "news value" of these political events has declined and the television networks have given them less coverage.

One of the most important strategic decisions a presidential candidate must make by the end of the convention is that of a vice-presidential running mate. Much political folk wisdom revolves around this choice, particularly the need to **balance the ticket** geographically or ideologically. The idea is to pick a running mate who differs from the presidential candidate in a way that makes the ticket attractive to a broader range of voters. Thus southern outsider Jimmy Carter picked northern insider Walter Mondale in 1976, western outsider Ronald Reagan picked eastern insider George Bush in 1980, and eastern liberal Michael Dukakis picked southern conservative Lloyd Bentsen in 1988. Bill Clinton broke with this practice in 1992 when he chose Al Gore, a moderate white southern male like himself, as his running mate.

The vice-presidency has long been the object of political scorn. Nevertheless, the offer of the vice-presidential nomination is something that few politicians

The climax of every presidential race is election night when the votes are counted. Late on the evening of November 3, 1992, President-elect Clinton and his wife Hillary were joined on stage by Vice-President-elect Al Gore and his wife Tipper as a crowd in Little Rock, Arkansas, cheered.

would sneer at. The amenities that go with the job are first-class, and recent presidents, particularly Jimmy Carter, Ronald Reagan, and George Bush, have gone to special lengths to see that their seconds have meaningful work. Perhaps most important is the fact mentioned earlier: The vice-presidency is the most direct stepping-stone to the White House. Of the 44 people who have served as vice-president, 14 have gone on to become president. No other job in the world gives its holder better odds of becoming president. However, the ascent typically comes by death of the president rather than election. Since 1800, only two incumbent vice-presidents have gone on to win a presidential election: Martin Van Buren in 1836 and George Bush in 1988.

The Electoral College

The main factor driving strategic decisions in the general election is the Electoral College. The election of the president of the United States is an indirect process. Citizens' votes elect *electors* and those electors, constituted as the **electoral college,** elect the president. Each state gets a number of electors equal to the combined number of its representatives in the Senate and House. Thus every state gets at least three electors, with additional electors depending on the size of its population. The District of Columbia currently gets three electors, under the terms of the **Twenty-third Amendment** (1961). (Figure 7.3 shows the number of electoral votes for each state.) The electoral college has 538 in all, with 270 needed to win the presidency. There is no constitutional requirement about how states choose their electors. That is left to the discretion of each state's legislature. All but two of the states have chosen to award all their electoral votes to the candidate (actually the slate of electors for that candidate) who wins a plurality in the state. The exceptions are Maine and Nebraska, which award two electoral votes to the statewide winner and the rest of their electoral votes by congressional district.

The members of the electoral college never actually meet in one place. The electors from each state meet in their state capitals to cast their ballots on or about December 15 of the election year. The results are sent to the U.S. Senate, where the president of the Senate (who is, of course, the vice-president of the United States) presides over the count of the results in the presence of the Senate and House of Representatives. A presidential candidate who has a majority (more than 50 percent) of the electoral votes is elected outright. If no candidate has a majority, the House of Representatives, with each state delegation casting a single vote, elects a president by majority from among the top three contenders. If no president can be elected by this process, the vice-president becomes acting president. A vice-presidential candidate who has a majority is elected outright. If no candidate has a majority, the Senate picks the vice-president from the top two contenders by majority vote of individual members. Ross Perot's presence and early popularity in the 1992 presidential contest raised the possibility that he would win enough states to deprive either George Bush or Bill Clinton of an electoral college majority and throw the election into the House. However, in the end, he won no states and no electoral votes. In fact, he managed to come in second in only two states, Maine and Utah.

FIGURE 7.3
Electoral Votes, 1992 Presidential Election

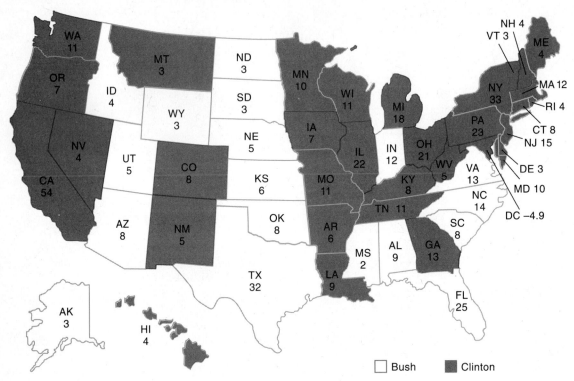

The electoral college has been, perhaps, the most prominent target of the advocates of electoral reform. Because a state's representation is determined by the number of senators as well as the number of representatives, small states are represented out of proportion to their populations. Electors are chosen state by state by plurality election, so a winner's advantage and a loser's disadvantage, no matter how slim, are magnified in the extreme. The greatest gains can be made at the smallest cost with narrow victories in big states, so candidates often focus their efforts almost entirely in the larger states. Further, persons chosen as electors for a particular presidential ticket are under no effective legal obligation actually to cast their ballots for that ticket (the **faithless elector** problem).

Worst of all to some people is the prospect of a popular-minority president, a president who gets fewer popular votes than the opponent, but still wins the presidency. This has happened three times in American history. In 1824 Andrew Jackson received more votes than John Quincy Adams, but the House chose Adams as president; in 1888 popular-vote winner Grover Cleveland lost to Benjamin Harrison. In 1876 the Democratic candidate Samuel J. Tilden outpolled Republican Rutherford B. Hayes, but a Republican-controlled commission appointed to settle a dispute over the electoral votes of three southern states awarded them—and thus the White House—to Hayes. The 1960 presidential contest between John F. Kennedy and Richard M. Nixon was the most recent near miss with this problem. Kennedy outpolled Nixon by only about 100,000 votes nationwide, and a shift of just a few thousand votes in certain states could have made Kennedy an electoral-vote winner but a popular-vote loser.

To repair all these alleged defects, reformers have come up with a variety of changes. The most sweeping proposal is to do away with the electoral college entirely and to replace it with **direct popular election** of the president and vice-president: Whoever gets the largest percentage of the national popular vote total wins the White House. This solves all the problems cited so far. But critics of direct national election see it as jeopardizing the delicate balance of the American political system. Simple plurality election would mean that presidents could be elected with the support of far less than half the people. Instituting a requirement of a majority or 40 percent of the votes to be elected might often mean a runoff election. That, in turn, would encourage more candidates to run in the first-round election. The result might be the end of the two-party, middle-of-the-road approach that has so long characterized American politics. Critics of popular election can easily point to one of the electoral college's greatest virtues: with only the three exceptions cited, it always produces a clear-cut winner.

Seeing problems with both the current electoral college and direct popular election, moderate reformers propose to steer a course somewhere between the two. One idea for reducing the impact of the statewide winner-take-all system with the resultant candidate emphasis on big states is to move to a winner-take-all system on the level of congressional districts, as Maine and Nebraska have done. This would reduce the tendency of large blocs of votes to be awarded on the basis of narrow popular-vote margins. Solutions to the faithless elector problem are to require electors to vote for the presidential candidate under whose banner they were elected or to do away with electors completely and simply tally up electoral votes.

Another call for reform focuses on the problems generated by a president who is compelled to spend the last half of a first term running for a second term. Critics of the current law, which limits a president to two full four-year terms, contend that single-term presidents do not have enough time to master the job and that first-term presidents who aspire to a second term are diverted from their duties by their efforts to get reelected. Defenders of the status quo argue that the limitation of two four-year terms gives good presidents plenty of time to achieve their objectives and allows the public ample opportunity to vote out poor presidents. A president limited to a single term, they say, would become an instant lame duck. One solution would be to allow the president one longer term, for example, of six years.[12]

Campaign Strategies

Presidential campaigns must pay careful attention to several strategic problems. One is image. Most candidates seek to fix an image of themselves in the public mind. For an incumbent, the choice is usually an easy one: to exploit as much as

---

[12] Tom Wicker, "Six Years for the President?" *The New York Times Magazine* (June 26, 1983): 16.

possible the resources of the presidency. Presidents often try to look fully occupied with governing the country and thus too busy to engage in partisan politics. For opponents the choices are harder. Should the challenger go on the attack against the incumbent president or instead play the role of the statesman? If the president is popular, the electorate may take the former as an attack on the country. The latter course is likely to attract little attention. Neither of these does the challenger much good.

How much to focus on issues is another strategic problem. Should the candidate present specific proposals regarding national problems or instead project a broad and necessarily fuzzy vision of the future? The American people continually decry candidates who do not take clear positions on issues because they deny voters a choice. But it is sobering to note that the two candidates in postwar history who gave the public the clearest choices, the conservative Barry Goldwater in 1964 and the liberal George McGovern in 1972, went down in two of the biggest defeats in American electoral history.

Nowhere are the questions of images and issues raised more directly and dramatically than in presidential debates. For an incumbent, a debate is close to a no-win proposition. It gives publicity to the opponent, puts the challenger on an equal footing with the president, and risks embarrassment either by an inadvertent slip or by an aggressive challenger. Only a desire not to appear afraid keeps a president from opting out completely. As a result, incumbents usually want as few debates and as much structure as possible. For a nonincumbent, a debate represents perhaps the best strategic opportunity of the campaign. It provides the greatest media exposure, "presidential" standing, a chance to flush the president (if the incumbent is the opponent) out of the Rose Garden, and an opportunity to display one's intellectual, political, and rhetorical wares.

The 1992 debates provided a case study on many of these issues. George Bush, as an incumbent tied to a weak economy facing an experienced and articulate debater in Bill Clinton, initially tried to avoid debates as long as possible. But Clinton's taunts that Bush was afraid to debate (accompanied by Clinton supporters dressed in chicken suits haunting Bush campaign appearances) and Clinton's persistent lead in the polls forced the Bush people to go to a heavy debate schedule as one of their few hopes of turning the election around.

In the debates, Clinton appeared presidential and Bush failed to deliver either a negative knockout punch or a positive vision of his plans for a second term. In fact, many saw Bush's fumbling response in the second debate to a young woman's question about how the bad economy had affected him personally as a clear sign that he was not going to be able to turn the election around. Bill Clinton, who followed up with a more articulate and sensitive response to that question, and Ross Perot, who scored overall with his homespun rhetoric and humorous one-liners, emerged as the overall winners.

The questions of campaign strategy are numerous and complex. The most vexing fact, though, is that strategy is always at the mercy of events. An unforeseen event can make a candidate look like a hero or a fool. A serious economic dislocation, a negative revelation about an associate, an outbreak of violence halfway around the world—any of these things can make one candidate look inept and another candidate look "presidential." Because incumbent presidents

Televised debates among presidential candidates first occurred in 1960 and have been a feature of each national campaign since 1976. The 1992 race witnessed three debates among the presidential candidates and one among the vice presidential candidates. Shown here is the second presidential debate of 1992 which took place on the campus of the University of Richmond in Virginia on October 15. The format featured questions from an audience seated around the three candidates, Ross Perot, George Bush, and Bill Clinton.

have the power to take action rather than just talk about events, they generally gain some advantage in such circumstances. But if events prove to be intractable, incumbent presidents can suffer badly. Jimmy Carter's futile struggle to free the hostages from the American embassy in Tehran, Iran, during the 1980 campaign and George Bush's poor economic record in 1992 stand as recent examples. Sometimes there is little anyone, even the president of the United States, can do to overcome events.

The Candidate's Perspective: Running for Congress

Running for Congress is much like running for president, except, of course, the stage is smaller—a state (for the Senate) or a congressional district (for the House) instead of the entire country. The basic strategic elements are the same: the problem of getting money; the two-phase contest of getting the nomination and then

winning the election; the impact of party, candidate appeal, and issues; the growing importance of the media; the long hours on the campaign trail; and so on.
However, different aspects tend to be particularly problematic.

Campaign Finance

Like presidential campaigns, House and Senate elections have become big-money
enterprises. Candidates need money for television advertising, direct mail operations to get their messages across and raise more money, polling to see how their
messages are playing, and expensive media consultants. According to Federal
Election Commission statistics, candidates for the House and Senate in 1988 spent
more than $457 million on their contests. The typical successful House campaign
now costs about $400,000, the typical Senate contest about $3.7 million.

Although public financing is an important resource for presidential elections,
congressional campaigns continue to operate without it. This leaves as the primary
resources for most congressional campaigns money donated or spent by individuals, parties, and PACs. Recent congressional elections have seen widespread
efforts by candidates and parties to get around the restrictions imposed by federal
campaign finance laws. Foremost among them were the increasing use of independent PAC expenditures to avoid the legal limits on direct contributions to
candidates and the use of soft money by parties.

A key question is whether this money actually helps a candidate. Research
suggests that it helps challengers more than officeholders. The more money a
challenger spends, the more likely he or she is to defeat the incumbent. This is
probably because money can be used to buy the name recognition and visibility
necessary to offset the advantages of incumbency. Incumbents who spend a lot
of money, however, do not do as well as those who spend less. This is probably
because incumbents tend to spend a lot of money only when they find themselves
facing a serious challenge.[13]

As in presidential campaigns, financing is a frequent target for reform in
congressional campaigns. The problems of the two are similar in some respects;
for example, too much PAC money, particularly for incumbents, and too much
soft money. However, the problems for congressional elections are exacerbated
by the lack of public financing of congressional campaigns. This makes congressional candidates much more dependent than presidential candidates on problematic sources of funds. Thus the most significant campaign reform would be public
funding of congressional campaigns. Congress has struggled repeatedly over the
last several years to institute this reform, but so far it has been unable to arrive at
any plan agreeable to both Democrats and Republicans. Many Democrats and
Republicans now say they want public financing. But the bone of contention is
public financing with or without spending limits: Democrats want limits because
they fear the wealth and fund-raising potential of some Republican candidates.

---

[13] Gary Jacobson, *Money in Congressional Elections* (New Haven, Conn.: Yale University Press, 1980),
p. 49.

Republicans, on the other hand, oppose limits because they think outspending the firmly entrenched Democratic incumbents is the only way to dislodge them.

Incumbency

Incumbency is even more an asset to members of Congress than it is to presidents. In 1988 and 1990 more than 95 percent of all representatives who ran for reelection won, and the success rate for incumbent senators was above 85 percent. It was predicted that 1992 would be the year in which anti-incumbent sentiment would be extremely strong. Although many House incumbents chose not to run because of redistricting in the wake of the 1990 census and fears about the impact of the savings-and-loan, House bank, and post office scandals, 93 percent of those incumbents who did choose to run were reelected. In the Senate, the reelection rate stayed at 85 percent.

The main reason for the difference between the House and Senate return rates is that about five out of six congressional districts are **safe seats.** That is, House districts tend to be homogeneous, and the division of party affiliation within them is lopsided enough that one or the other party is virtually assured of victory. Because senators represent states, their "districts" are often more heterogeneous, with a more even division between the parties. For both representatives and senators, incumbents are usually much better known than their challengers.[14]

As described in Chapter 8, incumbents in Congress continually boost themselves by taking credit for every beneficial activity the federal government undertakes in their states and districts. Incumbents also generally have a much easier time raising campaign funds. For example, in recent elections, more than 80 percent of all PAC money contributed to House campaigns went to incumbents. In addition, members of Congress are in a good position to use the resources of their offices to get reelected. One of the most valuable resources they have is the **franking privilege,** the right to send out official mail without any postage. Senators and representatives frequently use this privilege to send out newsletters extolling their activities on behalf of the district or questionnaires soliciting the public's opinion on current issues. In almost every case, the name and face of the legislator are prominently displayed. Another valuable resource is the staff. Most members of Congress use much of their staff's time to perform constituency services, mostly running interference through the Washington bureaucracy for constituents with problems. Needless to say, the hope is that the satisfied home voters will remember the favor on Election Day.

Critics charge that the high rates of reelection for incumbents have led to legislative stagnation and unresponsiveness. One solution that has attracted broad attention in recent years, and particularly in the 1992 campaign, is **term limits,** restricting the number of terms a person can serve in the House or Senate to, for example, 12 years. Term limits were on the ballot in 14 states in 1992 and won in all 14. Another solution is to reduce the perquisites that come with a seat in the

---

[14] Edie N. Goldenberg and Michael W. Traugott, *Campaigning for Congress* (Washington, D.C.: Congressional Quarterly, 1984), p. 136.

House or Senate, in particular to limit the amount of mail members of Congress may send at public expense under their franking privilege. Republicans attribute the high rates of reelection to gerrymandering of congressional districts by Democratic-controlled state legislatures and have worked hard to protect their interests in the redistricting that occurred after the 1990 census.

Parties, Candidates, and Issues

After incumbency, the single most important determinant of voting in congressional races is party. Both party and incumbency provide "low-cost" information cues to people facing a voting decision. The candidate's party is supplied on the ballot. The incumbent's name and generally positive reputation are known. Either may be used with little time and effort in information gathering—and either one may be substituted for the other.[15]

Earlier discussion indicated that the issues themselves usually do not play a major role in presidential campaigns. The same is even more true of congressional campaigns. The major problem is information, or rather a lack of it. If, as in many contests, voters do not recognize even the names of the candidates, they know even less about the candidates' positions and voting records on the issues.[16] Of course, the impact of issues can soar when differences between the candidates are sharp and well publicized on matters of importance. The only issue that consistently achieves salience with the public is the economy. In both presidential and midterm election years, the better the economy is doing, the better the congressional candidates of the president's party do.[17]

The other major factor in congressional voting, as in presidential voting, is the candidates themselves. Candidates for the House rest their appeal on such general qualities as trust and competence, and voters seem to respond most favorably to them.[18] Senate candidates, in contrast, are evaluated in more specific terms of experience and ability, closer to the values by which presidential candidates are judged.[19] This difference is probably because Senate candidates are generally better known than House candidates. Negative campaigning is as much a trend and an issue for congressional campaigns as it is for presidential ones.

The success of the congressional candidates from each party may be affected by the popularity of their party's president or presidential candidate. In the years when congressional elections coincide with a presidential election, a presidential candidate whose popularity appears to give a boost to his party's candidates for the House and Senate is said to have **coattails.** Ronald Reagan was said to have coattails in 1980 because his appeal seemed to help Republican congressional

---

[15] Barbara Hinckley, *Congressional Elections* (Washington, D.C.: Congressional Quarterly, 1981), p. 68.

[16] Thomas Mann and Raymond Wolfinger, "Candidates and Parties in Congressional Elections," *American Political Science Review* 74 (1980): 629.

[17] Edward Tufte, *Political Control of the Economy,* (Princeton, N.J.: Princeton University Press, 1978), pp. 113, 120.

[18] Richard Fenno, *Home Style: House Members in Their Districts* (Boston: Little, Brown, 1978), pp. 54–61.

[19] Hinckley, *Congressional Elections*, pp. 79–82.

candidates to do better than had been expected. In contrast, in 1988 George Bush was said to have no coattails because his party picked up no seats. In midterm elections, the Congressional vote is often interpreted as a referendum on how the president is doing. Historically, the president's party has tended to lose congressional seats in midterm elections. A gain or a small loss for the president's party is interpreted as an endorsement of the president and a big loss as a repudiation.

Summary

1. The American voter confronts two fundamental decisions on Election Day: whether or not to vote and, if so, how to vote. Qualifications for voting and registration in most states define the boundaries of the electorate. Beyond that, voting turnout varies substantially with social characteristics and psychological outlook toward politics.

2. The voter's decision on how to vote is similarly influenced by a broad range of factors. Throughout much of American history, partisanship has established a baseline in the division of the vote, but in recent years opinions about candidates and issues have caused voters to break from party lines.

3. Presidential candidates confront a challenge that is difficult in both strategic and physical terms. Strategically, a candidate for president confronts two separate contests: the intraparty race for the nomination and the interparty race for the White House. Physically, the candidate faces a grueling journey that begins not long after one presidential election and ends in elation or disappointment on election night four years later.

4. Congressional candidates confront a similar range of problems in getting elected. Money is an even greater problem because public financing has not yet come to congressional campaigns. Private contributions, particularly from PACs, remain a major source of political lifeblood. Because congressional elections are generally less visible than presidential campaigns, personalities and issues usually count for less and party and incumbency for more.

Key Terms

Fifteenth Amendment (p. 197)
Jim Crow (p. 197)
white primary (p. 197)
poll tax (p. 197)
Twenty-fourth Amendment (p. 198)
literacy test (p. 198)
Voting Rights Act of 1965 (p. 198)
female suffrage (p. 198)
Nineteenth Amendment (p. 198)
Twenty-sixth Amendment (p. 199)

residence requirements (p. 199)
Voting Rights Act of 1970 (p. 199)
registration (p. 199)
high-stimulus election (p. 202)
low-stimulus election (p. 202)
political alienation (p. 204)
Twenty-second Amendment
  (p. 208)
media consultant (p. 210)
horse race (p. 210)

exit polls (p. 211)
Federal Election Campaign Act
    (p. 212)
Presidential Election Campaign Fund
    (p. 212)
soft money (p. 214)
primary election (p. 214)
general election (p. 214)
open primary (p. 214)
closed primary (p. 215)
caucus (p. 215)

regional primaries (p. 215)
party conventions (p. 215)
balance the ticket (p. 216)
electoral college (p. 217)
Twenty-third Amendment (p. 217)
faithless elector (p. 218)
direct popular election (p. 219)
safe seats (p. 223)
franking privilege (p. 223)
term limits (p. 223)
coattails (p. 224)

Readings for Further Study

The voter's side of campaigns and elections is explored in two major works on voting, the classic *The American Voter* by Angus Campbell, Philip E. Converse, Warren E. Miller, and Donald E. Stokes (New York: Wiley, 1960), and the more recent *The Changing American Voter*, revised edition, by Norman Nie, Sidney Verba, and John Petrocik (Cambridge, Mass.: Harvard University Press, 1979). The former is based on surveys from the 1950s, and the latter updates and in some cases challenges the earlier study with surveys from the 1960s and 1970s. An excellent study of voting turnout is Raymond Wolfinger and Steven Rosenstone, *Who Votes?* (New Haven, Conn.: Yale University Press, 1980). The literature on presidential campaigns and elections is rich indeed: Virtually every election spawns at least one substantial account of what "really" went on. Most notable is the "Making of the President" series by Theodore H. White, particularly the classic *The Making of the President 1960* (New York: Atheneum, 1961). Herbert E. Alexander is a leading authority on the important topic of campaign finance; his *Financing Politics: Money, Elections, and Political Reform,* 2d ed. (Washington, D.C.: Congressional Quarterly, 1980), provides a good overview.

8 Congress

Thanks to the Constitution, Congress is the chief lawmaking body in the land. Because it is the branch of government established in Article 1 of the Constitution, Congress is sometimes called the "first branch." Of the three branches, Congress is also called the "people's branch" because its members are the public officials who seem most immediately responsive to changes in the public's moods and opinions. It is also the place in the national government where the political ideas of Americans are most visibly represented. Few legislative bodies possess greater authority over the lives, property, and happiness of a nation. Congress makes, or at least ratifies, fundamental decisions about national policy. Congress decides, for instance, whether the United States will have a military draft. Congress determines the fraction of every person's income the government will collect as taxes and the purposes for which that money will be spent. Key to understanding the first branch are the 535 individuals who serve in Congress: 435 as members of the House of Representatives and 100 as members of the Senate. Knowing who they are, what their job is like, what forces influence what they do, and how Congress is organized helps to explain how laws are passed.

The Constitutional Powers of Congress

The very first words of the Constitution declare that "all legislative powers herein granted shall be vested in a Congress which shall consist of a Senate and a House of Representatives." What are those powers? As summarized in Table 8.1, Congress may levy taxes, borrow and spend money, regulate foreign and interstate commerce, coin money, declare war, maintain the armed services, and establish federal courts inferior to the Supreme Court, to name but a few. Perhaps the most important grant of power is in the **necessary and proper clause,** which authorizes Congress to "make all laws which are necessary and proper for carrying into execution the foregoing powers and all other powers vested by this Constitution in the government."

TABLE 8.1
The Constitutional Powers of Congress

Responsibilities of Both House and Senate	Responsibilities of Senate Only	Responsibilities of House Only
Levy taxes	Try impeachments	Bring impeachments
Borrow and spend money	Ratify treaties	Originate tax bills
Regulate commerce	Confirm all federal judges,	
Regulate currency	ambassadors, cabinet	
Establish postal system	members, and other	
Provide for patents and	officials	
copyrights		
Establish federal courts		
below Supreme Court		
Declare war		
Maintain armed forces		
Govern the nation's capital		
Oversee national property		
Make laws "necessary and		
proper" to carry out		
above powers		

Article 1 of the Constitution grants many powers to Congress. In most cases, both houses must act, but in a few instances the Constitution specifies that one house or the other has a special role.

In *McCulloch* v. *Maryland*,[1] Chief Justice Marshall, speaking for the Supreme Court, found ample power in this clause for Congress to use all appropriate means to achieve its enumerated goals. In this case, discussed in Chapter 2, the Court supported the congressional power to create a national bank, even though this explicit power was not mentioned in the Constitution. Marshall made it clear that the necessary and proper clause added implied powers to those enumerated in the Constitution. With few exceptions, the powers of Congress have been construed broadly ever since.

But the Constitution does impose some constraints. First, the enumeration of specific powers limits what Congress can do to those powers and others implied from them. Second, Article 1, Section 9, contains eight specific limitations, including a ban on **bills of attainder** (legislative acts that declare an individual guilty and mete out punishment without a trial) and **ex post facto laws** (laws that make an act a crime after it was committed or increase the punishment for a crime already committed). As described in Chapter 3, the Bill of Rights places a set of personal liberties beyond the reach of Congress. For example, Congress cannot establish a state religion or abolish jury trials in criminal cases without violating the First and Sixth Amendments. But in the area of economic and social policy, Congress can roam broadly, deciding, for example, whether to regulate certain industries or to continue price supports for certain farm commodities.

The Constitution requires Congress to share many of its powers. This is the principle of **checks and balances** discussed in Chapter 1. The Senate ratifies treaties, but the president or his advisers negotiate them. Congress may pass laws, but the president can veto them (and can be overruled by a two-thirds vote in each house), and the Supreme Court can declare them unconstitutional. In foreign policy the president and Congress battle for control. Although Congress can declare war, the president commands the armed forces and can send them to far-flung places.

Congress also shares power within itself, for it is divided into two chambers—the Senate and the House of Representatives. The House, according to one of the Founders, George Mason, "was to be the grand depository of the Democratic principles of government." Each state was granted representation in the House according to its proportion of the national population, and members were selected by direct election. In 1964 the Supreme Court, in *Wesberry* v. *Sanders*,[2] took the principle a step further, requiring that each congressional district within the states be apportioned on the basis of equal population.

The delegates to the Constitutional Convention assumed that the House, being the most democratic of our institutions, would also be the most impulsive. Thus the Senate was to constrain the excesses of popular government. As Madison put it, "The use of the Senate is to consist in its proceeding with more coolness, with more system, and with more vision than the popular branch."[3]

---

[1] 17 U.S. (4 Wheaton) 316 (1819).
[2] 376 U.S. 1 (1964).
[3] Quoted in Roger J. Davidson and Walter J. Oleszek, *Congress and Its Members,* 3d ed. (Washington, D.C.: Congressional Quarterly, 1990), p. 23.

Apportioned two for each state, senators were originally elected by the state legislatures with the expectation that they would be more conservative and partial to entrenched economic interests. With direct election of senators required in 1913 by the **Seventeenth Amendment,** the Senate also became subject to the mass electorate, and the distinction the Founders considered so important faded away.

Yet differences between the House and the Senate remain, as Table 8.2 indicates. Almost all members of the House represent only part of a state, whereas each senator represents an entire state. Although the Constitution assigns both equal weight in writing laws, it commands unique duties to each. The Senate has the sole power to try impeachments, to confirm presidential nominations, and to ratify treaties. The House must originate tax bills (and by custom appropriation bills as well) and bring impeachments. Although neither chamber has ever consistently dominated the other, the prestige of a senator is greater than that of a House member. The reasons are obvious. There are fewer senators, and their terms are three times longer (six years versus two years). Representatives frequently give up their House seats to run for the Senate, but the reverse is seldom done.

TABLE 8.2
Differences Between the House and the Senate

Senate	House of Representatives
Senators represent entire states, with each state differing in population from other states	Members represent only part of a state (unless a state is assigned only one representative); House districts are equal in population
Senate contains 100 members	House contains 435 members
Senators serve six-year terms	Representatives serve two-year terms
Floor debate important in shaping outcome of legislation	Committee work important in shaping outcome of legislation
Unlimited debate	Limited debate
Riders (nongermane amendments) permitted	Riders prohibited
More prestige, media coverage, and visibility	Less prestige, media coverage, and visibility
Larger staffs for each senator, with size determined by population of state and distance from Washington	Smaller staffs of equal size for each member
Casework less important	Casework more important
Fewer committees	More committees
Source of many presidential aspirants	Few presidential aspirants
Vice-president is presiding officer	House elects presiding officer (Speaker)
	Rules Committee important

Although the House and the Senate are alike in many ways, differences give each a special character. In addition, the Constitution assigns to the Senate particular confirmation and treaty-ratifying powers and to the House the right to originate tax bills.

The Members of Congress

The powers the Constitution bestows on Congress present the opportunity for congressional action and influence on national policy. Much of what Congress actually does, however, is not specified in the Constitution but is largely a product of the values and interests of the 535 members who sit in the House and the Senate.

Who Are They?

The constitutional requirements for membership in Congress are simple. A House member must be 25 years old, a U.S. citizen for seven years, and a resident of the state (not the district) he or she represents. A senator must be 30 years of age, a U.S. citizen for nine years, and a resident of the state he or she represents. Although that opens the door to most of the adult population of the country, in practice the people who eventually go to Congress do not represent a cross section of the adult population. Members of Congress are predominantly white and upper-middle-class. In the One-Hundred Third Congress (1993–1995) the vast majority were lawyers or people who came from banking or business.[4] Some members—such as Senator John Glenn (D-Ohio), a former astronaut; Senator Bill Bradley (D-N.J.), a former professional basketball star; and Fred Grandy (R-Iowa), who played Gopher on "The Love Boat"—have cashed in on their celebrity status to gain election to Congress.

From its beginnings Congress was predominantly a men's club. The percentage of women serving in Congress in 1991 (5.8 percent) was only slightly higher than the percentage serving in 1953 (3 percent). Dubbed "the year of the woman" the 1992 election brought 24 new women to the House and four new women to the Senate. The percentage of women serving in the One-Hundred Third Congress practically doubled (10 percent). This figure will continue to grow in the coming years as more women are elected to state legislatures, a common launching ground for a congressional race.

Blacks were barely represented in Congress a generation ago. Between 1900 and 1928 there were no blacks in Congress, and until the passage of the Voting Rights Act of 1965 there were no blacks representing the South. Judicial interpretation of the Voting Rights Act has required that minorities be given maximum opportunity to elect their own to Congress. Consequently, in the 1992 election 13 new blacks and six new Hispanics won election to the House. In the One-Hundred Third Congress there were 39 blacks in the House and one in the Senate. Blacks still constitute only 7.4 percent of Congress, although they comprise 12.1 percent of our population. Table 8.3 on p. 233 is a profile of the members of Congress.

How Do They See Their Role?

The great eighteenth-century English political thinker Edmund Burke felt that an elected representative should seek to represent not his constituents' views but his own conscience and the broad interests of the nation. "Your representative owes

---

[4] *Congressional Quarterly Weekly Report,* November 7, 1992, pp. 8–9.

The election of 1992 resulted in a record number of women in Congress, including the three new senators shown here at a session of the Senate Committee on Banking: from the left, Barbara Boxer (D-Calif.), Carol Moseley Braun (D-Ill.), and Patty Murray (D-Wash.). Braun is the first black woman ever elected to the Senate. The success of many women candidates in 1992 may partly have resulted from the Anita Hill-Clarence Thomas affair, discussed in Chapter 11.

you," said Burke, "not his industry only, but his judgment; and he betrays, instead of serving you, if he sacrifices it to your opinion."[5] Such an understanding is known as the **trustee role.** Those who see themselves as simply voting their constituents' desires perform the **delegate role.** Most legislators combine both roles into what is known as the **politico style** of representation. These members consider their constituents' opinions and their own view of the national interest in making up their mind. The weight assigned to each varies with the issue involved. On bread-and-butter questions, such as public works and farm supports, members are more likely to follow their constituents' views than on moral questions, such as abortion or school prayer.

How Long Do They Stay?

In the early years, few members considered an actual career in Congress. Washington in the 1800s was a provincial, mosquito-ridden town, and most members lived in boardinghouses. Until after the Civil War it was not uncommon for half

---

[5] David J. Vogler, *The Politics of Congress,* 4th ed. (Boston: Allyn & Bacon, 1983), p. 76.

TABLE 8.3
Profile of the One-Hundred Third Congress (1993–1995)

	Senate	House
Average Age	58	51.7
Men/Women	94/6	388/48*
Blacks	1	39*
Hispanics	0	19†
Asians and Pacific Islanders	2	7‡
Religious Affiliations		
Protestant	63	269
Roman Catholic	23	118
Greek Orthodox	1	4
Jewish	10	32
Other and Unspecified	1	9
Occupational Backgrounds§		
Law	58	181
Clergy	1	2
Education	11	66
Politics, Public Service	10	87
Business, Banking	27	131
Medicine	0	6
Agriculture	8	19
Journalism	9	24

* Includes the nonvoting delegate from the District of Columbia.
† Includes the two nonvoting delegates from Puerto Rico and the Virgin Islands.
‡ Includes the nonvoting delegate from Guam.
§ Because some members have more than one occupation, totals exceed the membership of each house.
SOURCE: *Congressional Quarterly Weekly Report,* November 7, 1992, pp. 8–9.

The typical member of the One-Hundred Third Congress is a white, middle-aged Protestant male with a background in law or business, but less so than in the past. Reference to "nonvoting" delegates in the notes above requires some clarification. In 1993, in a move of dubious constitutionality, the Democratic majority in the House of Representatives (nonvoting delegates sit only in the House, and all nonvoting delegates are Democrats) allowed the nonvoting delegates to vote when the House sits as the Committee of the Whole, as it does much of the time. Because of the controversy this change generated, the Democratic leadership then restricted the votes of the nonvoting delegates to situations where their votes would not affect the outcome of a vote in the Committee of the Whole. Republicans charged that the Democrats were attempting to gain votes to offset their modest losses in the Democratic ranks in the 1992 elections.

the members of the House to be first-termers. Nor was it unusual for a representative or senator to resign in midterm to pursue a more lucrative profession. Few served longer than two terms.

Toward the end of the nineteenth century more members began to see service in Congress as a career. As the role of the national government expanded, the business of Congress seemed more urgent and exciting. Between

1850 and 1950 the average tenure for both senators and representatives increased, and the percentage of first-term members declined. In the 1970s those
trends began to flatten. Fewer members seemed interested in a lengthy congressional career, and the number of House members with 20 or more years'
service decreased by half.

In 1992, a record 53 members of the House, disenchanted with the demands
of the job, the low public esteem in which Congress was held, and the stalemate
between a Republican White House and a Democratic Congress, voluntarily retired
from the elective office. The 1992 election brought 110 new members to the House,
the most since 1948. In a reaction against career politicans and congressional
scandals, voters in 14 states approved term limitations for House and Senate
members. In all of these states senators were limited to 12 years, and in most
representatives were restricted to six years. Consequently, 181 members of the
One-Hundred Third Congress will be subject to term limits.

How Much Do They Do?

Today's legislators work almost 11 hours a day when Congress is in session, which
is approximately 300 working days a year. The business of Congress has expanded
in both volume and complexity. No longer does Congress have the luxury to
ruminate over the two or three issues of the day. In the Sixteenth Congress, when
James Monroe (1817–1825) was president, 480 bills were introduced. In the One-
Hundred First Congress (1989–1991) 10,352 were introduced, and they were
longer and more intricate and involved practically every area of our economic and
social life.

Their schedules are "long, fragmented and unpredictable." On any particular
day they may breakfast with a reporter; attend several committee hearings; meet
with constituents, lobbyists, or officials on legislative issues; discuss pending legislation with other members or staff, and attend floor debate. Evenings are often
consumed with meetings, receptions, and fund-raisers. Most of this is crammed
into four working days so that members may return home for a weekend of
campaigning. A 1987 survey of members showed that one-half had no personal
time and one-third had no time for family.[6]

What Do They Do?

The imperative of getting reelected motivates most members of Congress; therefore, they must cultivate the support and the trust of their constituents. How they
do that is described by Richard Fenno as a member's *home-style,* which involves:
(1) the members' allocation of time and resources to their district; (2) their personal
style; and (3) their explanation of their Washington activities. Sophisticated use of
the **franking privilege** (free postage for official business) has become an increasingly effective method for members to keep their constituents informed. In 1990

---

[6] Hedrick Smith, *The Power Game: How Washington Works* (New York: Ballantine Books, 1989), p.
108; Davidson and Oleszek, pp. 124–227.

the cost of the congressional frank exceeded $100 million. Computerized mailing lists allow incumbents to target their messages to particular constituencies.

A recent phenomenon is satellite-feed videotapes, whereby members can send prepackaged statements directly to a local television channel. Both parties have high-tech studios on Capitol Hill. For example, in the Hart Office Building the Senate Republicans have studios, film-editing rooms, and dishes on the roof so that Senators can do call-in shows or interviews for local cable channels.[7] With an advanced copy of the president's State of the Union Address, members can send their taped reaction to the speech to local television stations in time for the eleven o'clock news.

Members use a variety of methods to gain recognition and build support back home. They fight hard to see to it that their state or district gets its share of the governmental pie. Known as *pork barrel politics,* it involves gaining federal funds for sewage plants, housing units, and dams.

As eager as legislators are to denounce the size of the federal budget, they are far more anxious to secure a new federal office building, a bridge, or a hospital in their own district. But one cannot simply denounce Congress for such hypocrisy because it is shared by the public at large. Constituents expect their representatives in Washington both to cut the budget and to gain them a slice of the pork.

Beyond legislative work, members also are expected to serve as an **ombudsman** or go-between who intervenes with the federal bureaucracy on behalf of individual constituents. This is called **casework** and may include a student requesting information on a government scholarship program, a soldier interested in an early discharge, or someone with a tax or immigration problem. Such matters are usually handled by the staff through phone calls to the appropriate agency. If the case is difficult or involves influential people in the state or district, a member will deal with it personally.

How Do They See Each Other?

Legislative norms are the standards or unwritten rules of acceptable behavior in Congress. Some of these norms operate differently in each chamber, and time has altered others. First among the most important norms is **reciprocity.** Members are expected to extend support to other members in the expectation that the favor will be returned. An urban representative may support a farm bill in exchange for a rural member's vote for the food stamp program. This practice is known as **logrolling.** Among the general public it is considered vaguely disreputable, but members consider such conduct perfectly acceptable.

During the recent years of large deficits and budget cutbacks, legislation often requires that sacrifices rather than rewards be shared. In a form of negative logrolling, members will accept across-the-board reductions that limit all programs or benefits. If members can claim that everyone is taking their lumps, they can more easily avoid blame.[8]

Second, since political conflict is inherent in Congress, members are expected

---

[7] Ibid., pp. 130–131.
[8] R. Kent Weaver, "The Politics of Blame Avoidance," *The Brookings Review* 5 (Sprng 1987): 43–47.

to extend as much *personal courtesy* to each other as is possible. On the floor of Congress, colleagues refer to each other as "the gentleman from. . ." or "the gentlewoman from. . ." Members who engage in personal attacks on their colleagues are frequently rebuked.

Historically, because of the Senate's smaller size, its members have gotten to know each other better than those in the House. This has changed somewhat. The necessity of dealing with larger staffs, media demands, and frequent traveling have made it difficult for Senators to establish close friendships. The Senate's clubbiness and sense of esprit have consequently declined.[9]

Third, members are expected to *specialize* in one or two subjects, usually matters within their assigned committee. This gives Congress a degree of expertise on complex issues from arms control to acid rain. Specialization also makes a legislator's job manageable, allowing members to allocate their time and energy more efficiently. The degree of specialization is greater in the House than the Senate. Large staffs do an enormous amount of homework, enabling a Senator to become knowledgeable on a broad range of issues.[10]

In the 1950s, when Congress was dominated by older, conservative, and generally southern members, junior members were expected to serve a period of apprenticeship. They were expected to work hard, stay out of floor debates, and defer to their seniors; in brief, they were to be seen and not heard. Today a more independent and outspoken membership rarely observes that nicety. The liberal members elected in the 1960s and 1970s and the conservatives elected in the 1980s have been too independent and impatient. In the House, new members who recognize the need for some period of apprenticeship see it as months, not years. Junior senators feel no obligation to serve an apprenticeship, and senior members no longer expect it of them.

The Structure of Congress

Congress contains a complex network of party organizations, committees, subcommittees, and supporting agencies. Understanding each part of this network is important to comprehending the whole.

Party Leadership: The House

The **Speaker of the House** is the presiding officer of the House of Representatives. The position, established by the Constitution (Article 1, Section 2) is, according to the Presidential Succession Act of 1947, next in line to succeed the president after the vice-president. Although formally elected by the entire House membership, the Speaker is nominated by the majority party, all of whose mem-

---

[9] Barbara Sinclair, *The Transformation of the U.S. Senate* (Baltimore, Md.: Johns Hopkins University Press, 1989), pp. 98–100.
[10] Andy Plattner, "The Lure of the Senate: Influence and Prestige," *Congressional Quarterly Weekly Report*, May 25, 1985, pp. 991–998.

bers routinely vote for him. When the president and the Speaker are of the same party, the Speaker is expected to mobilize support for the president's program in the House and to represent House opinion to the president, seeing to it that unnecessary clashes are avoided.

The Speaker's power once rivaled that of the president, and toward the end of the nineteenth century, he was frequently referred to as a czar. The office reached its pinnacle under Speaker Joseph Cannon (R-Ill.) (1903–1911). Cannon had the power to make committee assignments and appoint and remove committee chairpersons. His impact on national policy was unmistakable. A thorough-going reactionary, Cannon helped to stifle much of President Theodore Roosevelt's (1901–1909) reform program on child labor, lower tariffs, and banking. In the 1910–1911 session of Congress a rising tide of progressivism (see Chapter 4) swept the House, and a revolt arose against Cannon in particular and the powers of the Speaker in general. The Speaker lost the power to make committee assignments and appoint committee chairpersons, and for some years after the revolt, the Speaker became once again a figurehead.

In 1975 the House Democrats increased the substantive power of the Speaker considerably. The Speaker became the chair of the party's *Steering and Policy Committee,* with the power to nominate all Democratic members of the **Rules Committee,** which clears major legislation going to the House floor. During his brief tenure as Speaker (1987–1989) Jim Wright (D-Tex.) aggressively exploited the new powers of the office to speed his legislative priorities through the House. He exerted tight control of scheduling and used the Rules Committee to restrict the amendments offered on the House floor. Wright referred pieces of major legislation to multiple committees with strict deadlines for consideration, a device known as "multiple referrals." He oversaw the passage of major trade legislation, a farm credit bill, and catastrophic health insurance. Wright resigned from the House in 1989 under fire for ethics violations. Yet, in two years he had transformed the office from a consensus builder to an agenda setter.[11]

The **majority leader** is the Speaker's chief deputy and the second most powerful figure in the majority party. Elected by the *party caucus,* the formal organization of House Democrats and House Republicans, the majority leader is his party's leader on the floor of the House, their chief spokesperson, and defender of the party's record from partisan attacks. He assists the Speaker in scheduling legislation and deciding party strategy in floor debates. Owing to his influence with the Speaker, the majority leader can help colleagues schedule legislation for floor consideration. When the president is of the same party, the majority leader confers regularly with him and frequently works to advance his programs. Since 1940 every Democratic majority leader has succeeded to the Speaker's job, as when Tom Foley (D-Wash.), majority leader in the One-Hundredth Congress, became Speaker in the One-Hundred and First.

The leader of the loyal opposition in the House is the **minority leader,** a post filled in the One-Hundred Third Congress by Robert Michel (R-Ill.). Because the Democrats have controlled the House since 1955, the job of minority leader

---

[11] Roger H. Davidson, "The New Centralization on Capitol Hill," *Review of Politics* 50 (1988): 358–359.

Contemporary Controversies

Ethics and Congressional Behavior

Congress operates in a fishbowl. Hovering around the Capitol are scores of ambitious investigative reporters and relentless federal investigators, whose inquiries not only cover public issues such as bribery or the abuse of office but also private questions of morality such as sexual conduct.

In 1977 the House and Senate passed separate, although largely similar, codes of ethics. Members and their spouses had to disclose their income, gifts received, financial holdings, debts, and other financial transactions. They were prohibited from accepting gifts of $100 or more from lobbyists or foreign nationals and from converting campaign funds to personal use.

In addition to ethics codes, the Constitution gives each chamber the power to unseat or punish its own members. Legislators, like members of most professions, are reluctant to condemn their own, and few are eager to serve on the committees that investigate such charges. Votes on censure or expulsion are considered the most distasteful a legislator can cast.

When a member has actually been convicted of criminal conduct, the issues are clear and easier for Congress to handle. The 1980 **Abscam** scandal was such an example. Six representatives and a senator were convicted of accepting money from FBI agents posing as wealthy Arabs who wanted help in getting federal grants and in arranging real estate transactions.

But some areas of congressional ethics are murky. For example, constituents expect members to pressure the bureaucracy for such things as veterans' checks, student loans, and disability benefits. But when does such pressure involve improper interference?

On April 2, 1987, four senators, at the request of one of their most generous contributors, Charles Keating, met with federal bank board chief Edwin Gray. The bank examiners were considering seizure of Mr. Keating's Lincoln Savings and Loan because of mismanagement and possible insolvency. After the meeting the board held off taking action against Lincoln for two years, when it eventually went bankrupt. The matter was investigated by the Senate Ethics Committee, which accused one of the senators, Alan Cranston (D-Calif.), of impermissible conduct that linked fund-raising and official activities. However, the Senate rules governing favors for constituents and contributors were vague, and Sen. Cranston could not be accused of violating any law or any specific Senate rule. The committee reprimanded him for "improper conduct that reflects upon the Senate." Cranston, in his own defense, insisted that his motives were "well-intentioned and honest" and that it was not unethical to intervene with the bureaucracy on behalf of a constituent simply because he or she was a contributor. But had Mr. Keating been an ordinary constituent who had given little or nothing to his campaign, would Sen. Cranston have gone to such lengths on his behalf?

has for more than three decades been held by a Republican. Being the leader of a minority can be dispiriting since one's party does not control the committee agenda and frequently loses votes on the floor.

The **party whip** acts as an assistant majority or minority leader. Whips are chosen by the party caucus. Although they have little independent power, they serve their party leadership by encouraging party discipline and floor attendance during important votes. This makes the whips the heart of the party communica-

Unethical or illegal conduct by senators and representatives may result in sanctions imposed on them by colleagues and by the voters. Following allegations of sexual misconduct in November 1992, Senator Robert Packwood (R-Ore.) apologized at a news conference on December 10, 1992, for "unwelcome and offensive" behavior toward female aides. When he traveled to his home state in January 1993, some Oregon residents demanded that he resign. In this photograph, demonstrators in Eugene, Oregon, try to gain entrance to a hotel meeting room as Senator Packwood's staff attempt to keep them out.

tion system. They poll members on crucial legislation and, when possible, pressure uncommitted members to follow the party line. They have the major responsibility of ensuring that the necessary members are present during important votes. The House Majority Whip's office is a large intelligence-gathering organization that includes a chief deputy whip, 7 deputy whips, more than 30 at-large whips, and more than 20 assistant whips.

The major arm of the Democratic caucus is the **Steering and Policy Com-**

mittee. This is a 34-member committee composed of the Speaker, the majority leader, the whips, the chief deputy whip, the chairs of four major committees, the congressional campaign committee chair, the chair of the caucus, the caucus vice-chair, 12 regionally elected members, and 8 members appointed by the Speaker. The Steering and Policy Committee was given the authority in 1974 to make Democratic committee assignments and to nominate the committee chairs, subject to caucus approval.

Committee chairs, who once received their position by reason of seniority, are now selected by a secret-ballot vote by the caucus prior to each Congress. On rare occasions the caucus has defied the principle of seniority. In 1975 the caucus rejected three committee chairs, in 1985 it rejected one, and in 1991 it rejected two. By this action, it sent a message to all committee heads that their behavior would be closely monitored.

Because the Democrats have dominated the House by swollen majorities for a generation, the influence of the Republican caucus on the workings of the House has been slight. Within the Republican caucus, known as the **Conference,** senior

Republicans and Democrats in Congress frequently disagree whether certain proposals from the president should become law. During President Clinton's State of the Union address on February 17, 1993, for example, Democratic members of Congress showed much greater enthusiasm than Republicans when Clinton called for a new system of health care. For such occasions, members have an advance copy of the president's remarks. Representatives and senators in the president's party usually have their copies already marked at the points where they are to cheer and applaud loudly.

members have more influence than their Democratic counterparts. Committee assignments are made by a **Committee on Committees** composed of one representative from each state having a Republican representative. Voting is weighted, and each member has as many votes as there are Republican members in his or her state. Starting with the One-Hundred and First Congress, the Republican leadership influence on the committee assignments increased. The minority leader and the whip now have 12 and 6 votes respectively on this committee.

Party Leadership: The Senate

Because of fewer members, party organization in the Senate is not as elaborate as in the House. Moreover, a tradition of independence cuts against attempts to regiment the membership along party lines. The *president of the Senate* and chief presiding officer is the vice-president of the United States. But the role is entirely ceremonial. It involves presiding over Senate sessions, which he rarely does, and voting only to break a tie, which happens infrequently. In addition to the vice-president, the Constitution also provides for a **president pro tempore** who may preside over the Senate in the absence of the vice-president. In practice the task of presiding over the Senate debates is given to a dozen or so junior senators in the majority party who serve about a half-hour each day. Since 1945 the post of president pro tempore has been regarded as largely honorific and given to the senior majority party member. The **majority leader** is the leader of the majority party in the Senate, elected at the beginning of each session. The **minority leader,** who leads the minority party, is also elected by party colleagues. But the majority leader is the dominant figure. As the floor leader, the majority leader is recognized first in debate, influences who will be recognized, and controls the scheduling of bills for floor consideration. Like the House Speaker, the majority leader may influence committee assignments of new senators and of other senators seeking to gain more desirable committee positions.

The Senate is far more difficult to lead than the House. Its 100 members, elected for six years, have a strong sense of independence and expect more deference to their wishes from the leadership than do House members. Only by a vote of 60 members can debate be terminated, and most routine Senate business is conducted by unanimous consent. Much of the majority leader's time is spent accommodating the hectic schedules of the individual senators. Rising constituent demands involve more service and visits to home states. The need for aggressive self-promotion and perpetual campaigning requires much from senators. Not only must they make frequent home visits, but they must engage in a constant round of media appearances, speeches, and fund-raising activities. Former Majority Leader Robert Byrd (D-W.Va.) once explained his role as "a traffic cop, babysitter, welfare worker, minister, lawyer, umpire, referee, punching bag, target, lightning rod [and] . . . the cement that holds his party group together."[12] Thus an effective

---

[12] Quoted in Samuel C. Patterson, "Party Leadership in the U.S. Senate," *Legislative Studies Quarterly* 14 (1989): 409.

majority leader must be a consummate diplomat, nurturing inflated egos, accommodating individual agendas, and smoothing ruffled feathers in order to pass important legislation.

The function of the party leader goes beyond managing the business of the Senate. The party leader is also a media personality and spokesperson for the party. That was an important reason why the Senate Democrats chose Sen. George Mitchell (D-Me.) as majority leader in the One-Hundred First Congress. Mitchell is considered a master of the brief, pithy comment that is so effective on the evening news.

The whip system in the Senate is smaller and less institutionalized than in the House. The *Senate whips* basically serve the floor leaders as vote counters and have not been major power brokers. Both the Senate majority and minority whips are elected by their caucus on a secret ballot prior to the beginning of each new Congress.

The Committee System

Contemporary lawmaking involves an understanding of numerous complex subjects. Members of Congress cannot be expected to master the details of the hundreds of bills that come before them. Through the committee system they can gain specialized knowledge of particular areas of policy and legislation.

There are three classes of committees: **Standing committees** (22 in the House and 16 in the Senate) are at the center of the congressional process. They alone can approve legislation and send it to the House or Senate floor for consideration. **Joint committees** are permanent committees made up of members from both houses. **Special** or **select committees** are created periodically to study particular problems or new areas of legislation not covered by the standing committees.

The concept of seniority, or privileges based on length of service, permeates Congress and is essential to understanding the committee system. **Congressional seniority** is based on length of continuous service in Congress. This can affect committee assignments, the amount of office space a member is granted, and even the deference shown a member during floor debate. **Committee seniority** is determined by the years of continuous service on a particular committee. The committee chair is usually the member of the majority party with the longest consecutive service on the committee. A member who switches committees must start at the bottom of the committee ladder.

Members consider desirable committee assignments crucial to their reelection. After each congressional election, freshman representatives and senators scramble to gain assignments suitable to their political fortunes and interests. Incumbents maneuver to gain more prestigious assignments. Assignments are first handled by a committee on committees in each house by each party, approved by the party caucuses (Democrats only), and then, in what is always a formality, approved again by the full Senate and House. Several criteria govern these assignments. For example, House Democrats rarely allow any member serving on what they call the "exclusive" committees (Ways and Means, Rules, and Appropriations) to serve on any other standing committee. Both Republicans and Democrats in the Senate agree that no member will receive two major committee assignments until every member has received one. Almost every senator now has the opportunity to serve on one of the four most prestigious committees (Appropriations, Armed Services, Finance, and Foreign Relations).

Members concerned primarily with reelection seek to join committees whose work has a direct impact on their constituents. A representative or senator from an area with considerable defense installations and large military contracts will probably seek membership on the Armed Services Committee, which handles the defense budget. Westerners are attracted to the House Interior and Senate Energy and Natural Resources committees, whose jurisdictions include mining, government lands, immigration, and environmental laws. Members from states that produce crops heavily dependent on government support programs (wheat, peanuts, tobacco, and sugar) seek membership on the agriculture committees. Those interested in influencing national policy seek membership on committees that consider broad public issues such as education, foreign policy, and civil rights. Some members, as they become more senior and more entrenched at home, seek to expand their influence within their respective chambers. They are drawn to committees that decide matters of importance to practically every member. These are the tax-writing committees (Senate Finance and House Ways and Means), the spending committees (Appropriations and Budget), and in the House, the scheduling committee (Rules).

Members cannot passively wait for their assignments. They must make their preferences known, urge senior members from their own states to lobby for them, personally meet with the chair or ranking minority member of the committee, and cultivate the support of the party leadership. Election results are barely known in November when senators and representatives descend on Washington to compete for the choicest committee seats. Committee assignments, one of the few benefits the congressional leadership can control, are employed when possible to promote party loyalty and responsibility.

At one time, committee chairs gained their position by sheer dint of seniority and ran their committees like feudal baronies. They appointed subcommittee chairs, abolished or created subcommittees, decided whether or not to call committee meetings, and hired staff. Although the chairs still retain many of these powers (influencing the agenda, hiring staff, controlling committee funds), they are no longer the autocrats of yesteryear.

The reforms of the 1970s limited and defined the chairs' power. In the House they lost the power to prevent committees from meeting, to designate subcommittee chairs, and to refer legislation to subcommittees. In the Senate chairs no longer control all staff appointments, and consequently they have lost their influence over this important group of experts. Chairs do not want to appear to be obstructing legislation strongly supported by a majority of the caucus for fear of losing their positions. But chairs still hold considerable power, although it is far from absolute. To get things done, they must use all their diplomatic and legislative skills. House Rules Committee Chairman Joe Moakley (D-Mass.) put it this way: "The days of snarling chairmen who look through junior members are long gone.

To survive, you have to be gracious even when you say no."[13] Nor can chairs exercise their authority behind closed doors. The Legislative Reorganization Act of 1970 opened up the committee process, which had previously been conducted away from the direct scrutiny of the public and the media (as well as the lobbyists). Open committee hearings are now required in most cases, and committee roll-call votes are available to the public.

Subcommittees

Most of the standing congressional committees are divided into subcommittees. In the One-Hundred Second Congress there were 131 in the House and 87 in the Senate. House committee chairs previously controlled their subcommittees by packing them with members who would follow their lead. Under such circumstances, subcommittees would rarely report to the full committee legislation that the chair opposed. When the era of the autocratic chair came to an end, there was a trend in the House toward "subcommittee government."

In 1973 the House Democratic caucus adopted a subcommittee "bill of rights." Democrats on every committee were given the authority to select subcommittee chairs, establish subcommittee jurisdiction, and provide the budgets for running the subcommittees. It required that all committees with more than 20 members be required to establish at least four subcommittees, ending the Ways and Means Committee's unique practice of operating without subcommittees. Subcommittee chairs and the ranking minority members were allowed to hire staff to work directly for them on their subcommittee.

Subcommittees assumed greater independence, conducting legislative hearings once held primarily by the full committee. Whereas only 30 percent of the legislative hearings in the early 1950s were conducted by subcommittees, by the mid-1970s the figure had risen to 90 percent. Subcommittees were also drafting more legislation and frequently gaining full committee approval. Subcommittee chairs were replacing committee chairs as the managers of legislation on the floor.

This movement toward subcommittee government is less prevalent in the Senate, where subcommittees primarily hold hearings and key votes are taken in the full committee. Yet in the Senate Commerce, Judiciary, and Labor committees, subcommittees have gained greater autonomy.[14]

The more democratic subcommittee government came with a cost. As more members exercised initiative and fewer could deliver the votes and call the shots, the committee system became increasingly unwieldy. With additional centers of power in Congress, party leaders had a far more difficult time building coalitions and constructing compromises.

---

[13] *Congressional Quarterly Weekly Report,* December 8, 1990, p. 406.
[14] Lawrence Dodd and Bruce Oppenheimer, "The House in Transition: Change and Consolidation," *Congress Reconsidered,* 2d ed. (Washington, D.C.: Congressional Quarterly, 1981), p. 42; Davidson and Oleszek, *Congress and Its Members,* p. 230.

Congressional Staff and Agencies

One hundred years ago senators and members of Congress performed their duties with only a few clerks, paid from members' own personal funds. By the 1990s over 14,000 people were employed on Capitol Hill as personal staff to representatives and senators or as committee staff, paid from public funds. This burgeoning congressional bureaucracy reflects the complexity of modern government. The issues have grown more intricate, the congressional work load has expanded, and Congress has felt the need to match the expertise of the executive branch. A typical congressional office will include a **legislative assistant** (LA) to analyze bills, draft laws, write speeches, and prepare position papers and an **administrative assistant** (AA) to act as the legislator's alter ego in dealing with colleagues, constituents, and lobbyists. In addition, most legislators have offices in their home states or districts to provide efficient constituent service and a personal touch. Who are these staff people? They are relatively young (average age slightly under 40), well educated (close to half have postgraduate or professional degrees), and predominantly male (over 70 percent). In an earlier time they may have been political operatives or cronies of the legislator, but today they are bright university graduates. The experience of being a staffer can be both exhilarating and precarious. Staffers are frequently in the center of dramatic legislative battles, but they have no civil service protection and can be fired by their representative or senator without cause or notice. Unlike the personal staffers, whose job it is to serve the member and his or her political interest, the *committee staffers* are responsible for developing the legislation that comes from the committees. They are appointed by the committee chair, subcommittee chair, or ranking minority party member. They organize hearings, conduct research, assist in the drafting of legislation, and prepare the reports that accompany bills sent out of committee. The chief committee aides—those most familiar with the details of a particular bill—may accompany the committee chair when the bill is debated on the floor. Because a member's time is stretched thin, staffers may act as stand-ins for the legislators themselves, negotiating with lobbyists, executive branch officials, and even other legislators to gain support for a particular bill. Like the rest of the congressional bureaucracy, the congressional committee staffs grew from about 400 in 1947 to over 3300 in 1989—an increase of over 750 percent.[15]

Has this expansion of staff solved the congressional need for more information? Some argue that members have become too dependent upon committee staff. Frequently staffers are the only ones who understand increasingly complex legislation such as the Clean Air Act of 1990. Others argue that more staff generate more legislation, diluting a member's ability to concentrate on what is important. Has the Congress simply transferred its dependency for information from the executive branch to its own staff?[16]

---

[15] Norman J. Ornstein, Thomas E. Mann, and Michael J. Malbin, *Vital Statistics on Congress, 1991–1992* (Washington, D.C.: Congressional Quarterly, 1992), p. 124.

[16] Michael L. Mezey, "The Legislature, the Executive, and Public Policy: The Futile Quest for Congressional Power," in James A. Thurber, ed., *Divided Democracy* (Washington, D.C.: Congressional Quarterly, 1991), p. 107.

In addition to staff, four agencies provide Congress with research and analysis of policy options:

1. The **Congressional Research Service** (CRS) serves the entire Congress—members, committees, and aides. On request, it conducts legal research and policy analysis and digests and summarizes legislation. Congress created the CRS to remedy the dearth of information at Congress's disposal, compared to the information resources long available to the president.
2. The **General Accounting Office** (GAO), known as the watchdog agency, reports to Congress on the efficiency and performance of federal programs. With over 5100 employees, its task is to see whether a program is achieving the objectives that Congress has prescribed.
3. The **Office of Technology Assessment** (OTA) was created in 1972 when Congress was concerned about its ability to confront the technical issues of energy and the environment. The OTA examines the impact of technology on policy and addresses such issues as the safety of nuclear reactors, the effects of a limited nuclear war, and the possibilities of solar and geothermal energy.
4. The **Congressional Budget Office** (CBO) provides essential analysis of the economy and the federal budget for Congress. Specifically, it provides an assessment of the inflationary impact of major bills, projects the five-year costs of proposed legislation, and forecasts economic trends. The CBO gives Congress an independent base of economic and budgetary expertise to challenge the economic assumptions behind the president's budget.

Congressional Procedures: How a Bill Becomes a Law

Ultimately Congress matters in American government because it is the chief law-making body. Presidents, parties, and interest groups may propose a host of programs, but unless Congress acts favorably, each proposal remains an idea, not a law. The legislative process in Congress is an obstacle course (see Figure 8.1). A bill can be stalled or defeated at various points along the way, and most are. Of the over 10,000 bills and resolutions introduced in the One-Hundred First Congress only 650 ultimately became law.

Committee to Floor Debate

The objective of guiding a bill through Congress is to have both houses pass the bill in identical form. Only then can it go to the president for signing. At the initial stage of the legislative process, only a member of the House or the Senate may introduce a bill, although the proposal frequently originates in the executive branch, an interest group, or a member's staff. Once a bill is introduced, it is sent to the appropriate committee; should a committee refuse to consider the bill, it is

FIGURE 8.1
How a Bill Becomes a Law

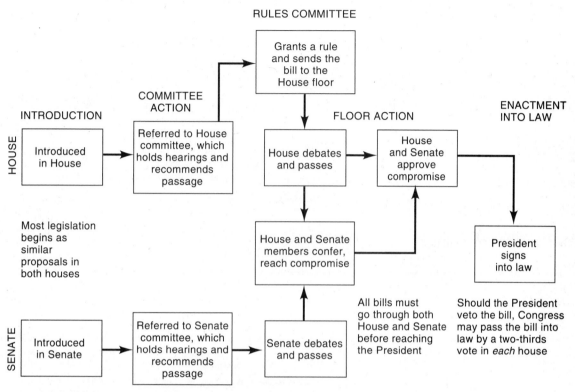

At each step along the way, a bill can be stopped, making this journey a genuine obstacle course.

consigned to an early death. If the bill is considered, it is usually assigned to a subcommittee for study, and the process begins. The subcommittee may then hold hearings inviting government officials and other experts to testify. These hearings serve not only to obtain information but also to test public opinion, build support for the measure, or perhaps delay ultimate consideration. Except in the case of national security matters, most hearings are open to the public. When the hearings are complete, the bill is **marked up.** This is the process whereby the subcommittee decides on the bill's precise language and on amendments. Like hearings, most mark-up sessions are open to the public.

The bill, if approved by the subcommittee, then goes to the full committee for consideration. If the full committee approves the·bill (it may mark up the bill or add its own amendments), it sends the bill to its respective chamber for consideration. Bills voted out of committee are often accompanied by an extensive report that explains the bill's purpose, the committee amendments, its effect on existing law, and its probable costs.

Floor Debate: The House

Bills finally reported out of committee are listed on one of the House calendars. Tax and appropriation bills are placed on the **Union Calendar.** Nonmoney bills go to the **House Calendar.** Private bills, such as one that granted citizenship to an 111-year-old Albanian woman so that she could vote in a free election before she died, are placed on the **Private Calendar.** Noncontroversial measures, such as one declaring National Dairy Goat Awareness Week, are placed on the **Consent Calendar.**

The Speaker and the majority leader determine when bills are called off the calendar and placed on the House floor. Bills on the Consent Calendar and the Private Calendar are brought directly to the floor usually by unanimous consent and passed with little debate. The Speaker may also bring other minor bills directly to the floor by a **suspension of the rules.** Under this procedure, which requires a two-thirds vote of the House, debate is limited to 40 minutes, and no amendments are allowed. Other matters are considered privileged and can be brought to the House floor at almost any time. But most major bills must take the route from the committee to the House floor via the Rules Committee. The Rules Committee decides the amount of time the House will spend debating a bill and dictates the amending process. The committee may send a bill to the floor with a **closed rule,** prohibiting all amendments except those from the committee that reported the bill; an **open rule,** permitting any amendments from the floor; or a **modified rule,** allowing a limited number of amendments. Tax bills reported out of the Ways and Means Committee are usually given the privilege of a closed rule. The Democrats on the Rules Committee are appointed by the Speaker, and the committee is thus an arm of the leadership.

When floor debate begins, the Speaker has a member of the Rules Committee from each party explain the rule under which the bill will be debated and voted on. Usually the Rules Committee specifies from one to two hours of debate, but it will grant controversial bills of particular importance up to 10 hours. Debate begins with a statement from the floor manager of the bill, by custom the chairperson of the committee or subcommittee that reported the bill. The floor manager has the responsibility of guiding the bill to passage. Frequently debate is conducted in the **Committee of the Whole.** This device allows the House to conduct business more quickly by relaxing the formal rules and by a quorum requirement of only 100, instead of the usual 218. But the full House must approve decisions made by the Committee of the Whole before they are official.

After general debate covering the pros and cons of the bill, the amending process begins. Here the fate of a bill may be decided. Opponents of the bill may try to amend it beyond recognition or else add objectionable provisions destined to kill it. The House rules require that amendments be germane to the bill under consideration. Amendments are debated no more than 10 minutes—5 minutes for the sponsors and 5 for the opponents.

An electronic voting system, installed in 1973, makes time-consuming roll-call votes unnecessary. Members may insert a plastic card into one of 40 voting machines and vote "yes," "no," or "present" (abstaining). The vote is recorded on an electronic display board on the wall of the chamber, and the process takes about 15 minutes. Members are alerted to floor votes by a series of bells that ring through the halls and offices of Congress.

Floor Debate: The Senate

The Senate, being smaller, has a more flexible set of procedures. First, there are only two Senate calendars: an **Executive Calendar** for presidential nominations and treaties and a **Calendar of General Orders** for all other legislation. Second, there is no equivalent of the House Rules Committee. Thus the Senate imposes no time limits on the general debate, no five-minute rule on amendments, and no restrictions on the number of amendments, and amendments need not be germane to the bill under consideration.

Nongermane amendments, called **riders,** allow a proposal to bypass a hostile Senate committee that otherwise would have considered and probably killed it. The rider must then only survive the conference committee if the complete bill passes the Senate. Riders are also used to force the president to accept a program that would be vetoed were it to reach him as a separate piece of legislation. This is done by attaching the rider to necessary legislation, such as a general appropriations bill, that the president will feel compelled to sign. One may ask how, with such permissive rules, does the Senate ever accomplish anything? It is done through **unanimous consent agreements,** which limit the terms of Senate debates. These agreements, usually secured by the majority leader in cooperation with the minority leader, are carefully negotiated to accommodate the desires of senators who wish to speak or offer amendments.

The best-known technique for forestalling the work of the Senate is the **filibuster**—continuing debate designed to prevent passage of a bill. A filibuster can be conducted by a single senator or a group of senators. The filibuster is essentially a political device to stop a bill that the minority does not have the votes to defeat, to win concessions on a bill, or to arouse public opposition to it. Defenders argue that the filibuster protects minority rights and requires the Senate to consider not only the extent of opposition but its depth and intensity as well. Critics claim that the filibuster thwarts majority will and allows a small minority to exercise disproportionate influence on a bill or even to defeat it altogether. Until 1917 the Senate had no way of ending debate except through unanimous consent. At that time the Senate adopted Rule 22, a **cloture** (debate-ending) rule that allowed two-thirds of the senators present to end debate. In 1975 the rule was amended so that 60 members (or three-fifths of the membership) can shut off debate. Once cloture is invoked, the Senate can continue consideration of the bill for only 30 additional hours. Prior to the 1970s a filibuster was a rare event, used primarily by southern Democrats to block civil rights legislation. Now it is almost commonplace and occurs on a wide range of issues. Cloture votes, which numbered six in the Ninetieth Congress (1967–1969), rose to 43 in the One-Hundredth. Owing to the time constraints on a busy Senate (more committee meetings, more recorded votes, more bills considered), even the threat to delay business by a filibuster can force a concession on a bill. (See "Politics and Ideas: Two Ideologues in the Senate.")

Armed with a 57-43 Democratic advantage in the Senate when his administra-

Filibusters are possible in the Senate but not in the House. They allow a minority to delay the vote on a bill, to block it entirely, or to bargain for compromises in a bill they find otherwise unacceptable. Filibusters can be particularly effective near the end of a session of Congress when there is a backlog of legislation to be considered. Shown here are senators resting in preparation for a long filibuster of a civil rights bill in 1960. From the left they are Clifford Case (R-N.J.), Norris Cotton (R-N.H.), Norman Brunsdale (R-N.D.), Russell Long (D-La.), Hiram Fong (R-Hi.), and Alexander Wiley (R-Wis.). A modest measure by today's standards, the bill eventually passed in amended form and provided for the appointment of referees to help blacks register to vote.

tion began, President Clinton felt no urgent need to negotiate with the Republicans in that body to secure the passage of his legislative agenda. He did not anticipate that the Republican minority, resentful of having been shut out of the process, would resort to a filibuster. In the spring of 1993 during the first months of the Clinton administration, the Republican members of the Senate successfully employed the filibuster to prevent the President's economic "stimulus package" (funding for job retraining, urban assistance, Head Start) from coming to a vote. In this case the filibuster was a warning shot to a new president that the Senate's rules permit a determined minority to exercise considerable influence.

Politics and Ideas

Two Ideologues in the Senate

Ideologues can rarely be called great architects of legislation. Consider two contemporary members of the Senate, Jesse Helms and Howard Metzenbaum. Standing at opposite ends of the political spectrum, Senator Howard Metzenbaum (D-Ohio) and Senator Jesse Helms (R-N.C.) are ideologues—people for whom it is more important to defend principles than to resolve differences.

Helms, a major spokesperson of the New Right, advocates a hard-line foreign policy, wants to see prayer allowed in public school, and opposes legalized abortion. He uses all his parliamentary acumen to influence the foreign policy of the executive branch and to force his Senate colleagues to take public positions on issues they would rather avoid. As a senior member of the Foreign Relations Committee, Helms has blocked or delayed the nominations of foreign policy officials whose views he does not share. By simply threatening a filibuster, Helms can cajole the Senate leadership, pressed with a busy agenda, not to bring up the nomination of an official he opposes. In 1985 Helms held up several dozen diplomatic appointments until he received assurances from the Reagan administration that they would find positions for six diplomats who supported Helms's conservative views.

Helms consistently seeks roll-call votes on abortion and school prayer in spite of clear evidence that they have no chance of enactment. None of this endears him to the Senate, which places a premium on cooperation and collegiality. It does, however, score points with the thousands of people across the country who contribute to his campaign. In his 1990 reelec-

tion campaign, Senator Helms raised over $12 million from direct mail and out-of-state conservative contributions.

While sharing few, if any, of Jesse Helms's views, liberal Senator Howard Metzenbaum employs some of the same techniques. Metzenbaum has used the filibuster rule to block or delay what he considers special-interest legislation. Toward the end of a session, when senators are eager to adjourn, Metzenbaum, in order to stop bills he opposes, will either threaten a filibuster or, failing that, introduce numerous amendments about which he has prepared extensive comments. Consequently, Metzenbaum has a pervasive, if unpopular, presence in the Senate. One senate colleague said of him, "When you prepare an amendment or a bill, subconsciously you're thinking about Howard Metzenbaum. Will it pass the Metzenbaum test?"

Both pay a price for their obstructionism. Sen. Alan Simpson (R-Wyo.), the Republican whip, put it bluntly, "Other senators go hunting with a passion for the bills that Helms and Metzenbaum want." This frequent threat or use of the filibuster by ideologues such as Helms and Metzenbaum makes the work of the Senate more difficult and the schedule less controllable. These maverick senators are more interested in using the Senate as platforms for their ideas than in forging coalitions and compromises. But senators are reluctant to alter the rules in order to make the Senate function more efficiently. Do Senators such as Helms and Metzenbaum raise important issues, or do they merely obstruct the business of Congress?

The Conference Committee: Resolving Senate-House Differences

Rarely do the Senate and House pass bills in identical form. If one house makes only minor changes in a bill passed by the other, the chamber that initially passed the bill will usually agree to the changes and send the bill on to the president for signature. But when there are major differences in dispute, a **House-Senate Conference Committee** must reconcile them. The conferees are named by the House Speaker and the Senate presiding officers on the recommendation of the chairperson of the committee that reported the bill. The majority from each delegation must be from the majority party in that chamber. Each chamber has one vote in the conference, which is determined by a vote of the majority of its delegation.

When the conference finishes its job, it sends the conference report or compromise bill back to the House and Senate for approval. Approval of the conference report by both houses constitutes final approval of the bill. Numerous traps await a bill before it gets to the president's desk. Bills must pass the Senate and the House within the two-year time period that makes up a particular Congress; otherwise, the bill must start through the obstacle course anew with the next Congress. It can be buried in committee or by the House Rules Committee, stifled by a Senate filibuster, or caught in a conference committee deadlock. Sponsors of a bill must know congressional procedure, be sensitive to key personalities such as the Speaker or the important committee chairs, and must at each crucial point weave a majority coalition for the bill.

Congress and the Political System

The legislative process alone does not explain why some bills become law and others do not. Congress is also part of the broader political system. Everything it does affects citizens as well as one or more interest groups and governmental agencies. These different constituencies labor mightily to influence congressional decisions.

The Lobbies

As the range of government programs, subsidies, and entitlements has grown, so has the number of interest groups with a stake in them. The result has been the proliferation of lobbies and lobbyists, as described in Chapter 6. Critics feel that lobbies distort the political process and give particular groups inordinate influence over legislation.

Lobbyists are most successful in affecting **distributive policies** (special-interest subsidies such as water reclamation projects, farm price supports, and new post offices). These programs usually provoke little opposition because they are perceived as providing considerable benefits at little relative cost. As a result, the entire Congress rarely pays close attention to these questions. Lobbyists can then concentrate their efforts on a key subcommittee or committee, simplifying its task. Open committee sessions allow lobbyists to monitor congressional action quite carefully. Rather than waiting outside a closed door while a committee mark-up session is going on, a lobbyist may be right in the committee room suggesting precise legislative language or a compromise amendment.

Lobbies have the most difficulty affecting **redistributive policies,** those that produce benefits to some segments of society at substantive cost to others. These include broad budget decisions that place social programs against defense spending or proposals for tax reform. Such issues are frequently resolved on the floor of Congress, not in committee. Because they usually involve conflicts among interest groups, the result is often a compromise, with no single lobby getting exactly what it wants.

Contemporary lobbying must go beyond working the halls of Congress. Moving legislation often requires affecting public opinion. Therefore, lobbyists must employ the techniques of mass marketing: targeted mailings, television advertising, and slick public relations campaigns. The National Rifle Association can generate millions of telegrams in 24 hours opposing a gun control measure; the retirees' lobby swamped Speaker Wright in one day with over 15 million postcards and letters warning against tampering with the cost-of-living formula for Social Security.[17] Much of this increase is a result of the weakened power of the committee chairs and the decentralization of power in Congress. Now that there are more committee members and staffers to be persuaded, more lobbyists are required to do the job.

The Bureaucracy

Interest groups are not the only lobbying force in Congress. The bureaucracy itself exercises considerable influence on the congressional process. Together with interest groups and congressional committees, bureaucratic agencies often develop informal partnerships called *subgovernments* or **iron triangles.** Each group scratches the back of the other. The agency gets its budget from the committee and political support from the interest group. The interest group gets favorable legislation from the committee and sympathetic treatment from the agency. The congressional committee members get campaign reelection support from the interest group and conscientious constituency service from the bureaucracy. These subgovernments have special influence over distributive policy.

An example involves veterans' programs. In this case the subgovernment includes the veterans' groups, the veterans' committees of Congress, and the Department of Veterans Affairs (see Figure 8.2). Together these pieces of the subgovernment conspire to protect veterans' programs from the budget-cutter's scalpel. Veterans' benefits are usually not matters at the top of the president's agenda, nor are they issues that excite broad congressional interest. They are, in fact, typical of the type of distributive policies that are shaped by subgovernments.

---

[17] Smith, *The Power Game,* p. 383.

FIGURE 8.2
The "Iron Triangle" and Veterans' Policy

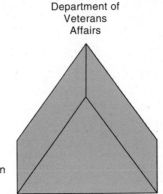

Department of
Veterans
Affairs

- House Commitee on
  Veterans Affairs

- Senate Commitee on
  Veterans Affairs

- American Legion
- Veterans of Foreign Wars
- Disabled American Veterans
- American Veterans Committee
- Vietnam Veterans of America

The triangular relationship among congressional committees, bureaucratic agencies, and interest groups indicates how relatively few people can determine public policy on some questions. The relationship does not mean that the groups are always in agreement, but it does mean that the dominant opinion represented here will usually have the largest say in setting veterans' policy. Sometimes the components in the triangle are more numerous. A proposed change in educational benefits, for example, would involve higher education lobbies and other committees and agencies. A change in job-training policy for veterans would involve the Labor Department as well as the labor committees in Congress.

To function effectively an iron triangle requires that the participants be shielded from the glare of publicity. Over the past decade the environment has changed and the effectiveness of these subgovernments has declined. The media are more aggressive in covering Congress, the number of lobbies with competing interests in legislation has increased, new public interest lobbies watch for special interest favoritism, and no committee has exclusive control over such broad issues as energy, foreign trade, and the environment. In the period of tight budgets fewer issues could be classified as distributive, providing benefits to a few without significant and visible costs to the many.[18]

What Role for a Changing Congress?

Largely through its own efforts, Congress democratized its rules and opened up its procedures. The seniority system is no longer sacred. Committee chairs do not control their committees. Committee sessions are now accessible to the public.

---

[18] Morris P. Fiornia, *Congress: Keystone of the Washington Establishment,* 2d ed. (New Haven, Conn.: Yale University Press, 1989), pp. 122–123.

Junior members can make an immediate impact, often serving as subcommittee chairs. And the creation of the Congressional Budget Office and the Office of Technology Assessment, plus the addition of more professional staffers, has put Congress in the position to challenge the expertise of the executive branch.

Many people welcome the resurgence of congressional will as a necessary corrective to the presidential excesses that produced the Vietnam War and the Watergate scandal. They argue that the openness of Congress is essential to a democratic society. But other observers question whether Congress has gone too far in its reassertion of power and independence. Congress cannot control inflation, negotiate arms agreements, or solve our trade deficit. They feel that the American government functions best under the leadership of the president. Only the president, they argue, can define national objectives that can arouse a majority of citizens. The historic statements of national policy, so the argument goes, were presidential not congressional: the Monroe Doctrine, the Emancipation Proclamation, the War on Poverty. Although Congress cannot lead, it does have an important role to play. It provides more citizen access to policymaking and offsets the impersonality of the bureaucracy. In a larger sense, Congress brings the parochialism of Main Street, the suburban kaffeeklatsch, and the union hall to Washington's corridors of power. The many and often confusing voices with which Congress speaks are the clatter of the democratic process.

Summary

1. Since 1819 the Supreme Court has granted Congress great leeway in legislating on social and economic matters. Both houses have equal weight in writing laws. But the Senate, owing to its longer terms, its special responsibilities (ratifying treaties and confirming presidential appointments), and its smaller size, seems to command somewhat greater prestige.
2. The task of members of Congress has many dimensions—mastering fields of legislation, bringing back a share of federal benefits for their state or district, meeting the needs of individual constituents, learning the norms and rules of their respective chambers, and voting on a wide variety of legislative questions. It is a demanding, complex, full-time job.
3. Power in the contemporary Congress is no longer the exclusive prerogative of a few senior members. In the House much of the power has flowed to the subcommittees. Individual senators have become increasingly assertive. Junior members feel under little obligation to serve a period of apprenticeship. Congress as a result is both more democratic and more unwieldy.
4. Leadership in Congress is based largely on persuasion and ability. Autocratic leaders are increasingly rare. The influence of the caucus requires that most congressional leaders be sensitive to the concerns of the rank-and-file members.
5. Before a bill can become a law, it must pass through a complete obstacle course. At each crucial point, successful sponsors must weave a majority coalition for their bill.

6. Congress, although influenced by presidential leadership, is not the president's rubber stamp and initiates much legislation on its own.

Key Terms

necessary and proper clause
  (p. 228)
bills of attainder (p. 229)
ex post facto laws (p. 229)
checks and balances (p. 229)
Seventeenth Amendment (p. 230)
trustee role (p. 232)
delegate role (p. 232)
politico style (p. 232)
franking privilege (p. 234)
ombudsman (p. 235)
casework (p. 235)
legislative norms (p. 235)
reciprocity (p. 235)
logrolling (p. 235)
Speaker of the House (p. 236)
Rules Committee (p. 237)
House majority leader (p. 237)
House minority leader (p. 237)
Abscam (p. 238)
party whip (p. 238)
Steering and Policy Committee
  (p. 239)
Conference (p. 240)
Committee on Committees (p. 241)
president pro tempore (p. 241)
Senate majority leader (p. 241)
Senate minority leader (p. 241)
standing committees (p. 242)
joint committees (p. 242)
special or select committees (p. 242)
congressional seniority (p. 242)

committee seniority (p. 242)
legislative assistant (p. 245)
administrative assistant (p. 245)
Congressional Research Service
  (p. 246)
General Accounting Office (p. 246)
Office of Technology Assessment
  (p. 246)
Congressional Budget Office (p. 246)
marked up (p. 247)
Union Calendar (p. 248)
House Calendar (p. 248)
Private Calendar (p. 248)
Consent Calendar (p. 248)
suspension of the rules (p. 248)
closed rule (p. 248)
open rule (p. 248)
modified rule (p. 248)
Committee of the Whole (p. 248)
Executive Calendar (p. 249)
Calendar of General Order (p. 249)
riders (p. 249)
unanimous consent agreements
  (p. 249)
filibuster (p. 249)
cloture (p. 249)
House-Senate Conference Committee
  (p. 252)
distributive policies (p. 252)
redistributive policies (p. 253)
iron triangle (p. 253)

Readings for Further Study

For a comprehensive overview of Congress, consult Roger H. Davidson and Walter J. Oleszek, *Congress and Its Members,*

3d ed. (Washington, D.C.: Congressional Quarterly, 1990), and Morris P. Fiorina, *Congress: Keystone of The Washington Es-*

tablishment, 2d ed. (New Haven, Conn.: Yale University Press, 1989). A collection of highly readable essays on the problems of the contemporary Congress can be found in Lawrence C. Dodd and Bruce I. Oppenheimer, eds., *Congress Reconsidered,* 4th ed. (Washington, D.C.: Congressional Quarterly, 1989). Up-to-date information and lively accounts of individual senators and representatives are available in Michael Barone and Grant Ujifusa, *Almanac of American Politics* (Washington, D.C.: National Journal), published every two years. A valuable collection of data appears in Norman J. Ornstein, Thomas E. Mann, and Michael J. Malbin, *Vital Statistics on Congress, 1991–1992* (Washington, D.C.: Congressional Quarterly, 1992).

9 The Presidency

The American presidency is an awesome and bewildering office. Its demands are numerous and often contradictory. The president is expected to be honest and trustworthy yet tough if not ruthless, to be a moral leader who is above politics as well as a political operator who can achieve results, to control government spending and taxes and yet provide extensive governmental services, and to preserve American honor against international threats and yet keep the peace. When the president extends his power, he is chastised for being imperial; when he fails to offer decisive leadership, he is considered weak and ineffective.

Even the most powerful American presidents have rarely been able to dictate the political agenda. They have had to lead, and leadership in a democratic society requires an ability to persuade without being tiresome, a capacity to administer without getting lost in details, and a sense of when to compromise and when to stand one's ground. The office is a complex mixture of authority and constraints, too subtle to capture in any one theoretical model. Some presidents have mastered the office, and some have been mastered by it.

Commentators on the presidency in the 1950s and 1960s stressed its great powers and the capacity of its occupant to accomplish great things. Franklin D. Roosevelt (1933–1945) was the model—a president who dominated Congress, shepherded through an ambitious reform agenda, centralized decision making in his own hands, fully exercised his powers as commander-in-chief, and inspired the nation with his speeches. Roosevelt's presidency influenced many to regard the office in heroic terms.

The fall from political grace of Lyndon Johnson (1963–1969) over Vietnam and Richard Nixon (1969–1974) over Watergate led later scholars of the office to warn against the dangers of an imperial presidency. Responding to the general public mood, Congress in the mid-1970s passed a series of laws constraining the president's power to impound funds, to authorize covert intelligence activities, to send troops into combat, to sell arms abroad, and to proclaim national emergencies. The two presidents of that period, Gerald Ford (1974–1977) and Jimmy Carter (1977–1981), thus besieged, seemed to be weak. Ford, upon leaving office, talked about an "imperiled presidency." Although weakened by the Iran-contra affair toward the end of his term, President Ronald Reagan (1981–1989) restored some personal power to the office but not its institutional authority. George Bush (1989–1993), who was unable to exert the mastery over domestic and economic policy that he had shown in the Desert Storm operation, was defeated for reelection.

The President and Symbolic Leadership

America has no purely symbolic head of state. Unlike most Western democracies, America does not separate the ceremonial **chief of state** from the actual **head of government.** We have no constitutional monarch, as in Great Britain, the Netherlands, and Sweden, and no ribbon-cutting ceremonial president, as in Germany, Italy, and Israel. The American president is both monarch and prime minister, reigning as well as ruling.

As the head of state, the president in a single week may meet with the winners of the high school Voice of Democracy essay contest, honor the teacher of the year, and prepare a humorous speech for the Washington Gridiron Club. Although a president usually spends no more than one or two hours a week on such activities, they are not as trivial as they may sound. Such ceremonies are important to a nation's morale, its sense of unity, and its recognition of common values.

The ceremonial presidency also has a political dimension. Because the president is our only symbolic head of state, the office carries with it a considerable fund of public goodwill and support. Presidents, no matter how narrow their election victory, find that in the weeks and months after assuming office they are the object of public adoration. According to opinion polls, their approval rating is rarely as high again.

During this honeymoon period some presidents have successfully translated public goodwill into notable political victories. Franklin Roosevelt, in his first hundred days, persuaded Congress to pass the bulk of his economic recovery program. Lyndon Johnson, soon after succeeding John Kennedy (1961–1963), pushed through Congress the far-reaching Civil Rights Act of 1964 (see Chapter 3); and Ronald Reagan, in the months following his first inauguration, won major victories on the budget and taxes.

In times of international crisis the public will often rally to support the office. When the nation perceives itself to be threatened or to have been wronged, the president is the symbol of unity. After the Japanese attack on Pearl Harbor in 1941, Franklin Roosevelt's popularity rose 12 percent; after the Korean War broke out in 1950, Harry Truman's (1945–1953) gained 9 percent; even after the ill-fated Bay

Recent presidents have spent much of their time on foreign policy. President Clinton, who came to office with mainly domestic economic concerns on his mind, is no exception. He promptly had to confront questions regarding the American role in hostilities in the former Yugoslavia, as this ''drop'' of food and medical supplies by an Air Force plane illustrates.

of Pigs invasion in Cuba in 1961, John Kennedy's support increased 12 percent; after the hostages were seized in Iran in 1979, Jimmy Carter's popularity increased a dramatic 31 percent; and immediately after hostilities commenced in the Gulf War in 1991, George Bush's approval rating soared to 89 percent.

But the fusion of symbolic and political authority in this office can result in a distorted public image of what its occupant can achieve. Just as the public will rally to the president in a time of crisis, so will people frequently blame him when events turn sour. Presidential popularity is often directly related to whether the news is good or bad. In other words, given the symbolic nature of the office, the public may both credit and blame a president for events over which he has little control.

Since the presidency has both symbolic and substantive power, a paradox is built into the office. The president is expected to be the symbol of national unity and the intensely political leader of the executive branch. Inevitably, the president must promote solutions to problems that will alienate some fraction of the public, and symbolic leadership will be sacrificed to the need for substantive leadership. The result is that presidential popularity frequently will decline from the time he enters office to the time he leaves.

Dwight Eisenhower (1953–1961) and Ronald Reagan were exceptions to the rule, being able to reconcile the two roles. Both completed two full terms and left office as popular as they entered (see Table 9.1). Eisenhower avoided taking on issues that he knew would cost him support, such as civil rights, and jealously protected his political goodwill. Reagan took controversial positions, but his reassuring personality and rhetorical skills generated much public trust. Both were fortunate in avoiding protracted and unresolved military conflicts and in presiding

TABLE 9.1
Public Approval Ratings of Presidents Roosevelt to Bush

	Beginning of Term	End of Term	High	Low	Average
Franklin Roosevelt*	—	—	84	54	75
Harry Truman	87	31	87	23	43
Dwight Eisenhower	68	59	79	49	65
John Kennedy	72	58	83	56	71
Lyndon Johnson	79	49	80	35	55
Richard Nixon	59	24	68	24	49
Gerald Ford	71	53	71	37	47
Jimmy Carter	66	34	75	21	47
Ronald Reagan	51	63	68	35	52
George Bush	51	49	89	32	61

* Polls taken 1938–1943 only.
SOURCE: *Gallup Opinion Index*, August 1986, January 1989; *Facts on File*, December 21, 1992.

Public approval ratings usually vary widely during a president's time in office. Sometimes they reflect the president's handling of events. At other times, they reflect public frustration over events largely out of a president's control.

over a period of general prosperity. This, above all, may be the key to presidential popularity.

The President and the Constitution

To understand the presidency, one must start with the Constitution. As with members of Congress, as discussed in Chapter 8, the Constitution is specific with regard to who may be president.

Only **natural-born citizens,** not **naturalized citizens,** qualify. Article 2 is the only place where the Constitution distinguishes between one kind of citizenship and another. (A natural-born citizen is one who has American citizenship by birth, although it is unclear whether a person born abroad of American parents qualifies as natural-born within the meaning of the Constitution. A naturalized citizen is an alien who has become a citizen by virtue of a procedure established by Congress.) Moreover, a president must be 35 years of age or older and a resident of the United States for at least 14 years.

Unlike representatives, who serve terms of two years, and senators, who serve terms of six, presidents have four-year terms. Although the Constitution in 1787 placed no limit on the number of terms a president could serve, George Washington's preference for a maximum of two terms set a tradition that remained unbroken until Franklin Roosevelt ran for his third term in 1940 and was then elected to a fourth term in 1944. Mainly in response to Roosevelt, the **Twenty-second Amendment** (1951) banned any future president from being elected president "more than twice." This amendment prohibits not only a third successive term but also an additional term even if a gap exists between the first two.

Executive Power

The Constitution confers many powers on the Congress but few substantive powers on the president. Indeed, Article 1, which establishes Congress, is more than two times the length of Article 2, which creates the presidency. Section 1 of Article 2 declares, "The executive Power shall be vested in a President of the United States." What do these words define? Does the phrase *executive Power* give the president an inherent authority to meet emergencies in the absence of any specific constitutional or legislative mandate?

Presidents have interpreted this power differently throughout history. At one extreme, President William Howard Taft (1909–1913) construed his powers narrowly. Taft claimed, "The president can exercise no power which cannot be fairly and reasonably traced to some specific grant of constitutional or legislative power." By contrast, President Theodore Roosevelt (1901–1909), Taft's predecessor, argued that the president could "do anything that the needs of the nation demanded unless such action was forbidden by the Constitution or by the laws."[1] Roosevelt's

---

[1] Quoted in Christopher H. Pyle and Richard M. Pious, *The President, Congress, and the Constitution* (New York: Free Press, 1984), pp. 68, 70.

broad interpretation of the office became known as the **stewardship theory** and Taft's narrow interpretation as the **constitutional theory.**

Between these somewhat extreme views is the more balanced approach of Supreme Court Justice Robert H. Jackson in the **steel seizure case,** discussed in Chapter 11: "When the President acts in absence of either a congressional grant or denial of authority . . . there is a zone of twilight in which he and Congress may have concurrent authority." In such a case Jackson implied that the Court would decide this constitutional boundary dispute on the basis of "the imperatives of events and contemporary imponderables rather than on abstract theories of law."[2]

Justice Jackson was close to the mark. Presidents since George Washington (1789–1797) have all possessed nearly identical formal constitutional powers, yet some have been far more influential than others. The reason comes from the *plasticity* of the presidency—the tendency of the office to be molded according to the energy and personality of its occupant in combination with the needs and challenges of the day.

The Power of Appointment

Section 2 of Article 2 states that the president "shall nominate, and by and with the Advice and Consent of the Senate, shall appoint Ambassadors, other public Ministers and Consuls, Judges of the Supreme Court, and all other Officers of the United States." For positions that require confirmation, the Senate generally allows the president to select people with whom he feels comfortable personally and ideologically. The Senate restricts itself in most cases to the personal qualifications of the nominee and to any possible conflicts of interest.

The president's power to appoint affects the judicial branch as well because he appoints Supreme Court justices and all federal judges. These judges serve until they retire or, in rare circumstances, are impeached. Franklin Roosevelt's nine appointments to the Supreme Court changed its character for a generation, and Ronald Reagan's three appointments and George Bush's two gave the Court a decidedly conservative cast in the 1990s (see Chapter 11).

The Removal Power

The Supreme Court in *Myers* v. *United States*[3] declared that the president's power to remove non–civil service appointees was unrestricted and beyond the reach of Congress. But later the Court ruled in *Humphrey's Executor* v. *United States*[4] that President Roosevelt could not fire a member of the Federal Trade Commission (FTC), an independent regulatory commission, because of policy differences. The FTC Act specified that the president could only remove a commissioner for "in-efficiency, neglect of duty, or malfeasance in office." The Court ruled that the

---

[2] Ibid., p. 130.
[3] 272 U.S. 52 (1926).
[4] 295 U.S. 602 (1935).

president's removal powers applied only to "purely executive offices." The FTC (and by inference all independent regulatory commissions) was a "quasi-legislative" and "quasi-judicial" agency, according to the Court, and the president's removal authority did not apply. (These commissions are discussed in greater detail in Chapter 10.)

Presidents cannot dismiss career civil servants except for cause (misconduct, inefficiency, incompetence, or criminal conduct). They can, subject to the procedures of the civil service laws, transfer or demote them. Presidents can also work through the budgetary process to reduce or eliminate funding for a particular agency, thus eliminating numerous jobs.

The Power to Pardon

Article 2, Section 2, gives the president the exclusive power to grant "Reprieves and Pardons for Offenses against the United States, except in Cases of Impeachment." The power includes the president's right to grant a full pardon, a conditional pardon, clemency for a class of people (amnesty), a commutation or reduction of a sentence, and the remission of fines. This power is limited to violations of federal laws and does not apply to state or local laws.

The use of this power rarely gains headlines, but it did in 1974 and 1992. On September 8, 1974, President Ford granted a complete pardon to former President Richard Nixon for any misdeeds that he may have committed during his presidency, which, of course, embraced the Watergate affair. Many criticized Ford's action as improper because formal charges had yet to be brought against Nixon. Without the benefit of trial, many argued, the full facts in Nixon's case and in the whole Watergate affair were unlikely to be uncovered. Others thought that Ford spared the country the unpleasant and disruptive sight of a former president placed on trial. On Christmas Eve 1992, President Bush pardoned former Secretary of Defense Caspar Weinberger and five others involved in the Iran-contra affair. The special prosecutor in the case, Lawrence E. Walsh, called the pardons a "cover-up" of misdeeds. Bush argued that Walsh's prosecutions did not represent legitimate law enforcement but were "the criminalization of policy differences." Notwithstanding their decisions, Ford and Bush were acting within their constitutional powers. The courts had established that a presidential pardon may be granted prior to a conviction or even an indictment.[5]

The President and the Executive Branch

In order to formulate and implement policy the president must appoint a considerable number of senior officials to whom he will turn for support and assistance. Who are these people? They include cabinet secretaries, undersecretaries, and the

---

[5] Louis Fisher, *The Politics of Shared Power: Congress and the Executive,* 2d ed. (Washington, D.C. Congressional Quarterly, 1987), p. 11.

administrators and deputies of the various independent agencies, all of whom require Senate confirmation. These officials, plus about 60 senior White House aides whom the president can appoint without Senate confirmation, make up **the administration**—the people who direct government policy on the president's behalf.

The Cabinet

Despite its prestige, the president's Cabinet (see Table 9.2) is not a collective high-level decision-making body. Because ours is not a parliamentary government, the president is not obligated to share responsibility with the Cabinet. Its officers serve at the president's pleasure, and he is under no obligation to consult with them individually or collectively.

Yet individual officers can have great significance for the president. As will be discussed in Chapter 10, they serve as the president's arm in controlling the massive federal bureaucracy and in imposing his political priorities upon it. The Cabinet also provides a mechanism for bringing into the administration people who represent different social, economic, and political constituencies. Often presidents will make appointments from constituent groups who did not support him but whose support he needs.

After several years in office, presidents become more concerned with controlling the bureaucracy than with decorating their Cabinet with people whose value is more symbolic than substantive. Thus they look for Cabinet officers who may be less well known but will be more loyal.

The selection of the right Cabinet is a difficult problem. Few Cabinet officers, whatever their temperament or background, can serve simply as the president's loyal agent. They must also represent to the president the perspective of their

---

TABLE 9.2
The Cabinet, 1993

Secretary of State	Secretary of Health and	Secretary of Veterans
Secretary of Treasury	Human Services	Affairs
Secretary of Defense	Secretary of Housing and	Ambassador to the United
Attorney General	Urban Development	Nations
Secretary of Interior	Secretary of Transportation	Administrator,
Secretary of Agriculture	Secretary of Energy	Environmental
Secretary of Commerce	Secretary of Education	Protection Agency
Secretary of Labor		

SOURCE: *Facts on File*, January 28, 1993, p. 44.

The Cabinet is composed of the heads of the 14 executive departments and certain other officials in the executive branch to whom the president has accorded Cabinet rank. The vice-president also participates in meetings of the Cabinet, and from time to time the president may invite others to participate in the discussion of particular subjects.

department and the *constituent groups* it serves. For example, the secretary of labor should have a good working relationship with organized labor; the secretary of the interior should have a solid relationship with the developers or the environmentalists, preferably both; and the secretary of agriculture must have a good rapport with farmers and the agribusiness community.

Not all Cabinet officers are created equal. There is often an **inner Cabinet** and an **outer Cabinet.**[6] The inner group consists of secretaries of state, defense, and the Treasury as well as the attorney general. These people handle issues of broad importance: national security, the economy, and the administration of justice. Of necessity, they have a direct and close working relationship with the president. The outer group is made up of the remaining members: the secretaries of agriculture, commerce, education, energy, health and human services, housing and urban development, interior, labor, transportation, and veterans affairs. These officers deal with sharply defined programs and are subject to considerable pressure from client groups. Only when a crucial issue arises will they gain frequent access to the president, and such instances are the exception. This lack of access by members of the outer Cabinet often leads to a sense of isolation from the president, gravitation toward the constituent interests served by their departments, and often a strained relationship with the White House staff.

To avoid this problem, President Reagan established the Economic Policy Council and the Domestic Policy Council, chaired, respectively, by the Treasury secretary and the attorney general. When these councils were to make a crucial policy decision, the president himself would chair the meeting. The councils consisted of relevant Cabinet officers and senior White House aides. They were designed to coordinate policy and to keep members of the outer Cabinet in close contact with the president and his thinking. Satisfied with this arrangement, President Bush kept the same system when he entered office.

From the president's perspective, the ideal Cabinet member should be clearly in charge of his or her department, sensitive to the department's constituency, able to distinguish between the president's interest and those of that constituency, and able to work well with Congress. Obviously, the job requires well-developed administrative and political skills. President Clinton was anxious to have a cabinet that "looked like America." Thus, out of 16 cabinet rank positions, Clinton appointed five women, four blacks, and two Hispanics. However, his cabinet included a higher percentage of millionaires than did President Bush's cabinet.

The White House Staff

Prior to the presidency of Franklin Roosevelt, White House aides played no role in policy. They were clerks—managers of files, appointments, and correspondence. Cabinet officers were the president's primary source of advice and counsel. Today the president's closest confidants are rarely his Cabinet members, who spend much of their time managing their departments. Presidents now rely heavily

---

[6] Thomas E. Cronin, *The State of the Presidency,* 2d ed. (Boston: Little, Brown, 1980), pp. 253–296.

on their White House staff. They select for senior White House positions people with whom they are comfortable and with whom they share a common background and political perspective. The loyalty of these people is not to a political party, an ideology, or their own political careers but to the president, first and last.

Responsibilities of senior White House aides involve the following tasks:

- Giving the president broad-gauged advice not influenced by a departmental or interest group perspective
- Setting legislative strategy
- Keeping check on the bureaucracy
- Reviewing the performance of Cabinet and sub-Cabinet officials
- Planning the president's time
- Saying no for the president to people who want something that he cannot give

Presidents manage the White House to suit their own personalities. Eisenhower and Nixon preferred a formalistic system and a highly structured staff. Eisenhower, who had spent most of his adult life in the military, was comfortable with a clear chain of command. At the opposite end of the spectrum was the competitive style of Franklin Roosevelt. Roosevelt had no rigid chain of command and was, in fact, his own chief of staff. He insisted on surrounding himself with strong-minded generalists who had divergent points of view and who could work on a variety of problems.

Although President Bush appointed a chief of staff, John Sununu, Bush's style was closer to Roosevelt's than Nixon's. Bush relied upon a process, known as **multiple advocacy,** which was designed to allow the president to hear all sides of an issue. White House aides would stage policy debates for the president's benefit. Dubbed "scheduled train wrecks," these debates would involve senior officials with sharply differing views on such things as clean air proposals. President Bush, who relished these debates, would take notes, interrupt with questions, and afterwards solicit the views of others in the administration or Congress. With his passion for secrecy and surprise Bush would often conceal his final decision from everyone, until he was ready for a public announcement.

The Executive Office of the President

Across a small side street from the White House is an imposing Victorian building that houses part of the **Executive Office of the President.** The EOP was created in 1939 as the managerial arm of the modern presidency when a presidential commission uttered its famous recommendation, "The President needs help." In its early years the EOP consisted of six administrative assistants and three advisory bodies—the National Resources Planning Board, the Liaison Office for Personnel Management, and the Office of Government Reports—all of which are now defunct.

The structure of the EOP reflects the dominant issues of the time. In the 1940s its agencies, such as the Office of Defense Mobilization, mirrored concerns with war and defense planning. In the 1960s and 1970s the EOP agencies (Cost of Living Council, Council on Environmental Quality, Energy Resources Council) paralleled the national concern with the problems of energy, the environment, and inflation.

During the Reagan years the EOP was pared back. One of its permanent agencies, the **Office of Management and Budget** (OMB), became one of its most important. Created in 1921 as the Bureau of the Budget and renamed the Office of Management and Budget in 1970, the OMB has three major responsibilities:

1. Helping the president to develop the annual budget he submits to Congress
2. Serving as a clearinghouse for legislative proposals submitted to the president by the various departments and assuring that all such proposals are consistent with presidential objectives
3. Monitoring the implementation of the president's programs and making sure they are administered efficiently

Presidents usually employ OMB to suit their own needs. Because the Nixon administration was interested in controlling the bureaucracy and in mobilizing the executive branch to support its programs, OMB had the primary responsibility of supervising administration programs in some detail. Under Ford and Carter the OMB played a relatively minor role.

During the Reagan and Bush administrations it enjoyed a significant comeback. Richard Darman, Bush's OMB director, was a powerful member of Bush's administration, shaping the contours of the budget and negotiating budget and tax policy with Congress. So long as budgetary politics dominate a president's agenda, OMB will remain a vital arm of the presidency.

The **National Security Council** (NSC), established by the National Security Act of 1947, is an essential part of EOP and is designed to provide the president with advice and policy coordination on questions of national security. Its members are the president, the vice-president, the secretary of state, the secretary of defense, and other officials the president may wish to add. As with OMB, presidents use the NSC to suit their own styles.

Truman and Eisenhower employed the NSC to coordinate policy but not to formulate it. Both relied on strong secretaries of state for policy advice. Under President Kennedy the council itself fell into disuse and was rarely convened. Instead Kennedy relied on the NSC staff headed by the national security adviser to provide him with information and expertise.

When President Nixon appointed Dr. Henry Kissinger to be his national security adviser in 1969, the role of the NSC grew substantially. With Nixon's encouragement, Kissinger and his staff not only dominated policy-making but became deeply involved in the actual conduct of foreign policy, shutting the State Department out of Nixon's major diplomatic initiatives. Kissinger conducted the negotiations that led to Nixon's historic visit to China, the Vietnam armistice, and the SALT I treaty.

Politics and Ideas

The Role of Ideology in Presidential Leadership

Presidents Jimmy Carter and Ronald Reagan had sharply different approaches to political leadership. Carter, a naval engineer and farmer, had not been actively involved in any of the struggles of the 1960s over Vietnam or civil rights. His approach to politics was not ideological. He approached government as a problem solver, seeking to find answers to a series of puzzles. He resolved each issue on its own merits. He was, for example, both an environmental liberal and a fiscal conservative. Carter's operation of the presidency fit his approach to politics. Without a broad ideological framework, he saw each issue as separate from any other. This made it difficult for him to set general guidelines for his subordinates to follow. He became engrossed in the details of each major problem that confronted his administration. He was a micromanager.

For example, Carter was deeply involved in framing energy legislation and negotiating the fine points of the SALT II treaty, the Israeli-Egyptian peace treaty, and the Iranian hostage crisis. Some feel that this style of leadership worked as a political disadvantage to Carter. Many held him personally responsible for the misfortunes of his term. These included the long gasoline lines and the failed Iranian rescue mission, both of which may have been beyond his control.

Ronald Reagan, by contrast, brought a clear ideological perspective to the presidency. Along with Barry Goldwater, he had been one of the major voices of conservatism in the 1960s and 1970s. He approached the job not as a micromanager but as a chairman of the board. He established the broad agenda, which was derived from his ideology: cut taxes, reduce domestic spending, and increase defense spending. The details were left to his subordinates. Reagan made certain that his ideology and agenda were shared by his Cabinet. Even his sub-Cabinet appointments were screened through a White House personnel committee, careful to protect Reagan's interests. Thus Reagan felt comfortable in broadly delegating authority, a style that created problems during the Iran-contra affair in 1986.

The public did not fault Reagan for many of the problems that occurred during his administration, such as the massacre of the marines in Lebanon or the resignation of his subordinates under a cloud of suspicion. Journalists dubbed his the "Teflon presidency" because—at least until doubts arose about his part, if any, in the Iran-contra affair—nothing bad stuck to him. Reagan's popularity well into his second term and Carter's failure even to win a second term may have been related to each man's approach to the office.

How important is ideology in shaping a president's style of governing? Do presidents need to have an ideological framework in order to delegate authority without losing control?

The NSC's involvement in the foreign policy operations reached its height during the Iran-contra affair. Congressional restrictions had barred direct aid to the Nicaraguan contras, fighting to overturn the pro-Soviet Sandinista government. Frustrated by the restrictions, President Reagan authorized the NSC staff to seek contra assistance from friendly governments such as Israel and Saudi Arabia. Marine Lt. Col. Oliver North, a senior NSC staffer, supervised this effort as well as those of private domestic groups seeking to provide funds for the contras. The president also authorized the NSC to oversee the secret sale of arms to Iran to encourage the release of our hostages. Without the president's apparent knowledge, part of the profits of that sale were diverted to contras. The affair seriously diminished Reagan's public support and resulted in extensive congressional investigations and lengthy criminal trials.

A presidential commission to examine the Iran-contra affair was appointed by Reagan and headed by former Texas Senator John Tower. The Tower Commission recommended that the NSC "focus on advice and management, not implementation and execution." President Bush's NSC adviser Brent Scowcroft, a member of the Tower Commission, appeared to follow his own advice and kept the NSC out of covert operations. Under Scowcroft the NSC functioned as an honest broker, coordinating advice from the bureaucracy and providing the president with policy options.

The **Council of Economic Advisers** (CEA), established by the Employment Act of 1946, is another permanent part of the EOP. Consisting of three members and a small staff, its chairperson, usually a prominent academic economist, is the predominant figure. The CEA's primary task is to analyze economic issues, make economic forecasts, and prepare the president's annual Economic Report to Congress. The CEA can be an important source of economic advice for the president, but it must share economic policy-making with the OMB, the Treasury Department, and the Federal Reserve Board.

The effectiveness of the CEA depends largely on the ability of the chair to gain the president's confidence and to translate obscure economic jargon into language the president can readily understand. President Reagan had little interest in the intricacies of economic policy, let the CEA wither on the vine, and even considered its abolition. Bush, who had a fascination with details, frequently consulted with the CEA and let its chair become a major player in his administration.[7] Clinton, who had promised in his campaign to focus on economic issues "like a laser," established a new National Economic Council to coordinate overall economic policy. It would have a status similar to the National Security Council. The chair of the CEA would now have to compete with yet another source of economic policy-making.

The **Office of Policy Development** (OPD), formed in 1981 from domestic policy staff within the White House, focuses on the formulation, coordination, and implementation of economic and domestic policy. The OPD also provides staff support to two Cabinet councils, the Economic Policy Council and the Domestic Policy Council.

The Vice-President

Until 1941 vice-presidents merely served in the ceremonial role as president and chief presiding officer of the Senate and had little influence on decisions in the White House. The office was a frequent target of ridicule and disdain, even by its

---

[7] Paul Strobin, "In the Loop," *National Journal* (March 24, 1990): 715–718.

occupants. The first vice-president, John Adams, called it "the most insignificant office that ever the invention of man contrived or his imagination conceived."

Later vice-presidents continued to find the job deeply frustrating. Harry Truman was not even aware of the existence of the secret atomic bomb project when he succeeded to the presidency upon Roosevelt's death. Richard Nixon, Eisenhower's vice-president for two terms, served as partisan "hit man," making attacks on the Democrats that Eisenhower felt were beneath the dignity of the president to do himself. This same demeaning task Nixon later assigned to his own vice-president, Spiro Agnew. Lyndon Johnson, who had been the powerful Senate majority leader, was given largely ceremonial responsibilities as John Kennedy's vice-president. Johnson, a proud and sensitive man, felt humiliated in the job and considered himself merely a spectator in the Kennedy administration.

The experience of Walter Mondale as Jimmy Carter's vice-president has given fresh hope that the office can become a vital part of the executive branch. Mondale served as President Carter's intimate adviser. He had an office in the White House West Wing, close to the president, and was given access to all important meetings and policy papers. Mondale had a private lunch every Monday with Carter so that

Presidents determine the role their vice presidents will have in an administration. During most of American history, presidents usually consigned vice presidents to respectful obscurity. Beginning with the Carter administration in 1977, however, vice presidents have been given significant responsibilities. Early in 1993, President Clinton instructed his vice president, former Senator Albert Gore, to oversee efforts to reduce "wasteful" spending.

he could give the president confidential and candid advice. By all accounts, Mondale was involved in all major policy decisions. The Carter-Mondale arrangement converted the vice-presidency from an office without a role into that of a senior policy adviser to the president.

Presidential Succession

Should a president be impeached and convicted, resign, or die in office, the vice-president automatically becomes president and fills the remainder of the term. Should a president become disabled and unable to fulfill his duties, the **Twenty-fifth Amendment,** ratified in 1967, provided a mechanism whereby the vice-president could serve as an acting president. The president can declare himself disabled and can authorize the vice-president to assume his job. Alternatively, the vice-president and a majority of the Cabinet can declare that the president is disabled, in which case the vice-president also assumes the job. The president may claim, however, at any time, that his disability is over and resume the office. Should the vice-president and a majority of the Cabinet disagree, the issue goes to Congress. If both houses decide by a two-thirds vote that the president is unfit to resume his duties, the vice-president continues as acting president.

The Twenty-fifth Amendment also established a mechanism to fill a vacancy in the vice-presidency. During our history six vice-presidents have died in office, two have resigned, and nine have succeeded to the presidency—in each case leaving the office vacant. The amendment now eliminates the possibility that the vacancy will stand for long. The president is authorized in the event of a vacancy to nominate a vice-president, subject to confirmation by both houses of Congress. This procedure was first used in October 1973 when Spiro Agnew resigned because of allegations of misconduct and President Nixon selected Gerald Ford as vice-president.

In the unlikely event of a simultaneous double vacancy in the presidency and the vice-presidency, the **Presidential Succession Act of 1947** applies. It establishes the following line of succession: (1) the Speaker of the House; (2) the president pro tempore of the Senate; (3) the Cabinet secretaries in the chronological order of the establishment of their departments, beginning with the secretary of state and ending with the secretary of veterans affairs.

The President and Congress: Foreign Policy

In foreign policy the Constitution divides formal power between the president and Congress. But the president does maintain the initiative. He negotiates treaties, mediates disputes, and proclaims friendship with new governments or works covertly to undermine them. Congress may reject these initiatives by refusing to ratify treaties, discouraging foreign arms sales, or outlawing covert activities. But when the president puts his prestige on the line, as President

Bush did in securing support for his Gulf War policy, he generally prevails. Why is that? Congress fears eroding presidential influence in international negotiations, a fear presidents use to their own advantage. But Congress also lacks access to classified information and often defers to executive expertise. The reality is that Congress can influence foreign relations, but only the president can conduct them, and the extent of Congress's influence is subject to the ebb and flow of history.

During the period from Pearl Harbor (1941) to the end of the Vietnam War (1973) the president dominated foreign policy, and congressional rebukes were rare and ineffective. The unpopularity of the Vietnam War produced a subsequent public disdain of future military involvements and with it an end to the era of presidential domination. The president still had the leading role in foreign policy, but he no longer controlled the play.

Over President Nixon's veto in 1973 Congress passed the War Powers Resolution, requiring congressional approval after 60 days of any presidential decision to send troops into combat. In 1974 Congress passed the Hughes-Ryan amendment, requiring congressional notification of covert operations conducted by the CIA. Emboldened by its new found authority Congress actually banned covert action in Angola from 1978 to 1983 and during the 1980s limited covert aid to the Nicaraguan contras. Presidential leadership in foreign policy now requires considerable skill and subtlety. Congress can be very independent unless a president carefully consults it and develops strong public support for his policies.

Negotiating Treaties

By the terms of Article 2 of the Constitution the president negotiates and signs treaties, subject to a vote of approval by two-thirds of the Senate. During the course of our history the vast majority of treaties have been approved by the Senate. But the most notable defeat came in 1919, when the Senate refused to ratify the Treaty of Versailles, which formally ended World War I and would have brought the United States into the League of Nations. This provided a profound object lesson for future presidents.

President Woodrow Wilson (1913–1921), who negotiated the Versailles treaty, did not include a single senator from either party in the negotiating delegation, nor did he provide the Senate with information on the progress of the negotiations. In shutting the Senate out of the negotiating process, Wilson failed to build broad bipartisan support for the treaty.

Presidents Franklin Roosevelt and Harry Truman were careful to avoid Wilson's mistake and included both Democratic and Republican members of the Senate Foreign Relations Committee in the negotiations for the United Nations Treaty (1945) and the North Atlantic Treaty Organization (1949). During the decade that followed World War II the Senate ratified without reservations or significant opposition mutual security treaties with over 40 nations. Since then the Senate has become more jealous of its prerogatives. Approval of important treaties is now rarely routine and often requires presidential concessions.

Executive Agreements

Presidents can avoid the political brambles of Senate ratification by entering into **executive agreements** with foreign governments. These agreements do not require Senate approval. Theoretically, a treaty involves a legal relationship between nations, whereas an executive agreement is merely an understanding between heads of state. In practice no distinction is observed, and the Supreme Court has provided no clear guidelines.

In the early years of the Republic, executive agreements involved relatively minor matters, such as the settlement of claims American citizens had against foreign governments. Beginning with Franklin Roosevelt, executive agreements became a serious tool of foreign policy. In September 1940 Roosevelt agreed to trade 50 American destroyers to Great Britain in exchange for leases of naval bases on British territory in Newfoundland and the Caribbean. Toward the end of World War II Roosevelt concluded a secret executive agreement with Joseph Stalin granting the Soviet Union territory and rights in the western Pacific previously belonging to China and Japan. In exchange Stalin agreed to enter the war against Japan.

Such secret agreements, unusual even in wartime, have now become almost commonplace. Of the 4359 agreements in force in 1972, almost 400 were classified and kept from Congress. Many involved commitments and informal alliances with other nations such as Spain, Laos, and Ethiopia.

To remedy what Congress considered an abuse of executive power, it passed the **Case Act** (1972), which placed some restrictions on the use of executive agreements, particularly secret ones. The Case Act requires that the secretary of state submit to the Senate the final text of any executive agreement. Should the agreement concern sensitive national security matters, it can be submitted in private to the Senate Foreign Relations Committee and the House Foreign Affairs Committee. The Case Act is largely symbolic and does not give Congress the power to alter or reject executive agreements. Moreover, compliance with the act is not easy to obtain. A 1976 Senate study disclosed that the executive branch had delayed submitting a number of executive agreements by almost a year and avoided submitting others by renaming them "arrangements."[8]

The President and Congress: The War Power

The war power is also divided in the constitution. The formal power to declare war is lodged in Congress (Article 1, Section 8: "The Congress shall have the power . . . To declare war"), and thus the power to *initiate war* rests with it alone. But the framers of the Constitution were careful to leave the president with some independent war-making authority. At the urging of James Madison and Elbridge Gerry, the Constitutional Convention changed the original phrase from "make

---

[8] Thomas M. Franck and Edward Weisband, *Foreign Policy by Congress* (New York: Oxford University Press, 1979), p. 142.

war" to "declare war." In changing this language, the framers intended to leave the president with the power *to repel sudden attacks on the United States, its territories, its possessions, or its armed forces.* The **commander-in-chief clause** (Article 2, Section 2) was not designed to alter this relationship nor to grant the president additional war-making powers. The clause simply established the principle of civilian control over the military. The president was to be, in Alexander Hamilton's words, "the first general and admiral."

The Mexican and Civil Wars

Presidents have used the power to control the armed forces in order to manipulate Congress and preempt the war power itself. President James Polk (1845–1849) in 1846, for example, ordered troops into the territory disputed by the United States and Mexico and set the stage for the Mexican War. The troops occupied high ground overlooking a Mexican village and aimed their artillery on the town square. The Mexican government, feeling threatened by the maneuver, responded militarily. Congress, at Polk's request, passed a declaration of war. Several years later the House of Representatives, feeling deceived by Polk's maneuver, passed a resolution that condemned him for a war "unnecessarily and unconstitutionally begun."

When Abraham Lincoln became president (1861–1865), he used the war power in a manner more consistent with the original understanding of the framers. After the attack on Fort Sumter (1861), which began the Civil War, Lincoln announced a blockade of the southern ports, increased the size of the army and navy, instructed the Treasury Department to spend $2 million to purchase military supplies, and in certain areas suspended the writ of *habeas corpus* (a judicial safeguard against unlawful imprisonment). None of these steps had been authorized by Congress, which was not in session. On July 4, 1861, Congress, back in session, ratified all of Lincoln's actions except the suspension of the writ of habeas corpus and the naval blockade. The Supreme Court in the **Prize Cases**[9] declared that Lincoln was within his constitutional powers "in suppressing an insurrection."

The Two World Wars

Twice in the twentieth century (1917 and 1941) Congress has formally declared war and delegated vast discretionary powers to the president. During World War I Congress granted President Wilson almost dictatorial control over the economy. This included the power to seize mines and factories, fix prices, license the distribution of foodstuffs, and take over railroads and telephone lines. Although Wilson did not exercise all this authority, he did assume unprecedented control over prices, consumption, and industrial production.

Congress granted Franklin Roosevelt similar authority during World War II,

---

[9] 67 U.S. (2 Black) 635 (1863).

but Roosevelt, who had a broad and expansive view of the office, asserted wartime powers independent of Congress.

The most dramatic and controversial of Roosevelt's actions came early in World War II. On February 19, 1942, Roosevelt decreed that 112,000 persons of Japanese descent living in the Pacific Coast region (70,000 of whom were American citizens) be removed from their homes, stripped of their jobs and property, and sent to detention camps. Concern about sabotage was the justification, although there was no evidence of its likelihood. Yet many of these people remained in the camps for the duration of the war. Congress later passed a law embodying the president's order and in effect ratifying it. In *Korematsu* v. *United States*[10] the Supreme Court upheld the exclusion program as within the combined war powers of Congress and the president. The entire case, repudiated by a government commission years later and the subject of renewed litigation in the 1980s, serves as a reminder of how difficult it is in time of war to maintain democratic standards and values.

The Cold War

Only when America became a global power after World War II did presidents assert independent war-making powers, in the context of the Cold War with the Soviet Union. The most dramatic example came in June 1950, when President Truman, on his own independent authority, ordered American ground, air, and naval forces to aid the government of South Korea against an invasion of North Korean forces. Truman declined even to ask Congress for a resolution authorizing this decision and simply cited his powers as commander-in-chief. Because the Korean invasion did not involve a sudden attack on American troops, citizens, or territory, Truman's unilateral action fell outside the framers' original understanding of the war power. Although Congress later implicitly ratified the decision by voting military appropriations for the war, Truman had nevertheless initiated American's involvement in a war that lasted three years and cost 30,000 American lives.

During the next two decades presidential war-making authority grew, nurtured by a new political consensus. Unlike the Americans of the eighteenth and nineteenth centuries, who believed in having no permanent military alliances, limited international interests, and a small standing army, Americans of the mid-twentieth century concluded that only through collective security and armed strength could war be prevented. Given this political climate, presidents felt emboldened to establish overseas bases, station troops abroad, and even send them into combat, all on the presidents' own authority. Congress did little to object.

In 1955 President Eisenhower requested from Congress a joint resolution authorizing him to use military force to protect Taiwan from a possible invasion by the People's Republic of China. The resolution stated that the president had the authority "to employ the Armed Forces as he deems necessary" to defend Taiwan. This undated check to the president to make war on his own terms passed

---

[10] 323 U.S. 214 (1944).

Congress overwhelmingly. The comments of House Speaker Sam Rayburn (D-Tex.) reflected the measure of congressional acquiescence to presidential authority in those Cold War years. "If the President had done what is proposed here without consulting Congress," Rayburn acknowledged, "he would have had no criticism from me."[11]

The Vietnam Trauma

As hundreds of thousands of American troops entered the Vietnam War in the mid-1960s, presidential control of the war-making authority continued to go unchallenged. An alleged attack on two American destroyers by North Vietnamese patrol boats off their coastal waters triggered action from President Lyndon Johnson, who sought broad authority from Congress. At Johnson's request Congress passed the **Gulf of Tonkin Resolution** (1964), which stated:

> The United States is, therefore, prepared, *as the president determines,* to take all necessary steps including the use of armed forces to assist any member or protocol state of the Southeast Asia Collective Defense Treaty requesting assistance in defense of its freedom.

The resolution, passed unanimously in the House and with only two dissenting votes in the Senate, recognized the president's claim to unilateral war-making authority.

As the Vietnam War lost public support, Congress sought to regain its constitutional authority, largely through its control of spending power. But the task was arduous and the results ambiguous. In 1970 Congress, fearing an extension of the war, barred the use of funds to "finance the introduction of the ground troops into Laos or Thailand." But President Nixon circumvented the law by ordering continued aerial bombing and paramilitary activities in Laos. After he authorized an invasion of Cambodia that year, Congress responded by prohibiting the use of funds for ground combat troops in that beleaguered country. Although Nixon eventually withdrew the ground troops from Cambodia, he continued the bombing.

The Paris Peace Accords (1973) ended direct American combat involvement in Vietnam but not the bombing of Cambodia and Laos. So the war continued, but with very little congressional support. Finally, in June 1973, Congress was able to use its power of the purse to control the power of the sword. President Nixon, weakened and distracted by the Watergate scandal, signed an appropriation bill that prohibited the further use of funds for *all* combat activities in Indochina as of August 15, 1973. However, all this occurred only after American combat activities against the North Vietnamese had ended and nine years after Congress had passed the Gulf of Tonkin Resolution.

---

[11] *Congressional Record* (January 25, 1955): 672

The War Powers Resolution

Chastened by the Vietnam experience and anxious to recapture its war-making authority, Congress in the fall of 1973 passed over President Nixon's veto the War Powers Resolution, which specified that the president could not commit troops to combat beyond 60 days unless authorized by Congress. The resolution also stipulated that before introducing troops into combat, the president was to consult with Congress in every possible instance.

The War Powers Resolution was criticized by both hawks and doves. Senator Barry Goldwater (R-Ariz.) argued that the 60-day cut off provision was an unconstitutional interference with the president's powers as commander-in-chief. Senator Thomas Eagleton (D-Mo.) claimed that the resolution placed no defined limits on when a president could take the country to war without prior congressional approval. So far the resolution has had little effect on presidential behavior, confirming neither the fears of its critics nor the hopes of its sponsors.

For years supporters of the resolution were concerned about the failure of presidents to abide fully by its provisions were the Congress to challenge the

Intending to fulfill a campaign pledge, in January 1993 President Clinton set in motion measures to rescind the military's ban on homosexuals. The Joint Chiefs of Staff, as well as some members of Congress, opposed the change. Shown here in a meeting with President Clinton and Vice President Gore to discuss the policy are: General Gordon R. Sullivan, Army Chief of Staff; General Merrill A. McPeak, Air Force Chief of Staff; General Colin L. Powell, Chairman of the Joint Chiefs; Secretary of Defense Les Aspin; and, Admiral Frank B. Kelso II, Chief of Naval Operations. Not pictured is General Carl E. Mundy, Commandant of the Marine Corps.

president. The effectiveness of the resolution depends on how seriously Congress takes its responsibilities. Such seriousness was not manifest until January 12, 1991. Then, the Congress granted President Bush the power, as authorized under the War Powers Resolution, to begin military operations to enforce the United Nations Security Council Resolutions demanding Saddam Hussein's military withdrawal from Kuwait.

So long as American foreign policy requires far-flung political commitments and a powerful mobile military, any limits on the president's role as commander-in-chief will be difficult for Congress to impose. The era of American isolation and neutrality has long passed, and along with it a small standing army. Contemporary presidents shape a large defense budget, select major weapons systems, control access to classified information, and send large carrier task forces around the globe. Thus congressional attempts to reassert its authority meet with mixed results.

The President and Congress: Domestic Policy

In domestic policy as well as foreign, the relationship between the president and Congress is rarely easy and never settled. The president's capacity to lead his legislative program through Congress is a strong indication of his power and often determines his historical impact on the office. Few presidents have been able to dominate Congress, and even then only for short periods. Presidents with an ambitious domestic agenda and aspirations beyond maintaining the status quo have a particular need for congressional support. Getting it requires great skill, a sense of what the public will support, and a capacity to persuade 535 independent-minded senators and representatives. What are the political ingredients that enable presidents to be successful leaders of Congress? Recent experience suggests several.[12]

Legislative Skills

A President Must Know the Legislative Environment   One of Franklin Roosevelt's advisers once explained that a president must understand who influences whom, who the key players are on an issue, and what a group wants that others can be persuaded either to accept or to tolerate. Lyndon Johnson made it his business to know as much as he could about the key members of Congress. By contrast, Jimmy Carter, whose legislative performance was less than spectacular, was unfamiliar with the ways of Washington and held himself aloof from the congressional leadership.

---

[12] The following discussion derives from Reo M. Christenson, "Presidential Leadership of Congress," in *Rethinking the Presidency,* ed. Thomas E. Cronin (Boston: Little, Brown, 1982), pp. 255–271.

A President Needs a Good Sense of Timing   He must know when to lead and when to pause. For example, wars often deplete the national energy for reform, and Congress itself can reflect such a national mood. Postwar presidents Warren Harding (World War I), Truman (World War II), and Eisenhower (Korea) were unable to get much reform legislation from Congress. Harding and Eisenhower did not even try, but Truman did and found the going very difficult.

Presidents Must Establish Their Priorities and Know Where to Concentrate Their Energies   No president will get everything he asks from Congress; therefore, he must put forward programs that are not only important but which also have a chance of success. Early successes may build a reputation for political mastery that can be translated into future legislative victories. Ronald Reagan focused on the budget and taxes in his first year and achieved astonishing success.

Presidents Must Have a High-Quality Legislative Liaison Office   They cannot personally keep in touch with all members of Congress. An effective liaison office gives members some access to the White House, if not to the president himself. It also provides the president with vital intelligence: how many votes he has for a particular bill, the members who need to be persuaded; what particular favors he can grant them to sway their votes. The liaison office can build crucial loyalty and support for the president and his policies.

Presidents Must Consult with Party Leaders, in the Opposition as well as in Their Own Party, When They Are Developing a Major Policy Initiative   A president needs to have a strong working relationship with those who can tell him the mood of Congress. Jimmy Carter failed to consult with the appropriate congressional leaders when he unveiled his energy program in 1977; to the surprise of very few, Congress extensively revised and rewrote it.

Wise Presidents Remember Jefferson's Advice: Great Innovations Should Not and Cannot be Forced upon Slender Majorities   Major innovations require broad bipartisan support or else they will fail. Truman worked closely with leading senior Republicans in Congress in order to gain support for the United Nations treaty, the Marshall Plan (economic rehabilitation aid to Western Europe after World War II), and the North Atlantic Treaty Organization. Presidents Kennedy and Johnson, in building a consensus for their civil rights program, cultivated Republican leaders in both houses. President Reagan's strong working relationship with conservative southern Democrats in the House (known as "Boll Weevils") was essential to his legislative success in 1981 and 1982.

The Presidential Veto

The president has a number of constitutional and statutory powers to use in his dealings with Congress, but none is more important than the veto. According to Article 1, Section 7, the president may veto a congressional bill within 10 days after it reaches his desk. He then returns the bill to the congressional chamber of origin with a message explaining his reasons and perhaps suggesting changes that could make it acceptable. Congress may override the veto by a two-thirds majority of each house of Congress. The bill then becomes a law without presidential approval. Should Congress announce its adjournment during the 10-day period, the president may employ a pocket veto. He simply kills the bill without a formal message and without the need of returning it to Congress. Congress cannot override a pocket veto. Presidents cannot veto constitutional amendments, but they can veto joint resolutions, which are formal expressions of congressional opinion and have the force of law. Table 9.3 summarizes presidential vetoes and overrides since Franklin Roosevelt.

The president, unlike a number of state governors, does not possess an *item veto,* which allows an executive to veto sections of a bill and sign the remaining portion. President Reagan, for one, has been a vocal supporter of the item veto. Its implementation would require a constitutional amendment. The president can under certain conditions refuse to spend part of an appropriations bill. Occasionally, a president may sign a bill and at the same time note that certain provisions are unconstitutional and cannot be enforced. The president's authority to do this has yet to be tested in court. As discussed in Chapter 8, a common congressional technique for avoiding a veto is to attach amendments (riders) to an appropriations bill. Frequently, the president cannot afford to veto such a bill without having the government run out of money. During the Vietnam War, Congress attached such riders to defense bills restricting the president's authority. President Nixon, in need of the appropriations to continue funding the war, was forced to accept these riders, which he otherwise surely would have vetoed.

Executive Privilege

Control over policy requires control over information; thus since George Washington presidents have claimed that personal communications with their advisers were immune from congressional or judicial scrutiny. Presidents have argued that they need the protection of confidentiality to ensure that they will receive frank and candid advice. The right of the president to refuse information requested by Congress and the courts is called executive privilege.

During the Watergate affair President Nixon attempted to enlarge the power of executive privilege. Nixon asserted that it included the authority to withhold from Congress and the courts information in the possession of any employee of the executive branch. In 1973 Nixon maintained that even the papers and tapes of conversations under subpoena by the Watergate special prosecutor were protected by executive privilege. Nixon's lawyer maintained that a president's claim of executive privilege was absolute and not subject to review by the courts or Congress. This broad definition suffered a setback from the Supreme Court in *United States* v. *Nixon*[13] when it ruled that although the president did enjoy a right to executive privilege, it was not absolute. The Court concluded that the need for

---

[13] 418 U.S. 683 (1974).

TABLE 9.3
Presidential Vetoes and Overrides

	Total Vetoes	Pocket Vetoes	Vetoes Overridden
Franklin Roosevelt (1933–1945)	633	261	9
Harry Truman (1945–1953)	250	70	12
Dwight Eisenhower (1953–1961)	181	108	2
John Kennedy (1961–1963)	21	9	—
Lyndon Johnson (1963–1969)	30	14	—
Richard Nixon (1969–1974)	43	19	5
Gerald Ford (1974–1977)	66	16	12
Jimmy Carter (1977–1981)	31	18	2
Ronald Reagan (1981–1989)	78	39	9
George Bush (1989–1993)	46	5	1

SOURCE: *Congressional Quarterly Weekly Report,* January 7, 1989, p. 7; *Congressional Quarterly Weekly Report,* December 19, 1992, p. 3925.

The veto remains one of the president's most significant constitutional powers. Yet the president does not possess an item veto—the power to reject part of a bill. The president must accept or reject the entire bill.

the tapes and papers as evidence in the Watergate trial outweighed the president's claim of confidentiality and ordered Nixon to produce the tapes and papers.

In the criminal trial of Admiral John Poindexter, the District Court Judge Harold H. Greene ordered President Reagan to turn over his personal diaries to the court. Judge Greene read the diaries *in camera* (in his private chambers), weighing the former president's claim of executive privilege against Poindexter's assertion that he could not get a fair trial without access to them. After reviewing 100 diary entries, Judge Greene declared that they furnished "no new insights" into the Iran-contra affair and concluded that Reagan's claim of executive privilege outweighed Poindexter's need for the material.[14]

United States v. *Nixon* and the Poindexter case addressed only the president's right to withhold information from the courts and not his right to withhold information from Congress. Since the Watergate scandal Congress has become more assertive against such claims and suspicious that they were used to cover up maladministration, if not corruption. In 1982 there were, in fact, charges of collusion between top officials of the Environmental Protection Agency (EPA) and corporations cited for allegedly dumping toxic waste. When EPA director Anne Burford refused to hand over to a House subcommittee documents relating to the enforcement of the toxic waste program, the House voted her in contempt of Congress.

President Reagan, claiming executive privilege for Burford, had the Justice Department challenge the contempt citation in federal court. The federal judge in

[14] *New York Times,* March 22, 1990. p. A1.

the case, reluctant to enter into this unchartered area of law, urged both sides to settle their differences out of court. The judge stated, "When constitutional disputes arise concerning the respective powers of the legislative and executive branches, judicial intervention should be delayed until all possibilities for settlement have been exhausted."[15] As a result of the political controversies that developed around the toxic waste program, Burford resigned, and President Reagan released all the documents to the relevant congressional committees. Presidents have to consider whether the assertion of a particular claim of executive privilege outweighs the political costs of withholding the information. In the matter of Anne Burford, President Reagan felt that the costs of asserting the privilege were too high.

Impeachment

In the struggle between the president and Congress, impeachment and removal from office is the ultimate congressional weapon. Article 2, Section 4, of the Constitution states: "The President, Vice-President and all Civil Officers of the United States shall be removed from Office on Impeachment for, and Conviction of, Treason, Bribery, or other high Crimes and Misdemeanors."

The actual impeachment resembles a criminal indictment in which the House acts as the grand jury. The investigation is done by the House Judiciary Committee, which votes its recommendation whether to impeach to the full House. The House can vote to impeach by a simple majority. The question of guilt or innocence is then determined by a trial, conducted by the Senate. The chief justice of the United States serves as the presiding judge over the proceedings involving the president or the vice-president, and a vote of two-thirds of the Senate is required for conviction and removal.

President Andrew Johnson (1865–1869) was impeached in 1868 by an overwhelming majority in the House but escaped conviction in the Senate by one vote. More than a century later, in 1974, President Richard Nixon faced a serious threat of impeachment. After eight months of hearings, the House Judiciary Committee voted three articles of impeachment charging Nixon with (1) obstruction of justice for encouraging perjury, destruction of evidence, and interfering with investigations by the FBI; (2) abuse of power for authorizing the FBI and IRS to harass his political opponents; and (3) contempt of Congress for refusal to comply with congressional subpoenas for tapes and papers relevant to the impeachment investigation. Before the House had an opportunity to vote on the Judiciary Committee report, Nixon resigned the presidency.

The Nixon experience did clarify the question of what is an impeachable offense. Treason and bribery are clear, and Nixon was charged with neither. But what constitutes a "high crime and misdemeanor"? The framers, especially Alexander Hamilton and James Madison, believed that the phrase included the abuse of political power. By including the abuse of power in the articles of impeachment, the House Judiciary Committee accepted the view of Madison

[15] *Congressional Quarterly Weekly Report,* February 12, 1983, p. 334.

⬈ Politics and Economics

The President and Economic Policy-Making

Nowhere is the gap greater between what the public expects and what the president can do than in economic policy. Accustomed to general prosperity, the American public demands full employment, stable prices, and an increased standard of living. Presidents who fail to provide all these things usually do not get reelected. Herbert Hoover, Gerald Ford, Jimmy Carter, and George Bush—all defeated incumbents—stand as examples. Hoover presided over the Great Depression, Ford served during a period of high unemployment; Carter contended with double-digit inflation, and Bush served during a recession and a slow recovery.

How much blame a president must share for such conditions is unclear. They act under severe constraints and it may seem unfair that they must take responsibility for things they cannot control. What are the constraints? First, the president can propose a budget and tax plan, but the Congress must approve. The president must deal with a complex congressional budgeting process and the powerful special interests that influence Congress. Often the budget the president gets does not resemble the one he requested (see Chapter 12). Second, the president's budget must be prepared 16 months before its enactment and during that period the economy can change dramatically. Third, the president must share power with the Federal Reserve Board, which sets interest rates and controls the supply of money in the economy. Fourth, much of the budget (approximately 75 percent) is controlled by legislation that is supported by powerful interests and hard to change—Social Security payments, Medicare, Medicaid, military pensions, farm support subsidies. The interest on the national debt, another legal obligation, now consumes about 15 percent of the budget.

In addition to the problems of budget making, the president must contend with the economy itself, which is complex and unpredictable. The cycles of inflation and recession frequently elude the economist's crystal ball. In addition, America is part of the international economic system and affected by events beyond the president's reach. The sharp increase in oil prices by the Organization of Petroleum Exporting Countries (OPEC) contributed to the high inflation of the 1970s.

Over the past two decades Japan, Western Europe, and South Korea have emerged as major economic powers, providing steep competition for key American industries such as steel, automobiles, textiles, and electronics. In the 1980s America became dependent upon Japanese purchases of government bonds to assist in financing our deficits and upon Japanese investments in the private sector to help in sustaining our economic growth. Changes in the behavior and economic fortunes of countries like Japan can have a significant impact on our economy.

Over the past two decades presidents have devoted increased time and energy to economic policy. Their economic advisers have become major players in the administration. The role of the OMB Director in providing the president with budgetary advice and negotiating that budget with Congress has grown; the Treasury secretary who must advise the president on international economic policy and the supervision of the savings and loan industry is usually a close confidant of the president; the president must also develop a good working relationship with the chairman of the Federal Reserve Board. Whether or not the economic conditions that prevail during his administration are the results of the president's policy, the public will hold him accountable.

and Hamilton that high crimes and misdemeanors involve "the violation of some public trust." Nixon's attempt to use the FBI and the IRS against his political enemies was considered by the committee 'a threat to political order and therefore an impeachable offense.

The President and the Media

Presidents and the media are usually involved in a love-hate relationship that resembles a bad marriage. They need each other, yet they have difficulty living together. Practically every president has complained about the press. George Washington charged that the unfavorable stories about his administration were "outrages of common decency." President Thomas Jefferson, a champion of a free press, stated that "even the least informed of the people have learned that nothing in a newspaper is to be believed." Richard Nixon, who suffered serious criticism of his Vietnam policy, had a considerable number of Washington reporters on his "enemies list." Ronald Reagan during the Iran-contra affair thought reporters were circling the White House like "sharks." George Bush championed a slogan during his unsuccessful 1992 reelection campaign, "Annoy the media. Reelect Bush/Quayle."

This conflict is built into the relationship. Chief executives are advocates of their own administration and want to see it portrayed favorably. They also feel the responsibility of suppressing information that, in their eyes, could damage national security. Presidents, therefore, are inclined to control the content and timing of information about their administration. Reporters by contrast want to get their hands on as much interesting and relevant information as possible, regardless of its sensitivity. Many a president has had his day ruined by seeing material from a highly classified document cited in the morning papers.

Editors want stories that sell newspapers or improve television ratings. Trivial stories, such as Nancy Reagan's purchase of expensive china for the White House, will often receive more attention than a complex and important one.

As much as presidents may grouse about the media, they are not above using it for their own purposes. Michael Deaver, a senior aide to President Reagan, spent much of his time constructing effective visual backgrounds for presidential stories on the nightly news.

Phases of the Relationship

The relationship between the president and the media can go through a series of phases. The first is cooperation and occurs in the early honeymoon stage of an administration. Presidents in this phase woo the media, grant numerous interviews, have nationally syndicated columnists for dinner, may visit influential reporters in their homes, and see to it that a reporter's calls to the White House are returned. During this time stories frequently appear, to the president's delight, about what a fresh breath of air his administration has brought to Washington.

The second phase begins after the administration has settled in, begun to develop some internal conflicts, seen some sensitive information leak, suffered through its first crisis, and received its first series of negative stories. Then the relationship turns to conflict. Presidents will try more vigorously to control leaks, may deny critical reporters access to top officials, and favor those writers who support the administration. After enjoying a honeymoon with the press and beginning to see stories critical of his leadership, President Kennedy said he was "reading more and enjoying it less."

The third phase can be described as detachment. The president becomes less accessible to the press. There are fewer press conferences, and he appears largely before sympathetic audiences. In the final months of his administration, Lyndon Johnson, under constant attack for his Vietnam policy, spoke primarily at military installations. Besieged by negative stories during the Iran-contra affair, President Reagan went months without holding a news conference. In this phase the media become more aggressive in seeking out stories. Their sources may be largely from those outside the White House or from disgruntled former officials. Consequently, the stories may grow more negative. By the end of a presidential term, the relationship has exhausted itself.[16]

The Imperial President Versus the Imperial Media

Both the president and the media have powerful weapons to use in dealing with each other. The president can decide what format to use in presenting his case to the public—a prime-time news conference, a fireside chat, or an off-the-record briefing. He can orchestrate his public appearances for the maximum visual effect. He can leak information to those reporters he favors and withhold it from those he disdains.

The media, in turn, can do extensive investigative reporting and take advantage of leakers in the administration who want to undercut a particular presidential policy. Reporters can pressure the president to release information through the Freedom of Information Act and barrage him with persistent questions at press conferences. They can portray presidential scandals as dramatic, unfolding who-done-its, as was done in Watergate and Iran-contra, whetting the public appetite for more information and placing the administration on the defensive.

The contest is usually a standoff. No president has been able to manage the press, and the media cannot make or break a president. The vast majority of American newspapers opposed Franklin Roosevelt and endorsed his opponents. Many Washington reporters had slight regard for Ronald Reagan's ability or wisdom. Yet this had little or no effect upon the ultimate judgment of the American people.

---

[16] Michael Baruch Grossman and Martha Joynt Kumar, *Portraying the President: The White House and the News Media* (Baltimore, Md.: Johns Hopkins University Press, 1981), ch. 11.

Summary

1. Because the president is the ceremonial head of state as well as the actual governmental leader, the office has strong symbolic power. The president can use it to rally the country behind him in time of crisis. But the power and visibility of the office can also mean that the public will hold the president responsible for events over which he may have no control.

2. The actual nature of the "executive Power" that the Constitution grants to the president is not clear, and presidents have given it different interpretations. The general contours of the specific powers of appointment, removal, and pardon are quite clear and leave little room for ambiguity.

3. Although the president has the complete power to appoint all his top advisers, he must be careful to appoint those who will both carry out his policies and run their department effectively.

4. In foreign policy the Constitution divides power between the president and Congress. The president retains the initiative, but Congress can limit his options, and in the period since Vietnam it has. For the president to lead in foreign policy, he cannot simply impose his will. He must persuade both the public and Congress to accept his leadership.

5. In domestic policy the task of presidential leadership is even more difficult. The president must be able to develop a close working relationship with Congress and have a clear sense of his priorities and the public mood.

6. Conflict is inherent in the relationship between the president and the media. The president wants the media to portray his administration favorably, and the media are anxious for news that gains public attention regardless of how the president and his administration are characterized.

Key Terms

chief of state (p. 259)
head of government (p. 259)
natural-born citizens (p. 262)
naturalized citizens (p. 262)
Twenty-second Amendment
(p. 262)
stewardship theory (p. 263)
constitutional theory (p. 263)
steel seizure case (p. 263)
the administration (p. 265)
inner Cabinet (p. 266)
outer Cabinet (p. 266)
multiple advocacy (p. 267)
Executive Office of the President
(p. 267)

Office of Management and Budget
(p. 268)
National Security Council (p. 268)
Council of Economic Advisers
(p. 270)
Office of Policy Development
(p. 270)
Twenty-fifth Amendment (p. 272)
Presidential Succession Act of 1947
(p. 272)
executive agreements (p. 274)
Case Act (p. 274)
commander-in-chief clause (p. 275)
Prize Cases (p. 275)
Gulf of Tonkin Resolution (p. 277)

Readings for Further Study

For a broad overview of the presidency consult Norman C. Thomas, Joseph A. Pika, and Richard A. Watson, *The Politics of the Presidency,* 3d ed. (Washington, D.C.: Congressional Quarterly Press, 1993), and George C. Edwards III and Stephen J. Wayne, *Presidential Leadership: Politics and Policy Making,* 2d ed. (New York: St. Martin's Press, 1990). An important collection of documents concerning the constitutional powers of the office is Christopher H. Pyle and Richard M. Pious, *The Presi-*

dent, Congress, and the Constitution (New York: Free Press, 1984). A highly readable collection of essays on the contemporary presidency can be found in Michael Nelson, ed., *The Presidency and the Political System,* 3d ed. (Washington, D.C.: Congressional Quarterly Press, 1990). A useful general reference is Leonard W. Levy and Louis Fisher, eds., *Encyclopedia of the American Presidency,* 4 vols. (New York: Simon & Schuster, 1993).

10 Bureaucracies

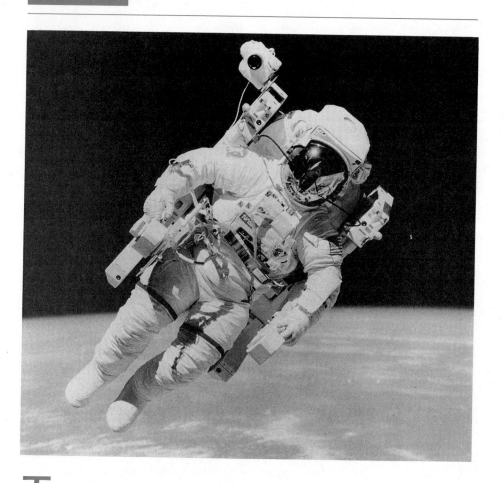

This chapter examines the work of the federal bureaucracy and its employees, who are called bureaucrats. Although bureaucrats have been favorite targets of criticism over the past several decades, the bureaucracy occupies an important place in American government. Congress and the president may attract more media attention. However, without bureaucrats, ideas might be discussed, speeches might be delivered, elections might be held, Congress might debate, presidents might sign bills, *but nothing would actually happen.* Ultimately, space stations are built, toxic waste dumps are cleaned up, and Social Security checks are delivered to the elderly because of the work of bureaucrats. This chapter describes who bureaucrats are and what they do, the major organizational types of bureaucracies, and the means the nation has adopted to ensure competence in the bureaucracy. The chapter also examines the problem of bureaucratic responsibility. As reflected in conflicts among interest groups, Congress, and the president, Americans do not always agree on what bureaucrats should do. Consequently, deciding to whom bureaucrats should be answerable is central to understanding bureaucrats and their place in the political system. Finally, the chapter explores how government regulations as issued by bureaucratic agencies illustrate the changing policy agenda and conflict over the appropriate role of government.

Bureaucracies As the Fourth Branch of Government

The Constitution contains specific articles on the legislature, the executive, and the judiciary, but the document only alludes to bureaucracy in several short phrases. Compared to 1789, Congress is now larger, the president has much greater staff help, and the number of courts and judges has increased. But the truly explosive growth in government has occurred in the development and evolution of bureaucracies. The result has been a U.S. government that employs about 3 million civilians and spends $1.5 trillion annually.

Bureaucracies: Translating Ideas into Action

Once an idea becomes public policy, that is, once Congress and the president agree to an idea and it becomes law, somebody must carry that idea into action. Bureaucracies exist because translating ideas into action always requires an organization of people and resources devoted to that task. For example, debate over the Social Security program is really a dispute over ideas and their attendant costs. Congress and the president decide whether the payroll tax should be cut or increased and whether benefit checks should be linked to increases in the cost of living. But they cannot translate those decisions into action. Implementation is left to bureaucrats, in this case employees of the Internal Revenue Service and the Social Security Administration.

Most Americans do not really ponder the intricacies of administering the huge Social Security program. Someone must determine who is eligible and the exact amount of money each will receive every month. The logistical demands inherent in the idea of a Social Security system inevitably require a group of people to administer the program on a day-to-day basis. Without bureaucrats, grandmothers and elderly uncles would simply not get their Social Security checks.

A **bureaucracy** is an organization that exists to accomplish certain goals. It consists of a group of people, hired because of specific duties they can perform and arranged in a hierarchy, an order based on rank where each member is responsible to a person at the next higher level. The goals or objectives of a bureaucracy are called **public purposes.** Max Weber, the great German sociologist, identified bureaucracy as a unique form of decision-making authority. For Weber, a division of labor, hierarchy, expertise, and impersonal rules characterize an "ideal-type" bureaucracy.[1] These ideal characteristics distinguish bureaucracy as a unique form of social organization designed to make decisions and get things done.

Who Are the Bureaucrats?

The term **bureaucrat** in American government generally refers to any individual who works in the executive branch of government. The Social Security Administration, for example, is comprised of some 60,000 employees who translate the idea of Social Security into action. Among these individuals are computer programmers and technicians, information officers, clerks, policy researchers, receptionists, and hearing officers, all in some way contributing to the execution of the Social Security idea.

Figure 10.1 shows a schematic organization of the United States government. It does not display actual patterns of authority or the real size (in numbers of people or dollars spent) of various units. But the chart does provide a general outline of the branches of government. In terms of numbers of people employed and dollars spent, the executive branch is the largest. It includes the president, and his Executive Office staff, and bureaucracies such as executive departments (like the Department of Defense), independent establishments (like the National Aeronautics and Space Administration), and government corporations (like the U.S. Postal Service). Because the president and his staff are politically separate in many ways from executive departments, independent agencies, and government corporations, these latter units are sometimes called a **fourth branch** of government.[2]

Distinguishing Characteristics of Bureaucracies

The most distinguishing characteristic of bureaucracies is that only they are responsible for executing public policies. The bureaucratic units in the fourth branch are also fundamentally different from the other three branches in size, diversity of purpose, physical dispersion, and relative anonymity. Approximately 65,000 people work in the legislative and judicial branches, a number which is dwarfed by the nearly 3 million civilian employees in the executive branch. As part of his cost-cutting efforts at the start of his administration, President Clinton ordered that

---

[1] A more extended discussion can be found in H. H. Gerth and C. Wright Mills, eds., *From Max Weber: Essays in Sociology* (New York: Oxford University Press, 1958), pp. 196–198.
[2] For an example of use of the phrase, see Kenneth J. Meier, *Politics and the Bureaucracy: Policymaking in the Fourth Branch of Government*, 3d ed. (Pacific Grove, Calif.: Brooks/Cole, 1993).

FIGURE 10.1

The Government of the United States

The jobs people have in the federal bureaucracy are as varied as the different tasks that government performs. Employees of the Bureau of the Census in the Department of Commerce, for example, have the enormous responsibility of counting all Americans every 10 years and recording all kinds of statistics about them. In a scene from the 1940 census depicted here, a census taker traveled by dog sled to locate some of the 60,000 persons living in what was then called the Alaska Territory.

100,000 of these positions in the executive branch be eliminated over a four-year period.

Bureaucracies are as diverse as the public purposes of government. Getting astronauts into orbit (National Aeronautics and Space Administration), protecting consumers from deceptive advertising (Federal Trade Commission), and collecting taxes (Internal Revenue Service in the Department of the Treasury) are each public services executed by individual bureaucracies. The degree of diversity among bureaucratic units in the fourth branch is so vast that it makes the other three branches appear almost monolithic in comparison.

FIGURE 10.1 (see facing page)   The fourth branch is comprised of executive departments, independent establishments, and government corporations. Although the president appears to be in command of the executive departments and other agencies, his actual control is measured by the degree of influence he is able to have on their decisions and programs. Most bureaucrats have civil service status and cannot be dismissed at the president's discretion. Only a relatively few administrative heads serve "at the pleasure of the president." Early in his administration, President Clinton established a new White House Office of Environmental Policy and proposed to Congress the elimination of the Council on Environmental Quality. This figure reflects the proposed change.
SOURCE: Updated from *U.S. Government Manual,* 1992/93, p. 21.

The Capitol, the White House, and the Supreme Court Building are familiar Washington landmarks. However, the bureaucracy has no such single physical symbol. Rather, individual bureaucracies are dispersed throughout the Washington area. Some are housed in highly visible and well-known places, such as the Pentagon or the J. Edgar Hoover FBI Building. But discovering where most bureaucracies are located requires initiative and enterprise. Indeed, 86 percent of bureaucrats work outside Washington in thousands of regional and field offices throughout the nation.

Most bureaucracies usually carry on their work with little sustained public awareness. The president performs his tasks in what seems like a fishbowl. Congress receives enormous media attention, and major Supreme Court decisions are given extensive news coverage as well. However, except for some highly visible Cabinet secretaries, most bureaucrats work relatively anonymously. Their names and exactly what they do are unknown to most citizens.

In the early decades of the nineteenth century only several thousand people worked for the executive branch. That number grew to about a quarter of a million by the beginning of the twentieth century. Executive branch employment expanded rapidly during the New Deal decade of the 1930s and reached its highest point ever at almost four million by the end of World War II. Over the past several decades, the number of civilians working in the executive branch has remained relatively stable at almost three million people.

Many government employees do not fit into the stereotypical view of bureaucrats as clerks and office workers. Practically every occupation is performed by someone working for the federal government. Executive branch employees include engineers, accountants, investigators, biologists, mathematicians, librarians, and veterinarians. Many blue-collar occupations are represented as well. The range of jobs in the federal service suggests the wide variety of public purposes. Generalizations about bureaucrats and bureaucracy, therefore, almost always refer in fact to *some* bureaucrats or *some* bureaucracies or *a portion* of the federal service.

Executive Branch Organization: Types of Bureaucracies

Individual bureaucracies are generally created in response to specific political pressures in a particular area of public policy. A mix of diverse demands and expectations in the political struggle to define the public purposes government ought to pursue produces an array of organizational types of bureaucracies.[3] In terms of size and visibility, five types are particularly important: the Executive Office of the President, executive departments, independent agencies, independent regulatory commissions, and government corporations.

---

[3] Harold Seidman, *Politics, Position, and Power: The Dynamics of Federal Organization,* 3d ed. (New York: Oxford University Press, 1980), p. 321.

The Executive Office of the President

The president has a variety of personal and institutional staff advisers, including the Office of Management and Budget, the National Security Council, and the Council of Economic Advisers. Beyond the economic and foreign policy advice they offer, **Executive Office** units are resources the president can use in his attempts to influence other bureaucracies in the executive branch.

Executive Departments

As a group, the executive departments are generally the largest and most visible bureaucracies in the national government. The heads of these departments comprise the president's **Cabinet,** a source of collective advice that the president may or may not seek as he sees fit. Cabinet status is naturally conferred on government purposes that are crucial by any standard, such as national defense. Beyond these crucial activities, just what purposes deserve Cabinet status is a political question.

For example, following President Reagan's endorsement of the idea, Congress in 1988 gave Cabinet status to the Veterans Administration. Creation of the Department of Veterans Affairs reflected the considerable political clout of veterans' groups in their demand for representation in the Cabinet. As recognition of the high place environmental issues have on the nation's policy agenda, President Clinton early in his administration pushed for legislation to elevate the Environmental Protection Agency to Cabinet status. The absence of departments of science and consumer affairs suggests the crucial role that political support plays in awarding public purposes a place in the Cabinet.

Table 10.1 shows that executive departments differ in their dates of creation, number of employees, and amounts of money they spend. Each department has a unique organizational history, and the dates of creation listed in the table mark either the beginning of Cabinet status or significant organizational change. For example, the Department of Defense was created in 1949 following the consolidation of the departments of the Army, Navy, and Air Force into the National Military Establishment in 1947. But the nation had a Department of War (the army) beginning in 1789.

In terms of number of employees, as Table 10.1 shows, the Department of Defense overwhelms all the others. With about 900,000 civilian employees (the additional 1.8 million military personnel are not included in the table), the Defense Department alone accounts for almost one-third of the total number of civilians working for the national government. Health and Human Services, largely because of the huge Social Security program, alone accounts for more than one-third of the total amount of money the national government spends.

Executive departments have presidentially appointed secretaries and assistant secretaries who provide direction. But departments are really organizational "umbrellas" or "holding companies" within which a variety of smaller bureaucratic units are located. For example, the Federal Bureau of Investigation (FBI) is a unit

TABLE 10.1
The Executive Departments

Department	Date of Creation	Employees	Expenditures (in billions)
Defense	1949*	922,000†	$294.9
Veterans Affairs	1988	234,200	37.7
Treasury	1789	163,100	318.9
Health and Human Services	1979	126,700	640.1
Agriculture	1862	110,800	63.0
Justice	1870	95,900	10.3
Interior	1849	76,000	7.2
Transportation	1966	69,300	39.1
Commerce‡	1913	35,500	3.3
State	1789	25,400	5.5
Labor‡	1913	19,300	37.6
Energy	1977	20,000	17.0
Housing and Urban Development	1965	13,300	28.9
Education	1979	4,800	31.0

* The War Department, predecessor of the Defense Department, was created in 1789.
† Number includes civilian employees only.
‡ A Department of Commerce and Labor existed between 1903 and 1913.

SOURCES: *U.S. Government Manual, 1992–1993, Budget of the United States Government, Fiscal Year 1994.* Data on employees are estimates for fiscal 1993. Employee data (full-time equivalent) are rounded. Expenditure data are 1994 estimates based on Clinton administration proposals.

Executive departments vary widely in terms of employees and budgets. But expenditures are not always related to size of staff, as the numbers for the Departments of Defense and Health and Human Services show.

within the Department of Justice. The Federal Aviation Agency (FAA), which is responsible for the safety of airports and airliners, is located within the Department of Transportation. The National Institutes of Health (NIH), overseeing what is probably the largest life sciences research program in the world, is an agency within the Department of Health and Human Services. The NIH has as its public purpose the satisfaction of one of the most persistent public expectations of the twentieth century, namely, that government discover the causes and cures of disease. Although it is only part of a Cabinet department, the NIH itself spends more money than the Department of State and employs more people than the Department of Education.

Independent Agencies

A third major type of bureaucratic unit is the **independent agency.** Among the best examples of such agencies are the National Aeronautics and Space Administration (NASA) and the Peace Corps. These units are called independent because they are located outside executive departments. The president can hire and fire their heads, and the amount of money these agencies spend must go through the regular appropriations process whereby the president and Congress make final expenditure decisions.

The determination of whether an agency shall be placed inside or outside an executive department is strongly influenced by political considerations. Some group may want an agency serving its purposes to be more highly visible, be unfettered by Cabinet control, or have more direct access to the president. Agencies can also be granted independent status because of the judgment that no executive department would be an appropriate home for the agency. For example, NASA was established as an independent unit to avoid the intermilitary service rivalry that marred the early space program and to give the nation's space program a nonmilitary cast.

Independent Regulatory Commissions

A fourth type of unit is the **independent regulatory commission.** As the title suggests, such units are headed by commissions (comprised of usually 5 to 11 people) rather than single individuals. The commission device was justified on the grounds that a group of experts in a particular field of economic activity, relatively insulated from partisan political considerations, could make reasonable and fair judgments on the basis of their technical knowledge.[4] The Interstate Commerce Commission, created in 1887, served as an organizational model for subsequent regulatory efforts.

Like independent agencies, the commissions lie outside executive departments. However, the independence of the commissions has greater significance, for they have a special status that insulates them to some degree from control by the president. The terms of the commissioners are fixed, so the president may appoint new commissioners only when vacancies occur. Often their terms are longer than the president's. In addition, the Supreme Court has ruled that commissioners can be removed by the president only for causes specified in statutory law governing the commission. Because the commissions are not purely "executive" agencies, the president's controls over them are more limited.[5]

Government Corporations

A fifth type of bureaucratic unit is the **government corporation.** Examples are the U.S. Postal Service, the National Railroad Passenger Corporation (Amtrak), the Federal Deposit Insurance Corporation, and the Resolution Trust Corporation, an agency Congress established in 1989 to take over the finances of failed savings and loan institutions. Government corporations provide services, such as delivering mail, offering insurance, or producing electric power, that are also provided by private corporations. In the provision of these services, government corpora-

---

[4] For a more detailed assessment of the commission form, see Marver H. Bernstein, *Regulating Business by Independent Commission* (Princeton, N.J.: Princeton University Press, 1966), pp. 23–30.

[5] *Humphrey's Executor* v. *United States,* 295 U.S. 602 (1934).

tions generally produce much of their own revenue. For example, people must pay a specific fee to the U.S. Postal Service to deliver letters and packages.

Historically, certain kinds of essentially commercial enterprises have been judged to be of sufficient public importance to merit substantial government involvement. A system of delivering mail to every corner of the nation and beyond at a reasonable price is such an enterprise. Compared to other public bureaucracies, such corporations have been granted a degree of financial and operational flexibility because of the essentially commercial character of their work. And because they generally rely on user fees, they are not tied to the regular appropriations process like other types of bureaucracies.[6]

The Search for Competence in the Civil Service

In assessing bureaucrats and their role, two questions are particularly important. First, how can the nation ensure that bureaucrats are competent? Second, to whom are bureaucrats responsive in the political system? The issue of responsiveness has become particularly important as government has grown over the last half-century, but concern over competence is as old as the Republic itself.

President Washington stressed the importance of "fitness of character" in appointments to high office. These appointees tended to be educated members of the upper classes who looked on government as a high calling. When the Jeffersonians took control from the Federalists after the election of 1800, many moderate Federalists remained on the job. This era has been called one of "government by gentlemen" because the "business of governing was prestigious, and it was anointed with high moral imperatives of integrity and honor."[7]

The Spoils System

The early period of integrity and honor is not nearly so widely known as the famous, or infamous, **spoils system,** the practice of making appointments to government jobs on the basis of party loyalty and support in election campaigns. The term *spoils system* comes from a statement made by Senator William F. Marcy of New York during a Senate debate over a presidential appointment in 1832: "They see nothing wrong in the rule that to the victor belong the spoils of the enemy."[8]

The beginning of the spoils system is ordinarily associated with the presidency of Andrew Jackson (1829–1837), which began a period of "government by the

---

[6] See Seidman, *Politics, Position, and Power,* pp. 265–276.

[7] Frederick C. Mosher, *Democracy and the Public Service,* 2d ed. (New York: Oxford University Press, 1982), pp. 58, 60.

[8] U.S. Civil Service Commission, *Biography of an Ideal: A History of the Federal Civil Service* (Washington, D.C.: Government Printing Office, 1973), pp. 16–17.

common man," a reaction against the elitism of government service in earlier decades.[9] The spoils system led to wholesale changes in government personnel after presidential elections. Government posts were openly bargained for and traded. Presidents spent much of their time not pondering great affairs of state but dealing with people whose needs were much more simple—they wanted government jobs. The result was a view of government as an employment agency and a perception, continuing even today, of government and politics as a corrupt and dirty business.

In one of those familiar ironies of history, the single most important contributor to the demise of the spoils system was an individual who sorely wished to take advantage of it. Charles Guiteau asked President James Garfield (1881) for an appointment as consul to Paris. Not receiving a government job, Guiteau shot the president, who died several months later. In galvanizing public opinion, an assassin's bullet accomplished what for so long eluded reasoned debate.

The Pendleton Act and the Merit Principle

President Garfield's assassination, combined with public reaction against scandals and corruption in the preceding Grant and Hayes administrations, led to the passage of the single most significant piece of legislation affecting public service. The **Pendleton Act** of 1883 established a Civil Service Commission given the task of introducing merit as a condition of government employment. Merit was to be determined by competitive examinations that tested an individual's ability to perform the job in question. Expertise replaced partisan political connections as the criterion of selection. In the beginning the Pendleton Act covered only about 10 percent of all government positions. However, as a result of a variety of executive and legislative actions over the past century, the vast majority of government jobs are now filled on the basis of merit. This emphasis on merit has been so strong that Congress enacted in 1939 the **Hatch Act,** which banned civil servants from participation in partisan political activity.

People get government employment through a variety of avenues. The military services have their own system of recruitment. Similarly, other agencies, such as the Postal Service, the FBI, and the State Department's Foreign Service, each have their own separate systems of hiring and merit. However, most government jobs are covered by the civil service system administered by the Office of Personnel Management, the agency that has assumed most of the functions of the Civil Service Commission, which was abolished in 1978. For many positions, particularly at lower levels, competitive examinations are required. But for others, individuals are rated on the basis of their experience and qualifications.

Clerical and administrative personnel within the competitive service are classified in a "general schedule" (GS) divided into 15 "grades" with stages within each grade. Specific grades are based on the experience and qualifications of individuals, as well as the job responsibilities they are assigned. Lower grades are assigned to

---

[9] Mosher, *Democracy and the Public Service,* pp. 64–66.

individuals who perform clerical, secretarial, or administrative support tasks. College graduates generally begin at grade 5 or above, whereas grades 13, 14, and 15 are "midlevel management positions."[10] Individuals with higher-level positions beyond GS-15 are generally in the Senior Executive Service discussed below. Presidential appointments are in a separate Executive Schedule.

The Civil Service Reform Act of 1978

As a candidate for the presidency, Jimmy Carter made reform of the federal bureaucracy one of his campaign themes. Among the most significant pieces of legislation enacted during his term was the **Civil Service Reform Act of 1978,** the most far-reaching attempt to change the civil service since the Pendleton Act. The act was intended to defend the merit principle and to provide incentives for high-quality work. It established a system of merit pay for mid-level managers and provided protections for whistle-blowers, individuals in the bureaucracy who report waste or fraud. The act also created the **Senior Executive Service** (SES), a group of about 8000 high-level civil servants who might be given bonuses, transferred among agencies, or demoted, all depending on their performance.[11]

President Carter established the **Office of Personnel Management** as the government's principal personnel agency with ultimate responsibility for hiring and maintaining the highest-quality work force. He also redesignated the Civil Service Commission as the **Merit Systems Protection Board,** charged with protecting individual employees against violations of the merit principle or actions taken against whistle-blowers.

The 1978 reform has not lived up to its promise. In the decade following passage of the act, the merit pay system was hobbled by a lack of adequate funds and perceptions of inequity in merit pay awards.[12] Hope that the SES would become a prestigious and respected group of senior civil servants was not met. SES members expressed dissatisfaction with their political superiors, their compensation, and the generally unfavorable public perceptions of the federal civil service.[13] Some change in these attitudes occurred in the early 1990s. For example, senior civil servants generally expressed satisfaction with their salaries after a generous pay raise in 1991.[14] The brief history of the 1978

---

[10] Many individuals who were formerly in grades 16, 17, and 18 (which have been abolished) are now members of the Senior Executive Service. See Meier, *Politics and the Bureaucracy,* pp. 34–36.

[11] Patricia W. Ingraham and David H. Rosenbloom, "Symposium on the Civil Service Reform Act of 1978: An Evaluation," *Policy Studies Journal* 17 (1988–1989): 311–312, provide a more complete list of the act's goals. The symposium contains a series of articles assessing the act from various perspectives (pp. 311–447).

[12] U.S. General Accounting Office, *Pay for Performance* (Washington, D.C.: Government Printing Office, 1989), p. 12.

[13] U.S. General Accounting Office, *The Public Services: Issues Affecting Its Quality, Effectiveness, Integrity, and Stewardship* (Washington, D.C.: Government Printing Office, 1989), p. 34.

[14] U.S. General Accounting Office, *Senior Executive Service: Opinions About the Federal Work Environment* (Washington, D.C.: Government Printing Office, 1992), p. 4.

act nonetheless shows that efforts to reform the civil service system are at once difficult and durable.

The Search for Bureaucratic Responsiveness: The Political Environment of Bureaucracies

Who determines what bureaucrats do is a matter of critical importance in any discussion of bureaucracy. Because the political system is one of dispersed power, the work of bureaucrats is shaped by a variety of individuals and institutions, including the president, Congress, the courts, and pressure groups. Both the president and Congress can point to specific clauses in the Constitution that give each a claim to control over the bureaucracy. Conflict between the two and their allies over who ought to control the bureaucracy is therefore inevitable.

The President

As the title "chief executive" suggests, the individual most responsible for the performance and actions of bureaucrats in the executive branch is the president of the United States. The Constitution charges the president with the responsibility to "take care that the Laws be faithfully executed." In addition, the Constitution authorizes the president to make appointments to head departments and allows him to "require the opinion, in writing, of the principal officer in each of the executive Departments, upon any subject relating to the Duties of their respective Offices."

Despite such constitutional authority, incoming presidents have discovered that they have to work hard to achieve bureaucratic responsiveness to their demands and requests.[15] The relationship sometimes resembles more a struggle among contestants than the easy downward flow of power suggested by neat organization charts.

Presidential control of bureaucracy is difficult for a variety of reasons. First, the sheer size and diversity of the executive branch means that close presidential control and direction of every bureaucrat is a literal impossibility.[16] Much of the work of government has a dynamic of its own, and each day, without direct presidential attention, the assigned tasks are accomplished.

Second, as specialists in some area of public policy, bureaucrats tend to be committed to their own work rather than to the person of the president. Such commitment is strengthened by the fact that they usually hold relatively permanent

---

[15] For a concise history of presidential efforts to get control of bureaucracy, see Francis E. Rourke, "Responsiveness and Neutral Competence in American Bureaucracy," *Public Administration Review* 52 (November–December, 1992): 539–546.

[16] Herbert Kaufman, "Fear of Bureaucracy: A Raging Pandemic," *Public Administration Review* 41 (January–February 1980): 3–4.

positions, whereas presidents are in office for a much shorter period of time. Perhaps most important, bureaucrats, taking advantage of the dispersion of power in the political system, can make alliances with other groups and institutions. Congress, its committees, and political interest groups are among the main sources of power bureaucrats can tap in their struggles with the president.

Bureaucrats can delay, take no action, or offer alternatives in response to a presidential request. But presidents determined to get action have at their disposal a variety of tools to make bureaucrats responsive. First, the president has the

The first female Attorney General, Janet Reno heads the Department of Justice. Prior to her confirmation by the Senate in March 1993, she was the state attorney (i.e., chief prosecutor) in Dade County, Florida. Unlike recent attorneys general, she had neither prior experience in federal law enforcement and the federal courts nor a prior close association with the president who nominated her.

power to make some 3000 appointments to the departments and agencies. These individuals, who include Cabinet secretaries, assistant secretaries, and the heads of independent agencies, are the people the president depends on to carry forward his programs in the executive branch. President Reagan, for example, skillfully used his appointments to help shape his public policy goals. President Bill Clinton won the presidency with the promise of new public policies to produce jobs and higher growth in a lagging economy. Meeting that promise depends in some measure on the people he has chosen to fill important executive branch posts in the Clinton administration.

Second, presidents can use the budget process to propose cuts or increases in the financing of specific bureaucracies. Although the president cannot independently determine expenditures, his proposals can significantly affect the size of bureaucratic budgets. For example, in his budget proposals President Clinton is the single most important individual shaping Defense Department spending and proposals to shift resources to new civilian technologies.[17] Finally, subject to congressional approval, the president can reorganize agencies to make them more compliant to his wishes. Using this power, the president can abolish agencies, create new ones, and rearrange lines of responsibility among existing agencies.

Congress

The president's most powerful competitor in the effort to ensure bureaucratic responsiveness is Congress. According to the Constitution, presidential appointments shall be made "by and with the Advice and Consent of the Senate." The document also grants to Congress taxing powers to provide for "the general welfare of the United States." And the Constitution grants what is probably the most potent power of Congress over bureaucracy by stating that "no money shall be drawn from the Treasury, but in Consequence of Appropriations made by Law." Like the president and his staff, Congress cannot hope to oversee consistently and in any detailed fashion the daily operations of every bureaucratic unit. Like the president, however, a Congress determined to make a difference can substantially shape bureaucratic behavior. First, Congress has the ultimate responsibility for the creation and abolition of agencies. Second, the Senate must confirm presidential appointments, particularly those at the highest bureaucratic levels. Although presidents generally get approval for their appointees, the Senate occasionally exercises its constitutional right to reject nominees. And the possibility of Senate rejection no doubt eliminates some candidates from consideration at the outset. Third, congressional power to enact a budget means that Congress may substantially shape both the amount and the purpose of money bureaucrats spend. Finally, pursuant to its constitutional authority to enact laws, Congress uses its power to investigate bureaucratic behavior. In hearings before its committees,

---

[17] For a good discussion of proposals to shift funding from defense to civilian technology programs, see William J. Broad, "Clinton to Promote High Technology, With Gore in Charge," *New York Times*, November 10, 1992, pp. C1, C14.

Congress can question bureaucrats about allegations of abuse of the purpose of specific legislation.

Congress engages in efforts to control bureaucracies partly because of self-interest. Members' reelection frequently depends on what bureaucrats do and how they do it. Indeed, one observer argues that the growth of big government and the expansion of bureaucratic involvement in the lives of citizens are in no small measure the responsibility of Congress itself. According to this view, members of Congress find electoral profit in "pork-barreling" and "casework" activities.[18] Pork-barreling means that members of Congress try to get as many federal dollars and projects to flow into their districts as possible. Casework refers to services to individual constituents having difficulties with government agencies, ranging from a lost Social Security check to getting a passport.

The Case of the Legislative Veto

As society has become increasingly technological and interdependent, Congress has delegated more generous discretionary authority to the president and executive agencies to grapple with the technical and complicated issues confronting government. To temper executive discretion, Congress also provided for a **legislative veto.** Under this provision, a vote by one or both houses of Congress—or even by a congressional committee in some instances—could halt an executive initiative. The president was bypassed in the process. Rather than initially specifying what could be done, Congress reserved for itself the right to react to what had been done. Congress wrote this legislative veto power into many laws. Among these have been statutes governing the rulemaking powers of regulatory agencies. In one of its best-known exercises of legislative veto power, Congress invalidated a proposed agency regulation that would have required used-car dealers to give potential buyers more extensive information about the cars. Critics of legislative veto power charged that the provision allowed Congress to interfere with executive prerogatives. In 1983, in *Immigration and Naturalization Service* v. *Chadha*,[19] the Supreme Court declared the legislative veto unconstitutional because it violated the separation of powers mandated by the Constitution.

However, the Court's ruling did not settle the matter, for "[t]he decision has been eroded by open defiance and subtle evasion."[20] The legislative veto power continues to be written into some statutes. In addition, informal arrangements provide that agencies will not take certain actions without consulting Congress. For example, NASA and the House Appropriations Committee have agreed that the agency will not exceed spending ceilings on NASA programs without informal

---

[18] Morris P. Fiorina, *Congress: Keystone of the Washington Establishment,* 2d ed. (New Haven, Conn.: Yale University Press, 1989), pp. 40–47 and 85–94.

[19] 462 U.S. 919 (1983).

[20] Louis Fisher, *Constitutional Dialogues: Interpretation as a Political Process* (Princeton, N.J.: Princeton University Press, 1988), p. 225. This discussion of the persistence of the legislative veto draws on Fisher's analysis, pp. 226–228. See also Fisher's *Constitutional Conflicts Between Congress and the President* (Lawrence: University Press of Kansas, 1991), pp. 146–152.

committee approval. The legislative veto continues because bureaucrats need to exercise some discretion as they administer federal programs, but Congress needs to place limits on that discretion without always resorting to the cumbersome process of enacting laws. The continuing use of the legislative veto is the practical result of these realities.

Interest Groups

Bureaucracies are engaged in day-to-day execution of public purposes, so political interest groups understandably try to shape what bureaucrats do. Practically every bureaucratic unit has the strong support of some group. In some cases groups have what amounts to a proprietary interest in specific departments and agencies. Veterans' groups consider the Department of Veterans Affairs "theirs," and farmers view the Department of Agriculture in much the same way. In other cases groups compete as they press their claims on the same agency. The Environmental Protection Agency (EPA) is consistently in the middle of a cross fire of conflicting demands from environmental groups, who charge that the EPA is not enforcing environmental laws vigorously enough, and industrial groups, who argue that the EPA is enforcing such laws too vigorously. Debate over public purposes naturally extends to the work of bureaucracies.

Groups can make direct appeals to the bureaucrats themselves, for example, by commenting on proposed regulations. But groups can also make claims on bureaucracies through other institutions, such as the mass media, the courts, and Congress. Groups can use press conferences or advertising campaigns to influence bureaucratic decisions. Or they can ask the courts to order bureaucracies to halt "unfavorable" actions or begin "favorable" actions. But most of all, groups can try to influence Congress to use its substantial powers to bring about the kind of bureaucratic activity that groups see as favorable to their own interests.

One of the most familiar models of decision making in American government is the **iron triangle,** comprised of interest groups, relevant congressional committees, and one or more executive branch agencies (see Chapter 8, Figure 8.2, for an example of the iron triangle and veterans' policy). Iron triangles characterize the decision-making process for many areas of public policy. One triangle, for example, consists of the Defense Department, congressional armed services committees, and corporate contractors who manufacture weapons systems.

Each of the sides of these triangles depends on and can support the other two because the triangles are held together by large doses of mutual self-interest. The development of a new aircraft or the continued production of an older one, for example, is a decision heavy with political and economic significance. Congressional appropriations for production not only satisfy units in the Department of Defense but also please aircraft companies, their suppliers and contractors, unions, and local communities, all of which benefit when government money is spent. Defense cuts strain these relationships. Attempts to cancel development of a new plane or to shift the contract for production to another company (and perhaps a different section of the country) are sure to provoke resistance from those who have the most to lose.

The Courts

The courts play a more passive role in the political environment of bureaucracies. However, in a variety of ways, courts can significantly shape what bureaucrats do. First, the courts can determine the constitutionality of some congressional or presidential action and, therefore, can affect the work of bureaucrats. More than a half-century ago, the Supreme Court ruled that Congress had unconstitutionally delegated its own powers to the National Recovery Administration, a New Deal agency created to help relieve the economic crisis in the Great Depression.[21] Although the Court since the New Deal has generally allowed Congress to determine the matter of delegation, controversial subjects like the legislative veto and claims of executive privilege have been tested in the courts in recent years.

Second, the courts attempt to ensure procedural fairness in the efforts of bureaucratic units to promulgate rules and regulations. If the courts determine that a group has not been given adequate notice or the right to comment, the rule may be struck down. Third, in discerning congressional intent behind legislation that is either vague or ambiguous, the courts can decide what bureaucracies can or cannot do. For example, if Congress in statutory law bans the use of public funds in "programs where abortion is a method of family planning," can the Department of Health and Human Services (HHS) issue rules that forbid medical personnel in federally funded clinics from even *discussing* with patients abortion as an option? Although President Clinton has since lifted the ban, in 1991 the Supreme Court in *Rust* v. *Sullivan* upheld the HHS regulations banning such discussion as a plausible interpretation of the congressional statute.[22] When Congress is not precise in what a bureaucracy should or can do in a specific instance, the courts ultimately decide the legitimacy of bureaucratic action.

Finally, as another example of judicial power over bureaucracies, the courts can determine whether rules issued by regulatory agencies are reasonable in light of available evidence. The courts must wait for cases to come to them, but judges can powerfully shape the work of bureaucrats.

Bureaucrats and Government Regulation

Given the great diversity among public purposes, bureaucrats engage in a wide range of activities, from doing research on AIDS to collecting taxes to building space stations. But issuing rules and regulations that affect a large number of individuals and companies throughout the nation has been the most controversial activity of bureaucrats over the past several decades. Regulations have produced sharp debate because of the costs and behavior changes they impose on the people affected. A review of regulatory policy illustrates the role of bureaucrats in public policy and the intensely political environment that shapes their work.

---

[21] *Schecter Poultry Corp.* v. *United States,* 295 U.S. 495 (1935).
[22] 59 U.S.L.W. 4451.

Regulation in Perspective

The Environmental Protection Agency has the herculean task of producing regulations required by the Clean Air Act Amendments that Congress enacted in 1990. For example, in the effort to limit the release of ozone-depleting chlorofluorocarbons (CFCs) into the atmosphere, Congress required the EPA to produce regulations on the servicing of motor vehicle air conditioners. The EPA rules are highly detailed and technical and an illustration of the role of bureaucrats in translating ideas into action, in this instance producing specific requirements that will change behavior to protect the ozone layer.[23]

Evidence of regulations in a wide range of policy areas is all around us. Electricity used in millions of homes may be produced by nuclear power plants regulated by the Nuclear Regulatory Commission. Radio and television stations are regulated by the Federal Communications Commission. The Food and Drug Administration certifies the safety of prescription drugs. The EPA sets detailed standards for safe drinking water. The physical safety of workplaces is regulated by the Occupational Health and Safety Administration. Baby cribs and toys are subject to regulation by the Consumer Product Safety Commission.

Government regulations touch people's lives at the most basic levels. For example, more than 300 federal regulations shape what goes into a pizza and how it may be sold.[24] Ingredients must meet specified nutritional requirements to pass federal inspection. Regulations similarly affect other common foods. The hamburger, an American staple, is shaped by 41,000 federal and state regulations.[25] Few people who eat pizza or hamburgers are aware of or give much thought to the dense network of rules that surrounds their meals. For those who produce and market pizza and hamburgers, however, these regulations are a constant reminder of the pervasiveness of government in even the ordinary activities of life. Such rules are intended to protect consumers from unsafe products and to try to ensure nutritional, high-quality meals.

One of the continuing issues in regulatory policy debate is whether regulatory agencies go beyond congressional intent in their creation of rules. Congress has delegated much authority to these agencies because members of Congress have neither the time nor the expertise to draft, for example, detailed safety standards for consumer products or rules on the servicing of car air conditioners to protect the environment. How to place limits on experts without crippling their expertise is a durable issue in the relationship between legislators and policymakers.

Regulatory Agencies and Types of Regulations

Regulations are rules devised by government to shape the actions of individuals and groups to achieve purposes mandated by law.[26] With the increase in public expectations and the general expansion of government activity, rules and regu-

---

[23] 57 Fed. Reg. 31242 (July 14, 1992).
[24] "A Pizza with the Works—Including 310 Regulations," *U.S. News & World Report* (May 31, 1982): 55.
[25] "Your Hamburger: 41,000 Regulations," *U.S. News & World Report,* (February 11, 1980): 64.
[26] This definition draws on Kenneth J. Meier, *Regulation: Politics, Bureaucracy, and Economics* (New York: St. Martin's Press, 1985), pp. 1–2.

lations cover practically every commercial activity to achieve a variety of policy goals. More than 100 agencies have regulatory powers.

The distinction between economic regulation and social regulation is useful in understanding the regulatory goals of government. In **economic regulation,** a government agency issues rules that shape the structure of some industry or ban or encourage certain business practices. For example, the Federal Trade Commission is charged with limiting monopolistic practices. In **social regulation,** agencies issue rules that are designed to achieve social goals, such as fair treatment in employment, clean air, or safe workplaces.[27] For example, the Equal Employment Opportunity Commission is charged with limiting employment discrimination. The consequence is the enhancement of the political and social status of some groups, such as women and blacks.

Regulatory agencies perform both **quasi-legislative** and **quasi-judicial** functions. In their quasi-legislative roles, agencies issue rules that, like legislation, apply to whole classes of people. For example, rules of the Securities and Exchange Commission (SEC) against stock market trading on the basis of insider information apply to all individuals and firms in the securities industry. As quasi-judicial bodies, agencies, like courts, can make decisions in individual cases. Because of action by the SEC, for instance, "junk bond" trader Michael Milken agreed in 1990 to pay $600 million in fines and compensation to investors for securities law violations.

As another example, consumers or competitors can complain to the Federal Trade Commission that a company is engaged in deceptive advertising. The commission can investigate the charge with an **administrative law judge,** who hears the case in what amounts to a trial proceeding. Administrative law judges were mandated by the Administrative Procedure Act of 1946 as part of a general effort to provide procedural protections for individuals and groups in agency proceedings. Administrative law judges hold an insulated status in agencies to protect their judicial function, and their findings in particular cases can be appealed to the commission and, if necessary, to the federal courts.

Table 10.2 lists selected regulatory agencies, their dates of creation, and their purposes. Major government initiatives to regulate the economy first occurred in the decades around the beginning of the twentieth century. As industrialization proceeded in the late nineteenth century, the relationships between the buyers and sellers of goods and services became increasingly national in scope. The growth of corporations and nationalization of the economy brought a variety of unsavory practices, such as price gouging, and structures, such as monopolies, to the marketplace. This led to demands that government remedy the imbalance between producers and purchasers. These problems frequently crossed state lines, so redress in many instances involved the national government.

Establishment of regulatory agencies has come in waves or groups, as Congress responded to persistent political demands. The first wave occurred around the turn of the twentieth century and dealt with the unprecedented size and impact of major industrial corporations and with the problems encountered by the buyers and sellers of goods and services. The second, in the 1930s, sprang from the

---

[27] See *Federal Regulatory Directory*, 6th ed. (Washington, D.C.: Congressional Quarterly, 1990), pp. 2, 5–13.

	Date of	
TABLE 10.2		
Selected Regulatory Agencies		
Agency	Creation	Purpose
Interstate Commerce Commission (ICC)	1887	To regulate interstate surface transportation, including trains, trucks, buses, and water carriers
Federal Trade Commission (FTC)	1914	To protect economic competition against monopoly or restraints on trade and protect against unfair or deceptive trade practices
Food and Drug Administration (FDA)	1930*	To protect the health of citizens against impure and unsafe foods, drugs, cosmetics, and other potential hazards
Federal Communications Commission (FCC)	1934	To regulate interstate and foreign communications by radio, television, wire, satellite, and cable
Securities and Exchange Commission (SEC)	1934	To provide protection for investors and to ensure that securities markets are fair and honest and, when necessary, to provide the means to enforce securities laws through sanctions
National Labor Relations Board (NLRB)	1935	To safeguard employees' rights to organize, determine through elections whether workers want unions as their bargaining representatives, and prevent and remedy unfair labor practices
Equal Employment Opportunity Commission (EEOC)	1964	To eliminate discrimination in employment on the basis of race, color, religion, sex, national origin, disability, or age
Occupational Safety and Health Administration (OSHA)	1970	To develop, promulgate, and enforce occupational safety and health standards
Environmental Protection Agency (EPA)	1970	To control and abate pollution in the areas of air, water, solid waste, pesticides, radiation, and toxic substances
Consumer Product Safety Commission (CPSC)	1972	To protect the public against unreasonable risks of injury from consumer products, to develop consumer product safety standards, and to promote product safety and research
Nuclear Regulatory Commission (NRC)	1974†	To license and regulate the civilian use of nuclear energy to protect public health and safety and the environment
Federal Energy Regulatory Commission (FERC)	1977‡	To set rates and charges for the transportation and sale of natural gas and oil by pipeline and for the transmission and sale of electricity and the licensing of hydroelectric power projects

* Assumed functions placed in the Department of Agriculture in 1906.
† Assumed many of the functions given to the Atomic Energy Commission in 1946.
‡ Assumed many of the functions of the Federal Power Commission created in 1920.

SOURCE: Statements of purpose taken, with some modifications, from *U.S. Government Manual, 1992/93* (Washington, D.C.: GPO, 1992).

Establishment of regulatory agencies has come in waves or groups, as Congress responded to persistent political demands. The first wave occurred around the turn of the twentieth century and dealt with the unprecedented size and impact of major industrial corporations and with the problems encountered by the buyers and sellers of goods and services. The second, in the 1930s, sprang from the economic dislocation caused by the Great Depression. The third, in the 1960s and 1970s, came in response to demands to remedy inequalities and to protect the environment and the workplace.

economic dislocation caused by the Great Depression. The third, in the 1960s and 1970s, came in response to demands to remedy inequalities and to protect the environment and the workplace.

In 1887 Congress created the Interstate Commerce Commission to regulate the railroads. The commission device was justified on the grounds that a group of technical experts in a particular field of economic activity, who were relatively insulated from partisan political considerations, could make reasonable and fair judgments. New industries and new demands for regulation came in the twentieth century, and the Interstate Commerce Commission served as a model for subsequent regulatory efforts. Other enactments followed, such as the Sherman Anti-Trust Act (1890) and the Federal Trade Commission Act (1914), which tried to limit the growing economic power of trusts and large corporations. The goal of regulation was to establish government as a counterweight to the concentration of economic power in a small number of businesses.

Another kind of regulation tried to protect consumers of specific products. In the ideal free market, companies compete with each other to sell products at the lowest price to consumers who make their purchase choices based on full information about the relative merits of the products. However, in the real world consumers either do not have access to such information or do not take the trouble to get it. Regulation of consumer products means that government action compensates for such market failures. Largely in response to publicity about unsavory practices in particular industries, Congress enacted the Pure Food and Drug Act (1906) and the Meat Inspection Act (1907) to protect unwary consumers. Such regulation continues, as contemporary rules on pizza and hamburgers suggest.

The next period of new regulatory activity occurred during the explosion of government initiatives during the New Deal of the 1930s. Regulation increased as part of the general response of government to the Great Depression. The drive for active government brought entire industries under federal regulation. Among the regulatory agencies created were the Securities and Exchange Commission for financial exchange markets, the Federal Communications Commission for electronic communications, and the Civil Aeronautics Board for the airline industry.[28] In the effort to combat unfair labor practices, the National Labor Relations Board was established to regulate employer-employee relationships in businesses in interstate commerce.

Until the past generation most government regulations had predominantly economic goals. The objects of regulation were relationships among businesses, rates, business practices, and entry into an industry. However, in the 1960s and 1970s new regulatory efforts went beyond economic concerns to encompass social goals, such as affirmative action, worker safety, environmental protection, and consumer product safety. Among the regulatory agencies established were the Equal Employment Opportunity Commission to fight discrimination in the workplace, the Environmental Protection Agency to limit environmental pollution, the Occupational Safety and Health Administration to promote worker safety, and the

---

[28] To deregulate and allow the operation of market incentives in the airline industry, the Civil Aeronautics Board has since been abolished.

Consumer Product Safety Commission to protect consumers from unsafe products. Social regulation has been the lightning rod drawing most of the conflict over regulation since the 1960s.

The Regulatory Process

Regulatory agencies make rules that can have real consequences easily discernible to most people. For example, almost everyone has had the experience of struggling to open a "childproof" aspirin bottle. Yet almost no one thinks about the circuitous route such regulations travel before they touch us. Figure 10.2 shows where regulations come from. All regulations ultimately have their roots in the

FIGURE 10.2
Where Regulations Come From

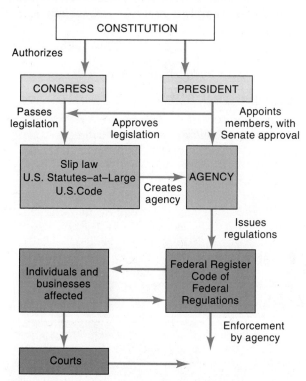

Authority for regulations lies in the Constitution, which authorizes Congress to enact and the president to approve the creation of departments and programs. A new piece of legislation appears first as a slip law and then in *U.S. Statutes-at-Large* and the *U.S. Code.* Established by such legislation, agencies issue and enforce regulations. These in turn appear in the *Federal Register* and later in the *Code of Federal Regulations.* Regulations may be contested in the courts.

Constitution, which grants Congress the power to pass laws and to establish agencies to accomplish specific purposes. Each act of Congress is published in the form of a **slip law,** which is the written text of the legislation. Depending on the subject matter, slip laws can range from a single page to several hundred pages in length. The slip laws passed by each session of Congress are bound together to form a volume of *U.S. Statutes-at-Large.* Laws currently in effect are classified by subject matter, such as transportation, labor, or public health and welfare, in the *U.S. Code,* a collection of dozens of volumes periodically revised to reflect changes in legislation.

Once established, agencies must abide by stringent procedural requirements in their promulgation of rules and regulations. To provide adequate notice and opportunity for hearing, under the provisions of the Administrative Procedure Act of 1946, agencies must publish proposed rules to allow anyone affected to comment on them. Such rules appear in the *Federal Register,* a daily government publication that also contains presidential proclamations and executive orders. The *Federal Register* on any given day may be several hundred pages in length, a fact that suggests the complexity and scope of the federal regulatory effort. All rules and regulations currently in effect are compiled by agency and subject matter in the *Code of Federal Regulations* (CFR), a collection of almost 200 volumes revised annually on a staggered basis. The regulations are arranged topically in the *CFR* just as statutes are arranged topically in the *U.S. Code.*

Regulations setting acceptable contaminant levels in drinking water traversed this process, as did those requiring childproof aspirin bottles to prevent accidental poisoning. In 1972 Congress enacted the Consumer Product Safety Act, which gave wide-ranging powers on consumer safety to the Consumer Product Safety Commission (CPSC). The act entered the *U.S. Statutes-at-Large* and the *U.S. Code.*[29] By publishing proposed rules in the *Federal Register,* receiving comment, and then issuing final rules, the commission establishes safety standards that a large number of consumer products must meet. The standards are compiled in the *Code of Federal Regulations.* The congressional act that established the CPSC is only 27 pages in length, but an entire volume of the *Code of Federal Regulations,* more than 600 pages long, is devoted to the commission and its rules. Among the detailed safety standards in the *CFR* are 21 pages on poison prevention packaging requirements, including rules on aspirin bottles.

Agencies themselves may go through a complicated internal sequence of steps before they issue a rule.[30] A variety of groups and individuals within the agency, including lawyers, technicians, scientists, and economists, shape the proposed regulation. The proposed rule is then reviewed by the Office of Management and Budget, after which it appears as a proposal in the *Federal Register.* After a period for public comment to take public reaction into account, the regulation is published as a final rule in the *Federal Register.* The process may not end here, for affected parties, such as a trade association, might contest the rule in the courts

---

[29] The act transferred responsibility for poison prevention packaging from the EPA and HEW to the new commission.

[30] For example, see Gary C. Bryner, *Bureaucratic Discretion: Law and Policy in Federal Regulatory Agencies* (New York: Pergamon, 1987), pp. 98–105.

or try to get Congress to change the enabling statute. Because regulators make choices, their work is naturally and continually shaped by the political demands of groups affected by those choices.

The Ebb and Flow of Regulatory Debate

Regulations have been a controversial political issue because they symbolize government interference in the daily lives of individuals and businesses. Some economic regulation in fact benefited the regulated industries by limiting competition and supporting the prices of services. In the name of economic efficiency and increased competition, some industries have been deregulated. For example, as part of the general effort to lighten the regulatory burden, the Civil Aeronautics Board, which set airline routes and rates, was eliminated in 1985. Congressional enactments have also limited the regulatory role of the Interstate Commerce Commission in the interstate trucking, railroad, and busing industries.

In response to criticism of regulation, recent presidents have made regulatory reform a policy objective. Emphasizing the view that regulatory costs threaten economic productivity,[31] President Reagan in particular made **deregulation** a major theme in his call to "roll back" the growth of government. He created a presidential task force on regulatory relief and appointed to regulatory agencies people who shared his interest in reducing the impact of regulations. The budgets of regulatory agencies were cut, and many new proposed regulations were suspended. The Office of Management and Budget assumed an active role in assessing the costs and benefits of new rules. However, as the box "Politics and Economics: Regulations and Cost-Benefit Analysis" suggests, OMB review of regulations has been controversial.

As the 1980s wore on, critics saw deregulatory efforts as attempts to strip government of its power to pursue worthy economic and social goals.[32] A turning point came early in the decade in the battle between Congress and President Reagan over the EPA. Congress in 1980 gave to the EPA the task of cleaning up toxic waste dumps with money drawn from a "superfund" financed by a tax on chemicals. Within a short time critics charged that the EPA was being too responsive to the interests of the chemical companies and was not vigorously enforcing the toxic waste law. The House of Representatives cited the head of the EPA (a Reagan appointee) for contempt of Congress for refusing to make available agency documents. Six congressional committees began investigations amid intense criticism that the agency reflected Reagan administration neglect of environmental concerns. To contain the political damage, the White House made sweeping changes in the agency's leadership and released the requested documents. The struggle uncovered the deep political support for strong governmental action in environmental protection.

---

[31] For a critique of regulation, see Murray L. Weidenbaum, *The Future of Business Regulation: Private Action and Public Demand* (New York: AMACOM, 1979).

[32] See Susan J. Tolchin and Martin Tolchin, *Dismantling America: The Rush to Deregulate* (Boston: Houghton Mifflin, 1983).

Politics and Economics

Regulations and Cost-Benefit Analysis

Regulations obviously cost money. Regulatory agencies require buildings, people, and sometimes sophisticated equipment and research capabilities, all of which must be funded by tax dollars. Agency rules can also require that other people spend money. The protection of workers may require that companies make expensive physical alterations in the workplace. Environmental quality standards may require that manufacturing plants install special equipment to reduce air emissions. Companies may be forced to spend scarce research and development dollars to meet mandated consumer product safety standards. One of the most durable and volatile issues in regulatory policy debate is whether these costs are worth the effort.

Cost-benefit analysis is one of the techniques used to assess the impact of regulations. In theory, cost-benefit analysis should enable government officials to determine whether regulations are worth their costs. The technique can take complicated mathematical forms. In general, the costs of a regulation are tallied and then compared with the benefits the regulation is designed to gain. For example, are the benefits of the lives saved from cleaner air worth the costs of EPA enforcement activities and air scrubbers used in manufacturing plants? The matter is complicated by the fact that progressively higher standards may require geometrically higher costs. For example, cleaning the air of 90 percent of its particulate matter may be equal to or less than the cost of cleaning the next 5 percent.

Efforts to make cost-benefit analyses an integral part of rule-making have been controversial. In 1981 President Reagan issued an executive order requiring that agencies assessing proposed or existing regulations be guided by an analysis of costs and benefits. According to the order, agencies can make rules only if "the potential benefits to society for the regulation outweigh the potential costs to society." Agencies proposing major rules, those having an impact of $100 million or more on the economy, must submit to the Office of Management and Budget a regulatory impact analysis before the rule goes into effect. Critics in Congress charged that the OMB used its powers of reviewing regulatory costs and benefits to delay or weaken proposed rules designed to enhance worker or consumer safety or to meet environmental goals. In the Bush administration, the White House Council on Competitiveness, headed by Vice-President Dan Quayle, assumed the role of regulatory watchdog as it diluted rules it judged to be too costly. The OMB and the Competitiveness Council were strongly supported by those who wanted to keep in check what they saw as unreasonably costly regulations. But the sharp criticism of the limits these agencies placed on regulations illustrates the political debate that can swirl around cost-benefit analysis.

The existence of the debate indicates that cost-benefit analysis does not offer easy answers for public officials. Efforts to tally costs and benefits can become mired in questions such as how much a life is worth or how the benefit of a smogless day can be calculated. Political interests are highly resistant to conclusions that do not support their positions, regardless of how mathematically sound they appear. Acknowledging the limitations of cost-benefit analysis, what questions can be asked about any proposed rule to assess its worth?

The Environmental Protection Agency (EPA) has been directed by Congress to control and abate pollution in air, water, solid waste, and toxic substances, among other things. Since 1980 employees of the EPA, like the one depicted here, have also had the unenviable task of cleaning up toxic waste dumps. Money for the clean-up operations come from a "superfund" financed by a tax on chemicals.

By the mid-1980s regulation as a volatile political issue temporarily receded, and renewed receptivity to government regulation became more evident. In 1986 Congress broadened environmental regulations on drinking water and toxic wastes.[33] Later in the decade some critics argued that the financial disaster of the collapse of savings and loan institutions could have been avoided had the regulatory atmosphere not been so lax.[34] However, as a lagging economy dogged his presidency, in his 1992 State of the Union address President Bush called for a "moratorium on any new federal regulations that could hinder growth." Predictably, the moratorium drew fire from consumer and environmental groups and support from those charging that regulations pose a costly burden. The scope of

---

[33] Michael E. Kraft, "Environmental Gridlock: Searching for Consensus in Congress," in Norman J. Vig and Michael E. Kraft, eds., *Environmental Policy in the 1990s* (Washington, D.C.: Congressional Quarterly, 1990), pp. 110–111.
[34] Jeff Gerth, "Regulators Say 80's Budget Cuts May Cost U.S. Billions in 1990's," *New York Times*, December 19, 1989, pp. A1, B10.

regulatory activity was an issue in the 1992 presidential campaign, and Bill Clinton's victory promised, as a contrast to the Bush moratorium, greater receptivity in the White House to consumer and environmental regulations. However, a knotty task that the Clinton administration confronts is making regulation more vigorous to protect the environment, workers, and consumers without limiting job growth and economic productivity.[35]

Regulatory bureaucrats caught in the middle of the cross fire of conflict surrounding regulation are really at the center of a debate over the appropriate role of government. The attempt to ban unsafe toys may be hailed by consumer groups but criticized by manufacturers. Environmentalists want to protect endangered species and wilderness areas, but loggers fear a loss of jobs. Handicapped citizens promote efforts to make buildings more accessible, but corporations and universities have worried about the high financial costs of providing such accessibility. Health groups vigorously support efforts to regulate cigarette advertising, but the tobacco industry views such regulation as a threat. Businesses cite the high financial burden of some worker safety requirements, but labor unions see efforts to limit such rules as increasing physical risks to workers. The contests over changes in regulatory efforts are more than differences over financial costs. The intensity of the debate may ebb and flow, but conflict over regulations springs from disagreement over what government should do, who should benefit from government action, and whether compromises among competing goals can be achieved.

Bureaucracies: Targets and Mirrors of Conflict

For much of the past generation, bureaucrats have been the target of biting criticism from elected officials, candidates for public office, and private citizens. Like lightning rods, bureaucrats have drawn criticism aimed at government in general. Four charges summarize the criticism.

First, bureaucrats waste or defraud precious public resources. Second, they wrap much of their work in what appears to be endless amounts of **red tape,** which can be defined as "unnecessary" procedural requirements that impede needed action. Third, bureaucrats do work that either duplicates or conflicts with the work of other bureaucrats. Fourth, and perhaps the most important, they play an independent and "political" role in public policy—that is, through their use of discretion, unelected bureaucrats make choices that either directly counter or go beyond the wishes of elected politicians.

Every large organization has individuals who work diligently and conscientiously and others whose work is either haphazard or detrimental to the goals of the organization. Given the size of the national government, waste and fraud exist. But there is no agreement on their extent. The national government spends huge

---

[35] For a discussion of the debate over regulations in the campaign, see Gerald F. Seib and Bob Davis, "Bush and Clinton Joust Over How to Regulate U.S. Business Activity," *Wall Street Journal,* September 23, 1992, pp. A1, A6.

amounts of time and money trying to limit waste and ensure integrity of work. The battle is always being fought.[36]

The criticism of red tape can be more accurately leveled at groups in the political system generally rather than at individual bureaucrats. One observer has argued that "one person's red tape may be another's treasured safeguard."[37] That is, what appears to be red tape is really the result of conflicting expectations on the part of different groups in the political system. For example, advocates of nuclear power may decry the long bureaucratic process of hearings, certifications, and licensing procedures that accompanies the construction of a nuclear power plant. Yet environmentalists and some local residents may see such procedures as absolutely essential to public health and safety. Perhaps red tape is more a reflection of the attempt to satisfy political values in our society, such as consideration of different points of view, than it is an effort by bureaucrats to paralyze action.[38]

Similarly, charges that bureaucrats engage in work that duplicates or conflicts with the work of other bureaucrats in large measure can be explained by outside expectations. For example, in granting college funds to veterans, the Department of Veterans Affairs (DVA) may be duplicating the educational programs of the Department of Education. Yet the political expectation that the DVA serve veterans encourages that agency to assume educational functions of its own. Similarly, the Agriculture Department represents the economic demands of tobacco farmers while Health and Human Services represents the demands of health groups. The conflicting demands of different groups in society are largely reflected in conflict among different groups of bureaucrats.

The most serious criticism of bureaucrats is that even though they are unelected, they independently make choices affecting public policy and in the process play an unintended political role. However, three qualifications need to be made about their political role. First, in executing policy purposes, bureaucrats obviously strive to achieve their institution's goals. For example, an administrator at the NIH may stress the importance of additional funding for cancer research. Defense analysts may call for the construction of a new weapons system. Executing policy is their work, and bureaucrats, not surprisingly, want the most favorable environment possible in which that work can proceed.

Second, bureaucrats cannot always exercise discretion in translating ideas into action. The Internal Revenue Service, for example, cannot decide to tax certain income groups at rates higher or lower than those prescribed by law. The greater the specificity of the idea written into law, the lower the degree of discretion bureaucrats have in translating that idea into action.

Third, if the law is vague or ambiguous, bureaucratic discretion is inevitable. In much legislation, Congress cannot possibly provide for every contingency or circumstance. These specific decisions fall to bureaucrats. For example, the Social Security Administration (SSA), in administering benefits to the disabled, must determine just what constitutes disability in individual cases. Depending on how

---

[36] See the discussion in Herbert Kaufman, *Red Tape: Its Origins, Uses, and Abuses* (Washington, D.C.: Brookings Institution, 1977), pp. 50–54.

[37] Ibid., p. 4.

[38] Ibid.

rigorous that determination is, the SSA, in effect, can make public policy toward the disabled.[39]

In many areas of public policy, different groups and institutions have conflicting ideas on what government ought to do. And they are interested in bureaucracy because they want to get their ideas translated into action. In large measure the issue of bureaucratic responsiveness centers on the determination of whose ideas ought to be translated into action. In an enlightening and provocative statement, a civil servant in the EPA declared during a controversy over environmental policy: "I signed an oath of office, and it was not to the President. It was to the American people."[40] In this political system, control over the bureaucracy comes to those who can successfully claim to determine what "the American people" want. The search for that determination, like the struggle to control bureaucracy, lies at the heart of political conflict.

Summary

1. The principal task of bureaucracy is the translation of policy ideas into action. Bureaucrats are people appointed to positions in the executive branch. Individuals responsible for executing public policies work relatively anonymously in bureaucracies. Compared to the other branches of government, bureaucracies are much larger, more diverse in purpose, and physically disperse. The three million government employees work in a great variety of occupations.

2. Executive Office units advise and serve the president. The executive departments generally contain a large number of smaller bureaucratic units. Independent agencies are placed outside the executive departments, generally in response to political demands for greater visibility. More insulated from presidential control than other bureaucracies, independent regulatory agencies monitor various sectors of the economy. Government corporations are public bodies engaged in essentially commercial enterprises.

3. Government service was seen as a high calling in the early decades of the Republic. In the spoils system, government jobs were rewards for political service. The Pendleton Act of 1883 established the merit principle as the basis for government employment. The Civil Service Reform Act of 1978 attempted to protect the merit system and rid the system of abuses, but its success has been questioned.

4. The president can shape bureaucracies by exercising his appointment, budget proposal, and reorganization powers. Congress can contest the president in the struggle to control bureaucracy through its statutory, budget, confirmation, and investigative powers. In iron triangles, interest groups can work with members of Congress to make claims on bureaucracies. The courts can shape

---

[39] See, for example, Susan Gluck Mezey, *No Longer Disabled: The Federal Courts and the Politics of Social Security Disability* (Westport, Conn.: Greenwood, 1988).

[40] Hugh B. Kaufman, quoted in Cass Peterson, "A Nagging Voice from E.P.A. Depths Now Singing from the Catbird Seat," *Washington Post,* February 14, 1983, p. A9.

the work of bureaucracies by declaring laws unconstitutional, ensuring procedural fairness, interpreting statutes, and judging the reasonableness of agency actions.

5. Regulation is a major policy of government that affects practically everyone in some way. Economic regulation centers on specific industries, and social regulation tries to achieve a variety of social goals. Major regulatory initiatives were made in the late nineteenth and early twentieth centuries, during the New Deal, and in the 1960s and 1970s. Regulatory agencies issue rules pursuant to powers they receive from congressional enactments. Debate over the regulatory role of government ebbs and flows with the debate over the appropriate role of government and who should bear the costs of government action.

6. Bureaucracies have been targets of sharp criticism over the past generation. Depending on the amount of discretion Congress allows in law, bureaucrats can make policy. The issue of bureaucratic responsiveness centers principally on determining whose policy ideas should be implemented.

Key Terms

bureaucracy (p. 290)
public purposes (p. 291)
bureaucrat (p. 291)
fourth branch (p. 291)
Executive Office (p. 295)
Cabinet (p. 295)
independent agency (p. 296)
independent regulatory commission (p. 297)
government corporation (p. 297)
spoils system (p. 298)
Pendleton Act (p. 299)
Hatch Act (p. 299)
Civil Service Reform Act of 1978 (p. 300)
Senior Executive Service (p. 300)
Office of Personnel Management (p. 300)

Merit Systems Protection Board (p. 300)
legislative veto (p. 304)
iron triangle (p. 305)
regulations (p. 307)
economic regulation (p. 308)
social regulation (p. 308)
quasi-legislative (p. 308)
quasi-judicial (p. 308)
administrative law judge (p. 308)
slip law (p. 312)
U.S. Statutes-at-Large (p. 312)
U.S. Code (p. 312)
Federal Register (p. 312)
Code of Federal Regulations (p. 312)
deregulation (p. 313)
cost-benefit analysis (p. 314)
red tape (p. 316)

Readings for Further Study

The United States Government Manual (Washington, D.C.: Government Printing Office) is a basic reference work that contains a history, relevant congressional enactments, and an organization chart for each bureaucratic unit. James W. Fesler and Donald F. Kettl, *The Politics of the Administrative Process* (Chatham, N.J.: Chatham House, 1991) is a comprehensive and erudite review of bureaucracies in the policy process. A classic work on the obstacles to the implementation of policies is Jeffrey L. Pressman and Aaron B. Wildavsky, *Implementation,* 3d ed. (Berkeley: University of California Press, 1984). A fascinating history and analysis of the public service in light of political culture can be found in Frederick C. Mosher, *Democracy and the Public Service,* 2d ed. (New York: Oxford University Press, 1982). An interesting analysis of bureaucracy and democratic theory can be found in Douglas Yates, *Bureaucratic Democracy: The Search for Democracy and Efficiency in American Government* (Cambridge, Mass.: Harvard University Press, 1982). William T. Gormley, Jr., *Taming the Bureaucracy: Muscles, Prayers, and Other Strategies* (Princeton, N.J.: Princeton University Press, 1989), reviews and analyzes efforts to control bureaucracy. Richard A. Harris and Sidney Milkus, *The Politics of Regulatory Change: A Tale of Two Agencies* (New York: Oxford University Press, 1989), examines the Federal Trade Commission and the Environmental Protection Agency within the context of regulatory politics in the 1970s and 1980s. A. Lee Fritschler's *Smoking and Politics: Policymaking and the Federal Bureaucracy,* 4th ed. (Englewood Cliffs, N.J.: Prentice-Hall, 1989) is an illuminating analysis of the Federal Trade Commission's attempt to regulate cigarette advertising.

The Supreme Court 11 and the American Judiciary

One of the distinguishing characteristics of American government is the major role the Supreme Court and other courts play in governing the nation. Because of the importance of the issues that confront American judges, their decisions weigh heavily in shaping the liberties, fortunes, and quality of life of many citizens. Chief among courts is the United States Supreme Court, the third branch of government. The Supreme Court enjoys prominence because of the Constitution and because Americans have been reluctant to place their fate entirely in the hands of elected officials and popular majorities. The Court, therefore, sits as an institution primarily responsible for interpreting the law of the land. Yet because the Court appears antidemocratic in a government that strives to be democratic, Americans have also been wary of giving

321

judges too much power. Explaining what judges do, discerning the Supreme Court's place in American government, and exploring how the Court decides cases are the objectives of this chapter.

The National Court System

A look at almost any recent term of the Supreme Court turns up decisions on subjects as varied as presidential powers, crime, taxation, religious freedom, and racial and sexual equality. The fact that the Supreme Court confronts important issues makes the Court similar to other major political institutions in Washington. Yet three factors distinguish the Supreme Court and other courts from the rest of the national government:

1. The judiciary operates only in the context of cases.
2. The cases develop in a strictly prescribed fashion.
3. Judges rely heavily on reason in justifying what they do.

The judiciary is distinctive because it is the part of government that speaks the language of the fundamental values of the political system.

Cases: Raw Material for the Judiciary

The judiciary acts by deciding cases. A **case** is a dispute handled by a court. Like most disputes, there are at least two opposing parties. A case may pit one individual against another, a government agency against an individual, a corporation against the government, and so forth. Cases are criminal or civil. **Criminal cases** result when the government begins legal action against someone following commission of a crime. A **crime** is a public wrong. That is, it is an offense, such as murder, against society at large even though it may have been committed against only a single individual. **Civil cases** encompass all noncriminal legal actions and commonly include attempts to redress a private wrong or to settle a private dispute. Divorces and recovery of damages following an automobile accident, for example, present civil law questions. They involve efforts by one party to enforce a right or to be compensated for harm caused by another.

By deciding cases, courts, like other governmental institutions, attempt to resolve conflicts peacefully. It is only a slight exaggeration that disputes that bring a regiment of soldiers into the streets of some countries summon a battalion of lawyers into the courtrooms of America.

Fifty-one Judicial Systems

Topped by the Supreme Court, the national court system contains both state courts and federal courts. The latter in turn consist of district courts, courts of appeals, and a few special courts.

References to **state courts** and **federal courts** can be confusing to anyone not familiar with the political features of American federalism (see Chapter 2). Concisely put, each state has its own system of courts, and the national government has its own system of courts (see Figures 11.1 and 11.2). The national courts are usually referred to somewhat misleadingly as "federal courts."

The two systems hear different kinds of cases. Almost all divorce and personal injury cases, for example, are heard in state courts, as are violations of state criminal laws. Antitrust actions and violations of federal criminal laws, by contrast, are adjudicated in federal courts. Someone charged with robbing a corner grocery will be tried in state court; someone charged with robbing a post office will be tried in federal court. The dual system of courts means that almost everyone in any of the 50 states is simultaneously within the *jurisdiction,* or reach, of two judicial systems, one state and the other federal. **Jurisdiction** refers to the authority a court has to entertain a case. The term has two basic dimensions: who and what.

FIGURE 11.1
The United States Court System

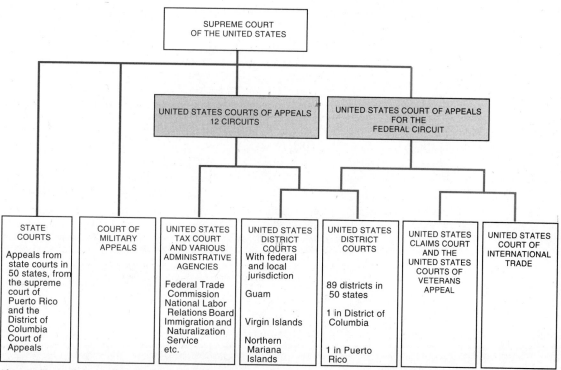

Almost all cases the Supreme Court decides each year are part of its appellate jurisdiction. These cases begin in the state and federal courts. SOURCE: Administrative Office of the United States Courts.

FIGURE 11.2
Typical Organization of State Courts

Each state has its own system of state courts. No system is exactly like another, but all are organized in a hierarchy similar to that pictured here. All states have courts of limited jurisdiction, courts of general jurisdiction, and a court of last resort. In Texas and Oklahoma, there are two separate courts of last resort—one for criminal appeals and one for all other types of cases. Most, but not all, states have at least one intermediate appellate court. In the 12 states that have no intermediate court, cases move on appeal from courts of general jurisdiction to the court of last resort.   SOURCE: National Center for State Courts.

The first identifies the parties who may take a case into a particular court. The second refers to the subject matter the parties can raise in their case.

Still, state and federal courts have at least two important points in common. First, the U.S. Constitution binds all American courts; second, the U.S. Supreme Court may decide cases that originate in both systems. Because the Supreme Court hears only a tiny fraction of all the cases looked at by judges each year across the land, however, the quality of justice in the nation depends largely on what these other courts and judges do. The Supreme Court weighs heavily in American politics not because it can literally oversee what every other court does but because these other courts consider the Supreme Court's decisions binding on questions of national law and policy.

State and Local Courts

State and local courts are organized according to the laws and constitutions of the 50 states. The resulting variety only serves to make them interesting, not insignificant. They handle the great bulk of legal business: Excluding minor traffic violations, the total number of cases filed each year in state courts exceeds 23 million. Felony criminal cases alone total over 1 million. Most crimes committed each year are violations of state laws and are tried in state courts, as are most disputes over estates, contracts, and property. As will be explained, a relative few are ever candidates for review by the U.S. Supreme Court. Most Americans, then, who go to court go to state courts and only state courts.

The judicial systems of most states are divided into four levels (see Figure 11.2). At the bottom are **courts of limited jurisdiction,** which hear particular kinds of cases in villages, towns, and cities, involving small claims, traffic violations, domestic matters, juvenile affairs, and minor criminal offenses. Such courts are variously labeled municipal court, county court, magistrate's court, traffic court, or recorder's court. Usually such cases are decided by a judge sitting without a jury. On the next tier are **courts of general jurisdiction,** with one usually located in each county. These courts receive appeals from the bottom tier and serve as trial courts for serious criminal offenses and civil suits involving substantial amounts of money. Again, the names vary from state to state: superior court, county court, or court of common pleas. Above these courts in many states, especially the more populous, are one or more **intermediate appellate courts,** which are labeled superior court or court of appeals and which accept appeals from the courts of general jurisdiction. At the top is a **court of last resort,** usually called the supreme court. Most states have only one "supreme court," but Texas and Oklahoma have two, with one specifically designated to hear appeals in criminal cases. (In New York the highest court is called the Court of Appeals, and a supreme court is a court of general jurisdiction.)

Unlike federal judges, who are appointed for life and removable only by impeachment, most state judges are elected. In some states judges run in nonpartisan elections or in partisan elections like legislative candidates. In other states the governor appoints judges from a list of nominees provided by a panel of lawyers and other citizens. This device is called the **Missouri Plan,** after the state that pioneered its use. Following initial election or appointment, judges may then be subject to retention votes every 5 or 10 years. That is, instead of running for reelection like other officeholders, judges have their names placed on a ballot alongside the question "Shall Judge X be continued in office for another term?" A negative vote creates a vacancy, and a new election is held or a new appointment is made. At present 21 states use a single method for selecting judges. Twenty-one use two methods, depending on the court involved (for example, appointment of supreme court judges by the governor and partisan election of all other judges), and in eight states judges are selected in three different ways.

Whether chosen by election or the Missouri Plan, the people can unseat state judges at the polls. Critics say that this possibility undercuts judicial independence, making judges too dependent on the voters and perhaps afraid to render unpopular decisions. Others reply that the people should retain control over all public officials, even judges. Experience shows that judges elected on partisan ballots are more likely than those chosen on nonpartisan ballots or under an appointment/ retention plan to be turned out of office by the voters.

United States District Courts

Of all federal courts, the Constitution requires only the Supreme Court. Article 3 left the creation of other ("inferior") courts to the discretion of Congress. Plausibly, Congress could have permitted the existing state courts to handle national business but chose instead in the Judiciary Act of 1789 to organize a separate court system for the nation as a whole.

Almost all federal cases (over 285,000 annually, excluding bankruptcy filings) begin in the 94 **United States district courts,** staffed by 650 judges. There are 89 district courts in the 50 states, plus one each in the District of Columbia, Guam, Puerto Rico, the Virgin Islands, and the Northern Mariana Islands. Each state has at least one district court, and no district crosses a state line. Some states have two or three districts, and the populous states of California, New York, and Texas have four each (see Figure 11.3).

The jurisdiction of district courts extends to cases that arise under the Constitution, laws, and treaties of the United States, as well as admiralty and maritime cases. Questions of state law (such as liability in an automobile accident) may get into district court through diversity jurisdiction. This occurs when the parties to a case are citizens of different states and when the amount at issue is greater than $50,000. As a way of reducing the volume of cases in the district courts, Congress has considered repealing diversity jurisdiction altogether. Should this happen, cases now qualifying for diversity jurisdiction would be decided by state courts, entirely outside the federal court system.

United States Courts of Appeals

Thirteen **United States courts of appeals,** staffed by 179 judges, occupy a middle position in the hierarchy of the federal judiciary. Twelve of these courts have a regional jurisdiction or circuit, as Figure 11.3 shows.

Although district judges sit individually in most cases, appeals judges normally sit in panels of three. In special situations cases are heard en banc, with most of a circuit's bench sitting at once. Cases in the courts of appeals number more than 40,000 annually. Most are appeals from disappointed parties in the district courts and the Tax Court (see Figure 11.1). Under exceptional circumstances cases may go from district courts directly to the Supreme Court, bypassing a court of appeals.

FIGURE 11.3
Geographic Boundaries of U.S. Courts of Appeals and U.S. District Courts

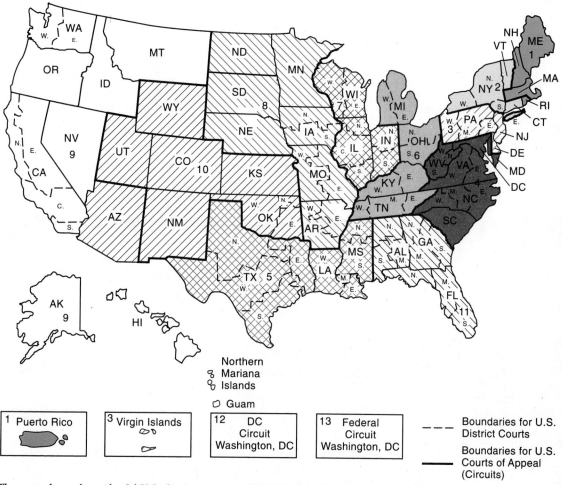

1 Puerto Rico	3 Virgin Islands	12 DC Circuit Washington, DC	13 Federal Circuit Washington, DC	- - - Boundaries for U.S. District Courts

Boundaries for U.S. Courts of Appeal (Circuits)

The map shows how the 94 U.S. district courts and 13 U.S. courts of appeals exist with the court systems of the 50 states and the District of Columbia. *SOURCE:* Administrative Office of the United States Courts.

Another large source of work for the appeals courts comes in the form of reviewing rulings of various administrative and regulatory agencies of the national government, such as the Federal Communications Commission, the Federal Trade Commission, and the National Labor Relations Board. The Court of Appeals for the District of Columbia Circuit hears more of these agency cases than any of the other appeals courts, making this court one of the most influential in the land.

The thirteenth appeals court is the newest and, unlike the other 12, has both a different and a national jurisdiction. The Court of Appeals for the Federal Circuit accepts appeals in patent cases from any district court as well as all appeals from the Claims Court, the Court of International Trade, and the Court of Veterans Appeals. For most litigants the courts of appeals are the courts of last resort in the federal judicial system because the Supreme Court accepts relatively few cases.

Special Courts

Congress has created other tribunals to hear particular kinds of cases, often where considerable specialization and expertise are desirable. Into this category fall the following:

1. The **Claims Court** hears suits involving monetary damages against the U.S. government.
2. The **Court of International Trade** adjudicates controversies concerning the classification and valuation of imported merchandise.
3. The **Tax Court** decides disputes between taxpayers and the Internal Revenue Service.
4. The **Court of Veterans Appeals** reviews decisions on benefits and entitlements from the Board of Veterans Appeals in the Department of Veterans Affairs. The newest special court, it heard its first case in 1990.
5. The **Court of Military Appeals** reviews judgments handed down by courts-martial in the several branches of the armed forces.

These courts rarely make the headlines, but they are quite important. In the first four, millions of dollars may ride on the outcome of decisions. The lives and liberties of hundreds of thousands of American citizens are in the care of the fifth.

The Supreme Court of the United States

It is from these courts, state and federal, that the nine justices of the Supreme Court receive almost all the cases they decide each term. At present some 5000 new cases appear annually on their docket, joining about 800 carried over from the previous term. All but a handful invoke the Court's **appellate jurisdiction.** Defined by Congress, this is the authority the Court has to review decisions of the federal courts as well as decisions of the highest state courts that raise **federal questions** (matters involving the interpretation of the Constitution, a statute, or a treaty of the United States). Today, almost all cases reach the Supreme Court on a **writ of certiorari** (Latin for "to be informed"). Except for a few cases involving the Voting Rights Act, review by the Supreme Court is plainly discretionary, not obligatory. It takes a minimum of four justices (one short of a majority) to agree to accept a case for review. This **rule of four** allows the Court not only to limit the number of cases it decides but to engage or avoid particular issues.

A very few cases each term are candidates for the Court's **original jurisdiction,** meaning that the case begins or originates there. Indeed, the number of "original" cases the Court decided between 1789 and 1992 totaled less than 200. The Supreme Court's original jurisdiction is spelled out in Article 3 of the Constitution and includes four kinds of disputes:

1. *Cases between one of the states and the U.S. government.* For example, in *United States* v. *Maine,*[1] the justices ruled that the national government—not the states—had control of oil deposits more than three miles offshore.

2. *Cases between two or more states.* In 1967 Michigan and Ohio each claimed the same piece of mineral-rich territory in Lake Erie, and in a series of cases, Arizona and California have battled each other over water resources.[2]

3. *Cases involving foreign ambassadors, ministers, or consuls.* In matters that could involve the nation's relations with other countries, the framers wanted those cases heard initially by the highest court.

4. *Cases begun by a state against a citizen of another state or against another country.* The **Eleventh Amendment,** however, requires suits initiated *against* a state by a citizen of another state or of a foreign country to begin in the courts of that state. The Eleventh Amendment came about because of a 1793 decision by the Supreme Court that a citizen of South Carolina could sue the state of Georgia in the federal courts.[3]

Only controversies between states qualify today exclusively as original cases in the Supreme Court. The justices have been content for Congress to grant concurrent original jurisdiction to the U.S. district courts for those cases in the other three categories. This means that although one of these cases *could* begin in the Supreme Court, in almost every instance the case will begin in a district court, unless it involves a dispute between two states of the Union.

The Supreme Court is headed administratively by the **chief justice of the United States** (the position has been filled since 1986 by William H. Rehnquist). Through the years the Court has usually been known by the name of the chief justice (the Marshall Court, for example), but the chief's vote in cases counts no more than the vote of any of the eight **associate justices.** The chief justice also presides over the Judicial Conference of the United States, which is composed of representatives of the lower federal courts and makes recommendations to those courts as well as to Congress on staffing needs and operating efficiency.

Federal Judicial Selection

The Constitution gives the president power to appoint federal judges, subject to confirmation by a majority vote of the Senate. In practice, a president rarely knows personally any of the district or appeals judges he appoints. Judges on the district, appeals, and Supreme Court benches serve "during good behavior," a provision

---

[1] 420 U.S. 515 (1975).
[2] *Michigan* v. *Ohio*, 386 U.S. 1029 (1967); *Arizona* v. *California*, 460 U.S. 605 (1983).
[3] *Chisholm* v. *Georgia*, 2 U.S. (2 Dallas) 419 (1793).

of the Constitution that effectively ensures lifetime tenure, with removal only by impeachment. In contrast to presidents and members of Congress, the Constitution spells out no qualifications, such as age or citizenship, for any federal judge. Federal judges do not even have to be lawyers, although since 1789 each has had legal training of some kind. Today, it would be unthinkable for the Senate to approve a nominee who is not a law school graduate and a member of the bar.

Although presidents overwhelmingly appoint members of their own political party to the federal bench (during the past 100 years, only in the Taft, Hoover, and Ford administrations has the figure dropped below 90 percent), the choices for the district courts are usually made by officials in the Justice Department working with political leaders from the state in which the appointment is to be made. Especially if they are of the same party as the president, a state's U.S. senators (one or both) ordinarily play a prominent role in the selection. There is some truth in the wisecrack that a federal judge is a lawyer who knows a senator. In contrast, appointment of appeals judges reflects more national and less local influence, with the attorney general and other officials in the Justice Department having a large say in the selection. Obvious choices for appeals posts are district judges because they have observable judicial "track records."

Under present policy of the Senate Judiciary Committee, a "blue slip" (indicating disapproval) from a home-state senator is sufficient to block a judicial nominee outright if the administration fails to consult with home-state senators before naming a candidate. This is an example of **senatorial courtesy,** the practice that allows home-state senators considerable control over the fate of presidential nominees. If a senator submits a blue slip after having been consulted, the committee considers the senator's objections but does not always reject the nominee.

An additional screening role is played by the Committee on the Federal Judiciary of the American Bar Association, the largest organization of lawyers in the country. Before the president sends a nominee's name to the Senate, the attorney general submits the name to the ABA committee for review. This committee then finds the candidate "well-qualified," "qualified," or "not qualified." Only occasionally will a president nominate someone the committee considers not qualified, but some are nonetheless confirmed by the Senate when he does. The significance of the ABA's participation is that a private organization in effect shares the confirmation role the Constitution assigns to the Senate. The committee's screening attracts the most attention when the president nominates someone to the Supreme Court.

In contrast to the other federal courts, vacancies on the Supreme Court occur relatively infrequently. Including the six original seats George Washington (1789–1797) filled, 106 persons had served on the Court through 1992. Supreme Court nominations are far more likely personally to occupy a president's time and attention. It is not simply that the Supreme Court decides important questions. Rather, once appointed, justices tend to stay on the Court a long time—usually far longer than the president who named them remains in the White House. Five considerations most often are at work as presidents make up their minds about whom to appoint:

1. *Professional qualifications.* How respected is the nominee?
2. *Acceptability to the Senate.* Will he or she be confirmed?

3. *Ideological fit.* Will the nominee support the president's program?

4. *Personal friendship.* Does the president want an old friend on the Court?

5. *Region, race, religion, gender, and other background factors.* Does a particular group need "representation" on the Court?

Since Washington's time, presidents have wanted a Court supportive of their administration. Yet they are not always successful in picking "right-thinking" justices. President Dwight Eisenhower (1953–1961) once remarked that appointing Earl Warren (1953–1969) chief justice was "the biggest damnfool mistake I ever made" after Warren turned out to be more liberal than Ike had supposed. President Richard Nixon (1969–1974) hardly approved of Justice Harry A. Blackmun's (1970–   ) authorship of the 1973 abortion decision,[4] and Presidents Ronald Reagan and George Bush were disappointed when three of their appointees [Justices Sandra O'Connor (1981–   ), Anthony Kennedy (1988–   ), and David Souter (1990–   )] voted against administration positions on school prayer.[5]

Frequently important in lifting or sinking one's chances to become a Supreme Court justice have been particular background factors. Most presidents have taken geographical region into account. Moreover, religion, race, and gender have sometimes been important considerations as well. Even so, Supreme Court justices have hardly been representative of American society. Of the 106 justices who sat through 1992, all but 17 were Protestant males of Anglo-Saxon origin. Justice Antonin Scalia (1986–   ) is the Court's first Italian-American member. Justice Thurgood Marshall (1967–1991) was the first black member of the Court, and Justice O'Connor is its first female member. Most of the 106 have come from economically comfortable and civic-minded families. All have been lawyers or have held law degrees. About one-third were graduated from the most prestigious colleges and universities in the United States. Most have been active in public affairs or have held political office, but some, including Justice Byron White (1962–1993), had no prior judicial experience. Moreover, Chief Justice Rehnquist is only the third chief justice (out of a total of 16 since 1789) to have been "elevated" directly from associate justice. All other chief justices were nominated from outside the Court. (By way of comparison, among state supreme courts as of 1992, only Minnesota had a majority of women on its high bench—4 out of 7. The high courts of Michigan and Oklahoma each had two women justices; the high courts of 26 states had one, and the remaining 21 states had none.)

Whatever a president's motivations, the Senate must still vote to confirm the nominee. That approval has been forthcoming most of the time, but on 26 occasions it has not. In this century, four presidents—Herbert Hoover (1929–1933), Lyndon Johnson (1963–1969), Nixon (1969–1974), and Ronald Reagan (1981–1989)—have had their choices blocked by the Senate. Nixon in fact struck out twice in succession before the Senate handily confirmed Judge Harry Blackmun, his third nominee for the same vacancy. When Reagan picked Judge Robert Bork

---

[4] *Roe* v. *Wade,* 410 U.S. 113 (1973).
[5] *Lee* v. *Weisman,* 60 U.S.L.W. 4723 (1992); Marcia Coyle, "The Court Confounds Observers," *National Law Journal,* July 13, 1992, p. 1.

Appointed to the Supreme Court by President Lyndon Johnson in 1967, civil rights pioneer Thurgood Marshall was the first black justice. As an attorney, he had directed litigation for the plaintiffs in *Brown* v. *Board of Education* in 1954. As a justice, he remained a strong advocate of busing to eliminate racial segregation in public schools and of affirmative action to erase centuries of deprivation suffered by American blacks during and after slavery. His retirement from the Court in 1991 created the vacancy that Clarence Thomas filled. Marshall died in January 1993 at the age of 84.

to succeed retiring Justice Lewis Powell (1971–1987), the Senate said no. Reagan's second choice, Judge Douglas Ginsburg, withdrew his name from consideration after acknowledging disclosures that he had smoked marijuana as a student in the 1960s and as a member of the Harvard law faculty in the 1970s. Powell's seat remained vacant until early 1988 when the Senate confirmed Reagan's third choice, Judge Anthony M. Kennedy.

The Clarence Thomas Affair

More recently, after Justice Thurgood Marshall retired in 1991, President Bush's nomination of Judge Clarence Thomas barely eked out enough votes in the Senate. Although Marshall had long been hailed as a tenacious advocate of civil liberties and civil rights, Democrats claimed that Thomas would threaten both, particularly in abortion and affirmative action cases.

Objection to Thomas's constitutional values led to a 7–7 split when members of the Judiciary Committee voted on September 27. Thus the nomination went to the Senate floor without a recommendation to confirm or reject. Still, press accounts predicted that Thomas would be confirmed easily in a vote scheduled for October 8.

Events, however, suddenly took an unexpected turn. A "leak" to the press during the weekend of October 5 quickly placed the nomination in doubt. Several weeks before the committee's vote, Professor Anita F. Hill of the University of Oklahoma School of Law had notified the committee's staff, in confidence, that Thomas had sexually harassed her from 1981 to 1983, during the time she was his assistant, first at the Department of Education and later at the Equal Employment Opportunity Commission (EEOC). At least some members of the committee were aware of Hill's accusations prior to their vote on September 27. Thanks to the leak of Hill's charges, virtually the entire nation knew about them.

To proceed with the vote on schedule now seemed hasty at best. Senators were themselves on trial for failing to take sexual harassment seriously. Accordingly, they sent the nomination back to the Judiciary Committee. What followed was a marathon television spectacle that left few satisfied: 28 hours of additional hearings marked by lurid details, bitter charges and countercharges, and equally bitter denials and counterdenials. Thomas told the committee that he was the victim of a "high-tech lynching for uppity blacks." Likened by some to a morality play or a psychodrama, the acrimonious hearings drew a larger viewing audience than the National League and American League play-offs going on at the same time.

The charges were grave and were potentially fatal for the nomination. Thomas, after all, had headed the agency responsible for enforcing the law against sexual harassment. Moreover, the charges undercut his principal strength. Because he lacked a record of legal scholarship or extensive judicial service, the case for his nomination had rested all along on character—precisely what Hill had called into question.

Unlike the baseball play-offs, however, the hearings concluded in a draw. There was no clear-cut victory in the court of public opinion for either Thomas or Hill. Although polls showed that more people seemed to believe Thomas's denials than Hill's accusations, polls also revealed that substantial doubts remained about the nominee. On October 15, such doubts helped to make the Senate's vote to confirm, 52 to 48, one of the closest on record for a successful Supreme Court nominee. Not since the controversy over membership in the Ku Klux Klan enveloped Justice Hugo Black (1937–1971) shortly *after* his confirmation in 1937 had a justice begun his tenure under a cloud of such suspicion.

No other Supreme Court confirmation battle seems ever to have had such a "spillover" effect. Anita Hill's accusations against Thomas have made many people more conscious of sexual harassment. By mid-1992, the EEOC (ironically the agency Thomas once headed) reported that sexual harassment complaints

Clarence Thomas's confirmation hearings in the Senate proved to be the most contentious in modern times, once Professor Anita Hill of the University of Oklahoma School of Law, who had been a former aid to Thomas in two federal agencies, made charges of sexual harassment against him. Testimony before a committee of Congress can be a lonely and uncomfortable experience. In this room used by the Senate Judiciary Committee to air Professor Hill's accusations, note the placement of the witness's table well in front of the dais where Senator Joseph Biden (D-Del.), who chaired the hearings, and the other senators sat. Although the Senate confirmed Thomas, Professor Hill's testimony made people more aware of sexual harassment on the job and encouraged many women to run for office in 1992.

filed in the first half of the fiscal year had increased by more than 50 percent, compared to the same period in the previous year.[6] Moreover, sexual harassment as a political issue galvanized both voters and candidates in the 1992 election.

What Courts Do

In the process of deciding cases, the Supreme Court and other courts perform several functions. These include constitutional interpretation, statutory interpretation, fact determination, clarification of the boundaries of political authority, education and value application, and legitimation. Not all courts perform each function in every case, and some courts do more of one than another. As will be noted, fact determination is largely, though not exclusively, the province of trial courts. Appellate courts are heavily engaged in constitutional and statutory interpretation.

---

[6] Jane Gross, "Suffering in Silence No More: Fighting Sexual Harassment," *New York Times,* July 13, 1992, p. A1.

Constitutional Interpretation

American government is constitutional government—government according to basic institutions, procedures, and values inscribed in a written document. The Constitution of the United States is not without ambiguity, however. Because some of its provisions are not clear and because the framers could not possibly have anticipated all contemporary issues, the document invites interpretation. This need for interpretation in turn guarantees disagreement over what the correct interpretation should be.

Interpretation involves the power of **judicial review,** first formally declared by the United States Supreme Court in the 1803 case of *Marbury* v. *Madison.*[7] Judicial review means that a court may set aside decisions made by elected representatives of the people if judges conclude that a law violates the Constitution. So judicial review allows contending political groups to continue their political skirmishes in the context of cases built around opposing interpretations of particular clauses of the Constitution. Groups that have not prevailed in executive offices or legislative chambers often resort to the courts. Whether the question involves education, immigration, or criminal justice, one side seeks to persuade the constitutional umpire that the other has broken the rules.

Statutory Interpretation

Many cases require courts to interpret statutes passed by Congress or state legislatures. In a typical term, about half the cases the Supreme Court decides involve the meaning the justices give to words the legislators have written. At first glance this task seems avoidable. Why are legislators not able to say exactly what they mean? Sometimes legislators expect judges to fill in the blanks, so to speak. A law will set up certain standards that judges are supposed to apply, or, as a way of avoiding controversy, legislators will deliberately choose language that is vague. Occasions also arise that the people who wrote the law simply did not anticipate. Judges will often try to figure out what the legislators would have done had they only known. This is called discovering **legislative intent.**

One of the first pages in this book refers to a *copyright.* The holder of the copyright has exclusive use and control of the work for a specified period of time. In this century copyrights have been extended to motion pictures and television programs. When Congress last rewrote the Copyright Act in 1976, provision was made for "fair use." "Fair use" allows one legally to make copies of protected material "for purposes such as criticism, comment, news reporting, teaching . . . , scholarship, or research," all without violating the copyright or paying a fee to the holder of the copyright. Is in-home videotaping of television programs an example of "fair use" or an infringement of copyright? Congress had said only that certain factors are to be taken into account in deciding whether something amounts to "fair use," leaving the task of adding precision to judges. With fuzzy guidance, different courts arrived at different conclusions. Finally, the Supreme Court an-

---

[7] The *Marbury* case and the concept of judicial review are discussed in Chapter 1.

nounced that in-home videotaping of copyrighted materials was "fair use" within the meaning of the statute.[8]

Fact Determination

Often the meaning of statutes and constitutional passages may be clear, and cases turn on the facts instead. Through fact determination judges select from competing testimony and evidence that which they accept as true and that which they reject as false. This task is inescapable because the judicial process in the United States is adversarial. That is, cases pit one side against the other. Each side attempts to build the stronger argument to persuade the judge or jury to accept its version of the truth. Fact discretion is perhaps most visible in a **trial court,** the place where the issues and merits of a case are heard for the first time. In the federal court system, trial courts are the district courts. In state courts systems, trials occur in both the courts of limited and general jurisdiction (see Figures 11.1 and 11.2).

Clarification of the Boundaries of Political Authority

As explained in Chapter 1, the Constitution mandates separation of powers—the division of political functions among the three branches of government. It is not obvious, however, where the legitimate power of one branch stops and another's begins. Courts sometimes try to resolve this built-in tension. In 1952, for example, President Harry Truman (1945–1953) directed the secretary of commerce to seize and operate the nation's steel mills. Labor disputes in the steel industry threatened the supply of war materials needed for American troops in the Korean conflict. Truman based his actions not on any statutory authority but on the president's responsibility for national security as commander-in-chief of the armed forces. Voting 6 to 3, the Supreme Court held that Truman had exceeded his powers under the Constitution. Although Congress might provide for such a takeover of industries by statute, Congress had not done so. Furthermore, the Court found nothing in the Constitution authorizing the president to act on his own.[9]

Education and Value Application

In deciding cases, judges teach and apply values. Even an ordinary criminal trial involves a judgment on what kinds of behavior are acceptable and unacceptable, on the part of both the suspect and the police. One of the hallmarks of constitutional government, after all, is that limits apply not just to the governed but to the governors as well. The constitutions and statutes of the state and national governments all represent value choices that define the kind of nation its citizens expect to enjoy. Judicial opinions give judges an opportunity to articulate those values. Of course, no one pretends that judicial opinions are widely read by the general

---

[8] *Sony Corporation* v. *Universal City Studios,* 464 U.S. 417 (1984).
[9] *Youngstown* v. *Sawyer,* 343 U.S. 579 (1952).

public. However, they are read and studied by journalists, scholars, and other opinion leaders, who in turn inform the public and help shape attitudes Americans have about the courts and the issues judges confront.

Legitimation

Judicial review means that courts are expected to make sure that actions of public officials conform to the Constitution and statutes. In the great majority of cases, judges uphold the challenged laws or policies, thus placing a "seal of approval" on what others have done. Securing legitimacy may be crucial when a policy emerges from a long and loud national debate. Winners look to the judiciary for support. Losers look to the judiciary for redress. Both typically see the courts as offering "the final word." During the civil rights movement of the 1960s, for example (see Chapter 3), Congress took the bold and controversial step of banning racial discrimination in restaurants, hotels, theaters, and other privately owned places of public accommodation. During debate on the bill in 1963 and 1964, opponents argued that the ban would be an unjustified intrusion into the right of owners of businesses to run their enterprises as they wished. The Supreme Court's decision upholding the constitutionality of the law virtually ended the controversy. Within a matter of months, most public agitation over the legitimacy of the new policy simply ceased.[10] A ruling can, however, inflame an issue, not soothe it. On occasion it may appear that the judges have thrust a broom handle into a hornet's nest, as the abortion controversy illustrates.

The Supreme Court at Work

Cases decided by the Supreme Court move through five distinct stages: petition for review, briefs on the merits, oral argument, conference and decision, and assignment and writing of opinions.

Petition for Review

Litigants who lose in lower courts begin climbing the steep slope toward the Supreme Court when their lawyers file documents called **briefs** with the Court's clerk. In these petitions for review, the opposing parties attempt to convince the justices that the issues the case raises are so important (or unimportant) that they deserve (or do not deserve) the Court's attention. As discussed previously, the Court will not accept a case for review unless a minimum of four justices agrees to do so.

From the thousands of cases on its docket each term, the justices will typically decide no more than 150 with full opinion, in accordance with the procedure laid

---

[10] *Heart of Atlanta Motel* v. *United States*, 379 U.S. 241 (1964).

out below. Other cases may be decided "summarily" without opinion by a directive affirming or reversing the lower court. Except for cases carried over into the following year's term, the justices deny review in all the rest. The result is that the lower court's decision stands (see Figure 11.4).

What factors seem to guide the Court in selecting cases for decision? Although the justices rarely explain their reasons for rejecting cases, chances for review by the nation's highest court are significantly increased if one or more of the following is present:

- The United States is a party to the case and requests Supreme Court review.
- The case presents a question that has been decided differently by different courts of appeals.

FIGURE 11.4
Caseload in the U.S. Supreme Court, 1950–1992

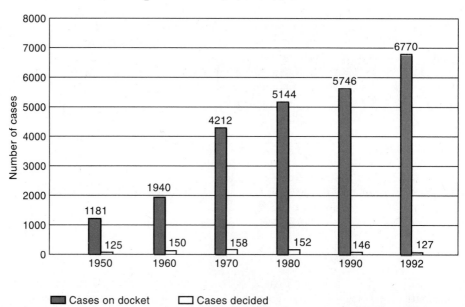

■ Cases on docket   ☐ Cases decided

The figure shows the number of cases on the docket of the Supreme Court in each of six years and the number of cases decided with full opinion. The justices decide other cases summarily each term. The number of summary decisions each term sometimes equals the number of cases decided with full opinion. The volume of cases has grown nearly sixfold since 1950, while the number of cases decided has varied only modestly. Indeed, since 1988 when 171 decisions were issued, the Court has been deciding fewer cases, a trend aided by the virtual elimination of the Court's obligatory appellate jurisdiction in 1988. Almost all of each year's cases come from the lower federal courts and the state supreme courts. Only a handful, at most, of original cases appears each term. A minimum of four justices must agree to hear a case.   SOURCE: Administrative Office of the United States Courts.

- The case involves an issue some of the justices are eager to resolve.
- A lower court has made a decision clearly at odds with established Supreme Court interpretation of a law or constitutional provision.
- The Court's work load permits accepting another case for decision.
- The case presents an issue of overriding importance to the nation.

Even if a case fits into one of the categories listed, the Supreme Court will not necessarily grant review. The thousands of cases on the Court's docket each term means that a litigant's chances of having a case heard by the justices are usually very long. Claims that someone will "take this all the way to the Supreme Court" are therefore more threat than promise.

Briefs on the Merits

Once the Court has placed a case on its "decision calendar," attorneys for the opposing sides file a second round of briefs. This time the arguments focus on the decision the justices should make, not on whether they should accept the case. Briefs of opposing counsel are supplemented by **amici curiae** briefs. Submitted by "friends of the court," these documents come from interest groups and others who are not parties to the case but who have a stake in its outcome.

One lawyer whose briefs the justices routinely read with extra care is the **solicitor general of the United States**—the third-ranking official in the Justice Department and the government's lawyer before the Supreme Court. In cases where the government has lost in a lower court, the "S.G." decides whether the United States will petition the Supreme Court for review. If so, the solicitor general is responsible for both written briefs and oral argument supporting the government's position. The job is important because the United States is a party in about half the cases that confront the justices.

Oral Argument

The most public part of the Court's work is **oral argument.** On about 40 days (always Mondays, Tuesdays, and Wednesdays), starting in October and concluding in late April, opposing lawyers face the justices. Cases are routinely allotted an hour, each side receiving 30 minutes. A spontaneous event, oral argument gives each justice an opportunity to ask questions about the case. Sometimes questioning from the bench is lively and intense. At other times it may seem that the justices are daydreaming or nodding off. At all times they rock back and forth in their leather swivel chairs, occasionally pass notes and whisper among themselves, and send pages on errands for documents and law books. The justices attach great importance to this step of the decision-making procedure. Whether argument changes many minds, however, is a question only the justices can answer.

An appearance before the Supreme Court can be intimidating even for the most seasoned advocates. Standing at the small lectern before the raised bench, an attorney can feel very lonely. Heightening the tension are the time limits, which the Court rigidly enforces. When five minutes remain, the marshal flicks a switch that turns on a white light at the lectern. A red light signals that time is up. The chief justice may allow counsel to complete a sentence or to answer a question, but Chief Justice Charles Evans Hughes (1910–1916, 1930–1941) is said to have cut off one attorney in the middle of the word *if.*

Conference and Decision

On Wednesday afternoons, after argument has finished at 3 o'clock, and all day on Fridays, the justices convene in a small room adjacent to the chief justice's chambers to discuss the cases they have heard that week. They also act on petitions for review. The importance of oral argument may be enhanced because the spoken words are fresh on the justices' minds when they take up a case in conference. The usual practice is for the chief justice to lay out his views first, followed by each associate justice, starting with the most senior. By the time all have had their say, each justice's position is often clear. If not, a vote is taken. These votes, recorded by each justice in a leather-bound docket book, are tentative. The decision does not become final until it is announced in court, weeks or even months later.

     In contrast to the openness of oral argument, the conferences are closed. No pages or law clerks are present in the room, only the justices. If something is needed, the most junior justice acts as messenger and goes to the door. What happens inside the room is very secret. In fact, the Court has the best secrecy record in Washington. Leaks, as prevalent in the nation's capital as the summer humidity, are so rare at the Court that they make headlines when they occur. Confidentiality is crucial, not just because it gives the justices freedom to talk and maneuver amid the most controversial issues of the day but also because political and economic fortunes often hang in the balance.

Assignment and Writing of Opinions

On Saturday or early in the week after the standard two-week session of oral argument, the chief justice circulates an assignment list to the justices. If part of the majority, the chief makes the opinion assignment in a particular case. If not, the task falls to the senior associate justice in the majority. The goal is an **opinion of the Court,** which is an explanation and justification of the decision agreed to by at least a bare majority of the justices. Between assignment of the opinion and announcement of the decision in open court, vigorous give-and-take routinely goes on among the justices. The justice writing an opinion has a draft printed in the Court's own print shop, all done in strictest secrecy. Copies circulate among the other justices. Those in the majority will insist on changes. It is not unusual for an opinion to go through a dozen or more drafts, or rewrites. Each opinion of the Court therefore represents the consensus of the majority, not merely the views of its author. Justices in the majority may write one or more **concurring opinions** when they reject the majority's reasoning while accepting its result. Or they simply may have other thoughts to add.

In only about a third of the cases each term do all nine justices agree on the result. For the rest, justices in the minority typically write one or more **dissenting opinions**. These help to explain what divides the Court and are written for the express purpose of undercutting the logic and/or exposing the folly that dissenting justices find in the majority viewpoint.

Majority, concurring, and dissenting opinions are later collected and published as the ***United States Reports***. This is the official record of the Court's work, now comprising over 500 volumes.

The Law Clerks

Assisting the justices are law clerks, recent law school graduates who typically serve a justice for a year. The justices use their clerks in a variety of ways: to do research, summarize certiorari petitions, and write and critique drafts of opinions. Justice Blackmun has confessed that his clerks manage to entice him to an Orioles baseball game at least once a term! Diversions aside, a clerk's day is long and includes evenings and weekends. Nonetheless, the opportunities for close association with the justices can be rewarding. Of former clerks, three (Byron White, William Rehnquist, and John Stevens) were justices on the Court in 1993.

The Supreme Court and American Government: An Assessment

Early in the nation's history, the justices assumed a prominent role in governing the nation. But this role has never been free from controversy. For most of its history the Court has seen itself as the guardian of preferred values. Years ago, for instance, the justices routinely censored social and economic legislation that they thought interfered unduly with property rights. In the years since President Roosevelt (1933–1945) confronted the justices in the "court-packing" fight of 1937 (see "Politics and Economics: The Supreme Court and Economic Policy"), the Court's decisions have emphasized civil liberties and civil rights instead. Now about half the cases each term involve a provision of the Bill of Rights or the Fourteenth Amendment.

Judicial Review and Democracy

As explained in Chapter 1 and as noted earlier in this chapter, the authority to interpret the Constitution carries with it the power of judicial review. Some critics assert that judicial review is antidemocratic because judges invalidate decisions

Politics and Economics

The Supreme Court and Economic Policy

Although Supreme Court decisions today may affect the economy just as they affect American life in other ways, between the years 1890 and 1937 the justices (and lower court judges too) played a far more active role in economic affairs. Then judges routinely reviewed the constitutionality of many kinds of social and economic laws that are now accepted without question.

In the decades after the Civil War, Congress and state legislatures passed hundreds of laws regulating working conditions, prices, wages and hours, and health in an effort to cope with the harmful effects of growth and industrialization. Opponents of such legislation advanced the arguments of laissez-faire economics, claiming that government regulation of business and the economy should be kept to a minimum. Soon justices of the Supreme Court decided that freedom from economic regulation was a constitutionally protected liberty. This did not mean that the Court turned aside all legislative attempts to improve the life of working people, but it did mean that the justices had what amounted to the last word on which regulatory policies were acceptable and which were not. For example, *Lochner* v. *New York*[a] struck down a law that set a maximum number of working hours for bakery employees, and *Hammer* v. *Dagenhart*[b] invalidated a congressional act banning interstate shipment of goods manufactured with child labor. The Court's role as economic censor came under sharp attack when laissez-faire economics faced the realities of the Great Depression in the 1930s. As states and the national government responded with policies to deal with economic dislocation, the Court proved to be a stumbling block. In 1935 and 1936 the justices invalidated 10 acts of Congress, cut-

ting the heart out of President Roosevelt's New Deal program of economic recovery.

After his landslide reelection in 1936, Roosevelt proposed legislation (dubbed by its enemies the **court-packing plan**) that would permit him to appoint one additional justice for every sitting justice over the age of 70, up to a total bench size of 15. Under the guise of aiding the justices with their work, the plan was a ploy to create seats for new justices who would support the president's programs. The plan never became law, but one or more justices quickly changed their positions in economic regulation cases to give the president the majority he needed. Tagged "the switch in time that saved nine," *National Labor Relations Board* v. *Jones & Laughlin Steel Corporation*[c] witnessed the Court upholding, 5 votes to 4, the far-reaching Wagner Labor Act of 1935, which created the National Labor Relations Board and guaranteed to unions the right of collective bargaining. The law remains the foundation of American labor policy. Thanks to changed views and a series of retirements and new justices, the Court soon made it clear that it was retreating from its old role as economic censor. Since that time the Court has by and large left economic policy-making to the president, Congress, and the states.

Recently, however, the Court has hinted that limits remain to a state's regulatory powers over property owners.[d] Does the Constitution require the Court to keep its hands off economic policy?

[a] 198 U.S. 45 (1905).

[b] 247 U.S. 251 (1918).

[c] 301 U.S. 1 (1937).

[d] *Lucas* v. *South Carolina Coastal Council,* 60 U.S.L.W. 4842 (1992).

made by elected representatives of the people. Moreover, they say that judicial review encourages citizens to rely on judges and not the political process to protect their rights. Without judicial review, elected officials would have to give more thought to the constitutionality of their actions. Besides, they maintain, individual rights survive in nations like Great Britain, where judges exercise no judicial review at all.

Others reply that the very idea of a written constitution means that a majority is not always supposed to get what it wants. Democracy American-style stresses not just majority rule but minority rights. Judicial review is but one of several constitutional features designed to control government power. Although citizens' control over their leaders through election is the primary check on government, judicial review can be an additional safeguard. Whatever the experience in other lands, enforcement of limits on government in this country seems to require the existence of institutions like the federal courts not directly accountable to the people.

Influences on Supreme Court Decision Making

Recognizing the important place the Supreme Court occupies in American politics leads to an examination of the major factors that shape its decisions. In the face of Chief Justice Marshall's broad self-denial that "courts are the mere instruments of the law, and can will nothing,"[11] political leaders have long recognized that justices do not decide cases in a vacuum. Surely "judicial decisions are not babies brought by constitutional storks."[12] Individual and institutional forces, as well as legal and extralegal factors, affect what the Court does.[13]

Foremost perhaps are the justices' own *political ideas*. A jurist adamantly opposed to capital punishment, for example, will be more inclined than one who is not to regard the death penalty as one of the "cruel and unusual punishments" prohibited by the Eighth Amendment. A justice who does not place high value on the free exchange of views will probably not be a strong defender of the First Amendment's guarantee of free speech. Indeed, research indicates that judicial decisions of most justices reflect a generally consistent ideological position.[14]

Akin to, but different from, political ideas is *role perception*.[15] What does being a justice mean to an individual named to the Supreme Court? Some justices have been *result-oriented*. That is, they see their task as one of writing certain political

---

[11] *Osborn* v. *Bank of the United States,* 22 U.S. (9 Wheaton) 738, 866 (1824).
[12] Max Lerner, quoted in Henry J. Abraham, *The Judicial Process,* 5th ed. (New York: Oxford University Press, 1986), p. 348.
[13] Tracey E. George and Lee Epstein, "On the Nature of Supreme Court Decision Making," *American Political Science Review* 86 (1992): 323.
[14] David W. Rohde and Harold J. Spaeth, "Ideology, Strategy, and Supreme Court Decisions: William Rehnquist as Chief Justice," *Judicature* 72 (1989): 247; Harold J. Spaeth and Stuart H. Teger, "Activism and Restraint: A Cloak for the Justices' Policy Preferences," in Stephen C. Halpern and Charles M. Lamb, eds., *Supreme Court Activism and Restraint* (Lexington, Mass.: Lexington Books, 1982), pp. 277–301.
[15] Harold J. Spaeth, *Supreme Court Policy Making* (San Francisco: Freeman, 1979), pp. 109–139; Mark W. Cannon and David M. O'Brien, eds., *Views from the Bench* (Chatham, N.J.: Chatham House, 1985), pp. 253–302.

ideas into their decisions. Other justices are *process-oriented,* hesitant to interfere with majority rule. Although they are prepared to apply the constitutional brakes to runaway legislatures, they are less inclined to do so than their result-oriented colleagues. Instead they believe that judges should allow maximum discretion to the people's elected representatives.

Jurists most eager to apply judicial review are **judicial activists.** Those most reluctant to do so are **judicial restraintists.** Yet, even by practicing judicial restraint the Court makes policy. Judicial restraint means upholding the judgment made by some other part of the political system. By affirming someone else's judgment, the Court is legitimating it and making that choice the Court's own. When the Court upholds the validity of a search of someone's home by police, for example, it is accepting the police officer's understanding of the Fourth Amendment (see Chapter 3).

Whether an activist or restraintist, no justice today writes on a blank slate. Although a new case is rarely identical to one the Court has decided in years gone by, prior decisions in similar cases called **precedents** may point the way to the decision the Court should render. This is the doctrine of **stare decisis** (Latin for "let the decision stand"), by which courts adhere to legal principles established in prior cases. Stare decisis does not mean that the Supreme Court must rule as it ruled 100 years ago, or even 10 years ago, but it does mean that justices are reluctant to overrule decisions that are already "on the books." They do so only when a legal principle seems plainly wrong or when public necessity dictates a change.

The power of precedent was an acknowledged factor in 1992 when five justices rejected the Bush administration's request to overrule the 1973 landmark decision *Roe* v. *Wade,*[16] which created a constitutionally protected right to abortion. Three of the five (Justices O'Connor, Kennedy, and Souter) indicated that they would not have sided with the majority position in *Roe* had they been on the Court in 1973. Nineteen years later, however, they believed that the Court should not turn back the clock.[17]

The Court's own decision-making process, described earlier in this chapter, also shapes its decisions. Briefs and oral argument inform the justices and define the issues the case presents. They may even supply the reasoning the Court uses in justifying its decision. The same kind of influence can derive from articles in *law reviews,* the scholarly journals law schools publish. Justices, like everyone else, are sensitive to evaluations of their work by others, and they pay attention to suggestions for evolution in the law that find their way into print. Moreover, because all justices participate in each case, *collegial interaction* becomes a factor. Discussion in conference and persuasive comment by one justice on an opinion drafted by another contribute to the form a decision eventually takes. They sometimes cause a justice to change positions in a case.[18]

Finally, justices are aware of *public opinion.* Justice John Stevens (1975–   ) is correct in asserting that "it is the business of judges to be indifferent to unpop-

---

[16] 410 U.S. 113 (1973).
[17] *Planned Parenthood of Southeastern Pennsylvania* v. *Casey,* 60 U.S.L.W. 4795 (1992).
[18] Walter F. Murphy, *Elements of Judicial Strategy* (Chicago: University of Chicago Press, 1964), ch. 3.

ularity."[19] Nevertheless public attitudes count in judicial decisions in at least two ways. First, public attitudes may influence the meaning justices give certain provisions in the Constitution. With capital punishment, for example, most states reenacted death penalty laws after the Supreme Court set rigorous new standards for capital punishment in 1972 (see Chapter 3).[20] State legislatures, in effect, were telling the Court that they did not think capital punishment was "cruel and unusual" but instead was a form of punishment the American people accepted. These new laws probably made it easier for some justices to decide in 1976 that capital punishment is not cruel and unusual.[21] Second, courts matter in American government ultimately because their decisions are accepted and applied, if grudgingly, by the rest of the political system. So public reaction to judicial decisions may affect compliance with them.

Checks on Judicial Power

Supreme Court justices and other federal judges enjoy substantial independence from outside political control. Thanks to the Constitution, they never face the voters in an election and may not have their salaries decreased by Congress. Yet, although the Court is a potent institution in American government, it does not enjoy unlimited power. Through *constitutional amendment,* Congress and the states may correct the Supreme Court's interpretation of the Constitution. Admittedly, amending the Constitution is not easy, but the justices have been reversed by amendment four times. The Eleventh Amendment (restricting federal court jurisdiction over the states) overturned *Chisholm* v. *Georgia.* The Fourteenth Amendment (granting both national and state citizenship to *all* persons born or naturalized in the United States) countered the infamous *Dred Scott* decision, which had held that the Constitution did not intend for blacks to be citizens. The Sixteenth Amendment (allowing for a national tax on incomes) reversed *Pollock* v. *Farmers' Loan and Trust Co.,* and the Twenty-sixth Amendment (establishing a nationwide voting age of 18) set aside *Oregon* v. *Mitchell.*[22]

Similarly, *statutory amendment* allows Congress to correct the Court's interpretation of a statute. Easier than amending the Constitution, passage of a law is still not an easy task, as Chapter 8 made clear.

Impeachment of justices by Congress may be only a "scarecrow," as President Thomas Jefferson (1801–1809) once said, but it is a weapon available in extraordinary situations. On grounds of misconduct, Congress has removed seven judges of lower federal courts through impeachment, including U.S. district judges Walter Nixon of Mississippi and Alcee Hastings of Florida in 1989, but never a Supreme Court justice. In fact, the Senate has held no impeachment trial for a justice since the Jefferson administration attempted to have Supreme Court Justice Samuel

---

[19] "Reflections on the Removal of Sitting Judges," *Stetson Law Review* 13 (1984): 215, 217.

[20] *Furman* v. *Georgia,* 408 U.S. 238 (1972).

[21] *Gregg* v. *Georgia,* 428 U.S. 153 (1976).

[22] 2 U.S. (2 Dallas) 419 (1793); 60 U.S. (19 Howard) 393 (1857); 158 U.S. 601 (1895); 400 U.S. 112 (1970).

Chase (1796–1811) removed in 1805. The House of Representatives might have begun impeachment proceedings against Justice Abe Fortas (1965–1969) after certain improprieties came to light, but Fortas resigned.[23] Five other federal judges have either been acquitted by the Senate or have had charges against them dismissed before a Senate trial began.

Congress may attack the Court by *withdrawing jurisdiction* to hear certain types of cases. Because Article 3 grants appellate jurisdiction to the Supreme Court "with such exceptions, and under such regulations as the Congress shall make," opponents of particular judicial doctrines can try to prevent certain types of cases from reaching the Court altogether. This is an extreme measure, frequently threatened but only very rarely carried out. Congress may also *change the size* of the Court. This was the heart of President Franklin Roosevelt's "court-packing" proposal in 1937. The plan failed, but the Court changed its interpretation of the Constitution to uphold the president's New Deal program (see "Politics and Economics: The Supreme Court and Economic Policy" on page 342).

Appointment of new justices by the president can place new ideas as well as new personalities on the bench. *Senate confirmation,* however, may limit the range of a president's choices. But judicial vacancies occur irregularly as well as infrequently. For example, President Nixon was able to name four justices between 1969 and 1971, whereas President Carter (1977–1981) was able to name none.

To be effective, Supreme Court decisions require *compliance.* Judges possess very little power actually to coerce obedience. Therefore courts depend on others to obey and to carry out their decisions. An absence of widespread compliance with the Supreme Court's school integration decision of 1954[24] (see Chapter 3) meant that for nearly a decade the decision went largely unenforced. Reaction to this decision was a reminder that the Supreme Court needs the support of both state and federal courts as well as other agencies of government to carry out its judgments. Hostile reaction to the 1954 school decision highlighted an additional check: *litigation.* Black families were sometimes afraid to initiate legal action against local officials who continued to disregard the Supreme Court's decision. Without a case, no court could act. Unlike legislators, who may introduce bills, judges do not initiate the cases they decide.

As cases bring issues old and new to the Court each term, the justices play a part in American government. For more than 200 years the Supreme Court has conducted a dialogue with the people that reflects the public's historic attraction to, and suspicion of, majority rule. "The people have seemed to feel that the Supreme Court," wrote Justice Robert H. Jackson (1941–1954), "whatever its defects, is still the most detached, dispassionate, and trustworthy custodian that our system affords for the translation of abstract into concrete constitutional commands."[25] The justices are the keepers of American constitutional morality. That truth is both a source of and limit on their power.

---

[23] Bruce Allen Murphy, *Fortas: The Rise and Ruin of a Supreme Court Justice* (New York: William Morrow, 1988).

[24] *Brown* v. *Board of Education,* 347 U.S. 483 (1954).

[25] *The Supreme Court in the American System of Government* (Cambridge, Mass.: Harvard University Press, 1955), p. 23.

Summary

1. As the highest court in the land, the Supreme Court of the United States annually confronts a variety of important political issues that appear in the form of cases. The system of courts in the United States consists of the federal courts and the courts of the 50 states. Major federal courts include the district courts and the courts of appeals, in addition to the Supreme Court. The justices and all federal judges are appointed by the president and confirmed by a majority of the Senate.

2. In deciding cases the Supreme Court and other American courts engage in constitutional and statutory interpretation, fact determination, clarification of the boundaries of political authority, education and value application, and legitimation.

3. Cases decided by the Supreme Court proceed through five major stages: petition for review, briefs on the merits, oral argument, conference and decision, and assignment and writing of the opinion of the Court.

4. The decisions of the Supreme Court are the products of several factors and have been a source of controversy during most of American history. Although the Court enjoys considerable political independence from Congress and the president, there are external checks on judicial power.

Key Terms

case (p. 322)
criminal cases (p. 322)
crime (p. 322)
civil cases (p. 322)
state courts (p. 323)
federal courts (p. 323)
jurisdiction (p. 323)
courts of limited jurisdiction (p. 325)
courts of general jurisdiction (p. 325)
intermediate appellate court (p. 325)
court of last resort (p. 325)
Missouri Plan (p. 325)
United States district courts (p. 326)
United States courts of appeals (p. 326)
Claims Court (p. 328)
Court of International Trade (p. 328)
Tax Court (p. 328)
Court of Veterans Appeals (p. 328)
Court of Military Appeals (p. 328)
appellate jurisdiction (p. 328)

federal questions (p. 328)
writ of certiorari (p. 328)
rule of four (p. 328)
original jurisdiction (p. 328)
Eleventh Amendment (p. 329)
chief justice of the United States (p. 329)
associate justices (p. 329)
senatorial courtesy (p. 330)
judicial review (p. 335)
legislative intent (p. 335)
trial court (p. 336)
briefs (p. 337)
amici curiae (p. 339)
solicitor general of the United States (p. 339)
oral argument (p. 339)
opinion of the Court (p. 340)
concurring opinion (p. 340)
dissenting opinion (p. 341)
United States Reports (p. 341)

court-packing plan (p. 342)   precedents (p. 344)
judicial activists (p. 344)   stare decisis (p. 344)
judicial restraintists (p. 344)

Readings for Further Study

A helpful survey of the role of the Court during much of the nation's history is Robert G. McCloskey, *The American Supreme Court* (Chicago: University of Chicago Press, 1960). Henry J. Abraham, *Justices and Presidents,* 3d ed. (New York: Oxford University Press, 1992), is the standard work on appointment of Supreme Court justices. *Behind* Bakke: *Affirmative Action and the Supreme Court,* by Bernard Schwartz (New York: New York University Press, 1988), takes a close look at how the Court reached its decision in a single case. David M. O'Brien's *Storm Center: The Supreme Court in American Politics,* 3d ed. (New York: Norton, 1993), explores the broader political environment in which the Supreme Court operates. Important decisions of the Supreme Court interpreting the Constitution are readily found in edited form in casebooks such as Alpheus T. Mason and D. Grier Stephenson, Jr., *American Constitutional Law,* 10th ed. (Englewood Cliffs, N.J.: Prentice-Hall, 1993). *Guide to the U.S. Supreme Court,* 2d ed. (Washington, D.C.: Congressional Quarterly, Inc., 1990) contains information on almost all aspects of the Court's work. Articles about the Court, past and present, appear in the *Journal of Supreme Court History,* published by the Supreme Court Historical Society.

12 Economic Policy, the National Budget, and the Deficit

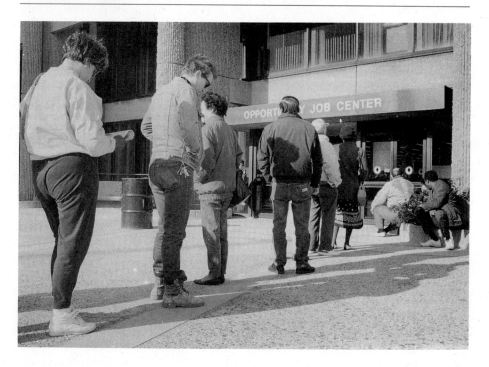

T his chapter addresses what public policy is and how it is related to the political process. Because government does so many different things, the chapter differentiates among different kinds of public policies, with special emphasis on economic policy. The chapter defines, as elements of economic policy, fiscal and monetary policy and outlines the tenets of three major schools of thought about what economic policy should be: Keynesian economics, monetarist economics, and supply-side economics. Given the importance of national budget policy in the 1990s, the chapter then pays special attention to spending choices in fiscal policy by surveying major categories of spending and addressing the issue of the deficit and why government expenditures are so hard to control. The chapter concludes with a review of how budget decisions are made and a discussion of the eternal search, driven by the persistence of high deficits, for better procedures in deciding how money will be spent.

Public Policy in the Political Process

Public policy can be defined in a variety of ways, but the simplest is: "public policy is whatever governments choose to do or not to do."[1] Financing cancer research, providing a Social Security system, cutting or raising taxes, initiating or halting development of a new weapons system, and attempting to clean up toxic waste dumps are all examples of public policies.

Some political debate seems to revolve around procedures, such as whether or not interest groups ought to be limited in the amount of money they can contribute to candidates. However, debates over procedures and rules are really debates over policy. For example, conflict over campaign spending limits is really debate over the degree of access that groups shall have to decision making in substantive areas of concern to them. All political debate ultimately hinges on what course of action government should take (or not take) in some policy area. The real significance of the institutions and processes of government lies in the policies they formulate and the effects of those policies on the lives of citizens. Those decisions invariably help some people and hurt others.

Conflict over the Ends of Government

Given the great differences among citizens in economic status, occupations, and political ideas, government is always subject to conflicting demands. Different groups will likely press for public policies in their own interest, regardless of the effect those policies might have on other groups. And from their perspective the use of rules, procedures, representatives, and institutions is important only toward the end of achieving public policies favorable to them.

The results of public policy mirror conflicts in demands. No governmental action can affect all citizens in exactly the same way. Whatever government does will have varying consequences for different groups. For example, placing limits on Medicare spending will provide some relief to taxpayers by reducing pressure for higher taxes, but those same limits will place economic strains on hospitals and other health-care providers. Increasing the money supply to reduce interest rates will help first-time home buyers by making mortgages easier to afford but will hurt senior citizens who depend on higher interest rates to bolster their investment income. Differences in demands and in the consequences of government action create political conflict. At issue in public policy debate is which

---

[1] Thomas R. Dye, *Understanding Public Policy*, 6th ed. (Englewood Cliffs, N.J.: Prentice-Hall, 1987), p. 2.

groups shall win and which shall lose in the effort to shape government actions to their own interest.

Stages in the Policy Process

In the real world of politics and conflict, the making of public policy frequently appears to be full of chaos. Groups demand or oppose, members of Congress respond or criticize, presidents agree or refuse, judges rule or defer, bureaucrats proceed or halt, and the mass media report or ignore. The making of public policy is not like a play where all the actors follow a predetermined script. Rather, in the making of policy, a group leader or a congressional representative may say and do things without knowing how others will respond or whether they will respond at all. In the efforts to shape policy, hope, uncertainty, and chance all play a role. Consequently, the policy process may seem to be a confusing clash of ideas, events, and personalities.

Public policy analysts try to break down the process of making policy into definable stages to order and make sense out of what appears to be chaotic.[2] Figure 12.1 portrays these stages in the evolution of public policies. In the real world, policies do not evolve in such neatly defined and apparently simple steps. Participants in the process make demands, offer responses, and make decisions without consciously following some analytical framework. Nonetheless, identification of these stages helps to make more understandable the evolution of public policies and the role of government procedures and institutions in the process. As Figure 12.1 shows, there are five stages in the evolution of policies.

1. *A problem or issue must somehow get on the agenda of government.* The **policy agenda** of government, comprised of the list of issues that engage the attention of elected officials, is like a kaleidoscope: The turn of decades results in constantly shifting patterns of issue concerns. In the 1990s the use of money as a public resource is the issue that seems to overwhelm and affect practically all others on the policy agenda. How much government should spend (and on what), how much and whom government should tax, and the impact of budget deficits on the economy and what government should do about them are the questions that drive most policy debate.

2. *Specific proposals to do something about the problem are discussed.* To say that government ought to "do something" about budget deficits is only a beginning. Achieving results requires a **policy strategy,** some specific course of action designed to deal with the originally defined problem. If the budget deficit is a problem, should we increase taxes, decrease spending, or press for a balanced budget amendment? Groups with different ideological beliefs are likely to propose different solutions to policy problems. To reduce budget deficits, for example, conservatives are likely to propose cuts in social welfare spending and liberals are likely to propose cuts in defense spending. The groups that benefit under one proposal will be hurt under the other.

---

[2] James E. Anderson, *Public Policy-Making,* 3d ed. (New York: Holt, Rinehart and Winston, 1984), p. 19.

FIGURE 12.1
Stages in the Policy Process

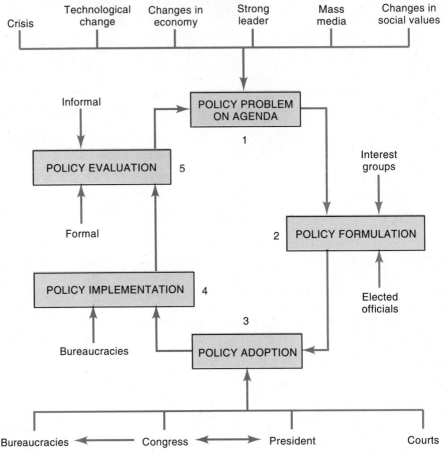

Policies do not always develop in such neatly defined steps. But an awareness of what happens in each step helps in understanding the process that occurs as government attempts to solve problems and accomplish goals. Any number and combination of persons and events can bring concerns to the attention of political leaders (step 1). Policymakers in the executive and legislative branches then study the range of choices open to them to meet those concerns (step 2). A variety of public officials may be involved in selecting a course of action or in deciding to do nothing at all (step 3). The policy than becomes the responsibility of bureaucrats to administer (step 4). Finally, evaluation occurs. Does the plan work? Is it worth its costs (step 5)? The evaluation may become a factor in encouraging further policymaking by government.

3. *Government officials adopt a policy by choosing some specific strategy for action from among the proposals considered.* Although an issue can get on the policy agenda and various policy strategies can be debated and discussed, nothing happens until **policy adoption** of a proposal by institutions of government. One specific strategy to deal with the problem of budget deficits might be a tax bill designed to raise revenue. If both houses can agree on a bill and if the president concurs on the wisdom and necessity of the measure, the resulting law is the formal adoption of a strategy for action.

4. *Bureaucrats implement or translate into action the adopted proposal.* **Policy implementation** is the translation of policy ideas into action. If Congress and the president decide to raise taxes to reduce the deficit, then bureaucrats in the Internal Revenue Service must change tax tables and in fact collect taxes under the higher rates. If Congress and the president decide on spending cuts to reduce the deficit, then bureaucrats in the appropriate agencies are responsible for making the actual spending changes those cuts require.

5. *The policy is evaluated to determine whether or not it succeeded in solving or ameliorating the originally defined problem.* Whether the adopted, implemented strategy in fact worked is the goal of **policy evaluation.** Most policies are not systematically evaluated. The evaluation of policies can range from infrequent, formal, controlled experiments to more frequent, informal assessments in policy debate during election campaigns. What has happened to the budget deficit after a period of higher tax rates and spending cuts? The evaluation process can be complicated by ideological opposition to the policy, such as conservative opposition to higher taxes and liberal opposition to spending cuts. That lower taxes and higher spending may be more attractive than a lower budget deficit to some groups can cloud efforts to define a "successful" deficit reduction policy.

Categories of National Government Policies

No single set of categories can adequately capture everything government does. However, even though overlaps occur, some divisions among policies can help make the scope of government activity more comprehensible. Over time the national government has taken on new functions and responsibilities in response to crises, changing technologies, citizen demands, and political pressures. Six substantive categories can help to bring some order to the scope of national government policies.

Foreign and Defense Policies   The oldest functions of the national government are to conduct relationships with foreign nations, such as trade negotiations with Mexico and Canada, and to maintain national security against threats from other nations, using physical force if necessary, such as the use of troops in the war in the Persian Gulf in 1991.

Social Welfare   In terms of the amount of money the national government spends, the growth of social welfare activities has been the most significant policy change in the role of government over the past half-century. Like a huge check processor, the national government takes money from taxpayers, or borrows it, and disburses cash or in-kind benefits like food stamps to millions of people who qualify because of old age, disability, unemployment, or poverty.

Protection of Legal and Constitutional Rights   The protection of legal and constitutional rights has been one of the principal sets of national government activities over the past generation. Supreme Court justices, presidents, and members of Congress have all brought to bear, to varying degrees, the power and influence of the national government to protect the rights of a variety of groups, such as political, religious, and ethnic minorities; the handicapped; and people accused of crimes.

Promotion of Science and Technology   Basic research, new technologies, and changing public expectations have drawn the national government into efforts to achieve certain public policy goals with the help of science and technology. Examples of such policies include the civilian space program, continuing research

Many government programs and projects, like the proposed space station advocated by the National Aeronautics and Space Administration (NASA), are "big ticket" items. Decisions on whether and how much to fund them have a major impact on the federal budget, the financial strength of certain corporations, and the health of local economies and the nation's economy generally.

efforts on genetic engineering and on diseases like AIDS and cancer, and the development of new civilian technologies to help the nation become more competitive in the world economy of the twenty-first century.

Regulation   Regulations are among the tools government uses to shape sectors of the economy. However, because their purposes go beyond economic goals, regulations can be considered a specific category of policy. As Chapter 10 indicated, government regulations are designed to structure relationships in specific industries, such as broadcasting and the marketing of securities, or to ensure social objectives like clean air and worker safety.[3]

Economic Policies   Given a national budget that is now $1.5 trillion, what the national government does (or does not do) in its spending, taxing, and borrowing policies has enormous consequences for the economy. Spending on education and on transportation and communication networks will shape the kind of economy the nation has in coming decades. Tax laws that eliminate or create tax deductions and tax credits influence investment decisions made by individuals and corporations. Large deficits can encourage higher interest rates, just as higher government spending can reduce unemployment rates. Through its control of the money supply, the Federal Reserve can also affect interest and unemployment rates and private investment decisions. Government efforts to shape the economy through its spending, taxing, borrowing, and money supply decisions comprise a major part of the policy agenda.

Government and Economic Policy

Some of the sharpest conflicts in a society are economic—who gains and who loses, who gives and who receives, who has and who has not. These issues affect the lives and well-being of millions of Americans. Further, with the development of an increasingly interdependent world economy, these issues affect billions of people around the world as well.

In its broadest sense, **economic policy** refers to the decisions a government makes that affect the production, distribution, and consumption of goods, the provision of services, the flow of income, and the accumulation of wealth. In a complex and interdependent modern economy such as that of the United States, virtually everything the government does has economic consequences. For example, President Kennedy's 1961 declaration to put a man on the moon by 1970 set off an explosion of research in metallurgy, electronics, and computers during the 1960s. This research in turn sparked the growth of new high-tech industries and the introduction of consumer goods like the personal computer.

Nevertheless, the term *economic policy* is usually confined to decisions government makes with the explicit intention of influencing the economy. These

---

[3] For a discussion of the purposes of regulation, see *Federal Regulatory Directory,* 6th ed. (Washington, D.C.: Congressional Quarterly, 1990), pp. 9–13.

decisions inevitably address fundamental questions about the role that government should play in the economy and society and, indeed, about the kind of economy and society the United States should be.

Basic Issues of Economic Policy

Economic questions have been part of American politics since the earliest days of the Republic. As Chapter 1 explained, unpopular British tax policies helped to spark the drive for independence before 1776. Barriers to trade and threats to creditors contributed to the call for a new and stronger national government in 1787. Political conflicts in the 1990s over taxes, deficits, trade, and alternative strategies for ensuring prosperity demonstrate the durability of economic issues on the nation's policy agenda. Current controversies illustrate five important economic issues that have recurred as themes through American history, from the beginning to the present.

First, *should government involve itself in economic affairs at all?* As discussed in Chapter 4, one long-standing philosophical view is that the government should stay out of economics and business. Known as **laissez-faire** (French for "leave things alone"), this idea maintains that completely free economic competition among individuals, each pursuing his or her own self-interest, will work naturally to the benefit of all.[4] Under laissez-faire, most economic regulations, such as regulation of the securities business, simply would not exist. This view contrasts starkly with **socialism,** which holds that people will be best off if economic decision making is completely under the control of the government and if government owns and operates most of the major industries. Although Americans have always favored laissez-faire much more than socialism, they divide over just where to strike the balance between the two.

Second, even if government involves itself in economic affairs, say, by insuring bank deposits, *should it try to stabilize the economy, or should it remain neutral?* Over the course of American history the economy has gone through periodic booms and busts. When the economy goes into a slump—a **recession** when the slump is relatively minor and short-lived, a **depression** when it is serious and sustained—or when it accelerates too quickly, some people argue that the government should not interfere but should rather allow the economy to correct itself in time. Others want the government to moderate the trend. Before the arrival of the New Deal during the Great Depression of the 1930s, the view that government should remain neutral prevailed. Since then the judgment that government should take an active role in stabilizing the economy has been dominant.

Third, if government is to maintain economic stability, *which policies work?* Some economists believe that government should adjust its spending and taxing decisions when the economy needs to accelerate or to slow down. Others think the government should try to shape general economic activity by adjusting the

---

[4] Eighteenth-century English economist Adam Smith called this idea the "invisible hand" in his classic *Wealth of Nations.*

money supply and interest rates to influence the willingness of individuals and companies to borrow money.

Fourth, aside from policies that affect the general health of the economy, *should government promote or discourage particular types of economic activity?* Some people believe that government should subsidize heavy industry, such as steel mills and shipyards, because they would be vital in time of war. A variation on this theme, often favored by the neoliberals discussed in Chapter 4, is the idea of developing a national "industrial policy," which plots out cooperation between government and industry in identifying and supporting particularly promising new products and industries. Others believe that certain industries, such as shoe and textile plants, need government help to protect them from foreign competition because they provide employment to many Americans. If necessary, government should engage in **protectionism** by restricting the flow of foreign goods into the United States. Advocates of **free trade,** by contrast, argue that a nation's economy will be better off in the long run if local producers who cannot compete with more efficient foreign producers are allowed to die a natural economic death.

The possibilities of success and failure suggest a fifth concern. *Should government foster economic equality among its citizens?* There is little support in this country for the idea that the government should ensure complete economic equality among all citizens. However, it is a principal tenet of contemporary liberalism that no citizen should be allowed to fall below a certain economic minimum. This view accounts for social welfare programs such as food stamps and medical care for the poor. A more conservative position is that government should see that every citizen has equal opportunity and then let economic forces work in their natural way. Extreme conservatives may find even this an unjustified intrusion into the economy.

Each of these five questions asks whether government should play an active or passive role. How each is answered has profound consequences for the kind of society in which Americans live. Should taxes be raised or lowered, should the supply of money be expanded or contracted, should social welfare spending be increased or cut, should the national government embark on a major program of capital investment or not? Such questions dominate most policy debate in the 1990s.

Fiscal and Monetary Policy

Economic policies are of two major types: fiscal and monetary. The two are conceptually and practically distinct, although political decision makers certainly must take the relationship between them into account. Some regulatory policy also involves economic issues, as discussed in Chapter 10.

Determinations of how much and whom to tax, how much and on what to spend, constitute the **fiscal policy** of the United States. The president makes tax and spending proposals and signs, if he agrees, legislation the Congress passes. The Constitution gives Congress the power "to lay and collect taxes, duties, imposts, and excises, to pay the debts and provide for the common defence and general welfare of the United States," and "to borrow money on the credit of the United States." Taken individually, decisions on these questions constitute much of the routine business of government. Should the savings from military spending cuts be put into constructing new bridges and highways? Should government raise the personal income tax or the corporate income tax to pay for new programs? Taken as a whole, these decisions by the president and Congress exert a powerful influence on the economic life of the nation.

Monetary policy, the second major type of economic policy, is the determination of how much money should circulate in the economy and what the cost of borrowing money, or interest rate, should be. The Constitution gives Congress the power "to coin money, regulate the value thereof, and of foreign coin." In the landmark case of *McCulloch* v. *Maryland,*[5] the Supreme Court recognized Congress's "implied power" to determine monetary policy when it held that the Congress could charter a national bank even though the Constitution did not explicitly give it that power (see Chapter 2). In other words, Congress possesses the power to set monetary policy for the United States. Pursuant to this power, Congress created the Federal Reserve System and delegated to it the power to make these decisions on the supply of money and the cost of borrowing.

The making of economic policy illustrates the classic interplay between institutions and ideas. In fiscal policy, the president and his **Office of Management and Budget,** an Executive Office agency that puts together the president's annual budget proposal, interact with Congress and its committees to produce a national budget. In monetary policy, the Federal Reserve shapes the economy by manipulating the money supply and interest rates. But as the box "Politics and Ideas: The Ideology of Economic Policy" shows, officials in these government institutions choose from among competing economic doctrines in the proposals and decisions they make. Conflicting ideas are the roots of economic policy debate.

The Deficit and the National Budget

Grappling with fiscal policy choices—that is, what taxes to raise or lower, what spending to increase or cut—dominates the policy agenda in the 1990s. Taxing and spending issues touch the president at almost every turn in his efforts to initiate and shape policy. Congress spends much of its time wrestling with the size and shape of the national budget. Elected officials find it much easier to approve spending increases than tax increases, and the resulting budget deficits loom as the most serious policy issue the nation confronts.

The Deficit as a Political Issue

College students can readily understand the concepts of deficit and debt. A **deficit** occurs when expenditures (tuition, room, meals, and so forth) exceed revenues (income from a part-time job and money from parents, for example). A student makes up the difference by borrowing money. **Debt** is the sum of the deficits of

---

[5] 17 U.S. (4 Wheaton) 316 (1819).

prior years. A student who borrows $2000 each year for four years graduates with a debt of $8000. This debt will not be erased until the student earns enough money to meet both current expenses and payments on those college loans.

The federal government today is in a similar position because the government's expenses routinely exceed revenues. Demands on government a century ago were not nearly so great as they are now. The national government in the nineteenth century had an almost embarrassing **surplus** (an excess of revenue over expenses) of funds. Difficult as it may be to believe, the national government had a budget surplus in 71 of the 100 years between 1800 and 1900. In 1834 the total public debt was $35,000—a paltry sum even by nineteenth century standards.[6] Even though the national government regularly ran surpluses in the nineteenth century, the existence of government deficits and debt today is really not a new phenomenon. What is new is their size and persistence, especially in the absence of war, which has always placed heavy demands for money on governments. Deficits have now become the norm in budget policy. The national government has not had a budget surplus since 1969!

Annual deficits and the federal debt have increased substantially over the last generation. In 1965 the annual deficit was a relatively modest $1.4 billion, but by 1975 the deficit began to exceed $50 billion annually. By 1985 the deficit was more than $200 billion. Over the relatively short period of 10 years, annual budget deficits quadrupled.[7] Inflation accounts for some of this increase. But a tax cut pressed by President Reagan in 1981 and higher defense spending in the 1980s contributed substantially to the growth in deficits. The deficit for fiscal year 1992 was $290.2 billion. And, in the absence of policy changes, things will get worse. The Congressional Budget Office (CBO) estimates that the deficit will drop somewhat in the mid-1990s but will rise to exceed $600 billion by the year 2003.[8]

The accumulated federal debt, the total amount of money government owes to lenders, such as government trust funds, banks, insurance companies, and the various financial institutions that purchase government securities, has also increased sharply over the past three decades. Federal debt rose from $322 billion in 1965 to almost $1 *trillion* in 1980. The debt was $3 trillion in 1990 and will exceed $5 trillion by 1995—about $20,000 for every person in the country. In 1992 the debt amounted to 68 percent of gross national product, higher than at any time since the mid-1950s.[9]

Some of the debate over the deficit is colored by the belief that government ought to be guided by traditional values in the matter of money, like "living within one's own means." However, as in other matters, economists disagree over the extent to which the deficit poses a problem. Some argue that government deficits are essential to stimulate consumer demand in a failing or even

[6] U.S. Bureau of the Census, *Historical Statistics of the United States: Colonial Times to 1970*, pt. 2 (Washington, D.C.: Government Printing Office, 1975), p. 1104.

[7] U.S. Office of Management and Budget, *Budget Baselines, Historical Data, and Alternatives for the Future* (Washington, D.C.: Government Printing Office, 1993), pp. 278–279.

[8] Congressional Budget Office, *The Economic and Budget Outlook: Fiscal Years 1994–1998* (Washington, D.C.: CBO, 1993), p. 38.

[9] *Budget Baselines*, p. 346; Office of Management and Budget, *Budget of the United States Government, Fiscal Year 1994*, p. 33.

Politics and Ideas

The Ideology of Economic Policy

In recent American history several philosophies of economic policy have vied for acceptance as official government doctrine. The dominant perspective among Democrats since the New Deal has been **Keynesian economics.** For many years its primary challenge came from advocates of **monetarism,** usually traditional conservative Republicans. But beginning in the Reagan years some less orthodox Republican conservatives embraced the new (or at least newly packaged) doctrine of **supply-side economics.**

Keynesian Economics

The brilliant British economist John Maynard Keynes saw the health of an economy as dependent on the relationship between overall supply and demand in the economy. **Supply** is the total amount of goods and services produced in the economy; **demand** is the total amount of goods and services consumed. Economic problems arose, he argued, when supply and demand were not in balance. If supply exceeded demand, businesses would build up a backlog of unsold goods, cut back production, and lay off workers. So supply exceeding demand would lead to unemployment. If demand exceeded supply, buyers would bid up the prices of goods, and inflation would result. Only if supply and demand were in balance would the economy experience maximum employment and minimum inflation.

Keynes argued that in complex modern economics, supply and demand would not automatically balance. The imbalance would lead to economic problems. Keynes's solution was to have the government use its fiscal policy to bring the two into balance. If supply exceeded demand and unemployment threatened, the government could spend more than it received in taxes—that is, it would engage in deficit spending and bring total demand and hence employment up to the optimum level. If demand exceeded supply and inflation loomed, the government could collect more in taxes than it spent—that is, it would run a surplus—and bring total demand and hence inflation down. In other words, Keynesians emphasize using government fiscal policy to adjust the level of demand to the point of balance with supply that will yield a low-inflation, high-employment economy. But a challenging economic policy puzzle in the 1990s is how much, at a time of high budget deficits, government spending can be used to create demand in a lagging economy.

Monetarism

Monetarists focus, as the name implies, on monetary policy. They see monetary policy rather than

sluggish economy. That is, by cutting taxes or increasing spending, government pumps money into the private economy to allow the kind of consumer spending that counters a depressed economy. Some maintain that the nation has had large deficits in the past, particularly in wartime, and those deficits actually spurred the economy.

Many other economists argue, however, that large deficits that are the product of a fundamental imbalance between revenues and expenditures can have the effect of slowing down consumer spending and economic growth. Government borrowing to cover deficits means that government competes with all other potential borrowers in the economy, such as corporations that want to build plants fiscal policy as the best way to control the level of demand for goods and services. If the Federal Reserve lets the amount of money grow too large and the cost of money (i.e., the interest rate) fall too low, consumers and business managers will borrow and spend so much money that demand will exceed supply and inflation will result. If money is in short supply and interest rates are high, consumer and business spending and borrowing will decline, supply will exceed demand, and unemployment will result.

One widely recognized monetarist prescription, advanced by the prominent economist Milton Friedman, is that growth in the money supply should be steady and gradual, roughly in pace with the growth in the amount of goods and services the economy produces. Anything more will lead to inflation, anything less to unemployment. Further, many monetarists, being conservative and suspicious of active governmental involvement in the economy, prefer adherence to this sort of general rule rather than "politically" exercised discretion about monetary policy.

Supply-Side Economics

As one might expect, supply-side economics focuses on how much is produced in the economy rather than on how much is demanded, as in the Keynesian and monetarist perspectives. According to supply-side economics' leading theoretician, Arthur Laffer, government can affect the balance of supply and demand in the economy better by adjusting supply than by adjusting demand. In fact, government is seen as having created the imbalance by setting taxes so high (particularly for the highest income groups) that people have little incentive to work or to invest and thereby produce. Only if government reduces taxes sufficiently to restore incentives and make money available will people begin to work harder, invest more, and produce more. The stimulus to economic activity created by lower tax *rates* will, according to the supply-siders, be so great that tax *revenues* will actually increase as a result of higher employment and consumption.

Supply-side concerns have played an important role in recent debates over whether to reduce the deficit by taxing the rich. Rejecting liberal concerns about increasing inequality in income distribution, supply-siders have argued that income tax rates on the rich and rates for capital gains taxes on everyone should be kept low. Their argument is that the rich especially are more likely than the poor to invest their money (rather than spend it), thereby stimulating greater production and prosperity.

or individuals who want to buy houses or cars. The deficit raises the cost of capital and the cost of doing business.

Most politicians and economists believe that persistent large deficits threaten severe economic consequences. The long-term health of a society depends on its ability and willingness to save and invest for future growth. Resources must be invested in basic research, new products, new technologies, and education. If present consumption limits the amount of saving required for such investment, the society risks a decline in the standard of living. The Congressional Budget Office reports that among the world's most developed countries the United States has had the greatest decline in national saving as a percentage of gross

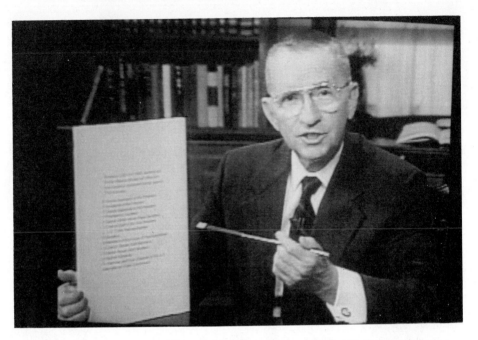

In the 1992 campaign, Ross Perot used television addresses (called "infomercials") to focus the attention of the electorate on the deficit and the national debt. The tireless efforts of Perot and his followers meant that Congress and the Clinton administration could not easily ignore deficit reduction as a priority of the federal government.

domestic product.[10] The federal budget deficit is a major contributor to this low national saving rate.

Persistent deficits figured prominently as a political issue in the 1992 presidential campaign. Third-party candidate Ross Perot skillfully used television to criticize both major parties for inaction on the deficit and the resulting public debt. Perot argued that paying higher interest costs on the debt steals from the nation's future by taking away needed resources from education, saving, and investment. He declared that "Our first priority is to balance the budget."[11] Perot clearly struck a chord with voters. He received 19 percent of the popular vote in the election, the best showing for a third-party candidate in 80 years.[12]

Perot's electoral strength placed pressure on elected officials to grapple seriously with the deficit. But their task is not easy. Reducing the deficit is so hard because of the sharp conflict over the alternative ways of doing it and the pain that lower deficits leave in their wake. Choosing among cutting expenditures, increasing taxes, or some combination of the two is really the essence of politics.

[10] Congressional Budget Office, *Assessing the Decline in the National Saving Rate* (Washington, D.C.: Government Printing Office, 1993) pp. 2–3. National savings rates were compared for the period 1960 to 1989.
[11] Ross Perot, *United We Stand: How We Can Take Back Our Country* (New York: Hyperion, 1992), p. 35.
[12] In 1912, after a split in the Republican party, Theodore Roosevelt, a former president, received 27 percent of the popular vote as the candidate of the Progressive party.

For example, elimination of the revenue-sharing program through which the national government granted funds to local governments lowered the deficit somewhat. However, elimination of the program also forced local governments to decide whether to increase their own taxes or cut services for local residents. As another example, building an orbiting space station or the superconducting super collider will be of great economic benefit to some contractors and some states. But these decisions also mean that either the deficit or taxes will be higher. Raising taxes will cut the deficit, but higher taxes also mean less money in the pockets of consumers. Researchers want more government money to do their work. Social welfare advocates want more spending on poverty programs. The beneficiaries of government spending, such as military contractors, researchers, and state and local governments, obviously press to maintain and even increase their benefits. At the same time, taxpayers do not welcome proposals to raise federal revenues by increasing taxes.

Major Components of the National Budget

Money's rise to the top of the policy agenda has deep roots in the past. Since the Great Depression of the 1930s government has treated the economic and social needs of groups like the elderly, the disabled, and the poor as *public* problems. Meeting such welfare demands has meant the expenditure of huge amounts of public money. War and the threat of war have also made their own heavy demands on public funds. Paying interest on borrowed money has itself become a major category of spending.

Figure 12.2 offers a graphic and useful summary of major budgetary trends over the past half-century. The figure divides the budget into four proportional categories: national defense, payments for individuals, net interest payments, and all other expenditures, which include programs such as cancer research, space exploration, highway construction, and environmental protection.

National Defense   The national government has constitutional responsibility to provide for the nation's security. Consequently, spending on defense has always consumed a significant portion of the budget. For example, of the $10.8 million that the national government spent in 1800, more than 55 percent went to the War Department (army) and the navy.[13] Figure 12.2 shows that almost 90 percent of the budget went to defense in 1945, at the height of World War II. After a postwar drop and then an increase in the early 1950s during the Korean conflict, the proportion of federal dollars going to defense began a general decline from almost 70 percent in 1954 to less than 23 percent in 1980. In absolute dollars, the amount spent on national defense increased over this period, but defense expenditures consumed an increasingly smaller proportion of the total budget. Other expenditure items in the budget were growing at a faster rate, and the proportional decline in defense spending became a major political issue.

---

[13] *Historical Statistics,* op. cit., pp. 1114–1115.

FIGURE 12.2
Federal Government Expenditures

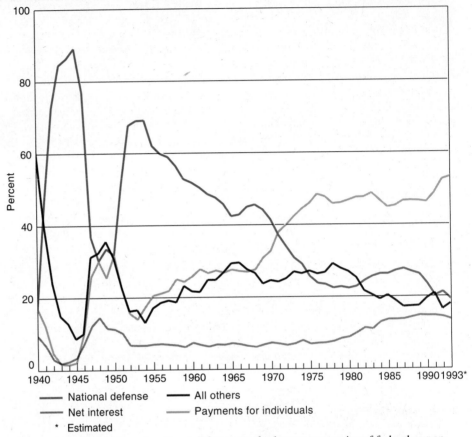

Payments for individuals and national defense are the largest categories of federal expenditures. Net interest alone was estimated to consume almost 14 percent of the budget in 1993.   SOURCE: U.S. Office of Management and Budget, *Budget Baselines, Historical Data, and Alternatives for the Future* (Washington, D.C.: Government Printing Office, 1993), pp. 340–345.

One of Ronald Reagan's (1981–1989) priorities was strengthening defense, and, as Figure 12.2 shows, the proportional amount of federal spending going to national defense increased in the 1980s. However, the breakup of the Soviet Union and the end of the Cold War have weakened the military's claim on the budget. The proportion of the budget spent on defense undoubtedly will go down in the 1990s. President Clinton has proposed reductions in defense spending, but battles loom over how large the cuts should be and where within the defense budget they should be made.

Payments for Individuals   Payments for individuals, the second major spending category in the budget, includes social welfare programs that are primarily a legacy of the New Deal of the 1930s and the Great Society of the 1960s, including Social Security, Medicare, unemployment compensation, food stamps, Medicaid, and supplemental security income. Retired and disabled citizens receive monthly checks through the Social Security program. Medicare provides medical care for the elderly and the disabled. The short-term unemployed receive weekly checks through the unemployment compensation program. Needy individuals receive food, medical care, or cash through programs such as food stamps, Medicaid, or supplemental security income. In administering these programs, the national government takes money from some groups in the form of retirement contributions or taxes and transfers it to other groups either in the form of cash, such as Social Security checks, or in the form of in-kind payments, such as food stamps.

This category of spending, compared to national defense, is a relatively new one for the national government. Only within the past half-century has the national government administered social welfare programs on such a comprehensive scale. This category has grown proportionally faster than any other since the 1940s, as Figure 12.2 graphically illustrates. In 1940 payments for individuals comprised less than 20 percent of all federal spending, a proportion that increased to 33 percent in 1970. This category of spending consumed more than half the total budget in 1993.[14]

Interest Costs   The third major category of spending, **net interest** represents the cost that government must pay the public for the use of borrowed money to cover budget deficits. Most individuals have at one time or another encountered the inevitability of making interest payments on goods they purchase. For example, most people who wish to buy a new home simply do not have enough cash to cover the full purchase price. If they want to buy a $100,000 home, they may have to borrow $80,000 from a bank or mortgage company to add to the resources they have to make the purchase. Borrowing money is really nothing more than using money that belongs to others. Of course, the right to use this money comes at a price, which is the payment of interest.

Money is among the most expensive items individuals can buy, and how much it costs depends on interest rates, which are in constant flux. If a home purchaser borrows $80,000 at 9 percent interest to be repaid over 30 years, the total repayment at the end of that period will amount to more than $230,000, or almost *three* times the original $80,000 borrowed! The amount of interest paid will vary with interest rates and the time period of the loan, but this simple example illustrates the high cost of using other people's money.

Individuals borrow money because they want things that cost more than the cash they have on hand. Governments borrow money for much the same reason. Because the money demands on government exceed the amount of money government receives in taxes, the resulting deficit must be covered by borrowing money from individual investors and financial institutions that buy government securities. And as the deficits rise, so too must the cost of borrowing money. In 1965 government paid $8.6 billion in net interest, about 7 percent of total federal expenditures in that year. In 1992 interest payments alone were $199 billion, more than 14 percent of total spending.[15] The proportional amount of the budget consumed by net interest has doubled since the 1960s.

---

[14] *Budget of the United States Government, Fiscal 1994,* pp. 31–35.
[15] Congressional Budget Office, *The Economic and Budget Outlook: Fiscal Years 1994–1998,* p. 128.

Mandatory Programs in the Budget

When the president and Congress begin to work on budget proposals every year, they do not begin with a clean budgetary slate. Present and future budgets build on past budgets in increments. This theory of **incrementalism** holds that "[t]he largest determining factor of the size and content of this year's budget is last year's budget."[16] Expenditures are difficult to control largely because present decisions are shaped by past decisions. Budget makers cannot decide to reduce total spending from $1.5 trillion to, say, $500 billion in a single year. Just as a rapidly moving freight train cannot be stopped quickly (and without much screeching of brakes), so too budget expenditures cannot be massively and rapidly reduced from one year to the next.

Much of the budget is comprised of **mandatory programs** in which spending automatically increases from one year to the next without specific annual appropriations action by Congress. Examples are **social entitlements,** programs in which eligible citizens receive benefits to which they are entitled by law. Entitlements include Social Security, Medicare, Medicaid, public assistance programs, unemployment compensation, and retirement programs for federal employees. The largest of the mandatory programs is Social Security, which alone accounts for about 20 percent of the total budget. According to the Congressional Budget Office, "[m]anaging the growth of federal spending . . . will be largely a matter of controlling the growth of mandatory outlays."[17] As an example, President Clinton has cited the control of health care costs in Medicare and Medicaid as crucial to limiting the growth of deficits.[18]

To illustrate the concept of mandatory spending, Congress and the president do not decide every year whether or not the nation should have a Social Security program. Once the program was established, and it is now a solid rock on the political landscape, eligible individuals receive benefits year after year. A person who has made contributions to the Social Security system via payroll taxes becomes automatically eligible for Social Security benefits upon retirement at age 65. Social Security expenditures are determined by the demographic movement of individuals into retirement age and by increases in payments because of inflation. Congress and the president could substantially reduce those benefits, but only at very high political and social costs.

A related program that illustrates the difficulty of cutting the budget from one year to the next is net interest. By law, interest on the debt must be paid. Failure to make such interest payments would destroy investor confidence in government securities and result in economic consequences too grave to contemplate. So Congress and the president do not have much choice in the matter of paying interest. The amount paid in a given year will depend on interest rates and the size of deficits. Because of the necessity to pay interest and the existence of mandatory programs, budget makers cannot easily make proportionally large spending cuts from one year to the next.

---

[16] Aaron Wildavsky, *The Politics of the Budgetary Process,* 4th ed. (Boston: Little, Brown, 1984), p. 13.
[17] Congressional Budget Office, *Reducing the Deficit: Spending and Revenue Options* (Washington, D.C.: Government Printing Office, 1993), p. 225.
[18] *A Vision of Change for America* (Washington, D.C.: Government Printing Office, 1993), pp. 11, 116–117.

In 1993 President Clinton's Office of Management and Budget estimated that without policy changes half of the fiscal year 1994 budget would be comprised of mandatory programs. Net interest payments and mandatory programs together would account for 64 percent of the total budget in 1994. Some changes can be made in social entitlements, but the programs cannot be cut drastically. And interest must be paid. The concept of mandatory spending illustrates the obstacles Congress and the president face in their attempts to cut deficits.

The President and Congress in the Budgeting Process

Most individuals know very little about the details of the national budget or how various governmental institutions work together to arrive at specific taxing and spending policies. However, taxpayers are acutely aware of the degree to which their salaries are reduced by withholding taxes, and beneficiaries of public programs notice even small changes in their benefits. From the perspective of individuals or specific groups, the politics of money is about maintaining or increasing the benefits of government spending while shifting the tax costs to someone else. If politics is the process of making choices among conflicting perceptions of national purpose, with different consequences for different people, then choices on the collection and use of public money are intensely political decisions.[19]

Budgets are essential because human wants must be tamed by the scarcity of resources. If human wants were limited, or if resources were unlimited, budgets would be unnecessary. However, because neither condition exists, the president and Congress are inevitably forced to wrestle with the necessity of coming up with a **budget,** or a planned statement of revenues and expenditures. One scholar has cited "the twin functions of a budget process as an opportunity for claiming resources and as a procedure for rationing limited resources among claimants."[20] Budgeting lies at the intersection of the inevitability of demands and the necessity to impose constraints on those demands. Continuing budget deficits are simply a reflection of the political fact that satisfying demands is more appealing than the distasteful business of imposing constraints.

Because the money pie cannot be expanded infinitely, making budget policy is a battle over the shares of the pie that different programs should receive. In addition to the inevitability of disagreement, putting together a budget is a complicated process for several reasons. First, determining how much government will collect in taxes and how much it will spend in a given year is largely a matter of estimation. Budget makers cannot accurately predict the flow of dollars into and out of the federal treasury in a particular year. Such dollar flows are greatly

---

[19] For the argument that "budgeting is at its very core political," see Donald F. Kettl, *Deficit Politics: Public Budgeting in Its Institutional and Historical Context* (New York: Macmillan, 1992), pp. 156–157.

[20] Allen Schick, *Congress and Money: Budgeting, Spending, and Taxing* (Washington, D.C.: Urban Institute, 1980), p. 570.

influenced by the performance of the nation's economy, a matter over which the president and Congress have little short-term control. Second, budgeting is complicated and difficult because constructing a budget is a highly *decentralized* process. That is, a large number of individuals and groups, both inside and outside government, help to shape the budget. The president and his Office of Management and Budget, the executive agencies, Congress and a variety of its committees and their staffs, interest groups, and sometimes even the courts all contribute to the making of budget decisions. At the center of political conflict, the budget process reflects the decentralization inherent in the political system itself. The process would certainly be more tidy and efficient if only one individual or committee could make all budget determinations. But the framers of the Constitution did not intend such a system. Especially in the budget process, ambition counters ambition, resulting in inevitable disorder and complexity.[21]

The Stages of Budgeting

The most important governmental actors in the budgetary process are the president and his staff, Congress and its committees, and the executive agencies. Budgeting can be divided into three separate stages, with each of these three groups playing a primary role in one of them.[22]

1. *Presidential proposal.* The president and his staff compile agency requests for funds, shape those requests to fit presidential priorities, and then submit to Congress a proposed Budget of the United States Government.
2. *Congressional response.* Congress and its various committees review the presidential budget proposals and mold them to meet congressional priorities. If the president agrees with those congressional actions, they then become law.
3. *Agency expenditure of funds.* The executive agencies spend the money pursuant to budget laws enacted by Congress and signed by the president.

Each stage occurs every year. Actual expenditures take place during a **fiscal year,** which for U.S. government budget and accounting purposes is a 12-month period beginning each year on October 1 and ending on September 30 of the following calendar year. The calendar year designation given to the fiscal year is the calendar year in which the fiscal year ends. For example, fiscal year 1995 begins on October 1, 1994, and ends on September 30, 1995. Starting the fiscal year on October 1 rather than January 1 is simply a human judgment or hope that Congress should be able to make budget decisions in the nine-month period

---

[21] See "Madisonian Budgeting, or Why the Process Is So Complicated" in Joseph White and Aaron Wildavsky, *The Deficit and the Public Interest: The Search for Responsible Budgeting in the 1980's* (Berkeley: University of California Press, 1989), pp. 1–17.

[22] An excellent brief review of the budget process can be found in *The Budget System and Concepts of the United States Government* (Washington, D.C.: Government Printing Office, 1992).

between the beginning of its session in January and October 1, the beginning of the fiscal year. That Congress does not always meet this deadline is one symptom of the problems Congress has in making difficult budget choices.

As Figure 12.3 shows, the three stages of the budgeting process take a total of more than two years to complete. For example, the president and his staff began to formulate proposals for fiscal 1995 in spring 1993, about 18 months before the beginning of the fiscal year in October 1994. Given uncertainties in estimating

FIGURE 12.3
Major Steps in the Budgeting Process

The steps in the budgeting process for each fiscal year take two and a half years to complete. If appropriation action is not completed by September 30, Congress enacts temporary appropriations (i.e., a continuing resolution). sources: Adapted from U.S. Office of Management and Budget, *The United States Budget in Brief, Fiscal Year 1990* (Washington, D.C.: Government Printing Office, 1989), p. 96, and information contained in U.S. Office of Management and Budget, *The Budget System and Concepts of the United States Government* (Washington, D.C.: Government Printing Office, 1992).

receipts and expenditures, planning for a fiscal year so long in advance is obviously no easy task. The second stage of congressional action began in February 1994, eight months before the start of fiscal 1995. Agencies actually spend the money in the fiscal year itself, October 1, 1994, through September 30, 1995.

Not all budgetary action by all three sets of budgetary actors concentrates on a single fiscal year at a time. At a single point in a given calendar year, each of the three stages may be in progress for three different fiscal years. In spring 1993, for example, agencies were actually spending money in fiscal 1993, Congress was reviewing presidential proposals for fiscal 1994, and the president and his staff had begun to plan for fiscal 1995. The need for planning and executing money decisions seems to be eternal, and so does the process of putting together a budget.

The President in the Budget Process

The president is the single most important individual in the process of constructing a budget for the national government. The president's central role in the budgetary process springs from his unique position in the political system. More than the words and actions of any other person, what he says about the budget and the priorities he establishes are especially important in shaping subsequent debate about the budget.

The president has two important powers that guarantee him a central role in the budgetary process. First, with the help of the Office of Management and Budget, the president *proposes a budget to Congress.* Proposal power does not mean that the president will necessarily get what he wants. Congress can and does work its own will on the budget. But the power to propose is a significant one, for the president's budget proposal sets the tone of debate and becomes the standard against which congressional changes are measured.

The president's budget proposals are really political statements, for, if enacted, they inevitably have different consequences for different groups. Depending on his budget priorities, the president can propose more (or less) spending on defense or housing or education. He can propose changes in eligibility standards for entitlement programs with the hope of saving money in future years. He can propose tax cuts or increases with consequences for the general health of the economy, the size of the deficit, and the economic status of different income groups. And he can do all of these things with the great flair of publicity—natural to the office of the presidency—which brings guaranteed and immediate attention to his proposals. President Clinton announced his economic plan in a speech to Congress one month after his inauguration, thus illustrating a president's power to structure discussion of the budget. The plan contained a wide range of initiatives to strengthen the economy, increase employment, lower the deficit, and redistribute the tax burden. Clinton's proposals included an energy tax, public investment expenditures, higher income taxes for many Americans and most corporations, reductions in defense spending, and limits on health care costs. Members of Congress can oppose presidential initiatives, but the president's proposals define the budget policy debate.

In addition to the authority to make budget proposals, the president has the constitutional power to *veto budget bills passed by Congress.* Appropriations bills go through the legislative process and must ultimately be signed by the president

Many officials in the executive branch help to shape economic policy for the nation. At this meeting in the White House on February 8, 1993, President Clinton meets with players on his economic team: (from left) Secretary of Commerce Ron Brown, Vice President Gore, Budget Director Leon Panetta, Council of Economic Advisors Chair Laura Tyson, Secretary of the Treasury Lloyd Bentsen, and Secretary of Labor Robert Reich.

before they become law and actual spending proceeds. The president may decide that he is opposed to an appropriations bill that Congress sends him because it diverges too much from his original proposal. However, he must veto the entire bill rather than portions of it. Congress can try to override his veto with an extraordinary majority (a two-thirds vote in each chamber), or Congress may try to recast the bill in terms more agreeable to the president. No other person has such power to stop the budgetary process in its tracks. The ever-present threat of a presidential veto dramatizes the critical role that the president plays in the budget process. But Congress has substantial powers of its own to shape budgetary choices.[23]

Congress and Budgeting

Congressional power to make decisions on the budget is firm and clear, for the Constitution states that "no money shall be drawn from the Treasury, but in Consequence of Appropriations made by Law." Presidential proposals cannot

---

[23] For a good review of relationships between the branches in the budgetary process, see Howard E. Shuman, *Politics and the Budget: The Struggle Between the President and Congress,* 3d ed. (Englewood Cliffs, N.J.: Prentice-Hall, 1991).

become law in the absence of congressional action. The first budgetary stage of presidential proposal is a triumph of simplicity compared to the second stage of congressional action.

Congress is a much more complicated institution than the presidency. By definition, the president is one individual to whom responsibility for budget proposals can be easily assigned. But Congress is a fragmented institution with 535 individuals representing different parts of the nation and inevitably reflecting conflicting views. By voting, each of these individuals can help to shape the budget that emerges from Congress.

Most of the important work of budget review and decision in Congress is done in committee. In addition to the authorizing committees (such as Agriculture and Armed Services), each chamber also has "money" committees, such as those on the budget, appropriations, and revenue (called Ways and Means in the House and Finance in the Senate). Each one of these committees can affect the budget in some way. Under the best of circumstances, the process of making budget decisions is never easy because the demand for government services always outruns the supply of money to fund those services. But this fundamental difficulty is heightened in Congress by the large number of individuals and committees, each moved by diverse and conflicting interests, with the capacity to shape the budget.

For most government programs, Congress must take two separate steps before money can actually be spent. The first step is program **authorization,** or the congressional decision to create (or continue) a program and the agency administering it. Such authorizations begin in substantive legislative committees, such as Agriculture, Armed Services, and Interstate and Foreign Commerce. Authorizing legislation ordinarily contains statements of program and agency goals as well as enabling powers to carry the program forward. Authorizations may be for one year, for several years, or open-ended. The legislation also contains a statement of money authorized to be spent on the program. For example, an authorization measure may state that an expenditure not to exceed $700 million is authorized for the following fiscal year for, say, certain pollution abatement activities carried on by the Environmental Protection Agency. However, no money can be legally spent as the result of such an authorization measure. Agencies do not have the legal right actually to spend money unless Congress takes the second step of appropriating funds pursuant to the authorization.

This second step is program **appropriations,** the congressional decision to fund an authorized program with a specific sum of money. Such appropriations decisions are shaped by recommendations from the Appropriations Committee in each chamber. The actual amount appropriated need not be the same as the amount authorized. For example, although $700 million may be authorized for pollution abatement, only $600 million may be actually appropriated.

The authorization-appropriations sequence does not apply to all government programs. For example, the authorization (creation and subsequent amendment) of most entitlement programs includes, in effect, a permanent appropriation to fund the program. By establishing the Social Security program, Congress has pledged that individuals reaching a certain age and meeting eligibility requirements will receive monthly checks. Congress can change the rules, but the amount of money spent in a given fiscal year is not dependent on specific congressional action for that year.

The Search for Better Budget Procedures

The deficit is proof of the extraordinary difficulty Congress and the president have in coming to grips with decisions on cutting expenditures and raising taxes. The substantive issues are so hard that policymakers have naturally considered whether different budget procedures might make their task easier. Would tough budget decisions be made more readily if procedures for arriving at them were different?

Proposed budget changes come in a variety of forms. The most controversial budget reforms are proposals to give the president **line-item veto** power and to add an amendment to the Constitution requiring a balanced budget. Under current rules, the president must sign or veto an entire bill sent to him by Congress. An appropriations bill may contain many specific programs, and the president must either accept or reject all of them in the bill. The line-item veto would give the president the power to reject some items in the bill and to allow others to become law. Governors in 43 states have line-item veto power, which, proponents argue, increases the managerial capability chief executives must have. With this power, its supporters say, presidents would not be forced to accept wasteful spending projects that members of Congress pack into a bill. Congress, however, has resisted granting the president this power. Many members fear that the line-item veto would result in a discernible shift in budgetary power from Congress to the president. Given the much larger number of options the power would afford, presidential flexibility in determining the shape of the budget would greatly increase. Congressional ability to mold the budget would correspondingly diminish.

The size of deficits and a growing public debt have also sparked interest in a constitutional amendment that would require a balanced budget. Proponents of a **balanced budget amendment** argue that only a constitutional mandate will force Congress and the president to produce balanced budgets. Opponents hold that the amendment risks tax increases and major reductions in a wide range of politically popular programs. Several times over the last decade, balanced budget amendment proposals have failed to get the constitutionally required two-thirds vote of the House and Senate before being sent on to the states for ratification. In 1992 Congress considered an amendment proposal that would have mandated a three-fifths majority in the House and Senate to allow deficit spending, except in a military emergency. The amendment did not receive the necessary two-thirds vote in either chamber. However, the amendment had substantial support, a sign that the political frustration of dealing with persistent deficits has led to a serious search for extraordinary constitutional remedies.

Although the line-item veto power and the balanced budget amendment remain proposals, in three laws Congress and the president have made fundamental changes in the process of deciding on budget expenditures as they wrestle with the pain of reducing deficits.

The Congressional Budget and Impoundment Control Act of 1974   Before 1974 Congress reviewed the president's budget in a highly decentralized, piece-meal fashion. Budget totals resulted from a process of summing up the work of separate committees rather than any conscious effort to consider the budget comprehensively. Nor was there institutionalized consideration of the relationship between spending and expected revenue, a violation of sound budget practice.

With increasing frequency, appropriations bills were not enacted by the beginning of the fiscal year. In the absence of appropriations laws, some agencies were forced to operate under a **continuing resolution,** a temporary funding measure passed by Congress. In addition, the relentless growth of the budget produced demands for more budgetary information. And the regularity of annual deficits sparked heated battles within Congress and between Congress and the president over who was to blame for the budgetary "red ink." In fact, in an unprecedented use of presidential impoundment powers, President Nixon refused to spend billions in funds already appropriated. He did so on the grounds that he was forced to take action to limit spending because Congress had not done so.

As a response to these problems, the **Congressional Budget and Impoundment Control Act of 1974** changed the fiscal year from a July 1–June 30 sequence to an October 1–September 30 sequence to allow Congress more time to review the president's budget; created the **Congressional Budget Office** (CBO), a congressional staff unit with the responsibility to provide Congress with needed information on the budget and the analytical expertise to sharpen budgetary choices for Congress; placed limits on the president's impoundment powers; created budget committees in both the House and Senate to provide a mechanism for comprehensive budget review by Congress; and established a timetable (revised by subsequent legislation) for the congressional budget review process.

The president submits his proposed budget to Congress early in the calendar year. Congressional committees review the programs within their jurisdiction and offer budget estimates to the budget committees by mid-March. With the help of the CBO, the budget committees pursue a more comprehensive budget review and report to the House and Senate a budget resolution containing targets for total revenues, total expenditures, and money to be spent in functional categories across the budget for the next fiscal year. The resolution is to be adopted by the full House and Senate by April 15. Legislation on appropriations and revenue is then to proceed in light of the budget targets set in the resolution. Congressional money decisions and budget targets are to be reconciled in time for spending to begin at the start of the fiscal year on October 1. However, in some years Congress has not been able to meet these procedural deadlines required by law. For example, in the fall of 1990 not a single one of the appropriations measures was enacted by the time the new fiscal year had begun.

Gramm-Rudman-Hollings   In response to the problem of deficits, Congress enacted the Balanced Budget and Emergency Deficit Control Act of 1985, more popularly known as **Gramm-Rudman-Hollings** after the senators who sponsored the legislation. The act as later amended mandated progressive annual cuts in the deficit and set into motion a process of automatic across-the-board spending cuts to achieve a balanced budget by 1993. The president ordered the cuts through the process of **sequestration.** Some programs, such as Social Security, Medicaid, and interest payments on the debt, were exempted from the cuts.

Gramm-Rudman-Hollings was enacted in the hope that the legislation would force Congress and the president to reduce the deficit. One problem with the deficit targets is that they encouraged the use of budget-reducing "gimmicks" which made it appear that cuts were made when in fact they were not. An example of a gimmick is pushing back a government payday several days from the fiscal year in question (say October 1) to the prior fiscal year (say September 29) so that the payroll will not be counted as an expenditure in the fiscal year under review. However, since the money went out anyway, if only at a different time, the cut was not real. The deficits continued, so Congress and the president tried a new law in 1990.

Budget Enforcement Act of 1990 Congress made fundamental changes in Gramm-Rudman-Hollings and tried a new approach to the deficit in the **Budget Enforcement Act of 1990.** The new procedures are aimed at specific congressional actions increasing the deficit. The 1990 act shifts the emphasis of congressional action from deficit reduction to the control of spending.[24] Rather than being driven by overall deficit targets, Congress is limited by caps on discretionary spending and by constraints on changes in mandatory spending.

For fiscal years 1991 through 1993, the law placed caps on spending in each of the three categories of defense, international, and domestic discretionary, that is, nonmandatory spending. The budget for the Federal Bureau of Investigation is an example of domestic discretionary spending because Congress can change FBI budget amounts from one year to the next. Examples of mandatory spending are Medicare payments to hospitals to fund health care for the elderly because eligible individuals automatically and regularly receive benefits without specific congressional authorizing action from one year to the next. If discretionary spending exceeded the ceilings, then sequestration cuts were to be made within the category in which excess spending occurred. Under the law, all discretionary spending is combined into a single category in fiscal years 1994 and 1995. In addition, mandatory program increases must be balanced by cuts in nonexempt programs or by revenue increases. The law also provides for overall deficit targets, but the president is given the flexibility to adjust them. Cuts are not required during war or a downturn in economic growth.[25]

Almost no one is satisfied with the procedures for considering and passing a budget. Elected officials and their staffs spend inordinate amounts of time dealing with budget issues. Congress has missed budget deadlines, government agencies have sometimes closed down temporarily for lack of spending authority, and the deficit continues. Critics wonder, "Is this any way to run a government?" Efforts to tinker with existing procedures will continue, and proposals for new ones are

---

[24] Congressional Budget Office, "The 1990 Budget Package: An Interim Assessment," December 1990, p. 2 (mimeo).

[25] U. S. House of Representatives, Committee on ways and means, *Background Material on the Federal Budget and the President's Proposals for Fiscal Year 1994* (Washington, D.C.: Government Printing Office, 1993), pp. 71, 82.

inevitable.[26] However, the tinkering with procedures is a symptom of a deeper political problem. Continuing entitlement programs at current levels, reducing the deficit, and avoiding both tax increases and deep cuts in general government spending cannot all be achieved simultaneously. Such budgetary pressures have placed obvious strains on procedures for deciding budget policy. Ultimately, those pressures and strains emerge from the intense political resistance to spending cuts or tax increases. As President Clinton's budget proposals illustrate, harnessing wants with available resources remains the quintessential challenge to government in the 1990s.

Summary

1. Public policy is whatever government chooses to do or not to do. Political activity springs from conflict within society over what government ought to do and for whom or to whom it ought to do it. Definable stages of policy-making are getting issues onto the agenda of government, formulating policy proposals, formally adopting policy, implementing policy, and evaluating policy.

2. Conflict over economic policy has been at or near the top of the political agenda throughout American history. Government makes two major types of economic policy: fiscal and monetary. Fiscal policy assesses the impact on the economy as a whole of governmental decisions to tax, spend, and borrow; monetary policy concerns the availability and cost of money and credit in the economy.

3. Budget deficits, the dominant policy issue Congress and the president face in the 1990s, can be reduced by cutting expenditures, increasing taxes, or some combination of these two strategies. Payments for individuals comprise the largest category in the national budget. The cost of borrowing money has become a significant national expenditure. Much of the budget is comprised of mandatory spending.

4. Given the decentralization of power in the political system, no single individual or group alone can decide the size and shape of the budget. The president has the power to make budget proposals, but money can be spent only after Congress reviews and revises those proposals and enacts them into law. Deficits persist despite procedural changes. Continuing calls to revise procedures are a consequence of the collision between the necessity to impose constraints and the political resistance to spending cuts or tax increases.

Key Terms

public policy (p. 350)   policy adoption (p. 353)
policy agenda (p. 351)   policy implementation (p. 353)
policy strategy (p. 351)   policy evaluation (p. 353)

---

[26] For a summary discussion of budget process reforms, see Rudolph G. Penner and Alan J. Abramson, *Broken Purse Strings: Congressional Budgeting 1974 to 1988* (Washington, D.C.: Urban Institute, 1988), pp. 109–129.

economic policy (p. 355)
laissez-faire (p. 356)
socialism (p. 356)
recession (p. 356)
depression (p. 356)
protectionism (p. 357)
free trade (p. 357)
fiscal policy (p. 357)
monetary policy (p. 358)
Office of Management and Budget
  (p. 358)
deficit (p. 358)
debt (p. 358)
surplus (p. 359)
Keynesian economics (p. 360)
monetarism (p. 360)
supply-side economics (p. 360)
supply (p. 360)
demand (p. 360)

net interest (p. 365)
incrementalism (p. 366)
mandatory programs (p. 366)
social entitlements (p. 366)
budget (p. 367)
fiscal year (p. 368)
authorization (p. 372)
appropriations (p. 372)
line-item veto (p. 373)
balanced budget amendment (p. 373)
continuing resolution (p. 374)
Congressional Budget and
  Impoundment Control Act of 1974
  (p. 374)
Congressional Budget Office (p. 374)
Gramm-Rudman-Hollings (p. 374)
sequestration (p. 375)
Budget Enforcement Act of 1990
  (p. 375)

Readings for Further Study

A good overview of public policy analysis and a variety of substantive policy areas can be found in Dennis J. Palumbo, *Public Policy in America: Government in Action* (New York: Harcourt Brace Janovich, 1988). Two quarterly journals of the Policy Studies Organization, the *Policy Studies Journal* and the *Policy Studies Review,* are sources of current scholarship on the field of policy analysis and on specific policy areas. For a thorough understanding of economic policy-making, there is no better starting point than a good text on economics, such as Paul Samuelson and William Nordhaus's *Economics,* 12th ed. (New York: McGraw-Hill, 1985). Analyses of current economic problems, along with an excellent compendium of useful economic data, are found in the "Annual Report of the Council of Economic Advisers," included as a part of the annual *Economic Report of the President* (Washington, D.C.: Government Printing Office). Comprehen-

sive information on the budget can be found in a document the Office of Management and Budget produces each year as the president submits his budget to Congress. *The Budget of the United States Government* contains extensive analysis of budgetary issues, detailed personnel and budgetary data for each agency in the government, and a variety of historical tables. The Congressional Budget Office also issues periodic reports that analyze the president's proposals, assess the state of the economy, and offer Congress spending and revenue options to reduce the deficit. Aaron Wildavsky's *The New Politics of the Budgetary Process* (Glenview, Ill.: Scott, Foresman, 1988) is a superb analysis of the political environment of budgeting and the enormous changes that have taken place in budgeting procedures since he wrote his classic *The Politics of the Budgetary Process* in 1964. Robert Eisner's *How Real Is the Federal Deficit?* (New York: Basic Books,

1986) is a provocative critique of the widely held concern about budget deficits. Allen Schick provides cogent analysis of budgeting and governing and of policy and process in *The Capacity to Budget* (Washington, D.C.: Urban Institute, 1990).

David P. Calleo's *The Bankrupting of America: How the Federal Budget Is Impoverishing the Nation* (New York: William Morrow, 1992) addresses the deficit's impact on America's ability to compete in world markets.

The Declaration of Independence

When in the Course of human events, it becomes necessary for one people to dissolve the political bands which have connected them with another, and to assume among the Powers of the earth, the separate and equal station to which the Laws of Nature and of Nature's God entitle them, a decent respect to the opinions of mankind requires that they should declare the causes which impel them to the separation.

We hold these truths to be self-evident, that all men are created equal, that they are endowed by their Creator with certain unalienable Rights, that among these are Life, Liberty and the pursuit of Happiness. That to secure these rights, Governments are instituted among Men, deriving their just Powers from the consent of the governed, That whenever any Form of Government becomes destructive of these ends, it is the Right of the People to alter or to abolish it, and to institute new Government, laying its foundaton on such principles and organizing its Powers in such form, as to them shall seem most likely to effect their Safety and Happiness. Prudence, indeed, will dictate that Governments long established should not be changed for light and transient causes; and accordingly all experience hath shown, that mankind are more disposed to suffer, while evils are sufferable, than to right themselves by abolishing the forms to which they are accustomed. But when a long train of abuses and usurpations, pursuing invariably the same Object evinces a design to reduce them under absolute Despotism, it is their right, it is their duty, to throw off such Government, and to provide new Guards for their future security.—Such has been the patient sufferance of these Colonies; and such is now the necessity which constrains them to alter their former Systems of Government. The history of the present King of Great Britain is a history of repeated injuries and usurpations, all having in direct object the establishment of an absolute Tyranny over these States. To prove this, let Facts be submitted to a candid world.

He has refused his Assent to Laws, the most wholesome and necessary for the public good.

He has forbidden his Governors to pass Laws of immediate and pressing importance, unless suspended in their operation till his Assent should be obtained; and when so suspended, he has utterly neglected to attend to them.

He has refused to pass other Laws for the accommodation of large districts of people, unless those people would relinquish the right of Representation in the Legislature, a right inestimable to them and formidable to tyrants only.

He has called together legislative bodies at places unusual, uncomfortable, and distant from the depository of their Public Records, for the sole purpose of fatiguing them into compliance with his measures.

He has dissolved Representative Houses repeatedly, for opposing with manly firmness his invasions on the rights of the people.

He has refused for a long time, after such dissolutions, to cause others to be elected; whereby the Legislative Powers, incapable of Annihilation, have returned to the People at large for their exercise; the State remaining in the mean time exposed to all the

379

dangers of invasion from without, and convulsions within.

He has endeavoured to prevent the population of these States; for that purpose obstructing the Laws of Naturalization of Foreigners; refusing to pass others to encourage their migrations hither, and raising the conditions of new Appropriations of Lands.

He has obstructed the Administration of Justice, by refusing his Assent to Laws for establishing Judiciary Powers.

He has made Judges dependent on his Will alone, for the tenure of their offices, and the amount and payment of their salaries.

He has erected a multitude of New Offices, and sent hither swarms of Officers to harass our People, and eat out their substance.

He has kept among us, in times of peace, Standing Armies without the consent of our legislature.

He has affected to render the Military independent of and superior to the Civil Power.

He has combined with others to subject us to a jurisdiction foreign to our constitution, and unacknowledged by our laws; giving his Assent to their acts of pretended legislation:

For quartering large bodies of armed troops among us:

For protecting them, by a mock Trial, from Punishment for any Murders which they should commit on the Inhabitants of these States:

For cutting off our Trade with all parts of the world:

For imposing Taxes on us without our Consent;

For depriving us in many cases, of the benefits of Trial by Jury:

For transporting us beyond Seas to be tried for pretended offences:

For abolishing the free System of English Laws in a neighbouring Province, establishing therein an Arbitrary government, and enlarging its Boundaries so as to render it at once an example and fit instrument for introducing the same absolute rule into these Colonies:

For taking away our Charters, abolishing our most valuable Laws, and altering fundamentally the Forms of our Governments:

For suspending our own Legislatures, and declaring themselves invested with Power to legislate for us in all cases whatsoever.

He has abdicated Government here, by declaring us out of his Protection, and waging War against us.

He has plundered our seas, ravaged our Coasts, burnt our towns, and destroyed the lives of our people.

He is at this time transporting large armies of foreign mercenaries to compleat the works of death, desolation and tyranny, already begun with circumstances of Cruelty & perfidy scarcely paralleled in the most barbarous ages, and totally unworthy the Head of a civilized nation.

He has constrained our fellow Citizens taken Captive on the high Seas to bear Arms against their Country, to become the executioners of their friends and Brethren, or to fall themselves by their Hands.

He has excited domestic insurrections amongst us, and has endeavoured to bring on the inhabitants of our frontiers, the merciless Indian Savages, whose known rule of warfare, is an undistinguished destruction of all ages, sexes and conditions.

In every stage of these Oppressions We have Petitioned for Redress in the most humble terms: Our repeated Petitions have been answered only by repeated injury. A Prince, whose character is thus marked by every act which may define a Tyrant, is unfit to be the ruler of a free People.

Nor have We been wanting in attention to our British brethren. We have warned them from time to time of attempts by their legislature to extend an unwarrantable jurisdiction over us. We have reminded them of the circumstances of our emigration and settlement here. We have appealed to their native justice and magnanimity, and we have conjured them by the ties of our common kindred to disavow these usurpations, which, would inevitably interrupt our connections and correspondence. They too have been deaf to the voice of justice and of consanguinity. We must, therefore, acquiesce in the necessity, which denounces our Separation, and hold them, as we hold the rest of mankind, Enemies in War, in Peace Friends.

We, therefore, the Representatives of the United States of America, in General Congress, Assembled, appealing to the Supreme Judge of the world for the rectitude of our intentions, do, in the Name, and by Authority of the good People of these Colonies, solemnly publish and declare, That these United Colonies are, and of Right ought to be Free and Independent States; that they are Absolved from all Allegiance to the British Crown, and that all political connection between them and the State of Great Britain, is and ought to be totally dissolved; and that, as Free and Independent States, they have full Power to levy War, conclude Peace, contract Alliances, establish Commerce, and to do all other Acts and Things which Independent States may of right do. And for the support of this Declaration, with a firm reliance on the Protection of Divine Providence, we mutually pledge to each other our Lives, our Fortunes and our sacred Honor.

John Hancock,

Josiah Bartlett, Wm Whipple, Saml Adams, John Adams, Robt Treat Paine, Elbridge Gerry, Steph. Hopkins, William Ellery, Roger Sherman, Samel Huntington, Wm Williams, Oliver Wolcott, Matthew Thornton, Wm Floyd, Phil Livingston, Frans Lewis, Lewis Morris, Richd Stockton, Jno Witherspoon, Fras Hopkinson, John Hart, Abra Clark, Robt Morris, Benjamin Rush, Benja Franklin, John Morton, Geo Clymer, Jas Smith, Geo. Taylor, James Wilson, Geo. Ross, Caesar Rodney, Geo Read, Thos M:Kean, Samuel Chase, Wm Paca, Thos Stone, Charles Carroll of Carrollton, George Wythe, Richard Henry Lee, Th. Jefferson, Benja Harrison, Thos Nelson, Jr., Francis Lightfoot Lee, Carter Braxton, Wm Hooper, Joseph Hewes, John Penn, Edward Rutledge, Thos Heyward, Junr., Thomas Lynch, Junor., Arthur Middleton, Button Gwinnett, Lyman Hall, Geo Walton.

The Constitution of the United States

We the people of the United States, in Order to form a more perfect Union, establish Justice, insure domestic Tranquility, provide for the common defence, promote the general Welfare, and secure the Blessings of Liberty to ourselves and our Posterity, do ordain and establish this CONSTITUTION for the United States of America.

Article I

Section 1. All legislative Powers herein granted shall be vested in a Congress of the United States, which shall consist of a Senate and House of Representatives.

Section 2. The House of Representatives shall be composed of Members chosen every second Year by the People of the several States, and the Electors in each State shall have the Qualifications requisite for Electors of the most numerous Branch of the State Legislature.

No person shall be a Representative who shall not have attained to the Age of twenty-five Years, and been seven Years a Citizen of the United States, and who shall not, when elected, be an Inhabitant of that State in which he shall be chosen.

Representatives and direct Taxes shall be apportioned among the several States which may be included within this Union, according to their respective Numbers, which shall be determined by adding to the whole Number of free Persons, including those bound to Service for a Term of Years, and excluding Indians not taxed, three fifths of all other Persons. The actual Enumeration shall be made within three Years after the first Meeting of the Congress of the United States, and within every subsequent Term of ten Years, in such Manner as they shall by Law direct. The Number of Representatives shall not exceed one for every thirty Thousand, but each State shall have at Least one Representative; and until such enumeration shall be made, the State of New Hampshire shall be entitled to chuse three, Massachusetts eight, Rhode-Island and Providence Plantations one, Connecticut five, New-York six, New Jersey four, Pennsylvania eight, Delaware one, Maryland six, Virginia ten, North Carolina five, South Carolina five, and Georgia three.

When vacancies happen in the Representation from any State, the Executive Authority thereof shall issue Writs of Election to fill such Vacancies.

The House of Representatives shall chuse their Speaker and other Officers; and shall have the sole Power of Impeachment.

Section 3. The Senate of the United States shall be composed of two Senators from each State, chosen by the Legislature thereof, for six Years; and each Senator shall have one Vote.

Immediately after they shall be assembled in Consequence of the first Election, they shall be divided as equally as may be into three Classes. The Seats of the Senators of the first Class shall be vacated at the Expiration of the second Year, of the second

Class at the Expiration of the fourth Year, and of the third Class at the Expiration of the sixth Year, so that one-third may be chosen every second Year; and if Vacancies happen by Resignation, or otherwise, during the Recess of the Legislature of any State, the Executive thereof may make temporary Appointments until the next Meeting of the Legislature, which shall then fill such Vacancies.

No Person shall be a Senator who shall not have attained to the Age of thirty Years, and been nine Years a Citizen of the United States, and who shall not, when elected, be an Inhabitant of that State for which he shall be chosen.

The Vice President of the United States shall be President of the Senate, but shall have no vote, unless they be equally divided.

The Senate shall chuse their other Officers, and also a President pro tempore, in the absence of the Vice President, or when he shall exercise the Office of President of the United States.

The Senate shall have the sole Power to try all Impeachments. When sitting for that purpose, they shall be on Oath or Affirmation. When the President of the United States is tried, the Chief Justice shall preside: And no person shall be convicted without the Concurrence of two thirds of the Members present.

Judgment in Cases of Impeachment shall not extend further than to removal from Office, and disqualification to hold and enjoy any Office of honor, Trust, or Profit under the United States: but the Party convicted shall nevertheless be liable and subject to Indictment, Trial, Judgment and Punishment, according to Law.

Section 4. The Times, Places and Manner of holding Elections for Senators and Representatives, shall be prescribed in each state by the Legislature thereof; but the Congress may at any time by Law make or alter such Regulations, except as to the Places of Chusing Senators.

The Congress shall assemble at least once in every Year, and such Meeting shall be on the first Monday in December, unless they shall by Law appoint a different Day.

Section 5. Each House shall be the Judge of the Elections, Returns and Qualifications of its own Members, and a Majority of each shall constitute a Quorum to do Business; but a smaller number may adjourn from day to day, and may be authorized to compel the Attendance of absent Members, in such manner, and under such Penalties, as each House may provide.

Each House may determine the Rules of its Proceedings, punish its Members for disorderly Behavior, and, with the Concurrence of two thirds, expel a Member.

Each House shall keep a Journal of its Proceedings, and from time to time publish the same, excepting such Parts as may in their Judgment require Secrecy; and the Yeas and Nays of the Members of either House on any question shall, at the Desire of one fifth of those Present, be entered on the Journal.

Neither House, during the Session of Congress, shall, without the Consent of the other, adjourn for more than three days, nor to any other Place than that in which the two Houses shall be sitting.

Section 6. The Senators and Representatives shall receive a Compensation for their Services, to be ascertained by Law, and paid out of the Treasury of the United States. They shall in all Cases, except Treason, Felony, and Breach of the Peace, be privileged from arrest during their Attendance at the Session of their respective Houses, and in going to and returning from the same; and for any Speech or Debate in either House, they shall not be questioned in any other Place.

No Senator or Representative shall, during the Time for which he was elected, be appointed to any civil Office under the Authority of the United States, which shall have been created, or the Emoluments whereof shall have been encreased, during such time; and no Person holding any Office under the United States shall be a Member of either House during his continuance in Office.

Section 7. All Bills for raising Revenue shall originate in the House of Representatives; but the Senate may propose or concur with Amendments as on other bills.

Every Bill which shall have passed the House of Representatives and the Senate, shall, before it become a Law, be presented to the President of the United States; If he approve he shall sign it, but if not he shall return it, with his Objections, to that House in which it shall have originated, who shall enter the Objections at large on their Journal, and proceed to reconsider it. If after such Reconsideration two thirds of that House shall agree to pass the bill, it shall be sent, together with the objections, to the other House, by which it shall likewise be reconsidered, and if approved by two thirds of that House, it shall become a Law. But in all such Cases the Votes of both Houses shall be determined by Yeas and Nays, and the Names of the Persons voting for and against the Bill shall be entered on the Journal of each House respectively. If any Bill shall not be returned by the President within ten Days (Sundays excepted) after it shall have been presented to him, the Same shall be a Law, in like Manner as if he had signed it, unless the Congress by their Adjournment prevent its Return, in which Case it shall not be a Law.

Every Order, Resolution, or Vote to which the Concurrence of the Senate and House of Representatives may be necessary (except on a question of Adjournment) shall be presented to the President of the United States; and before the Same shall take Effect, shall be approved by him, or being disapproved by him, shall be repassed by two thirds of the Senate and House of Representatives, according to the Rules and Limitations prescribed in the Case of a Bill.

Section 8. The Congress shall have Power To lay and collect Taxes, Duties, Imposts and Excises, to pay the Debts and provide for the common Defence and general Welfare of the United States; but all Duties, Imposts and Excises shall be uniform throughout the United States;

To borrow money on the credit of the United States;

To regulate Commerce with foreign Nations, and among the several States, and with the Indian Tribes;

To establish an uniform Rule of Naturalization, and uniform Laws on the subject of Bankruptcies throughout the United States;

To coin Money, regulate the Value thereof, and of foreign Coin, and fix the Standard of Weights and Measures;

To provide for the Punishment of counterfeiting the Securities and current Coin of the United States;

To establish Post offices and post Roads;

To promote the Progress of Science and useful Arts, by securing for limited Times to Authors and Inventors the exclusive Right to their respective Writings and Discoveries;

To constitute Tribunals inferior to the Supreme Court;

To define and punish Piracies and Felonies committed on the high Seas, and Offences against the Law of Nations;

To declare War, grant Letters of Marque and Reprisal, and make Rules concerning Captures on Land and Water;

To raise and support Armies, but no Appropria-

tion of Money to that Use shall be for a longer Term than two Years;

To provide and maintain a Navy;

To make Rules for the Government and Regulation of the land and naval forces;

To provide for calling forth the Militia to execute the Laws of the Union, suppress Insurrections and repel Invasions;

To provide for organizing, arming, and disciplining the Militia, and for governing such Part of them as may be employed in the Service of the United States, reserving to the States respectively, the Appointment of the Officers, and the Authority of training the Militia according to the discipline prescribed by Congress;

To exercise exclusive Legislation in all Cases whatsoever, over such District (not exceeding ten Miles square) as may, by Cession of particular States, and the acceptance of Congress, become the Seat of Government of the United States, and to exercise like Authority over all Places purchased by the Consent of the Legislature of the State in which the Same shall be, for the Erection of Forts, Magazines, Arsenals, dock-Yards, and other needful Buildings;—And

To make all Laws which shall be necessary and proper for carrying into Execution the foregoing Powers, and all other Powers vested by this Constitution in the government of the United States, or in any Department or Officer thereof.

Section 9. The Migration or Importation of such Persons as any of the States now existing shall think proper to admit, shall not be prohibited by the Congress prior to the Year one thousand eight hundred and eight, but a tax or duty may be imposed on such Importation, not exceeding ten dollars for each Person.

The Privilege of the Writ of Habeas Corpus shall not be suspended, unless when in Cases of Rebellion or Invasion the public Safety may require it.

No Bill of Attainder or ex post facto Law shall be passed.

No capitation, or other direct, Tax shall be laid unless in Proportion to the Census or Enumeration herein before directed to be taken.

No Tax or Duty shall be laid on Articles exported from any State.

No Preference shall be given by any Regulation of Revenue to the Ports of one State over those of another: nor shall Vessels bound to, or from, one state, be obliged to enter, clear, or pay Duties in another.

No Money shall be drawn from the Treasury, but

in Consequence of Appropriations made by Law; and a regular Statement and Account of the Receipts and Expenditures of all public Money shall be published from time to time.

No Title of Nobility shall be granted by the United States: And no Person holding any Office of Profit or Trust under them, shall, without the Consent of the Congress, accept of any present, Emolument, Office, or Title, of any kind whatever, from any King, Prince, or Foreign State.

Section 10.   No State shall enter into any Treaty, Alliance, or Confederation; grant Letters of Marque and Reprisal; coin Money; emit Bills of Credit; make any Thing but gold and silver Coin a Tender in Payment of Debts; pass any Bill of Attainder, ex post facto Law, or Law impairing the Obligation of Contracts, or grant any Title of Nobility.

No State shall, without the Consent of the Congress, lay any Imposts or Duties on Imports or Exports, except what may be absolutely necessary for executing its inspection Laws: and the net Produce of all Duties and Imposts, laid by any State on Imports or Exports, shall be for the Use of the Treasury of the United States; and all such Laws shall be subject to the Revision and Control of the Congress.

No State shall, without the Consent of Congress, lay any duty of Tonnage, keep Troops, or Ships of War in time of peace, enter into any Agreement or Compact with another State, or with a foreign Power, or engage in War, unless actually invaded, or in such imminent Danger as will not admit of delay.

Article II

Section 1.   The executive Power shall be vested in a President of the United States of America. He shall hold his Office during the Term of four Years, and, together with the Vice President, chosen for the same Term, be elected, as follows:

Each State shall appoint, in such Manner as the Legislature thereof may direct, a Number of Electors, equal to the whole Number of Senators and Representatives to which the State may be entitled in the Congress; but no Senator or Representative, or Person holding an Office of Trust or Profit under the United States, shall be appointed an Elector.

The Electors shall meet in their respective States, and vote by Ballot for two persons, of whom one at least shall not be an Inhabitant of the same State with themselves. And they shall make a List of all the Persons voted for, and of the Number of Votes for each; which List they shall sign and certify, and transmit sealed to the Seat of the Government of the United States, directed to the President of the Senate. The President of the Senate shall, in the Presence of the Senate and House of Representatives, open all the Certificates, and the Votes shall then be counted. The Person having the greatest Number of Votes shall be the President, if such Number be a Majority of the whole Number of Electors appointed; and if there be more than one who have such Majority, and have an equal Number of Votes, then the House of Representatives shall immediately chuse by Ballot one of them for President; and if no Person have a Majority, then from the five highest on the List the said House shall in like Manner chuse the President. But in chusing the President, the votes shall be taken by States, the Representation from each State having one Vote; a quorum for this Purpose shall consist of a Member or Members from two-thirds of the States, and a Majority of all the States shall be necessary to a Choice. In every Case, after the Choice of the President, the Person having the greatest Number of Votes of the Electors shall be the Vice President. But if there should remain two or more who have equal votes, the Senate shall chuse from them by Ballot the Vice President.

The Congress may determine the time of chusing the Electors, and the Day on which they shall give their Votes; which Day shall be the same througout the United States.

No person except a natural-born Citizen, or a Citizen of the United States, at the time of the Adoption of this Constitution, shall be eligible to the Office of President; neither shall any Person be eligible to that Office who shall not have attained to the Age of thirty-five Years, and been fourteen Years a Resident within the United States.

In Case of the Removal of the President from Office, or of his Death, Resignation, or Inability to discharge the Powers and Duties of the said Office, the same shall devolve on the Vice President, and the Congress may by Law provide for the Case of Removal, Death, Resignation, or Inability, both of the President and Vice President, declaring what Officer shall then act as President, and such Officer shall act accordingly, until the Disability be removed, or a President shall be elected.

The President shall, at stated Times, receive for his Services a Compensation, which shall neither be increased nor diminished during the Period for which he shall have been elected, and he shall not receive within that Period any other Emolument from the United States, or any of them.

Before he enter on the execution of his Office, he shall take the following Oath or Affirmation:—"I do solemnly swear (or affirm) that I will faithfully execute the Office of President of the United States, and will, to the best of my Ability, preserve, protect, and defend the Constitution of the United States."

Section 2. The President shall be Commander in Chief of the Army and Navy of the United States, and of the Militia of the several States, when called into the actual Service of the United States; he may require the Opinion, in writing, of the principal Officer in each of the executive Departments, upon any subject relating to the Duties of their respective Offices, and he shall have Power to Grant Reprieves and Pardons for Offences against the United States, except in Cases of Impeachment.

He shall have Power, by and with the Advice and Consent of the Senate, to make Treaties, provided two thirds of the Senators present concur; and he shall nominate, and by and with the Advice and Consent of the Senate, shall appoint Ambassadors, other public Ministers and Consuls, Judges of the supreme Court, and all other Officers of the United States, whose Appointments are not herein otherwise provided for, and which shall be established by Law: but the Congress may by Law vest the Appointment of such inferior Officers, as they think proper, in the President alone, in the Courts of Law, or in the Heads of Departments.

The President shall have Power to fill up all Vacancies that may happen during the Recess of the Senate, by granting Commissions which shall expire at the End of their next Session.

Section 3. He shall from time to time give to the Congress Information of the State of the Union, and recommend to their Consideration such Measures as he shall judge necessary and expedient; he may, on extraordinary occasions, convene both Houses, or either of them, and in Case of Disagreement between them, with respect to the Time of Adjournment, he may adjourn them to such Time as he shall think proper; he shall receive Ambassadors and other public Ministers; he shall take Care that the Laws be faithfully executed, and shall Commission all the Officers of the United States.

Section 4. The President, Vice President and all civil Officers of the United States, shall be removed from Office on Impeachment for, and Conviction of, Treason, Bribery, or other high Crimes and Misdemeanors.

Article III

Section 1. The judicial Power of the United States, shall be vested in one supreme Court, and in such inferior Courts as the Congress may from time to time ordain and establish. The Judges, both of the supreme and inferior Courts, shall hold their Offices during good Behaviour, and shall, at stated Times, receive for their Services, a Compensation, which shall not be diminished during their Continuance in Office.

Section 2. The judicial Power shall extend to all Cases, in Law and Equity, arising under this Constitution, the Laws of the United States, and treaties made, or which shall be made, under their Authority;—to all Cases affecting Ambassadors, other public ministers and consuls;—to all cases of admiralty and maritime Jurisdiction;—to Controversies to which the United States shall be a Party;—to Controversies between two or more States;—between a State and Citizens of another State;—between Citizens of different States,—between Citizens of the same State claiming Lands under Grants of different States, and between a State, or the Citizens thereof, and foreign States, Citizens or Subjects.

In all Cases affecting Ambassadors, other public Ministers and Consuls, and those in which a State shall be Party, the supreme Court shall have original Jurisdiction. In all the other Cases before mentioned, the supreme Court shall have appellate Jurisdiction, both as to Law and Fact, with such Exceptions, and under such Regulations as the Congress shall make.

The trial of all Crimes, except in Cases of Impeachment, shall be by Jury; and such Trial shall be held in the State where the said Crimes shall have been committed; but when not committed within any State, the trial shall be at such Place or Places as the Congress may by Law have directed.

Section 3. Treason against the United States, shall consist only in levying War against them, or in adhering to their Enemies, giving them Aid and Comfort. No Person shall be convicted of Treason unless on the testimony of two Witnesses to the same overt Act, or on Confession in open Court.

The Congress shall have power to declare the Punishment of Treason, but no Attainder of Treason shall work Corruption of Blood, or Forfeiture except during the Life of the Person attained.

Article IV

Section 1.   Full Faith and Credit shall be given in each State to the public Acts, Records, and judicial Proceedings of every other State. And the Congress may by general Laws prescribe the Manner in which such Acts, Records and Proceedings shall be proved, and the Effect thereof.

Section 2.   The Citizens of each State shall be entitled to all Privileges and Immunities of Citizens in the several States.

A Person charged in any State with Treason, Felony, or other Crime, who shall flee from Justice, and be found in another State, shall on demand of the executive Authority of the State from which he fled, be delivered up, to be removed to the State having Jurisdiction of the crime.

No Person held to Service or Labour in one State, under the Laws thereof, escaping into another, shall, in Consequence of any Law or Regulation therein, be discharged from such Service or Labour, but shall be delivered up on Claim of the Party to whom such Service or Labour may be due.

Section 3.   New States may be admitted by the Congress into this Union; but no new State shall be formed or erected within the Jursidiction of any other State, nor any State be formed by the Junction of two or more States, or parts of States, without the Consent of the Legislatures of the States concerned as well as of the Congress.

The Congress shall have Power to dispose of and make all needful Rules and Regulations respecting the Territory or other Property belonging to the United States; and nothing in this Constitution shall be so construed as to Prejudice any Claims of the United States, or of any particular State.

Section 4.   The United States shall guarantee to every State in this Union a Republican Form of Government, and shall protect each of them against Invasion; and on Application of the Legislature, or the Executive (when the Legislature cannot be convened) against domestic Violence.

Article V

The Congress, whenever two-thirds of both Houses shall deem it necessary, shall propose Amendments to this Constitution, or, on the Application of the Legislatures of two-thirds of the several States, shall call a Convention for proposing Amendments, which, in either Case, shall be valid to all Intents and Purposes, as part of this Constitution, when ratified by the Legislatures of three-fourths of the several States, or by Conventions in three-fourths thereof, as the one or the other Mode of Ratification may be proposed by the Congress; Provided that no Amendment which may be made prior to the Year One thousand eight hundred and eight shall in any Manner affect the first and fourth Clauses in the Ninth Section of the first Article; and that no State, without its Consent, shall be deprived of its equal Suffrage in the Senate.

Article VI

All Debts contracted and Engagements entered into, before the Adoption of this Constitution, shall be as valid against the United States under this Constitution, as under the Confederation.

This Constitution, and the Laws of the United States which shall be made in Pursuance thereof; and all Treaties made, or which shall be made, under the Authority of the United States, shall be the supreme Law of the Land; and the Judges in every State shall be bound thereby, any Thing in the Constitution or Laws of any State to the Contrary notwithstanding.

The Senators and Representatives before mentioned, and the Members of the several State Legislatures and all executive and judicial Officers, both of the United States and of the several States, shall be bound by Oath or Affirmation, to support this Constitution; but no religious Test shall ever be required as a qualification to any Office or public Trust under the United States.

Article VII

The Ratification of the Conventions of nine States, shall be sufficient for the Establishment of this Constitution between the States so ratifying the same.

Done in Convention by the Unanimous Consent of the States present the Seventeenth Day of September in the Year of our Lord one thousand seven hundred and Eighty seven, and of the Independence of the United States of America the Twelfth. In Witness whereof We have hereunto subscribed our Names.

Go. Washington, *President and deputy from Virginia; Attest* William Jackson, *Secretary; Delaware:* Geo. Read,* Gunning Bedford, Jr., John Dickinson, Richard Basset, Jaco. Broom; *Maryland:* James McHenry, Daniel of St. Thomas' Jenifer, Danl. Carroll; *Virginia:* John Blair, James Madison, Jr.; *North Carolina:* Wm. Blount, Richd. Dobbs Spaight, Hu Williamson; *South Carolina:* J. Rutledge, Charles Cotesworth Pinckney, Charles Pinckney, Pierce Butler; *Georgia:* William Few, Abr. Baldwin; *New Hampshire:* John Langdon, Nicholas Gilman; *Massachusetts:* Nathaniel Gorham, Rufus King; *Connecticut:* Wm. Saml. Johnson, Roger Sherman,* *New York:* Alexander Hamilton; *New Jersey:* Wil. Livingston, David Brearly, Wm. Paterson, Jona. Dayton; *Pennsylvania:* B. Franklin,* Thomas Mifflin, Robt. Morris,* Geo. Clymer,* Thos. FitzSimons, Jared Ingersoll, James Wilson, Gouv. Morris.

Articles in Addition to, and Amendment of, the Constitution of the United States of America, Proposed by Congress, and Ratified by the Legislatures of the Several States, Pursuant to the Fifth Article of the Original Constitution.

Amendment I [1791]

Congress shall make no law respecting an establishment of religion, or prohibiting the free exercise thereof; or abridging the freedom of speech, or of the press; or the right of the people peaceably to assemble, and to petition the Government for a redress of grievances.

Amendment II [1791]

A well regulated Militia, being necessary to the security of a free State, the right of the people to keep and bear Arms shall not be infringed.

---

* Also signed the Declaration of Independence

Amendment III [1791]

No Soldier shall, in time of peace, be quartered in any house, without the consent of the Owner, nor in time of war, but in a manner to be prescribed by law.

Amendment IV [1791]

The right of the people to be secure in their persons, houses, papers, and effects, against unreasonable searches and seizures, shall not be violated, and no Warrants shall issue, but upon probable cause, supported by Oath or affirmation, and particularly describing the place to be searched, and the persons or things to be seized.

Amendment V [1791]

No person shall be held to answer for a capital or otherwise infamous crime, unless on a presentment or indictment of a Grand Jury, except in cases arising in the land or naval forces, or in the Militia, when in actual service in time of War or public danger; nor shall any person be subject for the same offence to be twice put in jeopardy of life or limb; nor shall be compelled in any criminal case to be a witness against himself, nor be deprived of life, liberty, or property, without due process of law; nor shall private property be taken for public use, without just compensation.

Amendment VI [1791]

In all criminal prosecutions, the accused shall enjoy the right to a speedy and public trial, by an impartial jury of the State and district wherein the crime shall have been committed, which district shall have been previously ascertained by law, and to be informed of the nature and cause of the accusation; to be confronted with the witnesses against him; to have compulsory process for obtaining witnesses in his favor, and to have the Assistance of Counsel for his defence.

Amendment VII [1791]

In suits at common law, where the value in controversy shall exceed twenty dollars, the right of trial by jury shall be preserved, and no fact tried by a jury, shall be otherwise reexamined in any Court of the United States, than according to the rules of the common law.

Amendment VIII [1791]

Excessive bail shall not be required, nor excessive fines imposed, nor cruel and unusual punishments inflicted.

Amendment IX [1791]

The enumeration in the Constitution, of certain rights, shall not be construed to deny or disparage others retained by the people.

Amendment X [1791]

The powers not delegated to the United States by the Constitution, nor prohibited by it to the States, are reserved to the States respectively, or to the people.

Amendment XI [1798]

The Judicial power of the United States shall not be construed to extend to any suit in law or equity, commenced or prosecuted against one of the United States by Citizens of another State, or by Citizens or Subjects of any Foreign State.

Amendment XII [1804]

The Electors shall meet in their respective States and vote by ballot for President and Vice-President, one of whom, at least, shall not be an inhabitant of the same State with themselves; they shall name in their ballots the person voted for as President, and in distinct ballots the person voted for as Vice-President, and they shall make distinct lists of all persons voted for as President, and of all persons voted for as Vice-President, and of the number of votes for each, which lists they shall sign and certify, and transmit sealed to the seat of the government of the United States, directed to the President of the Senate;—The President of the Senate shall, in the presence of the Senate and House of Representatives, open all the certificates and the votes shall then be counted;—The person having the greatest number of votes for President, shall be the President, if such number be a majority of the whole number of Electors appointed; and if no person have such majority, then from the persons having the highest numbers not exceeding three on the list of those voted for as President, the House of Representatives shall choose immediately, by ballot, the President. But in choosing the President, the votes shall be taken by states, the representation from each state having one vote; a quorum for this purpose shall consist of a member or members from two-thirds of the states, and a majority of all the states shall be necessary to a choice. And if the House of Representatives shall not choose a President whenever the right of choice shall devolve upon them, before the fourth day of March next following, then the Vice-President shall act as President, as in the case of the death or other constitutional disability of the President.—The person having the greatest number of votes as Vice-President, shall be the Vice-President, if such number be a majority of the whole number of Electors appointed, and if no person have a majority, then from the two highest numbers on the list, the Senate shall choose the Vice-President; a quorum for the purpose shall consist of two-thirds of the whole number of Senators, and a majority of the whole number shall be necessary to a choice. But no person constitutionally ineligible to the office of President shall be eligible to that of Vice-President of the United States.

Amendment XIII [1865]

Section 1.   Neither slavery nor involuntary servitude, except as a punishment for crime whereof the party shall have been duly convicted, shall exist within the United States, or any place subject to their jurisdiction.

Section 2.   Congress shall have power to enforce this article by appropriate legislation.

Amendment XIV [1868]

Section 1. All persons born or naturalized in the United States, and subject to the jurisdiction thereof, are citizens of the United States and of the State wherein they reside. No State shall make or enforce any law which shall abridge the privileges or immunities of citizens of the United States; nor shall any State deprive any person of life, liberty, or property, without due process of law; nor deny to any person within its jursidiction the equal protection of the laws.

Section 2. Representatives shall be apportioned among the several States according to their respective numbers, counting the whole number of persons in each State, excluding Indians not taxed. But when the right to vote at any election for the choice of electors for President and Vice-President of the United States, Representatives in Congress, the Executive and Judicial officers of a State, or the members of the Legislature thereof, is denied to any of the male inhabitants of such State, being twenty-one years of age, and citizens of the United States, or in any way abridged, except for participation in rebellion, or other crime, the basis of representation therein shall be reduced in the proportion which the number of such male citizens shall bear to the whole number of male citizens twenty-one years of age in such State.

Section 3. No person shall be a Senator or Representative in Congress, or elector of President and Vice-President, or hold any office, civil or military, under the United States, or under any State, who, having previously taken an oath, as a member of Congress, or as an officer of the United States, or as a member of any State legislature, or as an executive or judicial officer of any State, to support the Constitution of the United States, shall have engaged in insurrection or rebellion against the same, or given aid or comfort to the enemies thereof. But Congress may by a vote of two-thirds of each House, remove such disability.

Section 4. The validity of the public debt of the United States, authorized by law, including debts incurred for payment of pensions and bounties for services in suppressing insurrection or rebellion, shall not be questioned. But neither the United States nor any State shall assume or pay any debt or obligation incurred in aid of insurrection or rebellion against the United States, or any claim for the loss or emancipation of any slave; but all such debts, obligations, and claims shall be held illegal and void.

Section 5. The Congress shall have the power to enforce, by appropriate legislation, the provisions of this article.

Amendment XV [1870]

Section 1. The right of citizens of the United States to vote shall not be denied or abridged by the United States or by any State on account of race, color, or previous condition of servitude—

Section 2. The Congress shall have power to enforce this article by appropriate legislation.

Amendment XVI [1913]

The Congress shall have power to lay and collect taxes on incomes, from whatever source derived, without apportionment among the several States, and without regard to any census or enumeration.

Amendment XVII [1913]

The Senate of the United States shall be composed of two Senators from each State, elected by the people thereof, for six years; and each Senator shall have one vote. The electors in each State shall have the qualifications requisite for electors of the most numerous branch of the State legislatures.

When vacancies happen in the representation of any State in the Senate, the executive authority of such State shall issue writs of election to fill such vacancies: *Provided,* That the legislature of any State may empower the executive thereof to make temporary appointments until the people fill the vacancies by election as the legislature may direct.

This amendment shall not be so construed as to affect the election or term of any Senator chosen before it becomes valid as part of the Constitution.

Amendment XVIII [1919]

Section 1. After one year from the ratification of this article the manufacture, sale, or transportation of intoxicating liquors within, the importation thereof into, or the exportation thereof from the United States and all territory subject to the jurisdiction thereof for beverage purposes is hereby prohibited.

Section 2. The Congress and the several States shall have concurrent power to enforce this article by appropriate legislation.

Section 3. This article shall be inoperative unless it shall have been ratified as an amendment to the Constitution by the legislatures of the several States, as provided in the Constitution, within seven years from the date of the submission hereof to the States by the Congress.

Amendment XIX [1920]

The right of citizens of the United States to vote shall not be denied or abridged by the United States or by any State on account of sex.

Congress shall have power to enforce this article by appropriate legislation.

Amendment XX [1933]

Section 1. The terms of the President and Vice-President shall end at noon on the 20th day of January, and the terms of Senators and Representatives at noon on the 3d day of January, of the years in which such terms would have ended if this article had not been ratified; and the terms of their successors shall then begin.

Section 2. The Congress shall assemble at least once in every year, and such meeting shall begin at noon on the 3d day of January, unless they shall by law appoint a different day.

Section 3. If, at the time fixed for the beginning of the term of the President, the President elect shall have died, the Vice-President elect shall become President. If a President shall not have been chosen before the time fixed for the beginning of his term, or if the President elect shall have failed to qualify, then the Vice-President elect shall act as President until a President shall have qualified; and the Congress may by law provide for the case wherein neither a President elect nor a Vice-President elect shall have qualified, declaring who shall then act as President, or the manner in which one who is to act shall be selected, and such person shall act accordingly until a President or Vice-President shall have qualified.

Section 4. The Congress may by law provide for the case of the death of any of the persons from whom the House of Representatives may choose a President whenever the right of choice shall have devolved upon them, and for the case of the death of any of the persons from whom the Senate may choose a Vice-President whenever the right of choice shall have devolved upon them.

Section 5. Sections 1 and 2 shall take effect on the 15th day of October following the ratification of this article.

Section 6. This article shall be inoperative unless it shall have been ratified as an amendment to the Constitution by the legislatures of three-fourths of the several States within seven years from the date of its submission.

Amendment XXI [1933]

Section 1. The eighteenth article of amendment to the Constitution of the United States is hereby repealed.

Section 2. The transportation or importation into any State, Territory, or possession of the United States for delivery or use therein of intoxicating liquors, in violation of the laws thereof, is hereby prohibited.

Section 3. This article shall be inoperative unless it shall have been ratified as an amendment to the Constitution by conventions in the several States, as provided in the Constitution, within seven years from the date of the submission hereof to the States by the Congress.

Amendment XXII [1951]

No person shall be elected to the office of the President more than twice, and no person who has held the office of President, or acted as President, for more than two years of a term to which some other person was elected President shall be elected to the office of the President more than once.

But this Article shall not apply to any person holding the office of President when this Article was proposed by the Congress, and shall not prevent any person who may be holding the office of President or acting as President, during the term within which this Article becomes operative from holding the office of President or acting as President during the remainder of such term.

Amendment XXIII [1961]

Section 1.   The District constituting the seat of Government of the United States shall appoint in such manner as the Congress may direct:

A number of electors of President and Vice President equal to the whole number of Senators and Representatives in Congress to which the District would be entitled if it were a State, but in no event more than the least populous State; they shall be in addition to those appointed by the States, but they shall be considered, for the purposes of the election of President and Vice President, to be electors appointed by the State; and they shall meet in the District and perform such duties as provided by the twelfth article of amendment.

Section 2.   The Congress shall have power to enforce this article by appropriate legislation.

Amendment XXIV [1964]

Section 1.   The right of citizens of the United States to vote in any primary or other election for President or Vice President, for electors for President or Vice President, or for Senator or Representative in Congress, shall not be denied or abridged by the United States or any State by reason of failure to pay any poll tax or other tax.

Section 2.   The Congress shall have the power to enforce this article by appropriate legislation.

Amendment XXV [1967]

Section 1.   In case of the removal of the President from office or of his death or resignation, the Vice President shall become President.

Section 2.   Whenever there is a vacancy in the office of the Vice President, the President shall nominate a Vice President who shall take office upon confirmation by a majority vote of both houses of Congress.

Section 3.   Whenever the President transmits to the President pro tempore of the Senate and the Speaker of the House of Representatives his written declaration that he is unable to discharge the powers and duties of his office, and until he transmits to them a written declaration to the contrary, such powers and duties shall be discharged by the Vice President as Acting President.

Section 4.   Whenever the Vice President and a majority of either the principal officers of the executive departments, or of such other body as Congress may by law provide, transmit to the President pro tempore of the Senate and the Speaker of the House of Representatives their written declaration that the President is unable to discharge the powers and duties of his office, the Vice President shall immediately assume the powers and duties of the office as Acting President.

Thereafter, when the President transmits to the President pro tempore of the Senate and the Speaker of the House of Representatives his written declaration that no inability exists, he shall resume the powers and duties of his office unless the Vice President and a majority of either the principal officers of the executive departments, or of such other body as Congress may by law provide, transmit within four days to the President pro tempore of the Senate and the Speaker of the House of Representatives their written declaration that the President is unable to discharge the powers and duties of his office. Thereupon Congress shall decide the issue, assembling within 48 hours for that purpose if not in session. If the Congress, within 21 days after receipt of the latter written declaration, or, if Congress is not in session, within 21 days after Congress is required to assemble, determines by two-thirds vote of both houses that the President is unable to discharge the powers and duties of his office, the Vice President shall continue to discharge the same as Acting President; otherwise, the President shall resume the powers and duties of his office.

Amendment XXVI [1971]

Section 1.   The right of citizens of the United States, who are 18 years of age or older, to vote shall not be denied or abridged by the United States or by any state on account of age.

Section 2.   The Congress shall have power to enforce this article by appropriate legislation.

Amendment XXVII [1992]

No law varying the compensation for the services of the Senators and Representatives shall take effect, until an election of Representatives shall have intervened.

PHOTO CREDITS

INDEX

Note: Page numbers in italics refer to figures, illustrations, boxes, and tables.

DATE DUE

Demco, Inc. 38-293